Agile ALM

Agile ALM

Lightweight tools and Agile strategies

MICHAEL HÜTTERMANN

MANNING

SHELTER ISLAND

For online information and ordering of this and other Manning books, please visit
www.manning.com. The publisher offers discounts on this book when ordered in quantity.
For more information, please contact

> Special Sales Department
> Manning Publications Co.
> 20 Baldwin Road
> PO Box 261
> Shelter Island, NY 11964
> Email: orders@manning.com

Manning Publications Co.	Technical editor:	Robert Aiello
20 Baldwin Road	Development editor:	Sebastian Stirling
PO Box 261	Copyeditor:	Andy Carroll
Shelter Island, NY 11964	Typesetter:	Marija Tudor
	Cover designer:	Marija Tudor

ISBN: 9781935182634
Printed in the United States of America
1 2 3 4 5 6 7 8 9 10 – MAL – 17 16 15 14 13 12 11

To my wife and kids

brief contents

contents

ix

preface

Welcome to *Agile ALM*. This book has three main goals. The first is to describe Agile Application Lifecycle Management (ALM) in practical terms and to provide a plan for rolling out Agile strategies and best-of-breed tools. The second purpose is to explain how to create ALM toolboxes based on standard tools used in advanced, real-world cases. The third goal is to give you some guidance on how to choose the best tools, use them correctly, and integrate them while applying Agile strategies. These three goals are the focus of this book.

In these pages, I have tried to present all the information you'll need to implement Agile ALM. I hope the book will also help you understand and put into practice the "tool chains" needed for automating builds, tests, and continuous integration for your applications, so you'll be able to deliver quality applications without wasting time on repetitive tasks or hunting for the right set of strategies and tools.

The book starts with an overview of Agile ALM and then takes you deeper into the details. First, we'll look at toolsets at a higher level and then dive into the essentials you'll need in order to achieve success. It's worth noting that while some version-specific information is bound to change over time, the overall approach of this book will remain relevant, even as tools and strategies mature and evolve. The tool explanations are timeless because they focus on basic concepts and how to use the tools, rather than on details that will change from version to version.

You will learn how to integrate tools that are effective and flexible enough to accompany the entire development process and yet, can be arranged seamlessly in an open architecture. You will also learn how to look at the tool infrastructure as a mashup so you can change and replace individual facets on the fly. The tools discussed in the book are free for the most part. In rare cases, where no free tool is available to achieve a specific task, or when the paid alternatives have worthwhile features, I'll introduce commercial tools. Still, most of the products described in the book are moderately priced.

Although ALM strives to be language-agnostic, the tools we'll look at in the book are Java-focused, for two reasons. First, Java engineers represent the largest target audience of this book. Second, as in most heterogeneous system environments, you will find one leading system that integrates subsystems. Java is one of the leading, if not *the* leading language and platform to influence other platforms (like .NET).

This book serves as a bridge between new innovative approaches to development like Scrum, BDD, and Scala and more traditional approaches, such as bridging the abstract Scrum template to traditional functional and technical release management, or to continuous integration with Scala and Cobol. This book doesn't promote any one set of solutions. Rather, it serves as an explanation and a reality check for different technologies; this can be useful to more conservative companies and adopters.

I have tried to find a balance between high-level management overviews (along with basic explanations) and technical details (with many hands-on examples). I hope that this combination will succeed in making this book a comprehensive "one-stop shop" for you.

acknowledgments

This book is based not only on my own expertise and experience, but also on commonly accepted best practices. With the goal of encompassing a wide range of ideas, including a variety of opinions, and maximizing quality, I reached out to a number of contributors as well as external reviewers as I wrote the book. The people I reached out to are the masterminds, founders, and power users of the tools and concepts covered in this book.

I would like to acknowledge and thank the following people, in no particular order: Julian Simpson, "The Build Doctor," for feedback on continuous integration; Prof. Dr. Michael Stal, principal at Siemens, for technical editing of the Scala chapter; Rainer Wasgint for providing the Siemens ALM field report and for discussing ALM; Radoslaw Holewa, Scala professional, for contributing the BDD/Scala section; Vaclav Pech (JetBrains), Groovy expert, for summarizing what Groovy is great for; Stephen Berczuk, author and SCM expert, for proofreading and technical editing; Lisa Crispin, author and testing expert, for proofreading and giving feedback; Simon Tiffert, development lead, for his contribution in the context of acceptance testing, including Excel, TestNG, and XStream; René Gielen, Struts 2 PMC chair, for contributing a Maven-related section and a section about the Git/SVN bridge; Heinrich Freiherr von Schwerin (Logica), Paul Lajer (Logica), Matthias Zieger (Microsoft), Sven Lindenhahn (T-Systems), Thomas Ferris Nicolaisen, Simon Brandhof (Sonar-Source), and Reinhard Borosch (IBM) for their feedback and for inspiring me; Matthias Weßendorf (Kaazing), for contributing the Maven releasing use case, which shows how a big project is released using Maven (derived from MyFaces' releasing process); JFrog, especially cofounder and tech lead Yoav Landman, for supporting me with their product Artifactory, discussing the releasing of Maven artifacts in general, and proofreading; Atlassian, especially Jon Silver and Don Brown for feedback, proofreading, and support; and Szczepan Faber for writing about Mockito and mocking in general. Also, a big thanks to Szczepan for the discussions, feedback, and ideas for chapter 5. Thanks to Max Antoni for his Maven contribution; Anne Horton, author, for ideas about the Hudson/Jenkins and continuous integration sections; JetBrains, for inspiration and support; Hadi Hariri (JetBrains), .NET expert, for his .NET contribution; Jonas Borgstrom and team for feedback on the section on Trac; Eric Torreborre, founder of Scala specs2, for editing and proofreading and supporting the migration of the Scala/specs chapter from specs to specs2; Brett Porter, author and committer to Maven, for technical editing and proofreading; Wesley Williams (founder of GivWenZen) for his contribution; Matt J. Duffy and Greg Bates, from "Oxford Editing," Roswell, Georgia, USA, for editing (on my behalf) and pointing me to the roundup; and Craig Smith for carefully proofreading the final manuscript.

At Manning, special thanks to Michael Stephens for guiding me through the detailed publishing process, Bob Aiello for his technical edit of the manuscript, Andy Carroll for his expert copyediting, and to many others who worked behind the scenes. Also, thanks to the following reviewers who read the manuscript at various stages of development: Andy Dingley, Christian Siegers, Michele Galli, Tariq Ahmed, Balaji D. Loganathan, Brad Gronek, Ben Ogden, Justin Tyler Wiley, Amos Bannister, Christophe Bunn, Dave Nicolette, Lasse Koskela, Robert Wenner, Benjamin Day, Deepak Parasam, Deepak Vohra, Carlo Bottiglieri, and Darren Neimke.

about this book

This book is divided into four parts. Part 1 gives an overview of Agile ALM and sets the stage for parts 2 through 4. Part 2 deals with the functional aspects of ALM, including functional release management and task-based development. Part 3 discusses integration management and releasing, and includes dependency management and technical releasing with Maven, productive development environments and tools, and additional recipes for continuous integration. Part 4 explains my view of outside-in development for barrier-free development and testing.

In addition, the book contains many examples. Chapter 1 gives pragmatic explanations and a field report from Siemens, where ALM is used. Subsequent chapters deliver details and numerous examples that implement the principles presented in the first chapter.

Roadmap

Here's a more detailed outline of the material we will be exploring.

In part 1, I provide the basics of what Agile ALM is, including its benefits and features. I also talk about Agile in general. Chapter 1 sets the stage and gives you a feel for what Agile ALM is. Chapter 2 introduces Agile including the message of the Agile manifesto and how it relates to ALM, and discusses Agile strategies (such as continuous integration). All the other chapters discuss and implement the building blocks illustrated in chapters 1 and 2.

In part 2, we'll focus on the functional, high-level part of ALM. Chapter 3 details how to implement the general management template called Scrum and how to bridge

Scrum to more traditional environments. It also provides strategies and tools for supporting the functional release of software. Examples of supporting vehicles are version-control hooks and release calendars.

Scrum can be thought of as an easy, compact, abstract framework. Although I also explain Scrum at a high level, I focus on the details of how to implement Scrum in real life. This is rarely covered elsewhere. Most books on Scrum are too high level to help you learn the essentials for successfully implementing these excellent Agile practices. Finally, chapter 4 discusses task-based development, illustrating two toolchains (including how you can orchestrate them freely). The first is based on JIRA, Bamboo, Mylyn, and FishEye, and the second is based on Trac. Although Trac is quite useful on its own, it can be combined with tools like Mylyn or Hudson/Jenkins. This chapter gives an overview of these tools.

With part 3, we leave the functional, high-level features of ALM and dive into its more technical aspects. This part is about integration management and the technical aspects of releasing software. As I'll explain, ALM is about iteratively integrating artifacts, building and testing them, and providing software releases that are high quality and free of defects. Maven is one of the market leaders in providing a comprehensive lifecycle and release process. In chapter 5, we'll discuss some of Maven's important features, especially dependency management and how it helps to host component repositories in different flavors. Here, I'll also show how you can use Maven in traditional environments without rolling out a full-fledged repository manager. We'll discuss Artifactory as one of the major full-fledged repository managers. Finally, we'll go through a complex real-world releasing process showing Maven in action. As you can see, all these topics provide valuable, advanced, best practices. Maven is a major backbone for the rest of the book. Subsequent chapters use or discuss Maven in some form.

Chapter 6 deals with productive development environments. Major topics include strategies and tools for enabling congruent builds as part of an advanced "workspace management" environment, as well as methods for integrating and working with artifacts on developers' desktops. Other facets of this chapter cover Mockito (for mocking), Cargo, TeamCity (for remote runs), and Maven's archetype feature. All these concepts and tools can help improve the productivity of development environments.

Chapter 7 delivers tools and recipes for advanced continuous integration. We'll review the basics, and then dive into advanced scenarios, including strategies and tools for continuous integration. The first section of this chapter covers concepts and tools for integrating languages that have suboptimal native build management integration (we'll look specifically at Cobol). Afterward, we'll look at how to integrate Microsoft .NET artifacts. You'll see that you don't need to buy Microsoft products to integrate .NET apps continuously and that you can use TeamCity (or Hudson/Jenkins) and Subversion to build and store assets. This also helps to unify the toolchain while integrating many different languages and platforms.

Another section of chapter 7 is about configuration and staging, which can be a big challenge in software projects. We'll discuss how to configure an application for different target environments without rebuilding the software and how to deploy Maven modules in an automatic, consistent way. We'll also talk about feature branching with Subversion and Git (to show how to bridge two VCS technologies) and discuss two popular continuous integration servers. The first is Hudson/Jenkins. You'll see how to use it for building software, auditing (together with Sonar), and staging Maven artifacts. The second is TeamCity, and we'll discuss .NET integration and demonstrate how easy it is to incorporate the use of cloud computing.

The last part of the book is about "outside-in development" as well as collaborative and barrier-free development and testing. Chapter 8 looks at an Agile ALM approach to requirements management and test management. Here, you'll learn about collaborative tests (where users, customers, testers, and developers work hand in hand), and we'll go through many advanced scenarios and toolchains. Starting with a basic data-driven infrastructure, we'll optimize the solution by managing data with XStream and Excel, to the point of writing acceptance tests. Further sections provide other views and possible solutions, using Fit and FitNesse. We'll also use GivWenZen for behavior-driven development (BDD).

Chapter 9 discusses polyglot platforms and the details of collaborative and barrier-free development. Here, we'll discuss Groovy and BDD with Scala and specs2. I'll show the potential of barrier-free development using Java, Scala, and Groovy.

Who should read this book?

This book contains advanced strategies and real-world scenarios for using Agile ALM tools. It's targeted to advanced users, but motivated beginners will also benefit. If you're a beginner, I'll lead you through the Agile ALM cosmos, teaching you about Agile ALM and providing brief explanations on how to get started with the various tools I'll discuss. If you aren't familiar with a particular tool (or a concept) yet, you'll get all the necessary introduction, along with pointers to further resources.

From a project management perspective, this book is for developers, testers, development leads, technical project managers, (technical) release managers, and all IT people who want to improve the development process. People with Java skills, especially those who already use or plan to use the tools introduced here, will benefit the most from this book.

The book will be most useful for the IT professional who wants to become familiar with Agile ALM, as well as for future users of the tools seeking advice for advanced use and best practices of applying Agile strategies.

Source code downloads

The most up-to-date source code for the book can be found here: http://huettermann .net/alm/. Code and tools that are mentioned in this book have different hardware and software requirements. Please consult the how-tos inside the downloadable source code, the respective sections in the book, and the resources for the specific tools for further details. The source code is also available from the publisher's website at www.manning.com/AgileALM.

The publisher and author have taken great care in the preparation of this book, but we make no expressed or implied warranty for the code and text due to any errors or omissions that might be contained in the book, in spite of our best efforts. An errata list will be posted on the publisher's website after publication and updated for as long as the book is in print.

About the title

It was a long journey to decide on the final book title. My first ideas for the title included terms like "configuration management" or "open source ALM." But neither of these was quite right. ALM is more than configuration management—although it is based on the discipline called software configuration management. In addition, while this book covers the best-of-breed lightweight tools, not all of them are open source.

The final title, *Agile ALM*, along with the subtitle, *Lightweight Tools and Agile Strategies*, best expresses the message of this book. It covers Agile strategies and lightweight tools through the complete software application lifecycle. What the title also suggests and the book explains in detail is that software development is not a unidirectional "fire and forget" activity. Rather, software development is done in cyclic loops, with iterations and increments, across all project phases, from requirements engineering to delivery, gaining feedback from users who work with the delivered software, to again start the loop.

When I submitted the manuscript to Manning in March 2010, the term "Agile ALM" was rarely used in the IT scene. Now, after the early access version of this book has been available for over a year, the expression "Agile ALM" is widespread. But the term is often used without a clear understanding of what Agile ALM really means. This book delivers a definition of Agile ALM and puts together the requirements that tools should implement in order to label themselves "Agile ALM" tools. Today, many tool vendors describe their products with words like "Agile," or "ALM," or both, to indicate that the tool supports application lifecycle management in an agile way.

In this book, "Agile ALM" is used only in an editorial sense with no intent to infringe on any trademark.

What this book doesn't do

This book will not teach you all the tools from scratch nor all facets of these tools. For instance, if you're new to Maven (which, as noted earlier, is a backbone for Agile ALM), you should consider consulting a dedicated resource on that tool, such as one of the many books on Maven that explain the tool from scratch. I also don't explain all strategies and concepts at every step. For instance, if you're interested in Scrum, you may want to consult books dedicated to Scrum. This book isn't meant to include detailed end-to-end descriptions of tools that are already discussed in other books dedicated to those subjects.

You probably will not use all the tools discussed in this book. Maybe you already use some of them, or you may prefer other tools. It's not possible to cover all the available tools in these pages, but the tools that are covered here are (or are likely to become) de facto standards, and most are already in widespread use. The individual choice of tools will depend on local conditions, personal preferences, and how your team operates. One could make arguments for or against each category of tool presented in this book, as well as for or against the tools I chose to cover, depending on context. From an Agile perspective, we want to find the "sweet spot" where we have all the tools we need for local conditions, and nothing more.

What's true for tools is also true for platforms and languages. This book is based on Java, although many examples show how to bridge to other platforms and languages. As with tools, it's not possible to cover all available platforms and languages.

Although most of the tools discussed in the book are open source and freely available, some tools are commercial, and worth the investment. Examples of commercial tools are the excellent products from Atlassian, such as JIRA and Bamboo, which you can use for setting up a task-based development toolchain, and TeamCity, which I discuss for running remote builds.

This book doesn't provide comparisons of tools. I take a different approach—instead of being tool-centric, I take a use case–driven approach. I show how to implement all major aspects of Agile ALM with specific tools, similar to a cookbook. In most cases, I discuss only one tool, but sometimes I use more than one in conjunction, or I integrate one with others. In all cases, I focus on best-of-breed solutions or toolchains for rolling out Agile ALM, but there are always other options you could use.

Author Online

Purchase of *Agile ALM* includes free access to a private web forum run by Manning Publications where you can make comments about the book, ask technical questions, and receive help from the author and from other users. To access the forum and subscribe to it, point your web browser to www.manning.com/AgileALM. This page provides information on how to get on the forum once you are registered, what kind of help is available, and the rules of conduct on the forum.

Manning's commitment to our readers is to provide a venue where a meaningful dialog between individual readers and between readers and the author can take place. It is not a commitment to any specific amount of participation on the part of the author, whose contribution to the book's forum remains voluntary (and unpaid). We suggest you try asking him some challenging questions lest his interest stray!

The Author Online forum and the archives of previous discussions will be accessible from the publisher's website as long as the book is in print.

About the author

A Java Champion, Michael Hüttermann (SCJA, SCJP, SCJD, SCWCD), is a freelance developer, architect, coach, author, and tutor for Java/JEE, ALM/SCM, and agile software development. He speaks at international conferences and was the responsible stage producer of the tooling track of Agile 2009. He is the founder and driver of the Java User Group Cologne, a java.net JUGs Community Leader, a member of Agile Alliance, on the board of the JetBrains Academy, a committer to FEST, and a Java contributor. Michael has written numerous articles and two German books: *Agile Java-Entwicklung in der Praxis* (O'Reilly, 2008), and *Fragile Agile* (Hanser, 2010).

Further information about the author, including ways to contact him, can be found at http://huettermann.net.

about the cover illustration

On the cover of *Agile ALM* is "A habitant of Brgud," a hamlet on the eastern side of the peninsula of Istria in the Adriatic Sea, off Croatia. The illustration is taken from a reproduction of an album of Croatian traditional costumes from the mid-nineteenth century by Nikola Arsenovic, published by the Ethnographic Museum in Split, Croatia, in 2003. The illustrations were obtained from a helpful librarian at the Ethnographic Museum in Split, itself situated in the Roman core of the medieval center of the town: the ruins of Emperor Diocletian's retirement palace from around AD 304. The book includes finely colored illustrations of figures from different regions of Croatia, accompanied by descriptions of the costumes and of everyday life.

In this region of Croatia, men wear black woolen trousers and jackets that are decorated with embroidered trim. The figure on the cover is wearing a vest and short jacket over a white linen shirt, black trousers, and a flat black hat that completes the outfit. The color and style of the embroidery, thin blue piping in this case, indicate the town or village of the costume's origin.

Dress codes and lifestyles have changed over the last 200 years, and the diversity by region, so rich at the time, has faded away. It's now hard to tell apart the inhabitants of different continents, let alone of different hamlets or towns separated by only a few miles. Perhaps we have traded cultural diversity for a more varied personal life—certainly for a more varied and fast-paced technological life.

Manning celebrates the inventiveness and initiative of the computer business with book covers based on the rich diversity of regional life of two centuries ago, brought back to life by illustrations from old books and collections like this one.

Part 1

Introduction to Agile ALM

Welcome to Agile ALM. In this part of the book, I will illustrate the basics of what Agile ALM is, from my point of view, including its benefits, history, and building blocks. We'll also talk about Agile in general and how Agile strategies can enrich application lifecycle management.

Chapter 1 sets the stage and gives you a thorough introduction to what Agile ALM comprises. Chapter 2 introduces Agile and Agile strategies. You'll learn how Agile can foster your project management and how Agile strategies (including continuous integration, component repository, and productive workspaces) can help to streamline your development process. You'll also learn how Agile ALM can counteract the illusion of control by operating as a change enabler.

After reading this part of the book, you'll be ready to explore Agile strategies in more detail and to learn how you can implement these strategies with lightweight tools.

Getting started with Agile ALM

This chapter covers

- An introduction to Agile ALM
- The evolution in software engineering leading to Agile ALM
- The aspects of ALM that are covered in this book

This book is about Agile application lifecycle management (ALM) and brings together the best of two worlds, Agile and ALM. I'll discuss ALM as a way to develop and release software in a coherent, integrated way, spanning all development phases, artifact types, roles, and business units. Bringing ALM and Agile together and using the right tools leads to a modern, efficient way of developing software. Consequently, you'll reduce costs, boost your productivity, and accelerate your team's collaboration. And you can make developing software a lot more fun.

Agile ALM enriches ALM with Agile strategies. In my opinion, ALM is based on software configuration management (SCM). SCM, in turn, is based on basic version control (see figure 1.1).

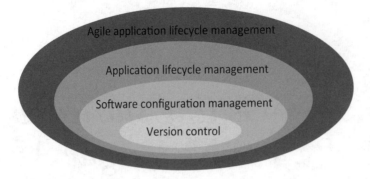

Figure 1.1   Agile ALM enriches ALM with Agile strategies. ALM is heavily inspired by and based on configuration management, which in turn is based on version control.

Agile ALM

- Helps overcome process, technology, and functional barriers (such as roles and organizational units).
- Spans all artifact types as well as development phases and project roles.
- Uses and integrates lightweight tools, enabling the team to collaborate efficiently without any silos.
- Makes the relationship of given or generated artifacts visible, providing traceability and reproducibility.
- Defines task-based activities that are aligned with requirements. This means that the activities are linked to requirements and that all changes are traceable to their requirements.

Agile ALM can be used with all kinds of process models and methodologies, including traditional ones, such as waterfall or spiral models. There are also ALM approaches that can hardly be called Agile or that are based on large-scale commercial tools; these can be difficult and expensive to implement. Agile ALM focuses on driving the process through people and not merely through tools. Where tools would be of benefit, such as continuous integration server, they should be lightweight and primarily open source. The Agile ALM approach results in processes and lightweight toolchains that are flexible, open to change, and high quality. This approach helps to make the ALM more Agile and leads to what I call Agile ALM.

This chapter introduces the concepts that are essential to understanding Agile ALM, including the evolution of software engineering with its migration to Agile ALM. I'll also discuss the essential impact that SCM (and version control) has had on ALM, including some of the first pilot projects to use Agile and ALM together. In addition, I'll explain my view that SCM is the basis of ALM and how these practices help develop ALM today. Many Agile books make the case that one doesn't adopt Agile practices, but rather one *becomes* Agile. It's important to establish an effective ALM through people, culture, processes, and tools. This chapter will also focus on open source and lightweight tooling along with the building blocks of Agile ALM. That's not to say that some large-scale commercial tools aren't worth using, but they won't be the focus of this book.

It's essential to take a stakeholder focus in any Agile effort; one must consider the role of releasing code in Agile ALM as well as the service orientation and application architecture. I place a strong emphasis on task-based development and the Agile ALM premise of aligning work to the customer's requirements (including setting up the most effective toolchain for a given context). I'll also explain one approach called "outside-in," which takes the customer's point of view in some specific (and important) ways. We'll consider the importance of configuration, customization, plug-ins, and our ever-growing, multilanguage, polyglot world, including my view that we can't forget the existing legacy systems that are often valuable to the organization. But first, let's take a step back and consider Agile ALM at a glance.

1.1 Agile ALM at a glance

ALM describes the coordination of development lifecycle disciplines, including the management of requirements, changes, configurations, integrations, releases, and tests. These functions span development phases, including requirements definition, design, code, test, and run, as shown in figure 1.2.

ALM is aligned with the engineering process, spanning development phases. This results in releases that are functionally and technically consistent. ALM also manages the relationships between various artifact types, including requirement documents, coding artifacts, and build scripts that are used or produced by the engineering process. By organizing, linking, and referencing activities and artifacts, you can track the development progress as a whole. Through the use of integrated toolchains, ALM helps you to overcome the biggest challenge in the software creation process: the technological and functional barriers that make it difficult to implement a transparent and consistent development process.

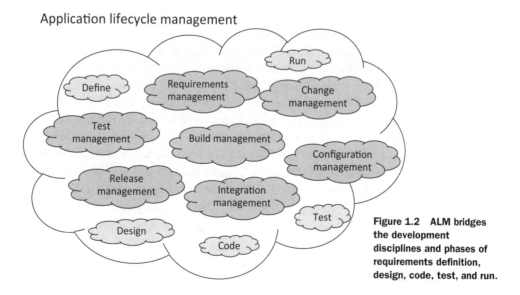

Figure 1.2 ALM bridges the development disciplines and phases of requirements definition, design, code, test, and run.

ALM is a task-based approach in which all activities are linked to requirements, and the relationships between all artifacts are visible; therefore, artifacts can be traced to the requirements they are based on.

> ### Agile ALM
>
> The Agile ALM approach
>
> - Is the marriage of business management to software engineering
> - Targets processes and tools working together seamlessly, without silos
> - Covers the complete software development lifecycle, including requirements management, coding, testing, and release management
> - Enriches ALM with Agile strategies
> - Is based on software configuration management and version control
> - Is based on a set of tools, enabling a team to collaborate efficiently

By using an Agile ALM approach, you'll gain from improved productivity that helps keep costs down, reduces time to market, and improves return on investment (ROI). All stakeholders have easy access to the information they need and can collaborate efficiently. They have real-time visibility and participation in the process lifecycle. This means that the technical infrastructure is aligned with business and business value. It also means that, through interactions between business and technical personnel, questions can be answered quickly in a user-friendly way. That leads to concrete, positive business outcomes.

Agile ALM's integrated approach leads to the protection of software assets, improved reuse, better requirements traceability, cleaner code, and improved test results. A high level of automation, seamless integration, and service orientation leads to a successful project and better team awareness.

An Agile ALM enriches a traditional ALM with Agile values and strategies. With a focus on communication and collaboration, ALM processes already have the prerequisites to support Agile software development. An Agile ALM has its major focus on human interaction ("peopleware"), increasing their communication and interactions by implementing Agile strategies (like continuous integration) and always weighing value and effort. The Agile approach uses lightweight tools as needed, based on concrete requirements. In this book, I will refer to large, bureaucratic, heavyweight systems as being *monolithic*, as discussed later in this chapter. A nonmonolithic approach uses open standards and helps to implement an Agile software development process. Agile ALM can also support other kinds of development processes.

In summary, Agile ALM consists of the following four major fundamentals:

1 *Collaboration*—All team members are aware of what others are doing. That way, choices can be made that best facilitate the progress of the entire project. This is achieved by focusing on personal interactions, the outside-in (customer-focused) development approach, and task-based development supported by tools.

2   *Integration*—Achieving business targets requires an enterprise infrastructure to integrate roles, teams, workflows, and repositories into a responsive software delivery chain. People must be connected wherever they are located (distributed, collocated) and must have the assets they need to get the information they seek. Integration occurs at several levels, including developer builds and integration builds, and is seamlessly maintained with comprehensive testing throughout the lifecycle.

3   *Automation*—The streamlining of the full lifecycle is heavily based on end-to-end automation.[1] For example, all of the steps in a build, including preparing the build system, applying baselines to source control systems, conducting the build, running technical and functional tests as well as acceptance tests, packaging, and deploying and staging the artifacts, are automated with the appropriate tools.

4   *Continuous improvement*—You can improve only what you can see and measure, so building and delivering software that minimizes manual work is a requirement for easily identifying where you are in your process. Comprehensive testing, regular retrospectives (where you discuss what went well and what needs improvement), project transparency, and project health (balancing work to eliminate work peaks) allow you to improve continuously.

To better understand ALM and its features and benefits, it's helpful to look at the history of software engineering in the context of ALM. We'll now take a quick tour through the evolution, from the pragmatic approach to software configuration management to ALM.

1.2   *Evolution of software engineering: moving to Agile ALM*

Software engineering has always focused on improving quality and productivity. This may involve reusing well-defined requirements or software components. Many companies spend years developing applications and continuously extend their portfolio with new ones. By repeatedly implementing the same requirements instead of reusing existing assets (which exist because you've implemented the same requirements before) and not using strategies for tracking artifacts (such as builds, test results, packages), the development team will be ineffective and inefficient. Developing software in a suboptimal way leads to poor quality, missed customer needs, and late arrival to the market.

From a technical view, without any comprehensive strategy for managing artifacts, integration is often a game of roulette that involves changing an existing application rather than merely transferring a set of changes into another stable and well-known system state. This is why technology professionals have worked hard to improve the application-development process and have tried to find answers to these common questions:

- How can I accelerate activities and exclude error sources?
- How can I improve communication in the team?

---

[1]   The end-to-end process, its people, and its processes are sometimes called the "value stream."

- How can I significantly improve the quality of my software?
- How can I keep in touch with the current state and quality of the developed software?
- Which tools fit my requirements and basic conditions best?
- How do the single building blocks of my infrastructure interact with each other?
- How can I set up a flexible infrastructure to secure the assets of my company?
- Which changes (requirements, bugs) are implemented in which artifacts?
- Which changes are provided in which builds/releases?

In order to appreciate this effort, we need to review software configuration management and its essential practices.

1.2.1   *SCM and the first ALM trial balloons*

Software engineering, from a historical perspective, is a young discipline. In the early stages, software development was seen more as a factory process and not as a complex activity aimed at implementing business objectives. In recent decades, software development has been evolving, initially to make life easier for developers and finally to answer internally and externally driven needs for productivity and quality.

THE BASICS OF SCM

Running an unreliable, fragmented development process doesn't empower a team to track and improve their work continuously. This is where software configuration management (SCM) can help. SCM helps improve the development process by tracking and controlling changes in the software. These processes are commonly implemented using version-control systems (VCS). SCM makes changes in the VCS visible, and it adds meta-information to the system to track *why* the change was made. Above all, baselines (identifying a specific version of the code suitable for release) and change-sets (linked to artifacts or work items) provide traceability to the development process and accelerate release management.

The following are the goals and values of SCM:

- Identifying and administering configuration items
- Controlling, versioning, and resolving conflicts for artifacts of any type (which impact the release) that may change over project time
- Documenting changes of all configuration items and their degree of maturity
- Supporting branching and merging
- Configuring software for use (deployment) on different target environments
- Performing functional auditing, reproducibility, traceability, and controlling configuration item dependencies
- Minimizing bad builds and detecting them early
- Reducing communication mistakes
- Providing a history of builds and releases in order to investigate issues
- Defining processes and tools
- Eliminating redundant tasks and streamlining processes

- Improving efficiency while orchestrating, packaging, and distributing software
- Establishing access control
- Saving time and money and satisfying the customer

Software configuration management

Software configuration management consists of four major functions:

- *Configuration identification*—Select and identify all configuration items and establish baselines on them so you can then control, audit, and report changes.
- *Change control*—Control changes to configuration items.
- *Configuration audit*—Ensure correctness, completeness, and consistency of baselines by examining the baselines, configuration items, and related processes.
- *Status accounting*—Report on the status of all configuration items throughout their lifecycle.

Using SCM, you can track incremental changes and compare and analyze stable baselines of the software. The SCM focus is primarily on physical changes as opposed to business objectives, as illustrated in figure 1.3.

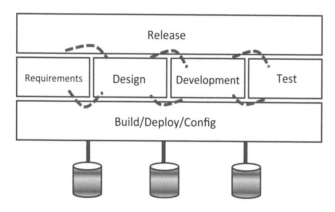

Figure 1.3 Development phases like design and development are often unreliable with unpredictable results, tools, and data. Phases are isolated and only loosely linked, as illustrated by the dotted lines in the figure. SCM activities like build/deploy are orthogonal to the phases and span them. They are often not reliable.

Configuration items

Configuration items refers to produced or consumed (used) artifacts or to (environmental) artifacts that created final artifacts. Depending on the point of view and the context, *artifacts* go by different names, products or deliverables (project management) or deployment units (software architecture), for example. The rules for identifying a configuration item may vary and depend on individual requirements. As a basic rule of thumb, a configuration item is any item delivered to a stakeholder. Examples include coding artifacts, design documents, user manuals, requirements, technical specs, test cases, build scripts, and so on.

> **(continued)**
>
> For a detailed discussion of configuration items, and configuration management in general, see the following sources: Alexis Leon, *A Guide to Software Configuration Management* (Artech House, 2000); Mario E. Moreira, *Software Configuration Management Implementation Roadmap* (Wiley, 2004); Mario E. Moreira, *Adopting Configuration Management for Agile Teams* (Wiley, 2010); Larry Klosterboer, *Implementing ITIL Configuration Management* (IBM Press, 2008); A. Mette and J. Hass, *Configuration Management Principles and Practices* (Addison-Wesley, 2003); Bob Aiello, *Configuration Management Best Practices: Practical Methods that Work in the Real World* (Addison-Wesley, 2010).

THE DEVELOPMENT OF SCM

In the early years of software development, the main challenges related to the fact that a team worked on software and data concurrently. Classic problems included the following:[2]

- The double maintenance problem, which arises from keeping multiple copies of software
- The shared data problem, arising from many people simultaneously accessing and modifying the same data
- The simultaneous update problem, arising from multiple people changing a piece of software at the same time

Database management systems and version-control software help us manage the daily challenges of software development, and the solutions are found in almost every project toolchain in use today. Yet the challenge of accelerating the development process and improving software traceability and quality remained difficult to achieve.

SCM strategies were developed and refined to further optimize the engineering process.[3] Over the years, it became increasingly clear that this wasn't enough. Focusing on only the technical view didn't improve the quality of software development.

Tracking the progress of the development efforts, and the changes on artifacts, including source code, design, and requirements documents, isn't always easy because it usually requires working with manual lists and accessing multiple data repositories. What makes implementing SCM even more difficult is the amount of manual work required, particularly for validating the current status of the software at any given point.

Technical release management is an explicit time-consuming activity. The solution was to focus on automating every aspect of SCM, from application builds to release packaging and deployment. For example, development managers need procedures for continuous auditing and change tracking. The release management process

---

[2] See Wayne Babich, *Software Configuration Management* (Addison-Wesley, 1986), 9ff.
[3] See Stephen Berczuk with Brad Appleton, *Software Configuration Management Patterns* (Addison-Wesley, 2003).

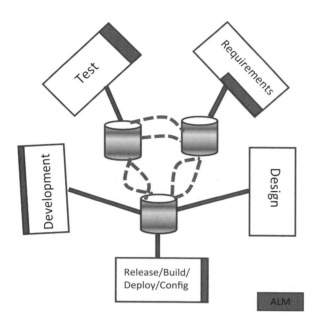

Figure 1.4   The first evolution of SCM toward an approach that can be called ALM spread over phases and synchronization. Unlike the design in figure 1.3, single phases now contain aspects of ALM but often have disparate data stores and processes, and there are challenges to sharing data and knowledge.

should be implicit, integrating across artifact types and development phases, with uniform or highly integrated tools and data repositories.

As a result of improved procedures for continuous auditing and change tracking, developers found themselves with a more integrated approach that was free of common obstacles. Instead of each organizational group suboptimizing its own work, barriers between areas were broken down and all stakeholders worked as a team for the company.[4] I refer to this approach as being "barrier-free." Figure 1.4[5] shows that SCM became more and more an implicit task embedded in all development phases. At this point, it becomes more appropriate to talk not only about SCM, but also about management of the application lifecycle (ALM).

THE TEST PHASE   There are many situations that warrant a separate testing phase, as shown in figure 1.4; other situations don't. In many projects and companies, the test activities can be part of the release/build/deploy/config block or part of the development block.

ALM features and activities are implicit throughout the entire lifecycle, meaning that all phases of the process include ALM features and activities now, instead of taking an orthogonal approach, as in the first evolution step. Early approaches to ALM resulted in significant improvements, but these early efforts were not always successful because many roles had their own tools, which were not integrated with the tools used by other team members. For example, there are many tools that are specific to requirements

---

[4]   See W. Edwards Deming, *Out of the Crisis* (The MIT Press, 1982), pp. 62–65.

[5]   Compare Carey Schwaber, *The Changing Face of Application Life-Cycle Management* (Forrester Research Inc., 2006).

engineering but that don't integrate well with other toolsets. In addition, many development teams grow attached to their specific tools and find it difficult to switch to using one integrated toolchain. The toolchain is often compared to a Swiss army knife, which has many clever tools but may not be completely effective for a specific task. As a result of all these issues, the wrong tool infrastructure may sometimes have slowed teams down instead of speeding them up! Additionally, some tools have their own proprietary data-storage approach, so tools were often not integrated and their database repositories can't share related information.

To span separate roles and phases, it's necessary to synchronize data among the various tools. This results in a more complex technical solution. Another idea to improve tracking software development is to set additional tools (such as a tool that aggregates the individual outcomes of other tools, or a dashboard) or manual activities on top of the infrastructure. In this way, information could be extracted or collected and offered at a central entry point.

In summary, the combined complexity and the missing "single point of truth" increases costs and may lead to inaccurate information. Tools that aren't aligned properly may lead to unneeded complexity. The lack of integration and collaborative features leads to a lack of transparency because requirements can't be traced throughout the lifecycle. All of these points make it a lot harder to align tools and processes.

Let's summarize the key issues in how ALM was commonly organized before the next evolutionary step occurred:

- *Alignment of tools, roles, and organizational borders*—The approach was mainly aligned at organizational borders and roles. As a result, there often was a single tool for each role or business unit. For example, let's consider a big integration project that has a central build/config/release business unit. In another business unit, the test management runs in isolation, starting its main activities only after the software is released. The isolated tool used by test management may enable writing test cases and tracking tests, but it isn't integrated into the other part of the toolchain; the organization may even have different accounts for those tools and micro workflows.

- *Suboptimal collaboration*—Another point where the toolchain wasn't balanced was in the lack of collaboration between team members and interaction features with other tools. For example, among the available (commercial) tools, none had a central wiki in which different users could discuss topics and exchange information. None enabled a shared view on information collected from multiple units, phases, or roles. This is like having a software application open on your desk in multiple isolated windows with no way to see the information as a whole or in different views.

- *Lack of transparent processes*—If you analyze how the workflows in companies and projects are implemented with tools—how the processes are implemented—you'll see that there are many proprietary scripts that drive and configure each tool, but that those individual tools are connected in clumsy and often proprietary ways. Single scripts can be versioned, but the whole integration itself can't be versioned or managed explicitly. This is suboptimal, because the companies' processes are part of their core assets, and you can't improve anything that you can't identify, describe, and measure.

■ *Unreliable data synchronization*—Tools and workflows extract information out of the development process, but tools often have their own proprietary data-storage mechanisms. Using a collection of unrelated tools (for instance, a requirement-tracking tool and a test tool) can quickly lead to a data-integration nightmare. Many tools have an open API to facilitate the sharing of data, or specific features that will handle data integration programmatically (for example, import/export via XML), but the results of programmatic synchronization are often cumbersome and error-prone, increasing the complexity significantly. The lesson learned is that just because you have a requirement-tracking tool and a test tool doesn't necessarily mean there is an ALM connection between these tools.

We need to consider these key issues, which have certainly impacted ALM.

1.2.2   *The dawn of ALM*

Years of experience with implementing software development lifecycles (SDLC) made many people realize there had to be a better approach. These improvements have evolved into what we call application lifecycle management (ALM) today. ALM is implicit in every phase of the lifecycle and impacts all roles, organization units, and development engineering phases, as shown in figure 1.5.[6]

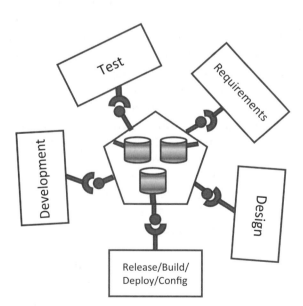

Figure 1.5   ALM is an implicit, pluggable hub: barrier-free engineering without redundant activities or redundant data. We now have neither orthogonal (as in figure 1.3) nor fragmented ALM aspects (as in figure 1.4).

---

[6]   Compare Carey Schwaber, *The Changing Face of Application Life-Cycle Management* (Forrester Research Inc., 2006).

All phases (and the stakeholders in those phases) should be involved with the complete ALM. All stakeholders have connection points to the uniform, comprehensive information hub. Let's look at three major facets of modern ALM:[7]

- *ALM is both a discipline and a product category.* There are many vendors selling full-fledged ALM suites, and others claim they have them in their portfolio. Lightweight, open source tools are also available and are often much easier and more cost-effective to implement. ALM doesn't rely on using any specific ALM tools suite. Your work with ALM should start with the concepts and ideas behind it, such as traceability, automation, and reporting. Also, ALM activities should be strictly based on the requirements of "task-based development," which we'll discuss later.

- *ALM keeps lifecycle activities in sync.* ALM doesn't introduce any specific new methods of developing software. It's more about introducing a supportive and implicit discipline to reduce complexity, keeping the people and processes in sync.

- *ALM integrates tools.* ALM isn't only about tools and using them but also about picking the right tools, using them effectively, and, above all, integrating them. Integration implies a barrier-free chain of tools that share a high-level workflow and consolidated data sets.

These aspects of the ALM approach led to the following key benefits:

- *Traceability of relationships between artifacts*—Created artifacts such as documentation, requirement documents, tests, build scripts, change requests, and source code (for example, changesets) are synchronized and traced automatically. A unified view of them is provided to gain continuous insight into the current status of the development process; this clarifies which requirements were implemented where and which were tested with what results.

- *Automation of high-level processes*—Technical people have been talking about automation for years, and continuous integration and other development-centric strategies are gaining momentum. ALM has continuous integration, but that's not all. When we talk about ALM, we also talk about high-level processes and workflows (such as those for releasing software) that are automated. These workflows should be unique and barrier-free across tools and organizational units. This is an evolved step in integration. ALM deals with maximizing business value, efficiency, flexibility, and the protection of company assets. This can be achieved only through a high-level approach that connects business and technology.

- *Visible progress of development efforts*—Often there's a big gap between the real status of the development and the view available to managers and developers. This

---

[7] Also see Carey Schwaber, *The Changing Face of Application Life-Cycle Management* (Forrester Research Inc., 2006).

gap often increases the higher you climb up the management chain. Frequently, the technical staff reports an overly optimistic view of the current software development status. Managers also do that when they report to their superiors, as they are eager to show they have reached forecasts, objectives, or milestones. But the end result is ugly: Deadlines are missed because risk management was removed from the process, and a lack of transparency conceals progress right up to the end. The goal of ALM is to collect the relevant information, transform that information into knowledge, and generate high-level insight into problems and progress. ALM circumvents old processes that extracted the view manually; communicated it personally; or generated project reports, status meetings, and the like. Instead, the ALM system provides the information continuously.

Obviously, there's a huge benefit to adopting an effective ALM. It's also essential to understand that one must *become* Agile in order to truly be successful in implementing Agile ALM.

1.2.3   *Becoming Agile: Agile ALM*

Agile teams produce higher quality work, deliver results more quickly, and are more flexible, allowing them to respond to changes in requirements (as those requirements are understood by all stakeholders), and making them more likely to create a greater (and often a quicker) return on investment (ROI). The dominance of single large projects is gone. In recent years, IT projects have become smaller and smaller. It's increasingly important to deliver low-cost solutions quickly, in small to midsize projects, or to use scoped milestones in big projects.

It's also important to set up an efficient, lightweight infrastructure in order to gain the benefits of knowledge and synergies. There's no "one size fits all" infrastructure for an ALM, mainly because every company and every project has its own basic conditions and culture. A plain-process or tool-centric approach obscures the fact that software is made by and for human beings, and therefore requires constant oversight by a human being. ALM can provide that oversight. This is one of the ways in which ALM helps to provide structure for Agile.

In this book, we'll also focus on the processes and tools that play a major role in supporting the ALM, but in the center of an Agile ALM project, people, culture, processes, and tools are important for establishing stability, or what I will refer to as *steadiness*. Figure 1.6 illustrates these relationships, with tools and

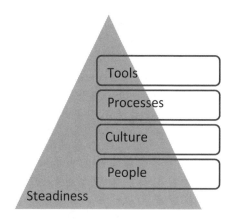

Figure 1.6   Pyramid of steadiness: People and culture own and drive the processes and tools. All four aspects are important.

processes at the top of the steadiness pyramid. People are the foundation of the steadiness pyramid, followed by culture. You don't want to use tools that will force you to practice specific processes. It needs to be the other way around: You identify and define the processes and decide on the tools to help you in applying those processes. To take the full path, you identify and define your goals as a first step and then use the processes best suited to achieving those goals.

Culture is heavily affected by former projects, historical events, and the collective experience and knowledge of the company. Though it's hard, culture must change if the organization is going to succeed with software development in the long run. Persuasion doesn't work. Management has to commit to delivering high-quality software by building in learning time and providing support for studying new practices and processes that will work better. They need to provide the right intrinsic motivators, such as autonomy and ability to innovate. The development team has to commit to building high-quality software. The development team needs to understand the definition of quality, and management needs to value quality preferably over time, scope, and cost. As people start to understand, they'll be allowed to "do things right," and then they'll be motivated to choose and learn the tools that best fit the process. Choosing the tools and the process is the easy part—it's easy to implement a framework like Scrum. But it's hard to flesh it out with a real commitment to quality and to business–technical collaboration.

All of this means that if you want to change a software development aspect in your company, you need both a bottom-up and a top-down approach. At the bottom level, you should persuade people to support the goals that you have articulated. It's much easier to overcome resistance to change when you have support from the key stakeholders, such as an experienced programmer who recommends or already uses a specific tool (often an open source tool). Relying on the opinions of experienced people is better than having a bureaucracy deploy large, cumbersome tools. At the top level, you also need a strong commitment from management to change processes or tools, because people become attached to using certain processes and tools and won't want to change without good reason.

Generally, stability is an advantage, so there should always be good reasons for changing something that's successfully in place. But developing software is about change, and Agile addresses exactly that. It can be hard to change to an Agile environment, so it's imperative to focus on selecting the tools best aligned to your flexible processes (not the other way around). These tools should have an open architecture, be simple to use, interchangeable, extensible, and interoperable.

Being flexible and *agile* in the classic sense requires an openness to change. Additionally, an integral, continuous risk management and review process is needed to quickly identify issues and their potential consequences. Modern software development consists of managing change and understanding all development activities as a defined and traceable process. Agile helps with change and risk management, independent of the overall development process you are using. Agile also focuses on the

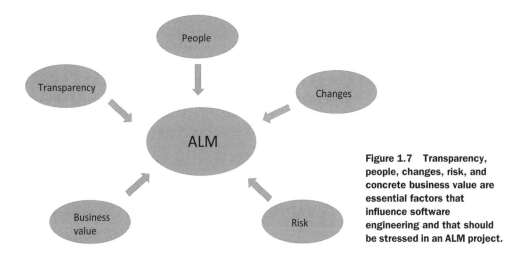

Figure 1.7 Transparency, people, changes, risk, and concrete business value are essential factors that influence software engineering and that should be stressed in an ALM project.

importance of transparency and on alignment with business value, as illustrated in figure 1.7.

We'll learn more about concrete Agile strategies in chapter 2 and we'll discuss lightweight, primary open source tools throughout the rest of this book. Right now, we'll look at the building blocks of Agile ALM. This information will give you the necessary preparation for subsequent chapters.

1.3 Building blocks of Agile ALM

What exactly is Agile ALM and what value does it add? In this section, we'll consider that question in the context of software releases and service orientation. We'll also discuss how important it is to be focused on the stakeholders' needs and to use a task-based approach. We'll consider configurable, pluggable systems and standards. Finally, we'll talk about what it means to use and cope with "polyglot" environments, with their many languages and technologies, and how to apply open source methods and automation. The tools we'll cover in this book will enable you to implement and support these building blocks. Tools are important, but it's also important to start with a stakeholder focus.

1.3.1 Stakeholder focus

Developing a software application isn't just about writing code. Once developed, code must be tested, approved, and deployed to the live environment where it must be maintained. Many programmers will expect their code to migrate to the live environment as soon as it's completed to see that their deliverables are used, whereas others understand that the release will be promoted when it's tested and approved.

> **INTERDISCIPLINARY ROLES** In this book, the *developer* is a person who not only develops or programs code but also has an interdisciplinary skill set. Developers are skilled in coding, but they should also know how to test, configure, and ship features. As a consequence, some people don't like to see the word

developer used for programmer. They argue that everyone involved in delivering software is a developer, including the testers. The DevOps movement (the word is a blend of development and operations) similarly brings development and operations together regarding communication, collaboration, and integration. All developers—programmers, testers, database administrators (DBAs), and other people on the team—need to take responsibility for quality and for ensuring that all testing, configuration, and deployment activities are completed at the same time as the coding takes place.

Depending on their role within the organization, each person may have a different focus.[8] For instance, a developer should usually work in an isolated environment (with an IDE) and then commit code only if it won't break the build for the rest of the team. Continuous integration (CI) provides immediate feedback to developers if code committed to the trunk can't successfully build. The release manager needs to have a clear overview of the status and must know whether the latest code (on the trunk) will build successfully and pass all relevant unit and automated tests. The release manager should also be kept advised on the state of QA testing and should know the current version in production. Production operators prefer an automated deployment process, where they can control the environment variables and flawlessly release a specific baseline of the code (or revert back if necessary). Finally, the CIO and CEO of a corporation (among other senior managers) want to see an automated and repeatable process with an audit trail.

ALM consists of several steps, including traditional versioning, and ends with deployment, always weighing the importance of the underlying business (the target domain). All those aspects are important for individual stakeholders, as outlined in table 1.1.

Table 1.1 **Stakeholder focus in an Agile ecosystem**

Why . . .	Developer	Production*	Management	Customer
Versioning?	Keep track of the changes	Easily revert to a prior version	No loss of data	Reliability
Continuous integration process?	Concentrate on developing software Early feedback Integrate with code from others	Get high-quality production code	Fewer errors Repeatable process Faster and shorter release cycle	Early feedback Working software
Automated build?	No loss of valuable time	Everything is coordinated by a script	Prevents mistakes	Fast feedback cycles

* For example, deployment, delivery, maintenance

---

[8] In *The Art of Project Management* (O'Reilly, 2005), Scott Berkun talks about three different perspectives: the business perspective, the technology perspective, and the customer perspective (chapter 3).

Table 1.1   Stakeholder focus in an Agile ecosystem *(continued)*

Why . . .	Developer	Production*	Management	Customer
Automated deploy?	Guarantee that production will receive the quality code Consistent and reliable process for deployment	No manual intervention reduces risk	Increases the possible release cycle frequency and productivity	High quality
Process?	Easier to build code for the test or production environment	Automate production deployment Reduce rework	Answers questions of who, when, why, and what occurred?	Comprehensive view Bridging technology and business

* For example, deployment, delivery, maintenance

We need to consider all stakeholders and their interests in an Agile environment (stakeholder focus). We also need to consider both the functional and technical views of release management.

1.3.2   Views on releasing and Agile ALM

Agile ALM can be split into a functional view and a technical view.

The goal of a functional view of ALM is to assign and track the implementation of requirements. Effective release management is at the core of successful Agile ALM, and this can be implemented with the help of Agile process frameworks like Scrum. Even if you don't use an overall Agile process model, applying Agile strategies can still improve the development process.

On the other hand, a technical view of ALM deals with integrating components (integration management) and increasing productivity by improving the development process, such as with continuous integration and installing productive development environments. A technical process and infrastructure *hub* enables automatic building and releasing, and incorporates testing, quality auditing, and integrating requirements.

In chapter 3, we'll discuss the functional view by implementing Scrum. In the same chapter, we'll bridge the gap between the functional and technical views.

Agile ALM also places a strong value on understanding the impact and value of the service orientation.

1.3.3   Service orientation, SaaS, IaaS, PaaS

Providing a service on demand (or Software as a Service—SaaS) isn't new. There have been a number of successful SaaS systems, including customer relationship management (CRM) systems such as www.Salesforce.com, which introduced this approach long ago. Today, there are many successful SaaS services, including several from Google: Gmail, Google Docs, and Google Calendar.

SaaS applications are often hosted on the providers' web servers to be used whenever the customer needs the service, and the vendor usually provides an API with a well-defined interface to make these services available. Normally, the functionality can be used by web services through a service-oriented architecture (SOA). With this approach, you distinguish business services from technical, isolated services. Technical services, for instance, encapsulate data (data access). The SOA approach introduces producers of services and consumers of those services. Reusing services and assets can help improve productivity. A repository of services on a consumer level is as important as a repository of technical components on a detailed, technical level. We'll look at this in more detail in our discussion of component repositories.

Besides SaaS, Infrastructure as a Service (IaaS) is also relevant today. A popular example is Amazon Web Services (AWS), a set of web services, and Elastic Cloud Computing (EC2), a big pool of hardware that can be used dynamically. A standard use case is to install your own images on those remote computers to extend processing power. Meanwhile, IaaS has become easy to use (a commodity). For instance, tools provided by VMWare provide a service to set up and roll out full images of computer systems and virtual machines.

Finally, Platform as a Service (PaaS) focuses on a platform that itself (the runtime environment) is hosted and scaled dynamically. An example of this is the Google App Engine, which lets you deploy and run your own applications.

Cloud computing is an example of IaaS that can also include PaaS and SaaS. Cloud computing describes scaled, configured, and dynamically provisioned infrastructure. The *cloud* can be publicly accessible on the internet, private (internally accessible), or a hybrid of the two. One cloud computing scenario in an Agile ALM context is to run agents (slaves) of a build agent in the cloud, adding additional, temporary power to your build grid as needed.

I refer to SaaS, IaaS, and PaaS collectively as (X)aaS. They are affected by Agile ALM, and vice versa. Although outsourced, the hosted items should be included in the ALM and not treated separately, though this isn't mandatory. You can use (X)aaS without any ALM in mind.

Agile ALM does comprise slicing services, focusing on core expertise while reducing costs and delivering reproducibility. You need to know which services and assets your project or company has in order to decide what you could add to this service "zoo" with an (X)aaS. This doesn't depend on the scope: On a business level, you benefit from knowing your services and the functions that they provide.

You may think this is obvious, but many companies don't know what functionality they have built up over the years. Identifying the services while starting with (X)aaS is a big value to begin with. You can't distribute a service into the cloud if you don't know which services you have. The same is true on a more technical level. You can garner huge benefit by identifying the components and their dependencies. Many companies don't know which technical assets they have, nor do they know the asset dependencies. They set out a big package of deployment units containing a nontransparent object meshwork without knowing if those units are necessary in that context. This is a use case where a build and release tool, such as Maven, can help to identify what units you have in your technical portfolio, including specific versions and dependencies.

1.3.4   *Task-based and outside-in*

Working in a *task-based* way means that, first, all activities are based on specific requirements or tasks, often called work items. Task-based also means tracing each task and the changes it creates, and this becomes even more appealing if you span the tracing over all roles, phases, and organizational units, including production. When are you close to the maximum of improving your process? When the production crew (and any other stakeholders) not only host final deployment units, but also know exactly which units are based on which sources. Additionally, you will know which sources were touched because of which changes were requested. This doesn't depend on languages, systems, and organizational barriers.

You can link requirements and defects to coding items, and vice versa. This referencing makes it much easier to validate that the work is done to plan and that the plan is getting done. This end-to-end referencing provides much more scale than using the plain story cards that are used by some Agile approaches, although this may be sufficient in many circumstances too. A common method is to add a ticket number to the check-in command so tools can cross-reference requirements with coding artifacts. An essential method is using change-sets. A change-set is a group of changes made to the system but processed as an atomic unit. Consider the different changes a developer must make to implement a new feature. Instead of checking in each change separately, they can be checked in as a single atomic transaction. This way, the system can verify that all changes are traced to their respective requirements and can update the status of the baseline.

A basic premise of Agile ALM is that work should be aligned to the customer's requirements. One approach to doing this is called *outside-in*. Too often, work isn't based on specific customer requirements, and sometimes requirements aren't defined at all or aren't tracked through the process. Other times, the technical staff and the customer, may be speaking different languages in defining the requirements of the software. The outside-in approach takes the right focus and it leads to a different approach in measuring success; it values customer satisfaction and other soft attributes. Its main drivers are as follows:[9]

- Understanding your stakeholders and the business context
- Mapping project expectations to outcomes more effectively
- Building more consumable software, making systems easier to deploy and use
- Enhancing alignment with stakeholder goals continuously

In this way, the customer requirements are implemented in the software development system.

Another important approach is known as a *balanced scorecard*, and it has much in common with outside-in. The customer (internal or external) requests a job and wants the job completed in a way that meets the business requirements. The customer

---

[9]   See Carl Kessler and John Sweitzer, *Outside-in Software Development* (IBM Press, 2008).

pays for functionality, not for technical solutions, design patterns, or prefactoring patterns on their own. The customer is interested in the resulting software and values working software more than comprehensive documentation. An unfortunate consequence of this approach is that you may deliver the software late. If you can deliver the product only when it's completed, the customer will expect that the release has been rigorously tested and is production-ready. Failing to communicate the status of the software and the development of the requirements to the customer is a missed opportunity at best, and will likely result in poorer quality software, as measured by the many bugs that will be detected late in the process. The outside-in approach is driven by communicating the status of the software to the customer early, which enables you and the customer to make decisions sooner rather than later.

You should communicate with the customer and the whole team in real time by setting up a task-based infrastructure. With the help of this infrastructure, all stakeholders, including the developer (in his workspace), the project or release manager, and the quality team, are kept informed about the implementation progress. The most important stakeholder—the customer—is also able to get honest answers about the project's current status.

> **OUTSIDE-IN AND BALANCED SCORECARD (BSC)**   There are parallels between the outside-in and balanced scorecard (BSC) approaches. Robert S. Kaplan introduced BSC as a strategic performance management and controlling tool. It also values nonfinancial measures and adds them to project reporting. BSC has four perspectives: financial, customer, internal business, and innovation/learning.

In chapter 4, I'll describe task-based development, and in chapter 8, I'll explain collaborative development and testing and provide a concrete implementation of outside-in. Acceptance tests and behavior-driven development (BDD) are properties of collaborative testing. Part 4 covers this major aspect of Agile ALM.

1.3.5   *Configuration, customization, and plug-ins*

The days of proprietary, heavyweight, monolithic tools that constitute the one-size-fits-all solution are ending. Tools that can be orchestrated and configured according to individual needs are the new trend. They provide features in an open, standardized way (for example, as a service), but they can also be configured and extended as needed.

Tools don't have to be reimplemented or extended programmatically to fit to the latest project needs. Continuous reimplementing is a nice business strategy for tool vendors, because it generates steady sales revenue, but companies change their minds and therefore require flexibility. Tools nowadays can be reconfigured extensively without touching the sources and without needing upgrades or replacement. Customization is easy enough that the project members can implement it on their own, without requiring a long learning curve.

Moving away from a more monolithic infrastructure, we can turn to a development system involving fine-grained modules. Application suites are customized as needed, and functionality is added where necessary with the help of plug-ins. These plug-ins may be part of the tool vendor's product portfolio, or they may come from a third-party institution or from the open source community. The overall tool integration infrastructure is evolving into what is known as a *mashup*, which refers to a toolset that combines data, user interface, and other functionality from two or more sources to create a new service.

Other key issues with monolithic infrastructures include the effort users have exerted to personalize an application to their needs and how many UI controls they must use to access their data. Today, role-based applications with complex dashboard functionalities are state of the art. Dashboards can be configured and customized to individual needs, and they offer many customization features out of the box, without the need to contact the vendor. Dashboards offer views on aggregated data and allow you to zoom in to get more details.

1.3.6 *The polyglot programming world*

We have already discussed the need to provide integrated access to the requirements and tests. But what happens with all those coding artifacts, themselves? Many big companies still use Cobol, for example. Others use only Java. To protect company assets, businesses integrate their legacy applications or partially enrich them with new technologies and components, such as providing new, more convenient user interfaces. Also, those different language sources have to be developed and should be managed in an integrative fashion. To enable that, integrated development environments (IDEs) support more and more development with different coding types. You can store all of those artifacts in one version-control system (VCS).

> **SOME WORDS ABOUT LEGACY CODE** Legacy code can sound pejorative, but *legacy code*, written in older languages, such as Cobol, may be an essential company asset. Billions of lines of Cobol code were created, and applications based on Cobol do their job continuously, and are still extended with new Cobol code. For other people, legacy code means code written by someone else last week. A third meaning of legacy code is code that neglects to include significant test coverage. For a detailed discussion of legacy code, see Michael Feathers, *Working Effectively with Legacy Code* (Prentice Hall, 2004).

Challenges in software development can be complex and individual. Having the choice of using a special programming language to solve a specific problem can be valuable. You can be more effective when you have an open landscape where you can use the technology and programming language best fitted to your task.[10] Whatever technology you use, it should be the best fit for the task.

For example, it could be better to write a neat file by copying scripts with the Ant tool than to set up a full-fledged Java application. Or you might use a dynamically

---

[10] See Andrew Hunt and David Thomas, *The Pragmatic Programmer* (Addison-Wesley Professional, 1999).

typed language like Groovy to write tests easily, or a statically typed language like Scala to enhance your software system, because it can be smoother to use these languages than Java, even though all these languages (Groovy, Scala, and Java) compile to byte-code and share the same JVM runtime environment. We look at Groovy and Scala in chapter 9, but the point isn't that you need to learn new languages, but rather, that you may have to cope with multilanguage environments.

In *The Productive Programmer* (O'Reilly, 2008), Neal Ford defines *polyglot programming* as "building applications using one or more special-purpose languages in addition to a general-purpose language" (p. 169). In this book, we'll talk about how you can integrate different artifact types in a continuous integration context. Furthermore, we'll discuss and look at examples of how to use and integrate other languages to accomplish special tasks within the overall process.

1.3.7   *Open source culture*

Development tends to rely more and more on lightweight, primary open source tooling, which supports using Agile strategies. Companies have learned they can't cope with time and cost pressures by focusing only on heavyweight processes and tooling. Lightweight tools can help here, and we'll discuss and integrate a lot of them in this book. But lightweight, open source tooling can require a cultural rethink within the company to overcome the tendency to resist change. Don't be afraid to change processes and tools where needed. Keep your solution aligned to your requirements as they evolve. Many tools don't evolve rapidly enough, others are evolving rapidly, and new tools are continuously entering the field.

With a lightweight toolchain, you should watch the market continuously and acquire new tools with better features as they become available. There are many open source tools available, but only successful open source products have a broad supportive community. If the community is supportive and the products are powerful, as well as easy to use, they'll maintain a leading market position by attracting more people to invest time in further developing the product.

If new open source competitors surpass a former market leader, it can be dangerous to ignore this development. A good approach is to be flexible in your decisions, to continuously monitor the market, and to focus on the tool mainline consisting of de facto standards and popular tools.

Buying commercial tools also requires you to watch the market. But once you've bought an expensive tool, you're often stuck with it for a long time. Another problem is that all vendors of commercial products claim their products are the best. Running an open source culture means being open-minded and preferring open, flexible solutions that can replace approaches and tools quickly with new and better ones. It also means you should constantly evaluate whether what you did yesterday still works best today and experiment with alternatives.

1.3.8   Open technology and standards

We've already talked about how Agile ALM facets and services should be orchestrated on demand, driven by the specific needs of a project. Tools have their interfaces, and ALM encourages the seamless integration of tools without barriers. Now the question is, how can we integrate those tools efficiently across different vendor products to provide services for the customer? For instance, it's pretty common to have multiple independent databases in your infrastructure. The minimum solution is to have open standards, such as internet protocols, to connect them. Integration shouldn't be done via data import/export routines, though; rather, data should be integrated where it's located.

What standards address these kinds of questions? The Open Services for Lifecycle Collaboration (OSLC, http://open-services.net) is a community-driven effort, mainly sponsored by IBM, to improve the integration of lifecycle tools. Members of the alliance are commercial vendors of ALM tools and other stakeholders, including IBM, Oracle, Accenture, Shell, Citigroup, Siemens, and many others. Commercial vendors drive the OSLC, which is aligned with feature-rich tools (like the IBM Rational product family), but the program is tool-category agnostic, meaning that it also encompasses open source tools.

The OSLC program established special interest groups working on individual ALM areas, including change management, requirement management, and software configuration management, providing public descriptions of interfaces for integrating these features. The interfaces are specified in a REST web service style.

The OSLC Open Source Project aims to encourage the creation of other components and contributions that can help support the OSLC community's goals. As part of the project reference implementations, sample code and test suites for testing OSLC service provider implementations are provided.

In this book, we'll discuss the concepts and solutions for ALM with lightweight, primarily open source tools and how to integrate them seamlessly. One benefit of choosing best-of-breed, lightweight, open source tools is that integrating them is often easier than integrating monolithic commercial tools. I call this the "Agile way." It's also based on technology standards, but without any cross-tooling interface standards.

OSLC has had a slow beginning. Although first specifications have been finalized, many are still in development, and the community is growing continuously. A prominent implementation of OSLC is available with IBM's Jazz platform (http://jazz.net). It's based on OSLC, extending it with its own Jazz Integration Architecture. IBM wants to further integrate its single Rational products with the help of that approach, including Rational Requirements Composer (a requirements management tool) and Rational Quality Manager (test management), and incorporate them with Rational Team Concert.

The impact of OSLC on Agile ALM development has to be monitored. Some people have reservations about big, traditional product vendors and their motivations. The question that many people will ask is, will OSLC have any significant influence on open source or commercial tools at all, or is it a "founder's toy"? If the latter is true, then only the original participants will benefit from this latest attempt at creating open standards.

1.3.9   *Automation*

Automation is the use of solutions to reduce the need for human work. "Automation can ensure that the software is built the same way each time, that the team sees every change made to the software, and that the software is tested and reviewed in the same way every day so that no defects slip through or are introduced through human error."[11] In software development projects, a high level of automation is a prerequisite to quickly delivering the best quality and getting feedback from stakeholders early and often.

Automating the most error-prone, repetitive, and time-consuming activities is most essential. Additionally, automation is necessary in all areas where you are interested in objective, reproducible results. Another good impulse to start with automating is if some parts of the process aren't transparent for the team. You should automate parts of the process that you don't understand so far; you can only automate what you understand and are able to describe. Finally, automation helps in areas where manual work is annoying—good developers have always automated repetitive aspects of their work.

A system can be evolved to have a high level of automation if the process is based on the building blocks of Agile ALM, as they are illustrated in this book. Continuous improvement should be part of your process. For improving the level of automation (and for improving anything in general), self-reflection is essential. You can best improve what you measure, and to measure something, you need a process that delivers results in a reproducible way.

1.4   *Comprehensive Agile ALM with lightweight tooling*

Complexity can take many forms. Organizational aspects create complexity, such as team size, distributed development, or antipatterns such as entrenching people. Technical and regulatory specifications are basic conditions that also influence complexity.

Small teams with low organizational or technical complexity can completely self-organize and choose the tools they want. But a loosely managed infrastructure may be unmanageable as soon as complexity increases. To improve awareness across the team in complicated scenarios, it's necessary to use leading tools and their powerful features. High demands for traceability and full automation, as well as for accelerating knowledge sharing, can only be fulfilled using integrated toolchains consisting of best-of-breed tools while driving an end-to-end approach.

A focus on integration occurs as complexity increases. Communication becomes more difficult, as does extracting knowledge from information and aggregating information from data. To reproduce and audit the full process at its most complex point, you should use a comprehensive end-to-end approach that includes all stakeholders, workflows, and configuration items. Tools that are seamlessly integrated will immediately add considerable value to the system. Understanding the overall process

---

[11] Andrew Stellman and Jennifer Greene, *Applied Software Project Management* (O'Reilly, 2006), p. 165

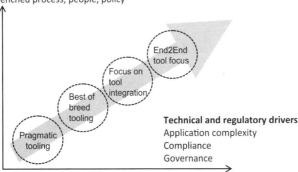

Organizational drivers
Team size
Organizational distribution
Entrenched process, people, policy

End2End tool focus

Focus on tool integration

Best of breed tooling

Pragmatic tooling

Technical and regulatory drivers
Application complexity
Compliance
Governance

Figure 1.8 Interdependency of complexity and tool usage: In complex environments, it's essential to use an integrated toolchain that glues together the best-of-breed tools to serve all stages of development in an end-to-end approach. Each circle must build on the previous one, so the end-to-end focus needs to be integrated, best-of-breed, and pragmatic.

and the status of both the project and the artifacts becomes a necessary part of coordinating the work.

In software development projects, an end-to-end approach delivers the best results, where you automate and integrate activities across phases, including building, developing and testing, releasing, deploying, and staging (configuring) artifacts with appropriate tools. Figure 1.8[12] shows the increasing importance of tools in the context of organizational and technical and regulatory drivers.

1.4.1   *Toolchains and accidental complexity*

The benefits of an integrated end-to-end tooling approach extend beyond coping with the complexity itself; it must minimize accidental complexity. *Accidental complexity* is that which is nonessential to the specific task to be performed. Whereas essential complexity is inherent and unavoidable, accidental complexity is caused by the approach chosen to solve the problem. An effective toolchain helps reduce complexity by providing traceability to show what has changed, when it was changed, who changed it, and who approved the change for promotion. A good toolchain also accelerates communication (for example, transparency and visibility) expressing the current state of the software, and it's the communication vehicle for all stakeholders.

The toolchain is both the glue that holds together the various components and phases of the application lifecycle and the oil that lubricates the smooth and efficient interaction of those components. It delivers an automated workflow, drives a continuous stream of activity through the development lifecycle, and efficiently coordinates and streamlines development changes.

VENDORS There are many proprietary, commercial (and expensive) tools and tool suites on the market, such as AccuRev AgileCycle, CollabNet

---

[12] Inspired by and derived from Scott Ambler, *Collaborative Application Lifecycle Management with IBM Rational Products* (IBM Redbooks, 2008), p. 41, Figure 2-14.

TeamForge, codeBeamer, MKS Integrity, Synergy, IBM Rational Team Concert, PDSA Agile ALM, Rally ALM, Visual Studio Team, and Borland Management Solution that can help (or that claim to help) implement an (Agile) ALM. Others, such as StarTeam and DOORS, provide support for single aspects in the overall process.

Chains of lightweight tools help you to deliver solutions across development phases, addressing even more stakeholders and keeping businesspeople and developers on the same page. Lightweight tools offer the features you need based on your project's requirements. They are customizable and straightforward to use, they have an open architecture, they're mostly free or moderately priced, and they can be easily integrated with other tools. My definition of Agile ALM results in processes and toolchains that are flexible, open to change, and high in quality. But always keep in mind that Agile ALM isn't only a product category, but also a discipline and a mental approach. Working with Agile ALM should start with values and people as well as the concepts behind it.

> **FREE AND OPEN SOURCE TOOLS**   This book doesn't strictly distinguish between free software and open source software, and it contrasts both to commercial software. There are many possible variations and license models, but in this book, I use *open source* in its classic sense: when the sources of the tool are available and the tool is free. We'll discuss lightweight and primarily open source tools. Open source tools covered in this book are considered to be lightweight too; some lightweight tools covered here aren't open source and cost money, but they're cost-effective and low-priced in comparison to feature-rich products from big traditional vendors. Examples of lightweight commercial tools are those from Atlassian, such as JIRA. Consult the individual tool licenses for the details on each tool.

1.4.2   Agile ALM tools

Some software development tools are too heavy, are monoliths, or offer functionality you seldom use. Often these tools are pretty expensive and difficult to roll out. Depending on your particular requirements, commercial, feature-rich tools or one-stop-shop tool suites may be a good fit for you, but these tools aren't the focus of this book. Recently, the ALM space saw a surge of integration with Agile concepts. Tool vendors understand more and more that it's crucial to become agile in order to cope with continuously changing requirements and contexts. This results in more and more companies using the term "Agile ALM" to describe their ALM suites. The origins of this book are different. Here, Agile strategies are introduced and implemented by lightweight tools. Chains of integrated tools lead to tailored, orchestrated ALM solutions.

An Agile ALM tool is one that fosters an Agile process. There's no strict checklist to categorize whether a tool is an Agile ALM tool, but the tool must enable you to become Agile—the tool must help the team do its job better, aggregating and providing information in an integrated, interdisciplinary way. An Agile ALM tool must add value to the system and improve the collaboration of the stakeholders. In my opinion, an Agile ALM toolchain must implement the essential Agile ALM strategies discussed in this book.

Some organizations use Agile ALM single-point solutions; others feel more comfortable with an orchestration of single tools. Both scenarios have their advantages and drawbacks. Too much complexity is a potential risk for both cases; the goal should be to minimize the accidental complexity. Relying on lightweight toolchains can dramatically improve flexibility because you can easily replace small units of the overall infrastructure without touching other parts. Many companies experience their best results (as the ratio of minimized complexity and optimized flexibility) while driving an open source culture. This means they use a mashup of configurable tools that offer exactly the features that are needed to solve a given task, and they evolve the infrastructure incrementally. Configurability, service orientation, and an open architecture (such as a plug-in system) can help to decrease complexity and increase flexibility. For "ready to go" tool suites, configurability is even more important. The market doesn't offer an Agile ALM tool suite that could serve as a golden hammer for all projects without having any configuration capability. Using a comprehensive one-stop-shop solution that can't be customized or extended as needed leads directly to "shadow processes" or retrofitting your process to work with the tool, which is a pretty bad approach.

There are Agile ALM tools or tool suites that cover (or claim to cover) many development phases. But it's not mandatory for a single tool to span all phases. Agile ALM tools can't and shouldn't automate everything. For example, consider build scripts: Tools should be able to trigger existing build scripts. But it's not the one-stop-shop Agile ALM tool suite that compiles the code; rather, it's the underlying solution that's already in place and successful.

1.4.3 Effective and efficient tooling

The process of picking the right tool should be aligned with your particular requirements. You may find that an out-of-the-box suite fits best to your individual context. Alternatively, you might prefer to orchestrate individual tools in a flexible way, where a single tool focuses on a special task and is able to easily integrate with the overall tool infrastructure. A toolchain that spans different development phases is sometimes called software development lifecycle (SDLC) tooling. Integration management integrates the work of your team and leads to technically and functionally consistent software. From a tool perspective, an Agile ALM tool integrates with other tools. An isolated, standalone tool, acting as a silo and satisfying only a minor subset of your stakeholders, will probably neither accelerate collaboration nor improve the time to market of your software product. You can also use tools successfully without connecting them to an overall Agile ALM ecosystem. Additionally, there are many great tools, market leaders in their field, whose users would never hit on the idea that they're using a tool that could be an essential part of an Agile ALM toolchain. I'll cover examples of those tools throughout the book.

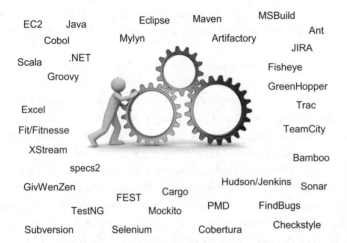

EC2   Java   Eclipse   Maven   MSBuild

Cobol   Mylyn   Artifactory   Ant

Scala   .NET   JIRA

Groovy   Fisheye

                              GreenHopper

Excel   Trac

Fit/Fitnesse   TeamCity

XStream   Bamboo

specs2

GivWenZen   Hudson/Jenkins Sonar

          FEST   Cargo

TestNG   Mockito   PMD   FindBugs

Subversion   Selenium   Cobertura   Checkstyle

Figure 1.9 Agile ALM integrates platforms, tools, and languages, all driven by people (illustration ©iStockphoto.com/ sellingpix).

Figure 1.9 gives an overview of the tools, languages, and platforms we'll discuss and integrate in this book. Lightweight tools are used throughout the complete development chain. In terms of languages and platforms, we'll mainly talk about Java, but we'll also discuss Cobol, Scala, Groovy, and .NET.

Normally, there's one leading tool that drives the process. It's the central entry point, which is generally also responsible for the workflow or that acts as a central dashboard. Building and releasing a software product involves many complex processes, roles, and deliverables, which need to be managed so they fit together, and streamlining these processes is a major effort, particularly when there are many people involved. An Agile ALM solution manages not only the simple versioning of your source code files, but it also facilitates support for continuous integration and build management. An Agile ALM solution also enables you to deploy the end result, and it offers approval processes and can manage complex runtime dependencies. Agile ALM tools have much more flexibility than the first-generation library tools that once enabled you to pump out a single software version at a time to a target library.

In modern Agile settings, the whole lifecycle is managed and tracked. With effective and efficient tooling, it's much easier to determine which requirements are already implemented in which artifacts and which bugs can be traced to specific artifacts. The artifacts can be compiled and deployed as a repeatable process. Continuous integration and audits can show the status of the development and provide synchronization points. But this doesn't happen manually—a toolchain should be used to connect and integrate both functional and technical release management.

In order to understand Agile ALM more clearly, let's consider an example use case.

1.5   *Example use case*

Let's look at an example Agile ALM use case. Before committing a change to the central VCS, the developer runs a private build on his desktop. This developer build is comparable to a *nightly build* (in continuous integration), which is often the same as an *integration build*. The difference is that the developer build runs in a local, isolated environment instead of the shared integration environment.

The required versions of identical, properly sliced component dependencies or transitive component dependencies are used, and if necessary they're replaced with mocks. Component developers include in their workspaces only those external components that are necessary to do their work. The external components are included as clean dependencies, which means that binaries, rather than sources, are included in their development environments. The dependencies are tested at a central place and are provided via a central component repository.

During the private builds, tests are run, including unit tests, component tests, functional tests, and smoke tests. The integration builds also run these tests, but they enrich them with more detailed integration tests.

> **NOTE** A *smoke test* (or *sanity test*) is a first test made to provide some assurance that the system won't catastrophically fail. In an IT project, a smoke test could be an automated test that starts the application and simulates a first user interaction by opening a visual control on the user interface.

Builds

A *build* is a standard repeatable and measurable compilation and packaging process done automatically. The specific steps of this process may vary. Some argue building means compiling. Others may include a preparation of the system, working on baselines in VCSs, compiling sources, running different sorts of tests, and packaging and distributing the configuration items. Build can also refer to the greater automation flow, including static code analysis, unit testing, and deployment. The output (the deliverables) of this process is often called a build.

The changes from multiple developers are integrated continuously and automatically. Each version of the build is the basis of later releases and distributions.

The build is completely configurable and can produce multiple versions that run on different target environments, including Windows and Linux machines. But be aware that even early in the process you should use environments (including operating systems) that match those you'll use in production.

This task-based build process overlaps different phases and roles. The developer codes according to tasks that are tracked and assigned. Part of the application is a bouquet of languages that are either company assets developed with commonly used, mainstream programming languages or targeted languages chosen to solve a specific programming task. For testing, Groovy and Scala are used, and all the tests are integrated into a seamless infrastructure without any cross-media conversations or friction losses.

The status of the software is always visible across the system. The toolchain is highly integrated and connects all developers and customers. In addition to the technical release infrastructure, the functional release management slices work items into more fine-grained tasks and assigns features to releases.

We'll discuss the different aspects of this example use case throughout the rest of this book.

Field report: "ALM at Siemens CT"
By Rainer Wasgint, program manager at Siemens Corporate Technology

At Siemens Corporate Research and Technologies, we're addressing cross-business sector topics and applied science and sharing best practices. Within the Global Technology Field (GTF) System Development Technologies, we're looking for the top tools and technology to give our development teams the best possible support. Over the last several years, we could clearly see software development infrastructures moving away from ad hoc toolchains and toward carefully considered, well-managed, and integrated solutions, now called ALM. For us, this meant finding an integrated solution that offers seamless project support to increase efficiency and provide transparency within the development process; impact analysis of potential changes and the identification of the involved parties; and project status reporting, including dashboarding for customers or upper management.

For example, when we were faced with the task of meeting the CENELEC/EuroNorm regulatory quality standards for motors, we needed a process and toolchain that was adaptable to different kinds of environments, ranging from small, colocated development teams to large, worldwide distributed project teams. It also needed to be applicable to different project processes, from heavyweight processes like RUP or the V-Model to Agile approaches.

To support such a huge range of potential ALM solutions, our approach is to implement scenarios based on a "meta-model" specific to each project. The meta-model describes the interconnection of the involved disciplines and the associated development artifacts like requirements, models, tests, and configurations. This allows us to control the resulting interaction paths in a structured manner. Rather than claim overall completeness for every thinkable relation, the model focuses on the information needed for traceability, impact-analysis, and the automation of tasks within ALM.

An optimal instantiation of this meta-model requires a flexible and configurable interaction between the software development tools used. Today, mainly interface-based, plug-in, or middleware-bus-based approaches dominate the markets, and unfortunately, there is no major standard for intertool communication and data exchange. We see a promising movement toward service-based and on-demand tools built on open standards, such as the Open Services for Lifecycle Collaboration (OSLC), which is community hosted and driven by IBM Rational to develop a specification for vendor-independent tool integration.

1.6   *Summary*

In this chapter, you learned about challenges common to software development. You saw how this prompted the evolution in software engineering that led to Agile ALM. You also learned what Agile ALM is for and what its features are.

The evolution of software engineering has moved from a cumbersome, fragmented approach to a more comprehensive, lean, integrated, crosscutting discipline that supports the whole development process. ALM evolved from software configuration management; it's a comprehensive activity spanning the entire development lifecycle, from requirements engineering to maintenance and production, iterating over those phases continuously. It can be understood as a continuous, comprehensive task that incorporates several management disciplines, including build management, release management, configuration management, test management, quality management, and integration management. This integrated approach is called *applied change management*. The goal is to provide high-quality, functionally and technically consistent software. Integration also means the ALM infrastructure provides a single view of the truth as opposed to multiple views.

Using Agile strategies, Agile ALM enriches ALM with further features like peopleware and transparency. Agile ALM is agnostic concerning process models, development categories (product versus project development), and project types (from greenfield to ongoing maintenance projects). It's also agnostic concerning tools and is applicable to both open source and commercial products. In this book, we'll focus on lightweight, primarily open source toolchains.

The remaining chapters provide more details on the different aspects of ALM and on how to implement them with lightweight tooling using Agile strategies. In chapter 2, we'll take a deeper look into Agile in the context of the ALM, and I'll describe my preferred Agile ALM approach.

ALM and Agile strategies

Everyone's doing it Agile today. Few will admit that they're not working in an agile way in its classic sense. But what about Agile software development? It comes in many varieties. Agile is a value system that emphasizes important aspects of software development, including communication and open, respectful collaboration, allowing errors and failures to be treated as valuable learning experiences. Agile promotes a safe-to-fail environment, where you can fail quickly and learn from your mistakes. Everybody makes mistakes; most of them are a result of initiatives based on poorly understood facts. Blaming people for mistakes eliminates their motivation to pursue innovation and leads to "management by fear." People who are afraid of expressing ideas won't ask questions and will act defensively.

Having motivated people is essential to further development; without them, your project will be stuck and will likely be a failure. Therefore, management must be careful to lead their teams by example, through coaching, and by improving basic work conditions. Management by numbers, management by objectives, or management by walking around doesn't work. Instead, prefer management through conversation, socializing, and leadership. Teamwork and leadership are much better when they promote education and improvements, provide a learning process (in which the team members lose nothing by admitting to weakness), and recognize the contributions of all people. "Everyone on the team has some unique contribution."[1] Enable people to have pride of workmanship. When there are issues, leadership shouldn't judge; rather, it should investigate possible causes and offer assistance during the daily work.[2]

Agile focuses on honest, open communication, including a pragmatic view of requirements that have proven to be effective. Management needs to create an environment that is conducive to productive and efficient work. Management by destructive criticism won't work!

A DEFINITION OF AGILE "You accept input from reality and you respond to it." —Kent Beck

Clear communication is essential in any project. Agile helps to facilitate clear communication and honest and open assessment of everything, from understanding user requirements to testing software.

Agile is a term applied to different process models. On the one hand, there are pure Agile models, such as Scrum, Extreme Programming, and DSDM (www.dsdm .org).[3] On the other hand, there are models that can implement an Agile approach, like the Rational Unified Process. Finally, Agile is also used to describe strategies that incorporate an Agile approach. Figure 2.1 illustrates these three dimensions as features of the Agile ecosystem.

In this book, I don't dictate any specific process model for developing software. You can use rich, full-fledged models like waterfall, spiral, or a hybrid type. The point is that you can enrich your current processes where it makes sense for you by using

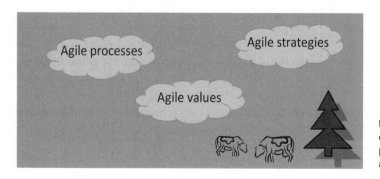

Figure 2.1 The Agile ecosystem: Agile processes, values, and strategies

---

[1] Gerald M. Weinberg, *Quality Software Management*, vol. 3 (Dorset House, 1994), p. 265.

[2] In *Out of the Crisis* (MIT Press, 1982), W. Edwards Deming lists 14 points for management that, in his opinion, lead to improved quality, increased productivity, and better team morale.

[3] For a detailed discussion of different Agile approaches, see Jim Highsmith, *Agile Software Development Ecosystem* (Addison-Wesley, 2002).

Agile strategies. Furthermore, these strategies aren't dependent on any specific tools (though I will recommend some). Think of Agile as a value system, a set of strategies, and a toolbox.

The waterfall

In 1970, Winston W. Royce published an article in which he described the "waterfall model." In the scope of software development, people often think about the waterfall model as a sequential chaining of phases, including design, implementation, and maintenance. They contrast it to the Agile approach, claiming they're completely different, but this isn't the case. Royce claimed that this static, sequential phase ordering wouldn't work. He recommended iterations, but this is often ignored when talking about the waterfall model.

What can we learn from that? First, don't believe everything others say. Second, don't think Agile is reinventing the world. And third, please don't think Agile is chaotic programming where we all do what we want without documentation or orderly control of changes.

In this chapter, we'll gain more insight into Agile strategies. Chapter 3 will introduce an implementation guide for Scrum, an Agile management discipline for functional releasing. This management framework is abstract enough that you can adapt it for many different, individual process flavors. We'll implement Scrum and make it concrete. Using the tools discussed later in this book, you'll implement those strategies.

2.1   *The Agile and project management*

Project management in an Agile environment requires an approach that can handle the frequent changes that exist in iterative development. Agile project management provides transparency and traceability in an environment that thrives on constant change. Everything the team does must add value to the system. The process must be open to changes and be highly organized and disciplined. Continuous cooperation and awareness are indispensable for responsibility, permanent reflection, and synchronization.

The Agile project management process is based on the magic barrel (also known as the magic square; see figure 2.2) and its four pitchers: quality, time, resources/costs, and scope (functionality and number of features). The total volume is limited, which means that features, resources, and time are also limited; in practice, you must save for quality. Agile projects invest much more in quality than traditional projects do.[4] Their high investment in quality is a fixed constant. Their investments in time (mainly in a time-boxed project where the times are fixed) and resources[5] are fixed constants as well, but the scope is variable.

---

[4] "The typical steps we take to deliver a product in less time result in lower quality." Tom DeMarco and Timothy Lister, *Peopleware,* 2nd ed. (Dorset House, 1999), p. 137.

[5] "Adding manpower to a late software project makes it later," Brooks's law, in Frederick P. Brooks, *The Mythical Man-Month* (Addison-Wesley, 1995), p. 25.

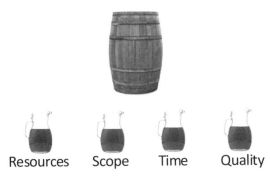

Resources   Scope   Time   Quality

Figure 2.2   The magic barrel. The limited content of the barrel is allocated among four pitchers. If one pitcher is full, then another pitcher will have less liquid. In Agile projects, the quality pitcher is filled to some reasonable amount, with the rest being balanced among the three other pitchers. (Illustrations ©iStockphoto.com/dja65, ©iStockphoto.com/thebroker.)

Software produced in an Agile way is designed, created, tested, and delivered in continuous iterations. An *iteration* is a collection of one to many increments of executable software. An iteration must follow a strict, well-defined process with the required discipline for all participants. The Agile approach is also based upon the fact that customers often don't know all their requirements up front. If customers don't have a complete set of requirements up front, developers often don't have all the information they need to write the code, or even to estimate the amount of time needed to create the application.

Increments and iterations

Increments and iterations are basic concepts in Agile projects:

- An *iteration* is a mini-project that may result in an increment of the software. Iterating starts with an idea of what is wanted, and the code is refined to get the desired result.
- An *increment* is a small unit of functionality. Incrementing allows you to build a better understanding of what you need, assembling the software piece by piece.

Although using both in parallel delivers the best results, this isn't required. You can increment more effectively when requirements are more stable (or you want them to be more stable) or better understood. Iterating allows a better response to changing or unclear requirements.

The Scrum Agile methodology uses both iterations and increments. Each iteration delivers a fully functional increment—a set of shippable features delivered to the end user. Although increments and iterations are highlighted by the Agile ecosystem, many other more traditional process models include these two basic approaches. Both increments and iterations have been around for years. In 1971, one year after Royce talked about iterations in his waterfall model, Harlan Mills from IBM wrote about the concept of incremental development in *Debugging Techniques in Large Systems*.

The Agile approach differs from the traditional approach of developing software. The Agile approach uses Agile values, processes, and strategies, all of which are sometimes viewed from the traditional perspective as an excuse for programmers to abandon project design and management. Table 2.1 lists some common practices used in Agile projects and briefly describes the Agile approach. The third column identifies common misunderstandings from the traditional viewpoint.

Table 2.1 Common Agile practices and associated misunderstandings

Practice	Agile approach	From the traditional perspective
Software development	Treats software development as an information process.	Software development is a manufacturing process.
Communication	Encourages and requires continuous interaction and feedback; the whole team is collocated.	Project members focus on their individual tasks first and often rely on documents more than on communication.
Courage	Encourages an open atmosphere.	There's a fear of missed deadlines and misunderstandings with customers.
Collective ownership	Specifies that program code and documents are owned and maintained by the team.	People feel responsible for only their piece of work.
Integration	Uses continuous integration to get early feedback and increase quality.	Integrations are rare, late, and felt to be a waste of time.
Test-driven development	Treats testing as of great value for design, code, and quality.	Tests are considered a waste of time. Many tests are done manually.
Customer involvement	Encourages customer participation.	The customer is often seen as the contracted party.
Refactoring	Accepts temporary suboptimal, pragmatic design; design is maintained and improved continuously.	Errors aren't allowed; created artifacts are supposed to run perfectly at once.
No overtime, sustainable pace	Follows regular working schedules that can be sustained over time.	Regular overtime is necessary to deliver on time while planning aggressively.
Iterations	Slices software into handy and convenient iterations.	No iterations are necessary; the work focuses on a single release, mostly a big bang release.
Stand-up meeting	Institutes daily structured exchanges.	Big, long, infrequent project meetings are used. The allocation of people and amount of time are often excessive.
Documentation	Uses documentation only where necessary, and when it adds value.	Documentation is considered an important artifact, written according to standards. In reality, it's seldom read.
Team	Treats the team as important, as a collection of individuals having their own strengths and characteristics. The team should be cross-functional.	The individual expert is in focus. Work is done in isolated islands of knowledge.

Table 2.1   Common Agile practices and associated misunderstandings *(continued)*

Practice	Agile approach	From the traditional perspective
Standards	Uses standards, where necessary, that are understood and agreed on by the team.	The work involves a strict process, with many heavyweight standards, often for the sake of having standards.
Quality	Is inherent in everything that the team does.	Quality is the first goal to be skipped when time and money get short.
Change	Considers change as a normal part of project work.	Change is more condemned than encouraged.

All projects address these practices in one way or the other.

The "Manifesto for Agile Software Development" (Agile Manifesto, at agilemanifesto.org) lists four value pairs, where one value is more important than the other.

- *Individuals and interactions over processes and tools*

    General approach—Projects and software development involve human beings. Software is developed by and for people; IT is a means to an end. The necessity of processes and tools is accented because a methodical process and the use of tools are essential, but individuals and interactions are even more important.

    ALM approach—Often people are frustrated when using a comprehensive release or even a lifecycle management approach, because the usage is typically combined with process formalities that are too complex and overloaded. Frequently, tools that provoke a rigid process are used, which isn't necessary. ALM processes and tools should support the work and not vice versa. Knowing and understanding the process will drive the need for a tool and its usage. The ALM infrastructure ought to be lightweight and support interactions. But while individuals and interactions are the primary consideration, processes and tools are also important.

- *Working software over comprehensive documentation*

    General approach—Although documentation of the software is important, a working program is more vital to the customer. Clients can't run their business by creating documentation; they must be able to run a working software system. Software doesn't lie; you can document something that is missing in the software, but you can't simulate executable software functionality just by documenting it. Documentation has to be created in those areas where it adds additional value. The software is self-contained, describing the system and keeping it maintainable for the future (which is often the task of good documentation).

    ALM approach—ALM automates the creation of software artifacts (and configurations). It can be based on "executable knowledge" instead of traditional documents. Rather than documenting processes, the processes are converted to an executable infrastructure. At any time, and starting early, executable software has the priority.

- *Customer collaboration over contract negotiation*

    General approach—Relying on contracts in business is standard. But customers and software developers are sitting in the same boat: Both parties want an optimal solution. Intensive collaboration, continuous exchanges, and active customer involvement are essential during the development.

    ALM approach—ALM can organize expectations and divert the communication and interactions of all stakeholders into coordinated communication and process channels. A targeted process and effective tooling make the project's status visible at any time. ALM delivers synchronization points and serves as a communication vehicle.

- *Responding to change over following a plan*

    General approach—It's important to deliver milestones at regular intervals. A fixed, rigid plan can suggest there's a certain security where none exists. There's often a mismatch between an officially described process and the real one used every day. Changing basic conditions and new insights are part of daily business in software development, and the process must be open to change. Change management is implicit in Agile projects.

    ALM approach—ALM makes change easier. ALM methods and tools facilitate development in a vital, enduring way. Synchronization points support identifying basic conditions as they change.

Agile values impact the entire application lifecycle and transform the way an organization operates in many important ways. In the next section, I'll give some examples of how to implement Agile strategies.

2.2   Agile strategies

Here, I'll describe a set of basic Agile strategies that demonstrate standard approaches to implementing ALM processes. The strategies don't say anything about tooling; they describe concepts and best practices. The strategies will be detailed later in the book and implemented with specific tools.

2.2.1   Version control and a single coding stream

First, it's important to store your artifacts in a version-control system (VCS), but which types of artifacts you store there depends on the project context and the requirements:

- Coding artifacts should be stored in the VCS. Although this sounds obvious, it's not always the case. Many projects, for example, patch their applications in production without having those changes under source control. In addition to source code, tests and build scripts need to be versioned.

- I recommend that you externalize (and version) your runtime configuration settings. It's best practice to control all variable configuration values externally from the application so they can be changed easily without recompiling the application.

- It's wise to place documents, such as use cases (written in Word, for example), into a version-control repository so that you can benefit from versioning and accessing change history.

Although common VCS tools like CVS or Subversion weren't invented to run as file servers, it's possible to store binary artifacts, such as Word documents, in them. Subversion is better equipped for this task than CVS, because it handles binaries more efficiently. This avoids the ugliness of storing documents on a central, shared file structure, which are then replaced randomly, with no history tracking or traceability. Using a VCS for documents is vastly superior to another common mechanism for sharing information: that of sending your documents by email and not having a central place to hold them. Unfortunately, this practice is often the norm.

Additionally, you should set up one central repository to store your assets, to avoid having multiple places where documentation might be located (for example, VCS, a file sharing server, and Notes in parallel).

When you check your artifacts into VCS, you'll have to decide how to arrange the files in the system and decide who works on which stream and why. The rule of thumb here is that you shouldn't open any additional streams for longer than necessary. If you're branching in your VCS, you should close the branch as soon as possible. But consider all developer check-ins and integration processes on one developing stream as synchronization points. This is also valid for distributed version-control systems like Git.

Keeping branches in use for too long is a bad practice.[6] The longer you wait to incorporate changes from one codeline to another, the more effort it takes to merge those lines and the more error-prone the effort will be. To facilitate progress, it's important to integrate code streams frequently. You should have one stream (for instance, a head or trunk) as the leading stream in your development.

There's no one-size-fits-all solution, though. Using branches is a good way to prepare releases (and to incorporate bug fixes on this stream after releasing). In an Agile context, you may only put a label (a tag) on a special source version (a baseline) while continuing to develop on the main code stream (the head/trunk). Then, if you find a bug that must be fixed in a release already promoted to production, you can create a *bugfix* branch, based on the existing tag or based on a given revision number (with Subversion). You can create these branches when needed. This makes the most sense when your velocity and release frequency are high.

In some environments, branches are often used as feature branches (for developing features or whole products or variants) or developer branches (with developers working on their own streams). In such environments, it can be obligatory to use several streams in parallel.

---

[6] See Kent Beck, *Extreme Programming Explained*, 2nd ed. (Addison-Wesley, 2005), p. 67.

2.2.2   *Productive workspaces*

Although frequent integration is essential to rapid coding, developers need control over how they integrate changes into their workspaces so they can work in the most productive way. Avoiding (or delaying) the integration of changes into a workspace means that the developer can complete a unit of work without having to deal with an unexpected problem such as a surprise compilation error. This is known as *working in isolation.*

Developers should always verify that their changes don't break the integration build by updating their sandbox with the most recent changes (from others) and then performing a private build prior to committing changes back to the VCS. Private workspaces enable developers to test their changes before sharing them with the team. The private build provides a quick and convenient way to see if your latest changes could impact other team members.

These practices lead to highly productive development environments. If the quality of the checked-in code is poor (for example, if there are failed tests or compilation errors), other developers will suffer when they include these changes to their workspaces and then see compilation or runtime errors. Getting broken code from the VCS costs everyone time, because developers have to wait for changes or help a colleague fix the broken build, and then waste more time getting the latest clean code. This also means that all developers should stop checking in code to VCS until the broken build is fixed. Avoiding broken code is key to avoiding poor quality.

Developers test their isolated changes, and then, if they pass the tests, check them into the VCS. But an efficient flow is only possible when the local build and test times are minimal. If the gap between making code changes and getting the new test results is more than 20 to 30 seconds, the flow is interrupted. If the tests aren't run frequently enough, the quality decreases. Decreased quality, in turn, means that broken builds aren't fixed immediately, and this becomes a vicious circle.

You can optimize test roundtrips by categorizing tests. Run smoke tests and unit tests in your private workspace, and then run comprehensive integration tests on a dedicated machine. It's important to automate the build process and provide a quick and easy procedure for building the code as a complete baseline. Do this by creating a build in the local sandbox or calling a dedicated build engine for a private build (perhaps using the same platform designated for the official production build).

> **BUGS**   There are always bugs in the system. This is normal. Tests can't guarantee the correctness of an application or ensure that it's bug-free. Tests can only find single bugs, and good testing should come as close as possible to finding all of them.

Having a local environment means the developer has their own local resources, such as a (local) server, or that their own database (or database scheme) enables testing. The local environment doesn't need to be physically on their desktop; it can also be on a central server (like an individual database scheme), but it must be reserved for the developer's individual use. A one-time investment in database schemes and similar tools increases productivity and application quality.

Furthermore, it's important to aim for a congruent build by comparing the developer and the integration views. Although the developer is working with a private build (which may use dummies and mocks), the build system itself should be identical to the central integration build. This helps avoid the "but it works for me!" syndrome and dramatically improves the start-up time for new peers. Most important, bugs can be identified and fixed quickly. The longer it takes to find them, the more expensive they're to fix when they're found.

This doesn't necessarily mean that the build on the developer's desktop (distinguished from the build system) will be identical to the one on the central build system. Because you want quick feedback, not all tests may run on the desktop—perhaps only the smoke tests. Or you may use mocks to simulate subsystems or components on the desktop but run full tests without mocks on a central integration machine. It's important to have a fast feedback loop on the developer's desktop, and if it isn't fast enough, the developer runs the tests too infrequently (or skips tests altogether) and the quality decreases. That can become a self-defeating process. Chapter 6 describes concepts and tools you can use to set up productive workspaces.

2.2.3 *Continuous integration*

Continuous integration (CI) includes code integrations that are run at least on a daily basis. The word *continuous*, as used in this context, denotes a repeatable process that occurs regularly and frequently. The word *integration* means that individually developed pieces of code that are stored in a source code repository are checked out as a whole; then they're compiled, packaged, tested, inspected, and deployed with build results integrated into web pages, or sent out as an email, or both.

> #### Continuous integration
>
> "Continuous integration is a software development practice where members of a team integrate their work frequently, usually each person integrates at least daily—leading to multiple integrations per day. Each integration is verified by an automated build (including test) to detect integration errors as quickly as possible. Many teams find that this approach leads to significantly reduced integration problems and allows a team to develop cohesive software more rapidly."—Martin Fowler[a]
>
> "The value of continuous integration is to reduce risks, reduce repetitive manual processes, generate deployable software at any time and at any place, enable better project visibility and establish greater confidence in the software product from the development team."—Paul M. Duvall et al.[b]

a. Martin Fowler, "Continuous Integration," http://martinfowler.com/articles/continuousIntegration .html.
b. Paul M. Duvall et al., *Continuous Integration* (Addison-Wesley, 2007), pg. 29.

There are numerous reasons why CI is effective. The more often the code is integrated, the faster it's to figure out exactly what caused a bug. That's because there are far fewer sources of errors to examine, debug, and resolve. For example, it's quicker (and much easier) to find the cause of a bug if there are only two changes to examine since the last integration rather than 50. In addition, it's easier to eliminate bugs (by first identifying the root cause) while the change is still fresh in the developer's mind, and they can remember exactly what they did, why they did it, and how they chose to implement it. Another reason CI is effective is that when multiple changes are integrated together, their combined impact can result in unpredictable bugs or, even worse, serious bugs that then get delivered to the customer. CI not only offers the preceding advantages, it's also "essential for scaling lean and agile development," as discussed by Craig Larman and Bas Vodde.[7]

The relationship between the effort of integration and the amount of time between integrations is exponential: As the number of days between integrations increases, the effort required to fix bugs skyrockets exponentially. Waiting another day to perform an integration build doesn't translate to merely one more day of effort, but often to several more (see figure 2.3).

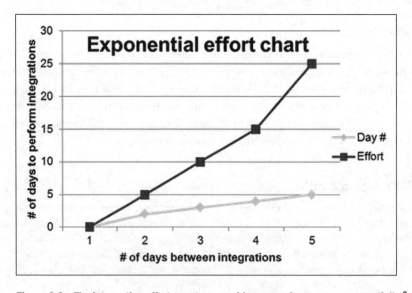

Figure 2.3   The integration effort spent on repairing errors increases exponentially.[8]

---

[7] Craig Larman and Bas Vodde, *Practices for Scaling Lean & Agile Development* (Addison Wesley, 2010), chapter 10.
[8] This illustration isn't based on an empirical study. Data is based on experience of the author and others.

CONTINUOUS INTEGRATION IN A NUTSHELL

Although project setups may differ slightly among teams or projects, the basic process of CI usually stays the same: A CI server captures all information needed to run a build and provides a general build environment, including the Java Virtual Machine (JVM), related runtime properties, and so on. The CI server executes a job definition to trigger project builds, which are reproducible based on a project's build management system. The build scripts should also be versioned and are separated from any IDEs; the CI server will continuously execute the build scripts, such as every time code is committed to the VCS.

Building and integrating software as soon as a developer checks in their changes is called *continuous build*. An *integration build* is the build that is created by a central build server. An integration build can be more complex than local builds that are triggered in developers' workspaces because it integrates more systems and runs more tests. In some environments, all that is needed is a nightly build. CI ensures that a given revision of code in development will build as intended or fail (break the build) if errors occur. The CI build acts as a "single point of truth," so builds can be used with confidence for testing or as a production candidate. An integration build may consume artifacts from a component repository and create artifacts and publish them to the component repository. CI should include all artifact types (configuration items), including coding artifacts, build scripts, database scripts, test cases, and so on.

Whether the build fails or succeeds, the CI makes its results available to the team. Reporting (dashboarding) ensures that the developers are notified about broken builds. The developer may receive the information by email, RSS notification, instant messaging (IM), IDE integration, or any other suitable notification mechanism. A build history provides an archive of former builds and their results. Reporting also contains generated documentation. With each build, documentation can also be created (such as API documentation, project site, and release notes) that reflects the recent state. Manually created documentation may be necessary (for instance, a user guide) but it should be minimized. Continuously updating manual documentation is error-prone and time-consuming. Worse, if the documentation doesn't correspond to the software, it quickly becomes useless.

You can implement "build-staging" according to your corporate standards. For example, validating special quality requirements on higher build stages prevents code from being promoted before it's ready. The initial staging area is the developers' workspaces.

After one experience with a development process incorporating CI, many developers tend to agree that it can potentially add value to their processes. Various positive effects can be triggered by incorporating CI into the development process. Each revision of the project source code that passes the CI build can be considered a release candidate, or at least a demonstrable product state, because the integration has proven to be successful. The team members may have reduced turnaround times, because they aren't required to do full builds and testing all the time. They can concentrate on verifying (unit) tests for the specific pieces of work that they're implementing in a task-based way, while the CI systems take the long-running builds and tests for the whole project. Most modern IDEs provide features that can help the developer with partial builds and isolated in-place tests.

Reduced turnaround times and the certainty of completing a working task increase the developers' sense of accomplishment as well as their productivity and motivation. This helps to keep the whole team focused on the feature tasks.

Before CI, most software projects had a dedicated integration phase. Integration was a painful part of the project, where developers did nothing but make their code work with that of their colleagues. Can you see what's wrong with this picture? First, the developers might think of code they wrote as their own. But the real owner of the code is the person who pays for it. Second, the developers could spend months doing nothing but merging many code branches together, delivering no value to the customer. That's staggering: stopping a project to make all of your developers' work compile. Continuous integration can eradicate this problem. By considering a project to be green if the code compiles and passes tests, or red if either or both fail, it's easy to make "keeping the build green" the norm.

Humans focus on improving their craft and not merely on improving their tools. Tools come in handy, but they can also come at the cost of maintaining one's discipline. It's all too easy to install a CI tool and then say that you're "doing" continuous integration. You're doing continuous integration if the team makes it a high priority to fix the build frequently and if your developers want to add their builds to your CI server. You are probably not doing continuous integration without some form of testing strategy (although you may start rolling out basic CI by automatically compiling and packaging software on a central machine). Proving that your code compiles isn't enough of a safety net for your developers.

AUTOMATIC TESTING AND INSPECTIONS

CI installs testing—particularly automatic testing—as part of the development process. Testing isn't a downstream activity; rather, the team's development and testing activities are integrated. In his book *Succeeding with Agile*, Mike Cohn says that testing at the end doesn't work. For him, it's hard to improve the quality of an existing product with testing at the end. Mistakes continue unnoticed, the state of the project is difficult to gauge, feedback opportunities are lost, and testing is more likely to be cut.[9]

Tests can be divided into functional tests and technical tests (unit, module, and component tests). Those test categories should be linked and reported on together. Unit tests make sure that modules, functions, and methods behave as they should. Functional tests ensure you've developed the right feature. Unless you can surround pesky regression bugs with tests, you'll have no confidence that the code is working and the required features are implemented.

Before you fully implement CI, your teams must possess the discipline to maintain tests and guarantee that the project's build is working and up-to-date. Automating

---

[9]   Mike Cohn, *Succeeding with Agile* (Addison-Wesley, 2010), pp. 308–310.

tests is the prerequisite to entering short development cycles, getting early feedback, and creating high-quality software. Testing must begin on the developers' workstations and lead into technical integration tests and to functional system tests. Pre-check-in tests should be applied before changes are checked into the version control. If a test case fails, that's an opportunity to build a first *quality gate*, which is a defined, special milestone during development, where special quality requirements are met. You can also think about using smoke tests or sanity checks to run basic operations on the application. They can check whether the application can be started or if the main functions are addressable.

If you detect a failure condition, an Agile approach is to write a new test that validates whether these errors do occur. It's interesting to measure the test coverage and to monitor the results. You can also introduce a quality gate that fails automatically when the coverage isn't good enough. It can be helpful to establish a build threshold that tolerates defects to some degree.

Metrics and audits should also be measured continuously. Some people claim that cycle time is the only valuable metric. *Cycle time* is the total time from the beginning to the end of your process; for example, from the definition of the scope of the release to the delivery of the software.

A continuous inspection analyzes the design and code and points to quality defects. This avoids long, manual review sessions. A prerequisite for a continuous inspection process is to have an open atmosphere and a transparent and collaborative project setting.

It's important to understand that quality doesn't come from inspection but from improving the process. Defects cost twofold: Somebody makes them and gets paid, and then another person (or even the same one) is paid to repair the defects. Measuring something doesn't improve the thing you've measured. Merely inspecting something won't build quality: "You cannot inspect quality into a product."[10] If suboptimal quality is the norm, this can only be addressed by improving the process.

Software craftsmanship

Driving an Agile ALM isn't enough for successful software delivery. Agile ALM is the backbone of your software development. The quality of the product does depend heavily on the quality of the software and the job the developers do. Software craftsmanship emphasizes the coding skills of the developers. For details, see *Clean Code: A Handbook of Agile Software Craftsmanship* by Robert C. Martin.

CONTINUOUS DELIVERY AND DEPLOYMENT

CI also includes continuous delivery and deployment. *Continuous delivery*[11] is an essential part of release management that addresses the "last mile" to provide the runnable

---

[10] W. Edwards Deming, *Out of the Crisis* (MIT Press, 1982), p. 29.
[11] See J. Humble and D. Farley, *Continuous Delivery* (Addison-Wesley, 2011).

(functional) release to the user. A change *may* result in a release and *may* start the whole release process. But no changes are applied to the production system without a process; most of the changes will be staged along the full staging path. The process and the infrastructure must enable the team to promote every change to production, if you want to do that.

Often there's a mismatch between how technical people perceive what constitutes "available" and the perception of the final customer—the user of the application. Software is only available for use when it's installed and distributed; it's not available if it's only packaged or deployed but can't be used. The software is available for use only if it's deployed on a system, the users have permission to work on the application, the database is available, and so on.

Specifications or versions of software in the developer's workspace can't replace versions of software available on dedicated test environments. Late binding "big bang" integrations are a bad idea—it's always best to release and deliver early and often. This can only be achieved by automating the delivery process. The more frequently the software is built and integrated, the more the process of delivery becomes a routine job (a repeatable process). If building and integrating doesn't become a daily routine, the people involved become worried about quality and delivery becomes more infrequent.

CI is a virtuous cycle. Once you've invested in the initial setup, your CI system will grow with your software hand in hand. Integration becomes a routine job, not a painful dedicated activity that's postponed downstream. The easier your CI is to use and the better optimized the CI process is, the more it will be used, the more it will be optimized, and the more it will be accepted. If you institute only heavyweight downstream integration, you'll experience a downward spiral; project members will probably have reservations against CI and will fail to integrate as much as necessary. Frequent deployments provide direct, timely feedback loops—a requirement for continuous improvement.

It's important that the technical target environment (the system to which you deploy) be similar, or ideally identical, to the final production system. This will help you detect errors quickly. Deployment should always be automated and should be part of the continuous development process. Preferably you'll have one unified deployment script for deploying the application to different target environments. A precondition for this is to decouple deployment and configuration. The deployment scripts should be self-testing to automatically verify their own output. The deployment should be started easily by executing one script (instead of numerous manual steps). Setting up a centralized machine to deploy your application to multiple target environments can further accelerate productivity.

CONWAY'S LAW

Why does CI (and ALM as a whole) sometimes have acceptance issues in companies? One explanation may be found in Conway's law: "Organizations which design systems . . . are constrained to produce designs which are copies of the communication structures of these organizations."[12] For example, consider a software application that has three development teams—developers, operations/deployment engineers, and QA. The system will likely have three subcomponents (or subsystems). Using the premise of Conway's law, the coupling between these three components and the quality of the interfaces between them can be predicted by the quality of the communication between the three teams. What implications does this have for CI? At least in bigger companies or projects, setting up integration and continuous integration requires strong cross-functional communication, synchronization, and uniformed solutions. Integration also means integrating across different organization borders and roles; for instance, development, deployment, and testing.

The software passes through the hands of these three distinct teams, and all these teams have individual problems and concerns. In the worst-case scenario, these concerns can lead to "empire-building," where a team attempts to acquire resources (more money, more employees) in order to increase its influence outside its areas and expand its size and power. Besides that, teams can have competing objectives. Consider the example of an operation crew that gets a higher bonus if the applications running in production have fewer bugs. An obvious (and counterproductive) maneuver would be to prevent applications from going into production at all. Rejecting new application versions and sending them back to development due to poor quality (even if it's not that bad) would improve that team's situation, netting the higher bonus. The operation team profits, but the whole company will suffer, as does the customer.

When you set up a cross-functional process, you must often address worries over losing power, competence, influence, and control. What could be worse for a huge testing department than to have a continuous process make them redundant? Agile aims to address these worries. Agile will overcome these reservations and focus on those invisible facets of software development. A strong management commitment to the chosen approach and shared objectives are needed to roll out a CI process and an ALM in general.

SYNCHRONIZATION AND CONTINUOUS IMPROVEMENT

ALM drives a comprehensive approach to software development. Whenever a developer commits changes, the system builds the software, the tests are run, and the customer reviews the deployed test version—this type of communication is known as synchronization. But you shouldn't apply CI that's strictly shaped to technical artifacts (such as sources and tests), although artifacts are good bases for communication, because synchronization isn't limited to artifacts. A comprehensive ALM approach also includes synchronization on other levels. Besides artifacts, clearly discussing tools and processes is also important. But tools and processes can't substitute for personal communication and interactions because software is made by and for humans. The technical infrastructure should accelerate communication by condensing the information and transforming information into knowledge.

---

[12] Mel Conway, "How do Committees Invent?" http://www.melconway.com/research/committees.html.

Key characteristics of Agile releasing are continuous reflection (improvement of the process), detection of process defects, and improvement of processes. Adaptation of your process and how you work is only possible if you know where you stand at any given moment. If you don't know where you stand—and without CI it's hard to know—trying to improve your process is like shooting in the dark. Setting up CI helps you to increase quality, detect issues early, and deliver software more frequently.

To build and integrate software continuously, it's best to create a repository to store essential artifacts and facilitate code and component reuse.

2.2.4   *Component repository*

Component repository is a logical expression. Physically, a component repository can be the same as a sources repository (for instance, Subversion). Alternatively, a component repository may be hosted by a VCS, a file system, or a database. In contrast to traditional version control (source repositories, like CVS, Subversion, Git), a *component repository* contains the binary versions that are the build result of sources (see figure 2.4). In Java those binary versions are the standardized deployment units, like JAR, WAR, and EAR.

In an Agile ALM context, it's mandatory to manage sources in a VCS to enable concurrent modifications and provide a reproducible version history. It's common for companies to have essential artifacts hosted in a couple of different repositories. In the best scenario, a single access repository contains the components your project or company uses, but this isn't necessarily the repository that the sources are housed in. You may choose to use more than one repository.

Minimizing media versus using a component repository

Using many different repositories in parallel, such as CVS, Subversion, file servers, and so on, inhibits efficiency. It's important to make the locations transparent so you don't know, and don't need to know, where exactly the assets are stored. On the one hand, it's wise to reduce channels and mediums if possible. On the other hand, it can be wise to use a component repository.

It's often efficient to store deployment units and their versions and dependencies in a medium other than a VCS. It's even more efficient to store derived artifacts beside the original sources (because you don't want to build the software on all environments again). In some situations, you *must* store binaries due to reproducibility reasons: Sources have a reproducible context by applying tagging in a VCS. Binaries also have a context that is resolved at build time, such as version ranges or dynamic properties.

Which approach you choose will depend on your specific requirements. For many projects, it's helpful to host the sources and their deployment units in two different locations.

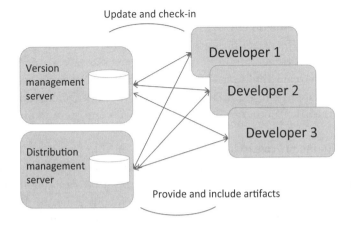

Figure 2.4   Version management servers store sources, and distribution management servers store binary artifacts

> ## Labels should be sticky
>
> Sources that are tagged with a VCS tag are labeled. A *label* is a snapshot that illustrates which state the software is in at the time. This approach is also known as *creating a baseline*. Suppose you use version 1 of a product that has the label 1.0b12. The twelfth build was the last successful one and was chosen to be the one for delivery to the outside world. It's not the twelfth version of 1.0b1.
>
> Don't move or change labels once they're set, keep them. If you change parts of the system after labeling, label them again. You should never work with moving targets, sometimes called *floating* labels.

Often it's necessary to reproduce software that's running on different machines. It can therefore be useful for a central release department to label final versions of the software and put the build artifacts into a build archive. This ensures binary integrity, which means that for each versioned software state, the same deployment units are delivered to each target environment (there's no recompilation for further environments). Such a component repository can also protect company assets and boost reusability, as well as minimize the number and complexity of dependencies. Additionally, the artifacts in the component repository can be included as binary dependencies. Chapter 5 details this concept and implements it with tools.

2.2.5   *Quality, standards, and release cycles*

Productivity increases as quality improves, because less rework is necessary and waste (parts of the solution not needed to solve the given problem or to implement the requirements) is reduced.[13] Simpler solutions lead to better quality, and quality improvements lead to lower costs, a better competitive position, and happier people

---

[13]   See W. Edwards Deming, *Out of the Crisis* (MIT Press, 1982), chapter 1.

on the job. In *Peopleware*, Tom DeMarco, and Timothy Lister state that "we all tend to tie our self-esteem strongly to the quality of the product we produce—not the quantity of product, but the quality" (p. 19), and they list "quality reduction of the product" as one of the negative "teamicide techniques" (p. 133). They also talk about having a "cult of quality" to foster team building (p. 151).[14] Quality begins with the intent, which is fixed by management and is pursued by the whole team. Quality can vary in different contexts. Gerald M. Weinberg states that "quality is conforming to some person's requirements."[15]

You need an identifiable process to be able to improve on your process. Therefore, having a systematic release process is always a good idea. For fast release cycles, developing and releasing is the top priority; it's necessary to aim for the best quality and to work according to the highest standards. Features and quality must be balanced. Refactoring to improve the design of the code without changing its functionality can help to improve existing code[16]—don't provide functionality at the expense of technical debt and poor quality!

The quality can be kept high by running tests frequently and automatically checking metrics (audits). Rules for designing and coding shouldn't only be described on paper, but also they should also be available as executable media. The integration build should run tests and audits to ensure that the quality requirements are fulfilled.

If the build fails, it's referred to as being *broken*. If a build doesn't fulfill the requirements, it's possible to break it automatically. In contrast to measurable tests and audits, nonfunctional requirements (such as usability) can't be tested automatically.

Lean software development

Lean software development, inspired by the success of the Toyota production system, claims to "stop the line" when defects are detected. If we transfer the picture of an assembly line being completely stopped when a bug is found on the staging ladder (not on the developer's workspace, because it's isolated), we have a CI landscape and builds that aren't passed through if standards are ignored or the quality falls below the requirements.

A second major message of the Lean approach is to create "just in time" releases and to avoid waste. The Lean approach is articulated in seven principles: eliminate waste, amplify learning, decide as late as possible, deliver as fast as possible, empower the team, build integrity in, and see the whole. For further details, see *Lean Software Development, Implementing Lean Software Development,* and *Leading Lean Software Development* (by Poppendieck and Poppendieck, Addison-Wesley).

---

[14] Tom DeMarco and Timothy Lister, *Peopleware* (Dorset House, 1999).
[15] Gerald M. Weinberg, *Quality Software Management,* vol. 1 (Dorset House, 1992), p. 5.
[16] See Martin Fowler, *Refactoring* (Addison-Wesley, 1999).

Results of tests and audits, as well as the verification of standards, should be handled according to fixed rules. Merely watching how tests fail, and then deploying the software anyway (perhaps after removing failed tests from the test suite), doesn't increase quality. Here, quality gates and a zero tolerance approach are the best practices for stopping the release when defects are detected. Otherwise, bugs will result in higher costs and missed deadlines.

In addition, an enterprise Agile ALM process as a whole should be standardized. It has to be carefully architected, with nonnegotiable elements. It should provide a mandatory framework that's capable of weaving together different elements to support each project's unique requirements.

Frequent releasing of software enables fast feedback, better measurability, and a meaningful picture of the software's status: "It forces you to get really good at doing releases and deployments."[17] Only built, integrated, and deployed software gives you an idea of what the software accomplishes and what it doesn't. The content of the release should be fixed before starting it. The dates should also all be fixed and published in a publicly accessible release calendar. Consequently, time, (high) quality, and resources (people) are three cornerstones of the releases that are fixed, constant, and balanced with your individual requirements. It's the number of features that should be variable: At the end of the release, if the implementation of features isn't finished or if tests fail, the features should be postponed for a future release. Short iterations and time-boxing are ingredients of good risk management. In a dynamic environment, individually chosen release lengths are a good way to keep requirements and basic conditions stable. Chapter 7 illustrates auditing with tools.

2.3   *The process pitfall, the illusion of control*

There's a conflict between having too much lifecycle management process and not having enough. This conflict can be named the *process pitfall*. An Agile approach advances and demands feedback and communication. The release management process should be effective, efficient, and targeted. In practice, though, many projects suffer from not having enough process.

To resolve this conflict, you need to focus on priorities, including the root cause of the process pitfall. Often, more process is introduced in order to address the problem of the illusion of control. Introducing too many rules or wrong process rules could suggest control that doesn't truly exist. In the worst case, you have a described process and a real process in parallel. Or you have a rigid process that dramatically decreases productivity. ALM and its major facet, release management, must be a balanced set of processes and tools aligned with your individual requirements.

---

[17]   Michael T. Nygard, *Release It!* (The Pragmatic Bookshelf, 2007), p. 326.

2.3.1 *Effectiveness and efficiency*

Effectiveness is doing the right thing, and efficiency is doing the right thing correctly. After consulting on a significant number of projects, I'm left wondering why some teams don't grasp this distinction.

If you have issues (or better, challenges), try a root cause analysis to detect the original evil. If you find it, you can think about possible improvements. Mostly, they all have pros and cons, so decide wisely which way to go. Choose only a few pain points, sign up for the actions, and track them over your next development iteration to ensure you complete them successfully. If you dig into challenges deep enough, you'll usually find communication defects inside the team. This is what Agile is all about: Communication and interaction are more important than processes and tools, as the Agile manifesto says. If you can solve the people issues, yet still see room for improvement, proceed to the processes.

Defects in processes are often a problem. For example, it's not possible to configure a workflow system to cover your processes unless you know what the processes are. If they're not described, identify and describe them. Sometimes, processes don't exist at all. Set them up; don't be satisfied if the whole team speaks about the task of "daily business." If you're managing the processes, and you know the requirements, then, and only then, can you think about tooling. There's no point in buying a full-fledged commercial ALM suite or using some of the great tools I'll introduce in this book if you don't know your requirements (and consequently can't determine whether the tools fulfill them).

You can work with prototypes, evaluation versions of tools, or a "release 0.0/zero" for setting up infrastructure. These provide good ways to get early feedback and gain some valuable experience. But always remember that you should stay flexible. It's often better to use a collection of lightweight, integrated tools that are de facto standards on the market and that do the best job in their domain. You can integrate and decouple your infrastructure while remaining quite independent and flexible.

If you want to kick-start your development of new components, you may decide to use a build tool, such as Maven, that provides component and build management and a neat archetype feature. If you want to integrate your system continuously, add a build server to your infrastructure. You may want to add tests and audits later. Little by little, you can extend your infrastructure in a requirement-based, focused way. And if you're not satisfied with one decision, you can replace one tool while still sticking with the other ones.

Managing the identification of configuration items is also important in ensuring your process matches your requirements.

2.3.2 *Agile ALM and configuration items*

ALM deals with the management of tasks and artifacts. Controlling artifacts is only possible if the artifacts are identified: Without determining which artifacts affect the release and the project and without putting the artifacts into the ALM system, it's not possible to control the artifacts or perform status accounting (to ensure completeness and provide a consistent version) and audits. Additionally, setting up an efficient ALM is only possible when processes and tools are optimally chosen, integrated, and standardized.

Identifying assets, controlling configuration items, and performing status accounting and audits are major tasks of traditional software configuration management (SCM). In an Agile ALM, you'll find the best fit to implement the traditional activities of a SCM—pure Agile projects implement SCM facets in an implicit way. There should be an SCM-aware expert on every Agile team or a traditional build manager or a (technical) release manager can drive the daily SCM needs of the business. This depends on how you slice your roles.

SCM is mainly about access to project artifacts. This includes not only tracking artifact versions over time, but also controlling and managing changes to them. Whereas in traditional SCM scenarios, you track every artifact, in an Agile ALM scope, you'll focus on final deployment units and important artifacts, including documents that influence the project (like requirement documents). For example, the Agile approach tracks EARs, WARs, and JARs independent of their contents (their packages and classes). The sources themselves are stored in the VCS. You won't store artifacts that you can generate out of other artifacts (unless you have good reason) or documents that won't change over time or that are written by multiple users (such as meeting minutes). See figure 2.5.

From an underlying SCM point of view, an Agile ALM focuses on aggregating and documenting the most important parts of the software necessary for release. For example, if you want to integrate further components or subsystems into your enter-

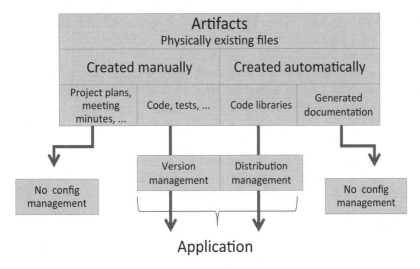

Figure 2.5 Artifacts in configuration management: Artifacts that are updated continuously and are of special interest are put into configuration management. Sources and tests are put into version control; libraries are put into distribution management.

prise SCM, you need basic information about these components, including their deployment units. Table 2.2 collects some of the major components in an SCM checklist. This is a much leaner approach than is promoted by traditional SCM. Depending on your particular situation and requirements, the checklist can be implemented in a smart way. If you use Maven, for instance, some of the checklist items are covered out of the box (such as documenting deployment units). Tools like Maven can help you define your SCM in an executable medium. This means, for instance, you have XML definitions that can be executed reproducibly.

Table 2.2 Approaching SCM in an Agile way: the SCM checklist

Group	Item	Details
Overview	Configuration elements	Complete list of all configuration elements, including scripts, database elements, deployment units, properties.
System	Deployment diagram	Deployment units (and their versions), packaging types, protocols, technical information (like a version of an application server), dependencies between configuration elements, nodes.
System	Infrastructure	Database elements (users, DDL), technical users, permissions, security.
System	Test environments	For all subsystems, mapping to other test environments where needed.
Build	Build system	System must provide its deployment units in a reproducible way (build must be provided by component development team).

Traditional SCM requires listings of configuration items and checklists. This can be necessary in an Agile context, too, but it's usually handled automatically by the ALM tools. But there are many possible usage models.

Release notes should be created automatically. You should also be able to audit the system automatically. For example, the JIRA issue and project tracking tool can be used to derive release notes based on a specific time interval or version number. Mapping sources to requirements to generate a list of what you're looking for is an effective way to create documentation automatically, along with applying active impact management with Mylyn or FishEye. Acceptance tests (for example, creating and running tests with the Fit tool) can also be part of this documentation.

Tests and audits (metrics) can be applied automatically as part of the continuous integration system. You can base these audits on tools like Checkstyle and Cobertura and your testing on Selenium, FEST, or something similar. Track your components in a component repository, where the system puts them continuously. If you already use Maven, you're familiar with this; if this is completely new for you, don't panic. Either way, this book will give you valuable tips.

Agile ALM minimizes overhead while maximizing benefit. It also acts as an enabler for change. We'll discuss this next.

2.3.3 Agile ALM as change enabler

All systems try to achieve stable states (*panta rhei*[18]). Being flexible in software development doesn't mean chaotic drifting, but rather, being able to change and transform from one stable state to another. Any substantial improvements must come from an action on the system.[19] This is management's responsibility of management and the ALM system can improve management's ability to know what's happening (meta-measurement[20]) and can improve insight into the best decisions.

The importance of lifecycle management will continue to grow. In this time of distributed, heterogeneous system landscapes, legacy systems that must be integrated, systems and components in many different versions, and (transitive) dependencies on different platforms, following a systematic release management approach has become a precondition to providing high-quality software in constant, short intervals. Agile ALM is the catalyst that enables the daily work of all project stakeholders. It also helps track and control the artifacts that were created during the project activities.

Agile ALM acts as a change-enabler. During the development of complex systems, change is a constant companion of the development process. Instead of being exceptional, changes are more and more the norm. A high percentage of projects miss their project goals because they don't grant enough space for changes in the process. Modern software development understands that changes are a major part of the project. They're part of the process of aligning the current activities with the valid requirements and basic conditions at any time (a process of continuous adaptation).

In the extreme approach, defects (bugs) and all kinds of functional and nonfunctional requirements are handled like a coordinated set of changes to the system. Following this paradigm, software development is the process of identifying and processing changes. ALM is evolving to be the hub of reproducibility and is the change enabler.

2.4 Summary

In this chapter, you learned about Agile and what Agile means in the context of ALM. We discussed continuous integration in detail and considered many aspects of the Agile ALM, concluding with Agile ALM being a change enabler. In the rest of the book, we'll implement an Agile ALM with lightweight tools and apply those Agile strategies. In the next chapter, we'll use Scrum to bridge functional releasing to technical releasing.

---

[18] Meaning "everything flows," here: it flows from one stable state to another.
[19] See W. Edwards Deming, *Out of the Crisis* (MIT Press, 1982), chapter 11.
[20] Gerald M. Weinberg, *Quality Software Management,* vol. 2 (Dorset House, 1993), chapter 12.

Part 2

Functional Agile ALM

Part 2 of this book focuses on the functional aspects of Agile ALM by discussing (functional) release management and task-based development.

Chapter 3 covers the functional release management aspect of Agile ALM. It details how to implement the general management framework, Scrum, and how to bridge Scrum to more traditional environments. It also details strategies and tools that support the functional releasing of software.

Chapter 4 is dedicated to task-based development. We'll track changes by linking requirements to software artifacts throughout the complete development process. After you've learned the necessary prerequisites, we'll explore example toolchains that help to implement this strategy.

Once you've finished this part of the book, we can leave the functional, high-level aspects of Agile ALM and focus on its more technical aspects.

Using Scrum for release management

If Agile ALM is about creating and tracking software, in which phases do you create the software? Using functional release management, you set up a guideline for how and when you'll provide releases and how you'll assign content to them. Together, functional release management and technical release management support and enable the development.

In this chapter, we'll talk about the release as the central unit in the development process. After covering the basics and core aspects of functional release management, we'll talk about vehicles that can support you in communicating your general release approach. I've based my release management approach on Scrum.[1] This method is popular, in part because it's simple and easy to implement.

Many teams say they're working in an Agile way, but they're only constantly planning and replanning, releasing something every two to four months. No one has ever clearly defined Agile release management, which has allowed a lot of dysfunctional projects to call themselves Agile.[2] Many projects use Scrum to support their release management. Scrum doesn't provide a full definition of release management; rather it's a rough management template—a framework, as discussed in the free Scrum primer and later in this chapter—and relying solely on the template increases the probability of complete failure. Many important details aren't described in Scrum at all.

With respect to lifecycle management, this chapter fills out the parts that are missing from what I call "textbook Scrum."[3] I'll also cover the basics of Scrum and put Scrum into context, as well as show you additional strategies to extend Scrum for Agile ALM. We'll implement Scrum and bridge from this approach (and its functional release management) to technical release management.

3.1   Getting started with Scrum release management

Figure 3.1 shows an example ALM lifecycle that starts with requirements management and then immediately begins the release management function followed by design, development, version, and build management. The release management collects functional and technical requirements to be implemented in a given iteration.

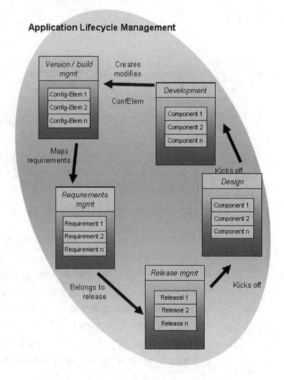

Figure 3.1   Software engineering goes through a workflow cycle: requirements management kicks off the development process. Requirements belong to releases. Release management triggers the design/ development of software, which in turn creates the artifacts implementing the requirements. Those implementations are then put into version and build management and are provided in releases.

---

[1]   See the free Scrum primer at www.scrumalliance.org/resources/339.

[2]   Unfortunately, a lot of dysfunctional projects call themselves Scrum as well.

[3]   For me, the term "textbook Scrum" (or "Scrum by the book") refers to how Scrum was initially described by Ken Schwaber and Mike Beedle in the book *Agile Software Development with Scrum* (Prentice Hall, 2001).

This approach drives the design and development of the software, which in turn creates and modifies the configuration elements.

The artifacts created include source code, binaries, configuration files, documentation, and test cases, which are all put into version control. It's important to trace requirements to the baselines that are approved for release. Requirements and changes are constantly being prioritized and assigned to iterations (and eventually releases); this is often handled by a specific change management function or by a release management function that's also responsible for monitoring and tracking releases. Acceptance testing, supported by tools and ultimately by the customer or their representative, determines when the release is ready to be promoted. From there, new requirements are determined, prioritized, and approved, which starts the lifecycle again from the beginning.

Releases, iterations, versions, sprints, and baselines

In Scrum (as described in books by Ken Schwaber), iterations are called *sprints*. The outcome of a collection of sprints, delivering a significant version of the software (such as a feature set that has value for the customer), is called a *release*. A common approach is to decouple the sprints from the releases (which have value for the customer).

A *version* is an arbitrary snapshot of the software. Releases are also versions, but not every version is considered a release. Important versions of the code are often called releases to indicate that the exact versions of the source code have been identified (often by a tag or version label). Releases are reproducible baselines of the code that can be built, packaged, and released to the customer.

How are common project phases, like defining requirements, creating the design, and the development (see figure 3.1), organized in process frameworks? As an example, we'll take a brief look at the rational unified process (RUP), which consists of four phases:

- *Inception phase*—Developing the core idea. By reviewing and confirming the core business drivers, the product feasibility is established and the project scope is defined.
- *Elaboration phase*—Defining the majority of use cases and system architecture. This is where risks are identified and a schedule is set up.
- *Construction phase*—Implementing a system that fulfills the requirements necessary to enter the transition phase.
- *Transition phase*—Ensuring all requirements are met to satisfy the stakeholders. Besides completing the software, documentation is also created. Often this phase starts with a beta release and ends with a software retrospective.

RUP is a popular iterative framework, and it has been successfully used in both small teams and large-scale development efforts.

This approach is valid for all kinds of development processes. Agile projects go through these common project phases as well, in an incremental and iterative way by defining requirements, designing the solution, implementing the requirements, and testing the solution. Although the Agile process uses an iterative approach involving different phases, it can be uneven and you can even slice the development process up into different processes that serve their primary stakeholders. One example of this is that Scrum is often used to manage the development process itself, whereas the overall process, including defining requirements and delivering increments, is managed by using a different process approach.

As a crosscutting discipline, release management acts as a progress-monitoring unit using different tools and data. The progress monitoring is mainly based on the information in the version-control system (VCS), where the artifacts are securely stored. Continuous build management delivers executable software increments that are configured and deployed in test environments.

Scrum as a comprehensive end-to-end approach

Scrum can be used as a comprehensive process framework covering all the major phases of the application lifecycle, from collecting requirements through to design, development, testing, and implementation. Scrum doesn't provide a lot of detail, so it's common to supplement it with best practices or guidance from other process models.

One popular framework is itSMF's IT infrastructure library (ITIL), which provides comprehensive guidance on all aspects of IT service management. In its volume on transition, ITIL provides a rich framework for implementing change and release management. You could also supplement your Scrum framework with guidance from the Capability Maturity Model Integration (CMMI), CobiT (Control Objectives for Information and related Technology), or even software development standards from the IEEE (Institute of Electrical and Electronics Engineers) or ISO.

Scrum release management includes an approach to assigning features to release iterations and burn-down charts that make it much easier to monitor progress. All of these process frameworks and industry standards help provide a common set of terminology that facilitates effective communication.

Heavyweight release-management approaches traditionally isolate phases or views. ITIL (IT infrastructure library) is one example. ITIL is a helpful collection of publications and a de facto standard for describing processes, roles, and tools. In its most recent version, it gives more weight to the creation of software, the management of knowledge, and the alignment of business needs, and not merely to managing software in production. ITIL has its origins in the management of infrastructure.

Scrum can also be used as a complete process framework. It offers a flexible skeleton that's open enough to accommodate changes that will occur during the development of software.[4] Although it's often limited to the construction of software itself,

---

[4] "The only thing you know about a plan is that things won't go according to it." Kent Beck and Martin Fowler, *Planning Extreme Programming* (Addison-Wesley, 2001), p. 95.

Scrum, as part of a comprehensive end-to-end approach, can cover the major parts of the software lifecycle. All phases of the lifecycle, from collecting requirements to rolling out the software, are important and shouldn't be managed in isolation. Although Scrum doesn't specify any particular methodology for managing lifecycle phases, it can be used in conjunction with a wide range of methodologies.

A benefit of frameworks such as ITIL or lightweight approaches like Scrum is that you have a template you can adjust for your environment as needed, and part of the template is a glossary. All stakeholders communicate using the same terms to express the same things. A common language is a big help.

Kanban

Kanban is a concept that was introduced at Toyota in 1947 and in recent years has been gaining momentum in software engineering. In software engineering, Kanban is influenced by Agile and Lean software development (see *Lean Software Development* by Poppendieck & Poppendieck). Kanban focuses on eliminating waste and bottlenecks as well as reducing waiting times. As a result, the overall throughput is maximized. Kanban uses a pull approach to take new tasks to where they can be completed (that is, to where the resources are available) and it focuses on the complete supply chain. In contrast to Scrum, Kanban doesn't use iterations but rather maximizes the flow by delivering software continuously.

In Scrum, the sum of the functionality to be implemented is located in the product backlog. Features are pulled from the backlog at well-defined points in the process. These points can be either when you're done with your latest task or when the team moves items from the product backlog to the release backlog to be implemented during the next release. Consequently, the complete product backlog is worked off over several releases. The target scope of one release is placed in the release backlog (see figure 3.2).

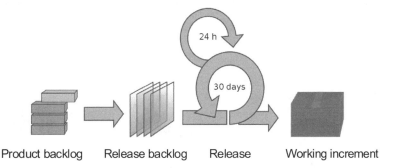

Product backlog   Release backlog   Release   Working increment

Figure 3.2 The Scrum process includes assigning items from a product backlog to a release backlog, and the items are then implemented as part of the release. The output of the release is a working increment (built and delivered software). A typical release duration is 30 days. The team synchronizes daily in a Daily Scrum meeting.

All stakeholders commit to the content of the release in a planning meeting that takes place before development begins. This is also known as the "release kickoff."

Many adopters of Scrum use the terms release, iteration and sprint interchangeably, and others prefer to talk about sprints that implement the release backlog. Some projects distinguish between releases and sprints, both having content and planning meetings, where a sprint is a sliced subset of the release. I will use the term release from now on, because, in my opinion, it's more consistent and more approachable in traditional, conservative settings. Due to possible paradigm mismatches, it's helpful to build bridges between the Scrum teachings and the existing organization's structure and culture, and that's what Agile ALM is intended to do.

The release should deliver a consistent, reasonable set of functionality that's developed incrementally and iteratively. Four weeks is a common release cycle that often works well and is a good starting point. Shorter cycles are possible and sometimes appropriate.

The final, finished release will be packaged and deployed on target environments, although doing this more frequently with continuous integration is helpful. The deployment cycle ends when the release is put into a system test environment available for the customer.

The team synchronizes itself on the status in a brief, daily stand-up meeting.

The major driver of the development process, and of the release particularly, is the set of customer requirements. The prioritized requirements emerge frequently due to changes in the business conditions or the technology used. Requirements are assigned to releases, always having the best ratio in mind between high value and low effort. The implemented requirement is shipped in an *increment*. Requirements are often sliced into fine-grained tasks, which are more practical to deal with during development. A requirement consists of one or more tasks. The approach of task-based development (see chapter 4) helps to focus on the current tasks and to make progress as well as delivery traceable, in an efficient way.

Figure 3.3 illustrates the process of developing software according to Scrum, highlighting the requirement as the driver of the development process and release.

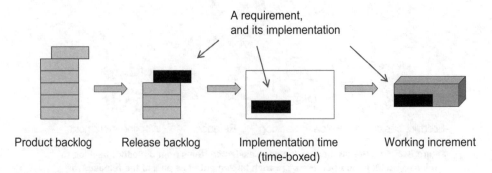

Figure 3.3 The Scrum process supports the user in transferring prioritized customer requirements into consistent releases and working increments.

Let's summarize the key artifacts and roles that are used by Scrum. In Scrum, the following artifacts are created:

- *Product backlog*—All work to be done. This is a list of items in the prioritized product backlog, containing new requirements to be implemented, open defects, and other work to be done.
- *Sprint (release) backlog*—A list of features to be implemented in one release, containing fine-grained tasks arranged in order of priority. The states of tasks are updated on a task board (such as "to do," "in progress," and "done").
- *Impediment list*—A list of issues preventing the team from performing work as efficiently as possible.
- *Burn-down chart*—A publicly displayed chart showing remaining work in the sprint backlog. The chart also shows the velocity of the work completed so the team and stakeholders can see the progress and whether they're on track to complete.

The Scrum template and common engineering activities

Although they're not explicitly mentioned in Scrum, essential activities of software engineering do still occur. For example, you will do some sort of requirement engineering (because the product backlog isn't filled by magic); you'll probably do some architecture work (but always the least that's required); you may do some architecture and design work up front (but maybe in release 0); and you may do some additional functional post-testing after the release, although this process has a high degree of automation.

Scrum has the following roles:

- *Product owner*—The major stakeholder (the user or the customer, or both) of the product or a representative (or proxy) if the stakeholder isn't collocated. The product owner can make timely decisions so the team can get on with the project.
- *Scrum master*—The person who maintains the process and looks out for impediments. The Scrum master mentors the team.
- *Team*—A cross-functional group that implements the requirements. The team is collocated and focused on the shared goal. It's self-organizing and self-accountable and is responsible for delivering a successful outcome at each release. Members of the team have different core competences; many are developers, others are testers. Besides strong technical skills, strong complementary skills are important such as skills in user interface design or design of processes and software architectures. Applying these skills during development makes a valuable solution out of a software application. Traditional soft skills such as strong communication skills are a must. Expertise and experience in the underlying busi-

ness domain is helpful. The team is open-minded in order to reflect and tune continuously and to complement one another.

> **NOTE**   Issues that will arise when using Scrum probably won't have anything to do with the method itself. Instead, Scrum makes existing issues visible. Already existing issues become obvious.

A key feature of Scrum is that customers work closely together with the development team. The customer is ideally collocated and participates in all relevant meetings. With its continuous deliveries, frequent meetings, and open management of issues, Scrum makes progress transparent. Issues are made visible, and no one can hide behind the supposed mistakes of others. Consequently, Scrum implicitly manages risk. Additionally, Scrum enables continuous improvement and improves team communication. This method emphasizes that every working day is as important as the next, regardless of whether the day is the first or the last during a release. This also means that Scrum enables the project to run at a sustainable pace to balance workload and to make sure that the release backlog consists of a sustainable amount of work for the length of the release.

3.2 *Implementing Scrum release management*

In this section, we'll take a closer look at implementing release management within the Scrum framework. Agile development, and Scrum in particular, rely heavily on excellent release management practices to support iterative development.

3.2.1 *The release*

The release isn't merely some functionality; it's numerous technically and functionally consistent configuration items that can be developed and distributed. Whereas versions (or iterations) may be created continuously, you only ship one final release.

Normally, the latest version that meets the requirements is named the final release. You should have measurable, testable acceptance criteria to verify that the software meets those requirements. You may also have customers looking at versions and deciding which will be chosen as the final one. The drawback to this second approach is that you can't clearly reproduce the decisions (it's better to have testable acceptance criteria). The most valuable approach is having the customer give feedback in addition to using testable acceptance criteria.

In a *timeboxed* approach, the resulting version at the end of the time frame (the timebox) is named the final release. Please keep in mind that you should release in a timeboxed way whenever possible, providing the final increment when the defined and fixed release duration is passed through. Timeboxing should be the preferred method. The development cycle is short in Agile, so it's much better to release the latest version within the allotted time frame and implement other features in the following release, than to shift the deadline. When you're approaching the release deadline,

Detailed requirements

Overly detailed requirements lead to overly specialized solutions that are less likely to be reusable. Such requirements can be difficult to create, are even more difficult to maintain, and take a long time, which delays getting starting and ultimately finishing. One excellent approach is to use high-level requirements that can be reused for other projects, and then supplement them with detailed information in the form of detailed test cases and scripts. Epics and stories have become popular, along with use cases that can be utilized to write acceptance tests.[a]

a. See Mike Cohn, *User Stories Applied* (Addison-Wesley, 2004).

it's also much better to take out a defective or uncompleted feature of the release instead of delivering defective software or moving deadlines.[5]

Releases are incremental, self-contained pieces of work. Implementation should be done iteratively and incrementally, which means that the software is provided in stages, with a later stage (a later release) providing additional functionality. This additional functionality can comprise new features or enhancements to existing ones. Changes and bug fixes are also possible. Many projects do track and approve changes on the software with the help of official change requests. To take it to the extreme, all types of changes (such as feature enhancements, bug fixes, and so on) that impact the state of the software are handled as changes, without further distinguishing between them. In Scrum, new features, enhancements, changes, and bug fixes are all items in the backlog that need to be prioritized.

Strategic foresight: estimating effort and content

Many approaches are available to estimate the complexity of functional content (that is, functional requirements) and to determine the costs and effort required for implementing release content.

Often, time-based estimations are used to estimate the effort that's necessary to implement the specified functionality. An Agile approach is to estimate the size of user stories with points and to relate the different stories to each other. Other, more traditional approaches include function point analysis to determine the complexity of the application. *Function point analyses* are calculated based on counts of particular types of elements in an application. This approach requires detailed design up front. Agile approaches use just-in-time design, so Agile projects don't have accurate counts of various elements prior to building.

Requirement-based approaches are different from metrics like Halstead that do compute the complexity of programs. Other metrics, such as "Lines of Code" can be faked too easily and aren't meaningful.

---

[5] In a "death march" project, the scope, as well as the deadline of the project, are moving targets.

Agile teaches us that software evolves over the course of many iterations. The Agile process continuously improves design, development, and testing until you have a finished product that meets the users' needs.

RELEASE TYPES AND CATEGORIES

Many projects find it helpful to distinguish release types and categories in order to improve planning and synchronization between all stakeholders, especially development teams, test teams with their respective test environments, and the production/operations teams.

Releases come in many different types and can vary in scope depending upon the sorts of changes implemented in the release. The release type defines the release on an organizational level. Typically, the release complexity, its implications, and the testing effort are metrics used to categorize releases. Some release types include structural releases, business releases, component releases, and emergency releases.

Structural releases are the biggest in terms of complexity and implications, because you change the underlying structure of the software. Common examples are structural changes in databases (data definition languages, or DDLs), which are normally put into this type of release. This comes in handy for communicating database changes to dedicated test and production departments that are responsible for maintaining and updating their respective databases. Test managers or database experts, such as database owners (DBOs) and database admins (DBAs), need to organize their activities. The impact of updating the structure of a database (with a DDL) is different from updating the data in the database (with a data manipulation language, DML), without changing the structure. Because of the difference in the impact and higher risks, structural releases are commonly targeted with a couple of months' notice to their delivery base. On the other hand, emergency releases to fix a severe production issue can happen at any time, based on a defined process.

The release category expresses the number of changes and is aligned at technical borders. The category name identifies which software artifacts are released. Typical approaches are delta releases, full releases, and package releases. A delta release provides a "diff" between the old and the new version; a full release provides the complete set of artifacts; and a package release contains single packages. Releases not delivering the complete set of artifacts are called incremental releases.

Although release types and categories are independent of each other, there are common traits found between them. For example, a structural release often is a full release, and an emergency release is generally a delta (or patch) release.

3.2.2   *The release duration*

The release duration—how long it takes the team to prepare the release—should be equal for all releases. This is important for planning reliability and for keeping the team organized in a flow. It's also considered a best practice to stick to the release flow regardless of any events that happen throughout the year (such as holidays, vacations, and so on). There's almost always a reason for one stakeholder to want to prevent frequent release; don't start with special cases to serve the individual wishes of one stakeholder at the expense of all other stakeholders, because every single stakeholder has their own individual preferences and wishes. It's important that all stakeholders commit to a unified approach. Reduce the number of features delivered in that release, if necessary, and eliminate the root causes of bottlenecks.

If you do change the release duration for one future release, communicate this at once and before the release starts. Put this into the public release calendar (as discussed in section 3.3.1 of this chapter). Don't extend the duration of the current release while it's running. If you think your work won't be done in time, reduce the amount of release content appropriately. You'll be better off if your releases are driven in a strictly timeboxed fashion, where all dates are fixed.

> **TYPICAL RELEASE DURATIONS** Every project is different and has its own requirements and basic conditions. My suggestion that release durations should be a matter of weeks is only a reference point. In projects applying Scrum, there are debates over whether two or four weeks is the best duration for a release (in this book's meaning of release). The traditional recommendation is four weeks, but more and more Scrum experts tend to recommend two weeks as the standard.

No single rule of thumb exists for the best release duration. In general, the shorter the release period, the better. Shorter release periods lead to early feedback, namely from the customer, who uses the software on staging environments (such as during acceptance testing). Continuous integration, automated testing, and productive development environments help to speed development and facilitate the Scrum short release intervals.

Don't confuse short release cycles with sequentially running releases at a high, unsuitable speed. A marathon runner won't choose the same pace for a marathon that a sprinter will for a short-distance race. Similarly, running releases at an unsuitable speed leads to what are often called *death sprints*, which result in an overheated project, burned-out people, and low quality software. The project may initially look like it's a success, but the quality of the code gets worse, new features become harder to implement, and new versions of the software introduce new bugs.

Some people say short releases don't pay off because too much effort has to be invested in the release process itself. Often this isn't the case: If you integrate, package, and deploy your software automatically, this process will become routine and will always take the same amount of time to run. This holds true even when you have a lot of manual work to do during releasing, but that's what you must reduce to zero. To take it to an extreme, examples exist where companies deliver new software several times a day.

RELEASE DURATION AND AUTOMATION

Automating the integration, build, packaging, and deployment steps will facilitate rapid iterative development. Automating the most error-prone, most repetitive, and most time-consuming activities is essential. Additionally, automation is critical in all areas where you're interested in an objective, reproducible result. Another good place to start automation is with processes that aren't transparent for the team, because this will force them to understand those processes: You can only automate what you understand and what you're able to describe. Finally, automation helps a lot in areas where manual work is annoying. Good developers have always automated repetitive aspects of their work because of this.

Automation can lead to improved flexibility. A good approach to quality control that leads to improved flexibility is to get the same automated results continuously. You can then step in immediately if the automated process reveals any defects. Besides that, in your daily work, you should focus on those aspects that require human activities. Humans shouldn't do the work of robots.

3.2.3   *The release content*

The content of the release is determined and committed to in the release planning meeting before the release starts. Agile approaches differ in dealing with changes that occur during the release. Many projects change the scope of the current release under the agreement that a similar amount of scope needs to be taken out of the backlog. As a general rule of thumb, it's often best to stick to the approach of text-book Scrum: The scope of the release and its content mustn't change during the release process.[6] This leads to stable requirements and basic conditions for implementing, and you can better measure what you're doing.

The one exception to this rule is that features can be removed from the release, particularly at the end of the release process, when it becomes obvious that a given feature can't be implemented or fails to meet quality standards. Quality standards can be defined through metrics and tests, and these standards should be fixed and defined before the release starts. It's not a good idea at the end of the release to remove some failed tests or to remove a metric that's not met by the application, just in order to pass the quality requirements and complete the release.

During the release, you'll further specify the features, and you may identify additional facets that are necessary. Specifying and implementing features will often result in new insights, leading to additional (or less) work.

Features taken out of one release go back into the product backlog. They may be put into the next release backlog, but this isn't always the case, because priorities may change. Consequently, a skipped feature may be implemented much later, or perhaps never.

> **RELEASE CONTENT** A release consists of software modules, installation routines (and other configuration items), and dependencies, including drivers, documentation, installation guides, help, user documentation, release notes, test cases, use cases, user stories, and requirement specifications. Most importantly, the release puts all these in the hands of the end user.

---

[6] For further discussion on how to handle bugs that come up during the release, see Rachel Davies and Liz Sedley, "Caring about Quality," in *Agile Coaching* (Pragmatic Bookshelf, 2009), part III.

THE RELEASE CONTAINER, AND RELEASE 0

It's important to understand a software release as containing all the artifacts of the required engineering effort (use cases, user stories, and others); source code (Java, Cobol, Scala, and so on) and its related artifacts, such as interfaces, copybooks, and build scripts; test cases (functional and technical); and other artifacts. A release is the reproducible container of all deliverables created in the release, or created before the release started but that become part of the release afterwards. Functional release management defines and tracks the number of changes applied to the software (major aspects of functional release management are planning releases, escorting the progress and delivering the final increment), whereas technical release management tracks and references all configuration units in physical terms (such as JAR, WAR, and EAR files).

A release 0 can be used to kick off the development and creation of the initial infrastructure. This can encompass setting up a continuous integration environment and rolling out tools to the developers. Further improvements and activities concerning infrastructure can also be done in later releases. It's important that you plan and track those activities.

In addition, a release 0 can help if you have a chaotic development status or don't know the software's status, perhaps because you recently introduced a new process model, are applying Agile strategies for the first time, or have only worked with software prototypes before. Collect everything you have (software, documents, and so on), and integrate and deploy it on target machines. Then you can identify the status of your software.

RELEASE CONTENT AND TESTS

The release content also includes tests, which should be implemented for all functionality. By writing unit tests, developers can find the best design and plan for future refactoring. Functional tests validate functionally correct implementations.

Functional tests that work as a specification for your application are also called *acceptance tests*. Acceptance tests are directly aligned with business requirements. In the best-case scenario, the customer writes the acceptance tests. This way, the tests are written in the customer's domain language, supporting outside-in development, as discussed in more detail in chapter 8.

Behavior-driven development (BDD) is a vehicle for expressing the behavior of the application that can then be coded as automated tests. BDD focuses on example scenarios of how to use the developed application. Basing the written tests on example use cases is often referred to as *specification by example.*

For speed, you should write tests at a lower level than the user interface, except for those tests that are explicitly testing the interface. Tests don't ensure absolute correctness: They can't verify that an application is error-free. They can only find errors, and hopefully they find a lot of them.

The goal should be to automate as many tests as possible—automated tests deliver the best value for the effort applied. You also need to be confident in the results of the tests, so you can use manual exploratory testing for any parts that aren't tested automatically. There are tools for doing that, which we'll discuss in more detail in chapter 8.

Tests and metrics (such as test coverage or design and code audits) are run continuously and should be required to pass, particularly in the endgame, when the release is finalized. The development team will have greater confidence if tests must always pass, and if failed tests and suboptimal metrics are addressed immediately. Tests and metrics (which yield their results) determine the further promotion of the software. Software will be staged only when quality requirements are met.

3.2.4   *Progress and size of working units*

To measure progress, Agile teams often use burn-down charts, illustrating the amount of work that has been completed and what still needs to be done. Both the amount of work completed and the amount of pending work should be visible.

The degree of work completed is often less visible, and the process of how to deal with uncompleted work is frequently done wrong. Consider the following bad practice: You work on a feature repeatedly over the span of two releases. At the end of each release, you state that the degree of completion is 80 percent. This is more about guessing than about transparency, and you won't gain insight into where you are with that feature.

In such a case, be sure to develop a fine-grained slicing of features and to communicate the progress in an objective, measurable way. It's much easier to go with the binary "done" or "not done" on small pieces of work.

A fine-grained horizontal slicing of functionality could use more units for specifying the same functionality. For instance, suppose you've started with two use cases to specify functionality. After the tailoring, you've got four separate use cases, expressing the same functionality, but they're more fine-grained. Their status is now more trackable and work progress on them is more measurable. This approach works for different units and aggregation levels; for example, if you aggregate use cases to features you can split both use cases and features.

The practice of vertical slicing is similar: you can break down the units into subunits in order to manage development and progress better on that level. A common example is to split features (or use cases, if you prefer to use them as the most fine-grained specification of functionality) into tasks where features are aligned with functional/business requirements, and tasks are the mapping from those requirements to fine-grained, technical tasks that have to be worked off to complete the requirement. If your most fine-grained planning unit is larger than two days, think about splitting it into more fine-grained parts. Mike Cohn suggests that you should create tasks with an approximate size so that each developer is able to finish an average of one per day.[7]

You don't have to do the slicing of features all at once, for all features. It's enough to do it for the high-priority items that you're going to implement next or for tasks

---

[7]   Mike Cohn, *Agile Estimating and Planning* (Prentice Hall, 2006), pg. 158.

that are clearly understood. On the other hand, larger units can be understood as placeholders for one or more additional units that will be added as soon as they're understood.

3.2.5 Release commitments

The whole project team works with release commitments. If you have a big project consisting of multiple organizational units, they may all have their individual backlog. Be aware that "when the team is specialized, its goals don't necessarily coincide with the overall goal of the project, or with the goals of another team."[8] The team can pull single items out of the backlog to contribute to a release.

On the other hand, occasionally, there's work that needs to be done that's outside the scope of the backlog. In Scrum, developers shouldn't be spending time scheduled for development on maintenance, support, or side projects, but such time can be scheduled in if you want to. These activities must be measured and made transparent. For example, you may reserve 20 percent of the time for other tasks besides working on the release backlog. Open issue lists of teams or individuals can be managed by issue parking lots or can be held in a document, such as an Excel spreadsheet.

Traditional environments often use a work breakdown structure (WBS) to define how the team and its members organize their individual commitments. A WBS describes who will do what, in which order, and what the individual pieces of work are, and it can be written in the form of a spreadsheet. Applying "rolling wave planning," the WBS is more detailed for the work that's done next. This means that the next commitments are well planned, whereas future ones are planned with a coarse-grained outline.

A team with a conservative posture may manage the development flow with a WBS, whereas a team with an aggressive posture "bets heavily on changes happening and on the ability of the project manager or lead programmer to manage the pipeline."[9]

Planning of individual and team work, and comprehensive overall release planning can be done simultaneously and in conjunction. As an example, a team of developers organizes their regular work with individual spreadsheet lists. At the same time, those who work in projects use the respective release backlogs of those projects.

The release commitment of the project (the release backlog) and individual team backlogs should be stored close at hand. The product and release backlog should be stored in a more formal way. The purist Agile approach involves writing cards and pinning them on the wall, but that's not mandatory and often doesn't scale well. You can also work with a lightweight ticketing system, like Bugzilla or JIRA. We'll discuss this further in chapter 4, which discusses task-based development.

CUSTOMIZING This chapter provides implementation practices for Scrum, in order to fill out the abstract Scrum template. These implementation

---

[8] Gerald M. Weinberg, *The Psychology of Computer Programming*, silver anniversary edition (Dorset House, 1998), pg. 107.

[9] Scott Berkun, *The Art of Project Management* (O'Reilly, 2005), p. 283.

practices have been proofed and found to be resilient in many projects. In your project, you should customize the approach where needed. No silver bullet exists that applies to all environments. Every company and every project is different in some way, so you need different configurations.

3.2.6   *Synchronization points*

ALM is all about synchronization. In every single moment, ALM synchronizes the state of the project. What adds important value in the context of functional release management is hosting regular meetings during your releases. Three main implementations for meetings are the daily stand-up, also known as the *daily Scrum* or daily stand-up meeting, the retrospective, and the release planning meeting.

DAILY SCRUM

In the microcosmic view, it's important for the team to meet every day to synchronize about the following questions:

- What have you done since yesterday?
- What are your blockers?
- What do you want to do by tomorrow?

Do this with a daily Scrum and focus on those three questions. Don't fall into verbose technical discussions. If a technical discussion is needed, arrange a technical meeting or a design session to discuss the design questions. The focus of the daily Scrum should be how this affects everyone in the team or how everyone in the team can help. The daily Scrum is the most essential meeting because it provides a chance to detect and address issues early, and it provides the chance to foster team communication and team building.

The strategy of not falling into verbose technical discussions is wise for any kind of regular status meeting. The stand-up shouldn't take longer than 10 to 15 minutes and should take place daily, always at the same time. Good times can be early in the morning or before going to lunch. The involved team should participate; other stakeholders can join, but they're not allowed to participate actively.

Responsibilities (during stand-up meetings)

Here's a story that spells out the distinction between being committed and involved, in which pigs are committed to the success of the work and the chickens are only involved:

A pig and a chicken are walking down a road. The chicken looks at the pig and says, "Hey, why don't we open a restaurant?" The pig looks back at the chicken and says, "Good idea. What do you want to call it?" The chicken thinks about it and says, "Why don't we call it 'Ham and Eggs'?" "I don't think so," says the pig. "I'd be committed but you'd only be involved."

> **(continued)**
>
> "Committed versus involved" is also valid in a broader sense. Developers are committed. They decide how much stuff goes into a sprint, whereas others in this case are bystanders.

RETROSPECTIVE

Communication is important, but action is more important. Too often people get bogged down in meetings where they fail to reach consensus and agree upon a course of action. One essential forum for discussion is a meeting in which the discussion focuses on what was done well and what can be improved. This is known as a *retrospective*.

The retrospective is done at the end of the release and before the planning meeting for the next release. A retrospective can also be done more often if required. The last release will be analyzed to look for areas where the process can be improved (and mistakes avoided). To be sure, there are things that can be optimized. If you detect several issues, focus on the most relevant and biggest ones. Talk about the issues, and find the root cause for the trouble. Only then can you find an adequate counterstrategy. This may sound simple, but it's often a challenge even for seasoned professionals.

> **BLAME STORMING AND FINGER POINTING** If you have people on your team blocking and hiding information (no, I don't mean the "information hiding" design principle of object-oriented software development) or waiting to blame someone in a status meeting, you aren't working the Agile way. For a retrospective to work well, you need the key values of honesty, trust, and courage and an environment where it's safe to speak out.

It's important not to blame anyone during the retrospective, but it's important to talk about what happened. By applying the appreciative inquiry approach,[10] you can underline positive relationships and the basic goodness in a person, a situation, and an organization, instead of focusing on gaps and problems.

In retrospectives, your thoughts and statements should be based on the agreement that, whatever the project members did during the release, they did it to help make the release a success. But this has limits. If you're working in a culture where people are acting to thwart a project or against the company's goals, you may need to quit the project as soon as possible, or you could at least establish that the team isn't being Agile, so that any improvements arising from a retrospective will probably add little value. Retrospective meetings aren't successful unless the entire team is contributing and feels free and safe to do so. Although this concerns the overall project atmosphere, in the beginning of the retrospective you can run a "safety check" to make people feel more comfortable. Entire books deal with how to set up and run retrospectives.[11]

---

[10] Recognizing the best in people while still exploring and discovering better ways of doing things.

[11] See, for example, Esther Derby and Diana Larsen, *Agile Retrospectives* (Pragmatic Bookshelf, 2006).

RELEASE PLANNING MEETING

During the release planning meeting, all important stakeholders will meet to discuss, synchronize, and commit to the content of the release. This doesn't replace other discussions that will occur during the development process. The planning meeting should be the final point at which the team commits to delivering the content identified in the release backlog. In many projects, the planning meeting is the event where stakeholders present their visions, break features into stories, and plan the release. Dean Leffingwell's *Agile Software Requirements*[12] offers great guidance in setting up agendas and checklists for such a planning meeting.

3.2.7 *Feature teams, component teams, caretakers*

Collaboration and teams are essential for reaching a project goal. "The manager's job with respect to a team is to start it when a team is needed, leave it alone when it's working effectively, and stop it when it's not."[13]

During release planning, feature teams are created where necessary. A *feature team* is a cross-functional team that traces and pushes the creation of a feature that has to be developed as part of the release to fulfill stakeholder needs. This team exists temporarily, working toward a common goal. A crucial benefit of feature teams is that the feature can be implemented using a strict focus that's free of organizational borders (which could have a negative impact on the architecture of the solution). The feature team takes care of its own organization, including times and frequency of meetings. It's created by the responsible stakeholder, usually the project management, and it's responsible for achieving the goal. The team may be led by a feature team leader or it may be completely self-organized. Possible challenges are escalated to the decision makers where needed.

In contrast to a feature team, a *component team* is a traditional team responsible for creating and maintaining a component in a system. It's more aligned at organizational borders or at architectural layers, such as the presentation layer or database layer.

Developers can work on both teams at the same time, although a full assignment to one team is often preferred to minimize time-consuming context switches. Developers who become part of a feature team leave this team either after a defined time or when the job is done. Typically, the feature team is retired when its goals are achieved. Then the created components are maintained and further developed solely by the component teams.

Figure 3.4 shows how feature teams and component teams coexist and how, in this example, one developer is part of both teams at the same time. A *caretaker* can be assigned the responsibility of achieving goals, tracking progress, or maintaining the process. This is often a special manager or expert who is good at achieving goals or solving problems. The Scrum master is an example of a caretaker. Often the caretaker

---

[12] Dean Leffingwell, *Agile Software Requirements* (Addison-Wesley, 2011), chapter 16.

[13] Gerald M. Weinberg, *Quality Software Management*, vol. 3 (Dorset House, 1994), pg. 264.

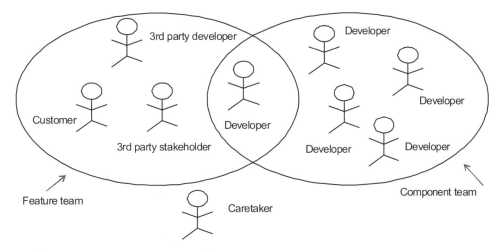

Figure 3.4 Feature team and component team in coexistence. The feature teams work cross-functionally on a feature, while the component teams work on a component. A developer may work as part of the component team and additionally be drafted into a feature team to work on a specific feature. The developer may work on both teams, or may solely work as part of the feature team for a defined period. A caretaker looks out for impediments and mentors a team.

isn't part of the team, but rather acts from outside the team. For instance, the Scrum master isn't part of the Scrum team. Another type of caretaker is someone who buys cold drinks after a long working day. Please let me know which pub you'll be in![14]

3.2.8 Delivery slots, frozen zone, and code freeze

Although you can create versions of your software continuously (for instance, every night with nightly builds), ultimately you want to complete your work and provide a final stable version. The final version is labeled in the VCS and distributed and communicated as such. The final version is the release.

You develop, integrate, and build your software from the first day of the release process, continuously adapting to change as it occurs. At the end, you want to stabilize the software and pay special attention to the quality, also verifying that the requirements are met. Some organizations call that part of the sprint the "endgame," the "frozen zone," or the "hardening phase." Here are several common strategies to focus on during the frozen zone:

- Code is committed only after it's peer reviewed (explicit review in a traditional project setup, organically through team collaboration and pair programming in Agile settings).

---

[14] In his book *Agile Software Development: The Cooperative Game* (Addison-Wesley, 2007), Alistair Cockburn mentions a use case where "getting seriously drunk together" helped to improve teamwork (pg. 231).

- No new APIs are implemented, meaning only bugs are fixed and no additional features are implemented (there's a feature-freeze, or features are feature-complete).

- If you don't have a complete integration build, including all components and databases, you want that to be done during the frozen zone at the latest. Scrum calls for a potentially shippable solution increment to be delivered in each sprint; the solution increment isn't potentially shippable unless it includes a complete integration build.

- If you have timed builds—once a day, for example—you may want to increase the number of builds to get more feedback.

- The development team might continue to work on the trunk while the release branch is frozen.

The duration and the start of the frozen zone vary. Typically, it takes days. If you get good at Agile ALM, you may reduce this time interval to a minimum, but in a 30-day release, having a frozen zone of two days isn't uncommon.

The frozen zone isn't the same as a code freeze (see figure 3.5). The *code freeze* is a short interval at the end of the frozen zone that spans a few hours, such as the last hours of the release or the last afternoon of the release. The code freeze is the slot where no one can commit anything, not even new features or bug fixes. It's the time where the releasing team creates the final release. But the procedure of creating the release should be the same as creating the continuous versions. The purpose of the code freeze is obvious: to eliminate any changes to the artifacts. Changes made during the last moments of the release dramatically increase the probability that the next (and final) build will be broken. Although you did build the software continuously, no

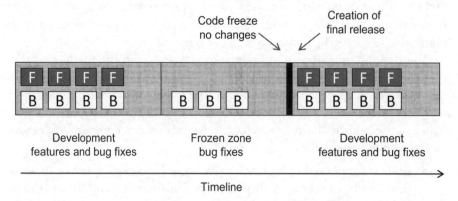

Figure 3.5   The frozen zone and the code freeze for stabilizing and finally releasing the software before the next release is developed (F = feature; B = bug). The way testing is done in an Agile environment often eliminates the need to have a project phase dedicated to detecting and fixing last-minute bugs. There may be a few last-minute bugs, but the dedicated phase should be as short as possible. In the best case, the number of last-minute bugs doesn't justify a scheduled phase in the lifecycle.

former build took the last (changed) sources, so the last build can fail. Because the release is strictly timeboxed, it's important not to have any surprises on the last day or get any new bugs later.

If you detect some final showstopper bugs, they should be fixed. But only one person or a special group should work on those bugs, under the highest quality restrictions. Restricting access on the VCS can be done by conventions. You can email your team and tell them not to change anything in the VCS (they may continue work in their individual workspaces), and then send another email later, releasing the code freeze. In some environments, though, this lightweight approach doesn't work. If you have a chaotic team, hypermotivated people, or too many team members to inform with emails, you may want to support the code freeze technically (see section 3.4). Code freezes are important for providing stability and the chance to complete a releasable unit of work. Success also depends on a good release plan.

3.2.9 *Staging software*

Staging software is the process of completely and consistently transferring a release with all its configuration items from one environment to another. The process of staging releases consists of deploying software to different staging levels, especially different test environments. Staging also involves configuring the software for various environments without needing to recompile or rebuild the software. Staging is necessary to transport the software to production systems in high quality.

It's not always necessary to put a release that won't be shipped to the customer into the complete releasing process, including promoting it on higher staging environments. But like other processes, the releasing process should be done automatically and continuously. If you skip deploying the software on higher staging environments, you'll miss an important synchronization point. You're done with delivering the release only after you have put the software onto the target machine with all its facets (including, for example, creating a technical user account that's used by the system) and verified that it runs successfully. Many Agile projects try to optimize the cycle time between development software and the point when the end user is able to use the software in production. But having a software release available on a test environment can be of much value, especially if you don't need or don't want to put every single release into production.

Only a deployed and available software release illustrates the current status. No substitute exists for that—not any working software in a workspace, and surely no specification or other document in Microsoft Word. Often, and particularly for those projects in the biggest chaos, a complete deployment on a real machine is the only thing that demonstrates the quality of the software and what set of features is implemented and available.

Every significant release of the code needs to be deployed to a testing environment. Sometimes you'll need to stage the release so that the current testing phase can be completed without interruption. You need to balance the stability of the testing effort with the value added by continuously integrating the code. If you postpone a release in order to include more features, you're more likely to postpone uncovering

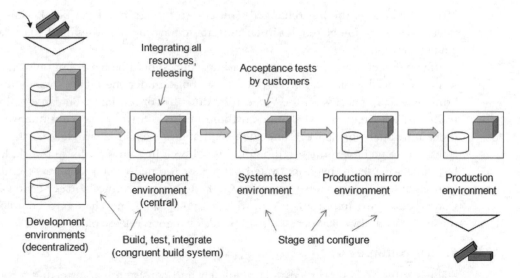

Figure 3.6   Staging software: requirements will be implemented in the developers' workspaces. The central development environment integrates all respective configuration items and is the base for releasing. Software is staged over different environments by configuration, without rebuilding. All changes go through the entire staging process.

serious integration issues, but deploying while QA is in the middle of an automated test run is also a bad idea.

The release itself shouldn't be dependent upon any specific target environment, although obviously there may be required runtime environments, including external data feeds or other resources. You should be able to reconfigure any release for a specific environment without having to rebuild the entire codebase. Figure 3.6 summarizes how software is developed and integrated on lower staging (or promotion) environments and then is promoted to higher staging environments by configuration only.

All software changes must climb the whole staging ladder, from the lowest rung on the ladder to the highest rung, sequentially. (Commonly, this ladder is illustrated on its side, as in figure 3.6, with the higher rungs being the boxes further to the right.) It's good practice not to skip any rungs during staging, such as by deploying a software version that was created in a local workspace to the system test environment. Exceptions in staging may be made for emergency patch releases, but how you handle emergencies must be planned wisely. The process for handling emergency patches must define rules for how to retrofit the changes back into the test environments and the current version in the development phase, to prevent environments from getting out of sync. In a complex projects, many companies minimize such synchronization issues by moving production versions of specific configuration items back to lower levels of the staging ladder.

Many projects define fallback strategies for reverting to an older release in case the deployment of the new one fails. Rolling back to an older (usually the most recent) version can involve redeploying all artifacts that were deployed on that staging level before the new release was unsuccessfully deployed.

Rolling back is a valid approach, but it's better to always move forward and stage all the different types of artifacts, including database dependencies. Reverting a release on a staging level back to a previous release isn't always feasible, especially in complex settings with many dependencies between configuration units. Database elements are often on the critical path during releasing new versions. Upgrading a database to a new release is often a one-way path, where the old version of the database structure and data can't be fully recovered to the old version. This is a good reason to use a well-defined staging process and to test the delivery of your software on lower rungs of the staging ladder.

If you can't revert to a previous release, you need to plan and test the entire release process to minimize risk and to address any possible issues that may arise. It's always best for the test and production environments (and delivery processes) to be identical. This is the only way you can do a dry run of your production delivery. All staging is a set of changes that further develop the system, as opposed to rolling something back.

3.2.10 Quality gates

Quality gates allow the software to pass through only if it meets their requirements. Figure 3.7 shows the staging ladder with quality gates injected. Developers commit code to the VCS in order to update the central test environment only if the code satisfies the defined quality requirements; for instance, the local developer build may need to run successfully and have all tests pass locally. Build, test, and metrics should pass out of the central development environment, and then automated and manual acceptance tests are needed to pass the system test. The last quality gate to pass is the one from the

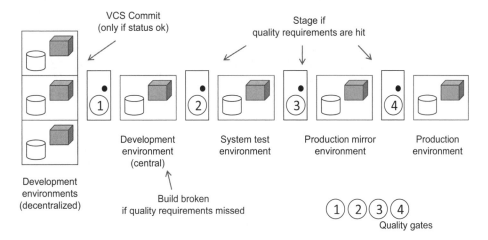

Figure 3.7 The staging of software is allowed only if it successfully passes through the defined quality gates. Quality gates have an obligatory character, validating the defined quality requirements (tests and metrics).

production mirror to production. Here, for example, specific production tests are done or relevant documents must be filled in and signed.

It's mandatory to define the quality requirements in advance and to resist customizing them after the fact, when the software has failed. Quality gates are different at lower and higher stages; the latter normally consist of a more severe or broader set of quality requirements, and they often include the requirements of the lower gates.

Feature specification tests aren't always available when the release starts; it's normal to detail the specifications of requirements, features, and tests during the release process. Bug fixing occurs not only on coding artifacts, but also on tests. Tests must be corrected and detailed where necessary. Tests must also be put into a VCS and baselined along with the contents of the release.

3.3   Release planning vehicles

It's always best to create release plans and then communicate them to all stakeholders. A release plan is a central and important utility, and a couple of vehicles are available to express and communicate these plans.

In chapter 4, we'll look at a tool-driven approach based on JIRA and Trac for setting up releases with milestones and plan and track contents. But that's the second step. The first step is to set up and create a release overview that communicates the timeboxed slots, indicating when important things happen. This overview can have different implementations. One is a release calendar; another is a release screenplay.

3.3.1   Release calendar

The release calendar is set up and updated by a release manager, if one exists. If not, it may be the project manager. It shows all times for all releases and the key activities required within each. The goal is to provide a comprehensive view of the process with dates, and the calendar broadcasts the information. This calendar is lightweight and not locked down; it's open to change if required. The release calendar provides the exclusive view of the releasing of one project.

Figure 3.8 shows an extract of a release calendar. In the first column you see the days, and in the second you see a shaded link expressing some activities spanning days. The third column contains comments about what has to be done during those days. This is only an example; the calendar will vary from case to case.

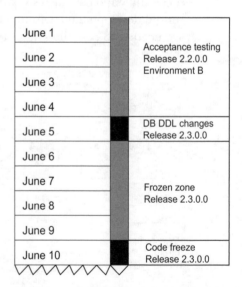

Figure 3.8   The release calendar defines the dates and activities. It's the single view on the timeboxed releasing that may include activities and deliveries.

In this example, during the first four days in June, the focus is on acceptance testing release 2.2.0.0 of the software on environment B. On June 5, a mandatory delivery is defined: structural database changes influencing release 2.3.0.0 must be finalized and communicated.

During the next four days, the team and the software go through the frozen zone. Here, you also see a common pattern. Structural database changes are often handled differently compared to coding artifacts. In the best approach, all artifact types are managed identically, but in practice this may vary for database elements: database changes must often be defined earlier, as expressed in this example. On June 10, the code freeze for the new release happens and the release is finalized.

You may want to distinguish between a project release calendar and a corporate, central release calendar. The corporate release calendar aggregates all of the distributed releases.

3.3.2   *Release screenplay*

The *release screenplay* is a timetable balanced at a zero point, which is normally the day of release. It's further aligned with important activities and responsibilities. Figure 3.9 shows such a schedule that's balanced at day X—the moment when the release is created. Looking back from this time, you can see different milestone activities, like the start of the frozen zone two days before.

Other actions can start when the database structures are frozen, when the creation of target environments begin, and so on. Looking at the time interval after day X, you can see actions such as deploying in target environments or special bug-fixing slots. Typically in this timetable, there's a column that lists the person in charge of the action. It can also be helpful to mention the major stakeholders in an additional column.

Time	Action	Responsible	Stakeholder
Starting day X-5	Preparing, setting up	DB team	Release manager; team
Day X-3	Frozen zone start	Team	Release manager
Day X-2	Writing reminder mail	Release manager	Dev-team
Day X-2/X-1	Functional tests	Customer proxy	Dev-team
Day X-2/X-1	Last bug fixes	Dev-team	
Day X	Creating release branch, tagging	Releasing team	Dev-team
Day X+1	Deployment environment A	Release manager	
Day X+2	Drinking coffee	Team	
Day X+3	...	...	...

Figure 3.9   Release screenplay balanced at day X (release day), aligning times, actions, responsibilities, and the stakeholder.

Let's look at one example: Calling out and starting the frozen zone is the task of the central releasing or software configuration management team, and one stakeholder is the complete development team. A screenplay for this scenario can be set up centrally for common use. It can also be implemented for every concrete release, so you'll have to transform the variable times to concrete dates. Then the screenplay will increasingly match the release calendar we discussed before.

Another derivative of the release screenplay looks at dates and activities from one role's perspective. Consider the development team or the release manager. The latter can set up a schedule that describes all actions from their point of view. Figure 3.10 shows an example.

Time	Action
Starting day X-5	Sending GO to DB-team for DML changes
Day X-3	Communicate frozen zone
Day X-2	Check status
Day X-2/X-1	Monitor functional tests
Day X-2/X-1	Check status
Day X	Creating release branch, tagging
Day X+1	Deployment environment A
Day X+2	Drinking coffee
Day X+3	...

Figure 3.10   Release screenplay, aligned with one role.

3.4   *Supporting strategies with Subversion*

We've discussed the basics of functional ALM and have talked about Scrum and the fundamental aspects of releasing. We've also talked about calendars as tools for rolling out and supporting releasing. In this section, we'll cover technical strategies and tools you can use to bridge the functional and technical releasing. We'll look at technical strategies to support functional releasing.

One strategy is to use hooks (sometimes also called triggers). Another wise choice is to use locking. Both strategies are tool-agnostic.

Some VCS tools use a distributed approach (like Git), whereas others use a more restrictive approach (like ClearCase); the examples in this chapter are based on Subversion (see http://subversion.apache.org). A distributed VCS has a different usage for branches, but the illustrated approaches are useful for both, particularly for handling a main trunk (or a main stream that's necessary for continuous integration). In chapter 7, we'll discuss how to bridge different version-control systems (such as with Subversion or Git) to enable feature branching.

Why bother with hooks and locking? Technical releasing collects configuration items for inclusion in releases, and they're primarily stored in a VCS, checked out by developers, updated, and again checked in. Access to the VCS should be aligned with Agile strategies leveraging the overall release process.

3.4.1   *The one-medium approach*

Many tools are available on the VCS market. At their core, they all have the same intent and functionality: Artifacts should be stored centrally; stakeholders must be able to retrieve the artifacts, update them, and provide the new versions to the others. This holds true for all artifact types, not only source code. But opinions differ about whether the VCS is the right tool to use for managing all artifact types, including binaries (for example, Word documents), and acting as a file server. In my opinion, it's better to reduce the number of different channels, to avoid, for example, having a separate file server for storing binary documents. Using Subversion as a file server has the advantage that you benefit from version control and know who has touched which artifact, and when they did so. The information about which is the most recent version of the artifact isn't always available when using a plain file server.

If lots of large binaries in the VCS slow down the checkout, consider improving the folder structure in the repository. But not all stakeholders are interested in the same artifacts and don't have to check out all the artifacts. For example, a project manager may be primarily interested in the project archive, including project protocols, whereas an architect is more interested in design documents. Refining the project definition to include roles, the roles' access paths to the Subversion repository, and the roles' permissions is often a good way to organize the work with the VCS.

If you have team members who don't want to store large documents in the Subversion repository, you should gather your requirements and consider the alternatives. For example, pin down what large means. You may also consider storing references to large artifacts, and not the artifacts themselves.

Subversion is a lightweight, open source tool that enables a team to apply Agile strategies. As CVS's successor, Subversion is popular and its use is widespread throughout the industry.

Subversion is a good tool for storing all kinds of artifacts, including binaries (through its efficient storage strategies). By using it when working on different artifact types, you always profit from Subversion features like version history (which is important for tracking changes) or hooks and locks.

Another advantage of using Subversion is that all stakeholders can access the tool and the artifacts stored in it. Artifacts in their versions can be accessed by developers (via Subversion integration in the IDE) or by nontechnical stakeholders, who can use the free TortoiseSVN tool. Once installed, TortoiseSVN adds Subversion commands to the directory explorer of your local operating system (see figure 3.11).

Both Subversion and TortoiseSVN are easy to use, though it may take a bit of training to get the team up to speed on using them.

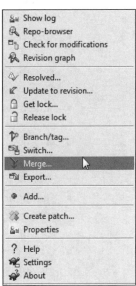

Figure 3.11 Accessing Subversion on Windows with TortoiseSVN. Menu action items are part of Windows Explorer after installing TortoiseSVN.

Another interface for accessing the repository is a browser. You can peruse the central Subversion repository and its content with a web browser (if the repository is hosted via Apache, which is the recommended strategy). This way, you can provide read-only access when necessary.

Subversion has several interfaces that make it much easier to use. Automating common tasks through scripts, known as hooks, also helps improve Subversion's usability.

3.4.2   Hooks

A *hook* is a program or script that's started when entry conditions apply. For example, a trigger could be thrown due to a Subversion repository event. These events are aligned with significant VCS lifecycle operations. A *commit* is an operation, for example.

A hook is a self-contained piece of work. It knows its context, including who did (or wants to do) what. The hook can have output or a return status that can influence the further behavior of the system. Hooks are powerful vehicles for synchronizing the technical and functional worlds.

Hooks are used in the niche between functional and technical releasing and they can allow you to enforce certain rules, such as the following:

- During code freeze, developers aren't allowed to check in changes to VCS.
- During code freeze, only lead developers are allowed to check in changes to VCS, on demand.
- Multiple users can simultaneously update source/ASCII artifacts.
- Multiple users can't simultaneously update binary artifacts like Word documents.
- Stakeholders must enter a commit message (with a minimum length of *x* letters) for all updating actions.
- Stakeholders must enter a commit message, including a ticket number, to enable task-based development.
- Stakeholders aren't allowed to access the repository when the administrator wants to drive a repository backup.
- Stakeholders should receive emails with details of updating operations.
- Stakeholders aren't allowed to update frozen versions of the software. This system must prevent updating changes on repository paths that contain *tags* (after you update a Subversion tag, it becomes a *branch).*
- When synchronizing a ticketing system with changes in the VCS (depending on the commit message), you change the state of tickets; for instance, you close or comment on them.

Hooks are helpful, but having too many can slow down the response time of the VCS and cause unexpected (and undesirable) outcomes.

In the Subversion cosmos, after creating a Subversion repository, you also create a directory named *hooks* inside the repository. All executables put in that directory are

Project role: Captain Hook

Using hooks can be helpful in application development. Often hooks are used for extending or modifying runtime behavior. Hooks are valid OO tools for designing good APIs. Examples occur in the context of delegation and inheritance—such as in the template method design pattern.

Please use hooks and the word itself sparingly. There are people (let me call them *Captain Hook*s) who patch and hack sources and add functionality systematically on a daily basis, while calling that *hooking*. Tinkering with sources without caring about the design, extensibility, and sustainability of software isn't using hooks; it's tinkering.

By the way, hooking a hook script is a bad idea—as bad as modifying the Subversion repository with operating system commands instead of the intended interface. If you need to extend Subversion, use the dedicated API!

automatically run in their individual context, depending on the trigger event. Here are the most important hook triggers available in Subversion:

- *Start-commit*—Runs before commit transaction begins
- *Precommit*—Runs at the end of the transaction but before commit
- *Postcommit*—Runs at the end of the commit
- *Postlock*—Runs after a repository path is locked
- *Post-unlock*—Runs after a repository path is unlocked
- *Pre-unlock*—Runs before an exclusive lock is destroyed

Subversion hooks are used by convention. The hook script in the directory must be executable (often the hook scripts are Python scripts) and named with the intention and context you want that hook to be applied to. For example, if you want to create a start-commit hook with Python, you would name the file *start-commit.py*. On Windows, executable extensions are *exe* and *bat*. To make it easier, the directory already includes hook templates named correctly. Subversion uses the extension *.tmpl* for templates, which you can easily rename.

> **WARNING** You can run Subversion and host Subversion repositories on many different platforms, including Windows and Linux. But be aware of platform-specific peculiarities. For example, Subversion configuration is case-sensitive and Windows is case-insensitive. The decision of what platform to use can depend on many different factors; for example, if you want to run Subversion with 64-bit Apache, this installation isn't as mainstream on Windows as on Linux.

Further details about hook scripts can be found in the free *Version Control with Subversion* book, available at http://svnbook.red-bean.com.

3.4.3   Flow and locking

Subversion naturally supports Agile workflow because it uses the copy-modify-merge model as an alternative to the classic lock-modify-unlock model. Copy-modify-merge is optimistic about locking where files aren't generally locked initially. This means all stakeholders can work on and change a file at the same time. Developers have local copies of the central repository (or parts of it). They work simultaneously, modifying their private copies, and after their work is done, the private copies are merged together into a new, final version. Subversion assists with merging, but you'll still have to make sure that the merges are performed correctly.

This approach can dramatically accelerate the development flow and the velocity, because work can be done in parallel and waiting times are reduced (idle time is *waste*). The drawback is that someone has to deal with the merges, particularly the merge conflicts. Agile suggests frequent small commits to avoid large merge conflicts. The alternative is to apply pessimistic locking, where only one person at a time can work on a file, but merging scenarios are much easier to handle.

Copy-modify-merge is based on the experience that in software projects, it's rare that more than one person is working on one file. If multiple people work on one file simultaneously, they (mostly) work on different parts of the file so there's no reason for additional communication—the tool can merge such cases automatically.

Tools like Subversion automatically merge different developers' versions into a central, leading version. In cases where this isn't possible, the tool can provide merging information. The human in front of the keyboard must then decide what the new version of the final file should look like.

> **LOCKING AND COMMUNICATION** Locking doesn't replace communication. Rather, it supports releases and communication. Stealing or breaking locks is technically easy with Subversion. Please use the locking features wisely and in cooperation with your peers. There are good and bad scenarios for stealing locks. First, a good one: A colleague is on holiday and forgot to release his lock. And a bad one: Hey, the guy on the other side of my table locked the file; but it's my file, and I want to update it now.

Subversion's support for merging binaries is limited. That's no surprise. How should the tool, for example, merge two versions of a Word document or a JPEG image? For binary files, a stricter approach is helpful when working with locks. With the Subversion command `svn lock word.doc`, you lock the file word.doc. This command runs directly on the file in the repository. After it's applied, other people can't change the file; the file is locked for your changes. Conversely, `svn unlock word.doc` releases the lock again (also, a `commit` releases the lock by default). These operations will work only when the file isn't locked by another user. You can overwrite another user's lock by using the `force` attribute—for example, `svn unlock --force word.doc`. This is known as *breaking* or *stealing* locks.

> **NOTE** Working with locks and properties is also conveniently possible with Subversion clients like TortoiseSVN or SmartSVN.

It's also helpful to tell Subversion to expect locks for individual artifact types by default. This means that setting locks isn't optional but mandatory before you can change a file of a special type. In such cases, or if you want to simulate a complete lock-modify-unlock approach, you can configure Subversion to operate accordingly. Subversion can deal with properties (metadata) to achieve that. They can be set (and likewise also edited after being added). Setting the `needs-lock` property then looks like `svn propset svn:needs-lock yes file.doc`. This is something that happens in your local sandbox first (you don't run the command changing the attributes directly in the repository). This means you have to commit this in the same way you commit other changes to files.

This is convenient for single cases. But you have to do that for all your file types or files individually and manually. Your local Subversion client installation contains a conf directory, and you can set it so that for all newly added files of a special type, the property is added automatically:

```
[miscellany]
# enable-auto-props = yes
[auto-props]
*.doc = svn:needs-lock = true
```

This snippet activates automatic property setting and defines the individual property rule. You can combine locks with a precommit hook that ensures that the property is set on newly added files. You can also use prelock and pre-unlock hooks to let administrators decide when to permit lock creation and lock releases. With these hooks, you can prevent certain users from breaking or stealing locks, or allow them to do so.

> **TIP** In the same neat configuration file, you can also customize which editor to use for merge tracking and many other things.

Subversion is a popular open source VCS and lends itself nicely to Agile development.

3.5 Summary

In this chapter, we looked at what functional ALM is, and we introduced Scrum as a popular high-level management template. We talked about releases as the central item in the functional releasing process and discussed releasing strategies inspired by Agile strategies. You can use the strategies in pure Agile projects and in rich, traditional approaches. We also discussed expressing and communicating release plans. Release calendars and release screenplays are valuable tools for defining and communicating the functional releasing process. Tools for version control like Subversion support running an Agile approach. Running the copy-modify-merge optimistic locking pattern increases flow and velocity. In special cases, Subversion still allows administrators to create stricter enforcement policies through the use of locks or hook scripts.

In the next chapter, we'll discuss using toolchains to provide functional and technically consistent releases in a task-based way.

Task-based development

4

This chapter covers

- Approaches and different tools for implementing task-based development
- Lightweight tools for planning and tracking tasks
- Example toolchains, including JIRA/ GreenHopper, Bamboo, Eclipse, FishEye, Mylyn, Trac, for planning and tracking tasks

Traditionally, work items (or tasks) are spread across artifact types and tools. Tasks are an abstraction level for coping with the general information overload and the challenges of parsing information from many different sources. A task is a fine-grained, measurable unit of work, extracted from a broader scope, like a use case or a feature. Leffingwell states "for more detailed tracking of the activities involved in delivering stories, teams typically decompose stories into tasks that must be accomplished by individual team members in order to complete the story."[1]

With a task-based (or task-focused) approach, the task is the unit of interaction and the base of work. *Task-based development* is the technique of linking work items

---

[1] Dean Leffingwell, *Agile Software Requirements* (Addison-Wesley, 2011), pg. 38.

(issues, defects, tasks, and so on) to the specific set of changes (such as an atomic changeset) made to complete the work described in the work item. For example, if you're fixing a defect that's listed as defect 4711 in JIRA, task-based development requires that you link the exact set of changes to defect 4711 in JIRA.

Task-based development is powerful and significantly improves your productivity by making it easy to track changes to the approved change request that authorized the modification. Working in a task-based way, the functional and technical consistency of releases is improved.

This chapter will examine task-based development by providing numerous compelling examples. Tools aggregate knowledge and improve traceability and visibility. They aggregate content and provide views to improve the release process. I will describe toolchains consisting of JIRA/GreenHopper, Bamboo, Eclipse, FishEye, Mylyn, and a product called Trac, which provides much of the same functionality. You might be using a different set of tools in your organization, but you'll likely find that the functionality described is similar.

First, let's discuss a few basic prerequisites that are commonly found in task-based development.

4.1 Prerequisites for task-based development

Every set of changes should be documented with a brief comment that explains the reason for the change when you check changes into the VCS. I recommend that you use change comments to explain *why* you made the changes to the code base. Merely describing *what* you have done doesn't usually add any value. For example, comments such as "checked changes in" aren't helpful; "fixed defect #136—date calculation error" is more useful.

In Agile, it's also essential that you commit your changes frequently so that you're continuously integrating your code. Before you commit your changes, always refresh your sandbox to ensure that your changes won't break the build for someone else. Basic quality gates are also important for analyzing static code, testing, and ensuring that the code can successfully compile.

There's more, but these are the basics we'll focus on now. Here are more details about the practices.

4.1.1 Coordinating changes

Task-based development is valuable when you're coordinating the changes of a large team of developers who may be located in one place or distributed across several locations. Managing the changes of a group involves handling complex dependencies, and it demonstrates the value of continuous integration.

For example, suppose you want to commit your changes to the Subversion (SVN) repository. Before you do so, you should update your sandbox (your workspace) with incoming changes. Afterward, you need to ensure that your classes compile and your tests run successfully (including all of the required quality gates, such as static code analysis). Other developers are also refreshing their sandboxes and committing their changes to the repository at the same time. Each commit causes the Subversion repository revision number to be incremented by one and the changes to be documented in the log.

Once all specified features are implemented, the release is finished, and the changes from each member of the team are successfully integrated, one developer (often the lead developer) should tag the revision of the code, which creates a *baseline*. This is often done in the code freeze phase, as you learned in the previous chapter. Some teams use branches to help organize their work (especially when they're close to a release). Your colleagues can always see what you have changed, and by browsing the changelog, they can see the set of changes that was committed to fix a particular bug or implement a feature.

You should commit your changes to the VCS often and continuously. A general rule of thumb is to synchronize with the central repository and commit your own changes at least twice a day, perhaps in the morning and evening. This doesn't mean you must close tickets in your bug tracking system twice a day. Instead, tasks can be updated and be "in progress." Therefore, one task could lead to multiple check-ins, although one commit for one small-grained task is even better.

The VCS system should be used to track different changes as frequently as possible. Additionally, issue management systems should track tasks with different changes; one task could be related to several changesets (check-ins), and each changeset could link to several files. But keep in mind that your commits should be aligned to tasks, so you need to slice your tasks accordingly. Fine-grained, focused tasks will give you greater confidence and are easier to track. If tasks take days or weeks to implement, they're too coarse-grained and the approach definitely needs to be improved.

4.1.2   Using changesets

Modifications that are dependent on each other because they implement the same task should be grouped in one atomic VCS commit. This enables the VCS and other tools that connect to the VCS (like an IDE) to track these changes as a single changeset.

Matthew B. Doar states that a changeset is "a group of related changes to a set of files; the changes are applied all together or not at all."[2] This changeset can be propagated as needed and contains all the modifications that lead to a new revision in the VCS. On the other hand, by doing atomic, bulk commits aligned with tasks (rather than committing separate, single files), you assign one change commit to the full batch. This allows you and others to track the impacts and results much better. Changesets allow a technical view on an entire group of changes.

Allow me to provide an example: You're working on a bug fix that requires you to modify a couple of files. After you finish your work, you commit the changeset to a VCS (for example, Subversion). In Subversion, this single transactional commit will increase

---

[2] Matthew B. Doar, *Practical Development Environments* (O'Reilly, 2005), pg. 42.

the revision number by one. Your colleagues can see what you have changed and, by browsing the change log, they can confirm that these changes belong together. You (and others) can easily reproduce the different software versions—the one version from before the changes and the resulting one after applying them. By accessing the Subversion revision number, you can do this even without using Subversion tags.

If you use a VCS that doesn't handle commits in a transactional way, such as Concurrent Versions System (CVS), mistakes or problems can occur because of incomplete transactions. Consider using a continuous integration infrastructure where a new build is triggered after a developer commits changes in order to integrate the changesets with the central repository and with the work of your peers. You can also use the task management system (for example, JIRA) to trigger an integration build. For instance, when the task is marked as complete, continuous integration will trigger the build and related testing.

After a commit occurs, the build server often has to wait several intervals (or a specific scheduled time) to start the build. If you don't commit the changes all in one step, you may kick off a new build that's based on an inconsistent state.

4.1.3 Associating changesets with tasks

The next important step is to associate every changeset with a specific task and indicate the task number (for example, defect 136) in the comment that you enter when you commit the changeset. (*Task* here means a ticket in the ticketing system, such as JIRA or Trac.)

By associating changesets with tasks, the tasks (change requests, new features, or bugs) are traceable through the system. Many tool integrations make this connection a two-way function that automatically tracks the changesets to the defect number that authorized the changes. This means that you can look up the defect in JIRA and see the revision number of the changesets that implemented the bug fix. You can also see the defect number in Subversion that explains why the changeset was committed. This two-way traceability improves quality and productivity.

If this all sounds complicated, it is. But it's more complicated, even impossible, to track without task-based development! These different aspects of enabling task-based development, coordinating changes, using changesets, and associating changesets to tasks, are important considerations, and I'll soon explain how to implement an example solution. Right now, though, let's consider a high-level solution from a logical point of view.

> **COMMIT MESSAGES AND VCS HOOKS** Task-based development is enabled by using a special commit message that references the task identifier. You can make referencing the ticket numbers in check-in messages mandatory by using VCS hooks.

Figure 4.1 shows what a high-level solution looks like, from a logical point of view (without any specific tools). The system infrastructure contains a ticket system, where you manage your tasks (work items, requirements, bugs, features, and tasks).

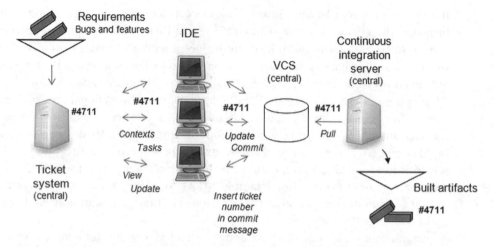

Figure 4.1   The Agile ALM infrastructure: the unique ticket number of a task connects the different participants (nodes) in the system. This results in traceability and transparency, and it ensures the alignment of activities with specific requirements.

The developers use an IDE to update tasks in the ticket system with (specific context) information. Developers can update the tickets in the ticketing system (which tracks the changes on the task description) without leaving their development workspace and tools. This information is distributed to other developers who are working on these tasks too. Their workspaces are aligned with tasks and artifacts, which are necessary to accomplish the specific task.

Code sources are managed with a VCS. The developers share their code via the VCS and perform *update* (pull changes) and *commit* (put changes) operations on the code base. In order to work in a task-based way, they add the ticket number to their commit messages.

A central continuous integration server pulls the source code and builds the software. By referencing the ticket number to the changes, the build server can retrieve this meta-information from the VCS, and reference the changes to the build artifacts.

Consequently, the Agile ALM system delivers information about which artifacts contain what features or bug fixes (which tasks motivated changes on these artifacts) and which tasks are solved by working on which artifacts. This is called *traceability*, and it ensures the alignment of activities with concrete requirements.

The ticketing system allows you to manage requirements (such as bugs, features, and tasks) from a logical point of view. This helps facilitate the Agile business view of the development process. The developers may also be using an IDE that has a plug-in installed to allow easy access to the information in the ticketing system. Workspaces should be created and aligned to organize the work in a logical way (using Eclipse, you can use working sets to logically group the artifacts in your workspace) whereas the code is managed in the VCS (such as Subversion). This approach provides traceability, improving both productivity and quality.

In the next two sections, we'll look at how to implement task-based development using two different toolchains. The first uses JIRA/GreenHopper, Bamboo, and Fish-Eye with Mylyn.

4.2 *Our first toolchain—JIRA, FishEye, Bamboo, and Mylyn*

In this and the next section, we'll look at how to implement task-based development using two different toolchains. The first toolchain, discussed in this section, is based on the commercial tools JIRA/GreenHopper, Bamboo, and FishEye. The second toolchain is primarily based on Trac, which is an enhanced wiki and issue-tracking system for software development projects—it's covered in section 4.3. Regardless of which toolchain you use, you can add a product known as Mylyn, which is a task framework for Eclipse. Both toolchains can (and should) be integrated with a continuous integration server.

Remember what we discussed in chapter 1. Your tool infrastructure should be flexible and open to changes. If you feel more comfortable with different tools in your toolchains, you can replace them with your favorites, keeping the rest of your toolchain unchanged. Other toolchains are possible by integrating different tools of the same tool types. For instance, if you prefer Jenkins over Bamboo, you can easily replace that one specific tool in the overall chain either during initial setup or at any time later.

JIRA (and its plug-in GreenHopper), FishEye, and Bamboo are commercial products developed by Atlassian.[3] These lightweight tools span different phases of the development process, including requirements engineering, development, and delivery. Different project roles gain benefit from this highly integrated toolchain:

- The team (developers and testers), project managers, and product owners can use JIRA to manage the requirements and to align their work with those requirements.
- Developers can access the tasks from within their IDEs with Mylyn.
- The team can use Bamboo for CI, and developers can use it to start builds from within their IDEs.
- The team, project managers, and product owners can use FishEye to track source changes, providing real-time notifications of code changes plus web-based reporting, visualization, searching, and code sharing.
- The team can track changes by ticket. This means the team is aware of which tickets were completed in specific builds (via Bamboo and FishEye), which sources were modified to complete a specific ticket (via JIRA and its connection to FishEye/Subversion), and which tasks they should work on (via Eclipse and Mylyn). Because developers have all this information at their fingertips, the approach is often also described as developer-centric.

---

[3] See www.atlassian.com to find comprehensive online documentation for installing and configuring these tools.

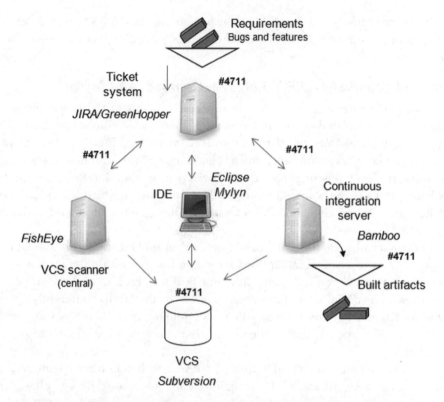

Figure 4.2   This toolchain enables task-based development. It's based on JIRA, FishEye, Subversion, Bamboo, Eclipse, and Mylyn. Requirements are managed with JIRA. GreenHopper enriches JIRA with further features for Agile development. The CI server pulls sources from the VCS to build the software. FishEye is a convenient VCS browser that makes changes visible in a convenient way. Both Bamboo and FishEye are integrated with JIRA. Developers use Eclipse with Mylyn to work on code; they access code with Eclipse and the plug-in that's available to connect to the VCS that's used.

These tools are lightweight (and inexpensive) but they still provide full tracking of tasks to changesets, which is the main point of task-based development. This toolchain is illustrated in figure 4.2.

As you already know, the ticket system contains your tasks. In this specific solution, JIRA is the ticket system, and its GreenHopper plug-in enables JIRA to support Agile development. Developers use Mylyn to access JIRA tasks directly from within the Eclipse IDE to work in a task-based way. The sources are managed in a VCS, which in this case is Subversion. FishEye monitors code changes in the VCS, and the FishEye integration allows you to browse your source-control repository from inside JIRA. Bamboo, as the CI server, provides build information and makes it visible inside JIRA, as part of the ticket.

Let's take a deeper look at these tools.

4.2.1   *Managing tasks with JIRA*

JIRA is most commonly used for issue tracking, but it can also help with project and release management. You can configure JIRA for your needs. For example, you can configure your own workflows (transition rules), and you can modify issues so they contain information about bugs, enhancements, requirements, or a customized work item. You can configure JIRA to track different change types that contain different information. As a result, JIRA can also be used for tracking requirements and tasks, which makes it appealing.

JIRA can be integrated with a VCS, like Subversion. JIRA displays all changes in Subversion with their respective commit messages, including the JIRA ticket number. Besides its powerful configurable features, it also has an extensible open architecture. There are plug-ins that you can easily add to the system, and you can also write your own plug-ins using the documented API.

Some of JIRA's main features include the following:

- Release management support (roadmaps, versions, milestones)
- Ticketing system
- Fine-grained permission system, Lightweight Directory Access Protocol (LDAP) support
- Open for integration with Atlassian Confluence wiki, Atlassian Bamboo, and other Atlassian products like Crucible
- Multiproject support
- Extensibility and configurability (for reporting, issue types, features, and so on)
- Feature-rich approach enabling Agile development
- A configurable state machine (a workflow engine) for handling issue transitions
- Support for task-based development
- Support for Agile processes, including burn-down charts and cards (via Green-Hopper)

BUG-TRACKING TOOL = PROCESS SMELL?   Some teams track defects separately from other tasks, and some teams treat a defect the same as any other work item. Many mature Agile teams call the existence of a bug-tracking tool a *process smell*. Other teams have such a severe problem with legacy code that they need a bug-tracking tool to find a practical starting point to improve their code base. The choice of tools will depend on local conditions and on how the team operates. JIRA's advantage is that you can track all the different types of changes, including bugs and tasks. You can customize JIRA to hold issues of type task and bugs in parallel, making JIRA more a task-tracking tool.

GreenHopper is an optional JIRA plug-in that improves JIRA's ability to prioritize and visualize priorities, and it thereby empowers JIRA to support Agile project management. To that end, GreenHopper introduces cards that can be assigned to issue types and target releases. GreenHopper also adds burn-down charts to JIRA, visualizing progress through the release. Installing GreenHopper into a running JIRA instance is easy. In newer versions of JIRA, you can install the plug-in through JIRA's admin screen.

CODE REVIEWS WITH CRUCIBLE   Crucible is Atlassian's tool for reviewing work as a continuous process. Crucible enables code review and is highly integrated with JIRA, supporting Subversion, Git, and other VCSs. One common use case for Crucible is to provide a workflow that transitions a ticket from Open to Under Review to Resolved. Another scenario is a postcommit review, done automatically after code changes are checked in.

After you have completed the well-documented JIRA installation process, you'll have JIRA running on your machine on port 8080, which is the default. After you've started JIRA, you can create and work on tickets.[4] The ticket overview shows all relevant information belonging to one ticket, including the component the ticket belongs to and the affected and target versions, as can be seen in figure 4.3.

On the right side of the screen, the ticket reporter is listed as well as the current assignee. You can assign other people to continue the work on that issue. Voting for a ticket is a nice feature: You can vote on tickets to express the importance of the ticket and the team can determine how many developers consider the ticket important. You can watch a ticket and its progress to keep informed of ongoing activities. You'll automatically get emails advising of any changes to tickets you're watching. The right panel also includes information about when the ticket was created and last updated.

The upper panel of buttons provides functions for working on this ticket, such as editing the attribute of the ticket (the type of the ticket, for instance), commenting on

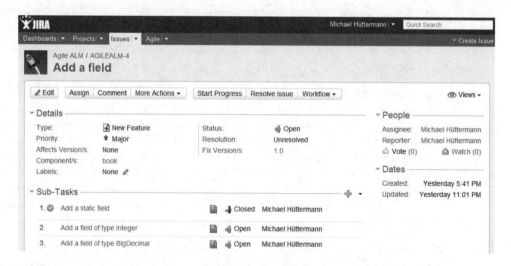

Figure 4.3   The ticket AGILEALM-4 is of type New Feature and is linked to three subtasks.

---

[4] For further discussion of how to set up roles and permissions, please consult the documentation.

the ticket, indicating that you've started work on the ticket, or assigning others to work on the ticket.

Being assigned to work on one ticket doesn't automatically mean that you've started the task. If you work on the item, you can document that by using the start progress feature. This way, the amount of time you spend working on that ticket is recorded. Furthermore, the ticket is added to the in progress list, which can be displayed on the dashboard. After completing work on an issue, you can resolve it. The possible transition states are also configurable.

The main middle section of the page identifies attributes of the ticket that were entered when the ticket was created, such as the issue type or the ticket's priority, as well as status information.

By configuring JIRA, you can work on personalized items and attach your own custom fields to the ticket, your own issue types, your own priorities, and so on. You can also configure dependencies of tickets, such as relationships between them. One common example is configuring a ticket to be a subtask of another ticket. In the example in figure 4.3, the ticket with the unique identifier AGILEALM-4 identifies a feature that was sliced into three subtasks. One subtask is already implemented and closed; two others are still open and still must be implemented.

Integrating Confluence wiki

Atlassian also provides an enterprise wiki called Confluence. You can integrate Confluence in different ways. An easy way to integrate JIRA with Confluence is to link from Confluence to JIRA with the combination of Confluence shortcuts and JIRA's quick search.

In Confluence, you can create a shortcut for JIRA and use it inside your Confluence page with [ALM-1@JIRA] to reference the ticket in JIRA. You can also use the {jiraissues} and {jiraportlet} macros to embed JIRA reports and portlets into your Confluence site.

Another scenario is to integrate Confluence project documentation into a build. In this use case, you maintain project documentation with Confluence. Then, in the automatic release process of your software, you export static HTML out of Confluence. This can be done with Maven in its assembly phase, for example. (Technically, you create a zip file after calling wget via Ant execution.) This is embedded in the Assembly Plugin for Maven.

A third integration scenario is quite different: pushing content to the Confluence wiki after a build is created. In this case, wiki content is created and uploaded in Confluence's xmlrpc interface. One solution is to use Maven and its Confluence plug-in.

Another way to organize your work is to create target versions of your software. Tickets can be assigned to target versions in JIRA, and these JIRA versions map to releases (or iterations) in your development process. You define a JIRA version with a version ID

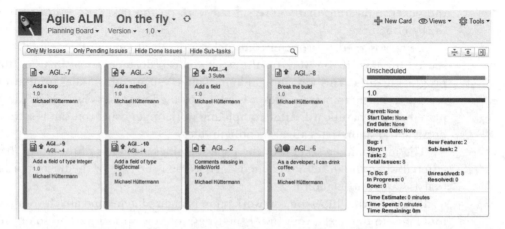

Figure 4.4   GreenHopper's planning board: Visualizing tickets as cards enables you to create new ones or change their status. Cards can be filtered to show only cards that are open or only your tickets. The GreenHopper view also visualizes target versions and uses different icons to express information such as priorities.

(for example, "1.0" or "Important-0.1"), a description, and a release date. By using a schedule, you can define its position in the list of existing versions. A *roadmap* collects a list of upcoming versions.

You can monitor the development progress in different ways. One way is to use charts of newly created and closed tickets, or you can use GreenHopper's burn-down charts. In addition to the burn-down chart, GreenHopper adds planning and tracking facilities to the system to help with Agile development. Figure 4.4 shows the planning board for planning and tracking issues.

Instead of the linear, text-based JIRA approach, you can simulate working with cards, with a card being like a traditional JIRA ticket. The planning board can be opened via the Agile menu at the top of the JIRA screen. Here, you can create new cards and modify existing ones. You also can change the target version of cards by dragging them to a different area on the display. For instance, a card that was assigned to be part of version 1.0 can be assigned to be unscheduled by dragging the card to the Unscheduled area on the page. A transition rule must exist to perform that operation, and you can set up transition rules as part of JIRA's state/workflow system.

Requests for developing a bug fix or a new feature lead to tasks. You'll have different configuration settings, like priorities, but a good approach is to manage all tasks similarly. That's why it's named "task-based development" and not "development based on feature requests" or "development based on bug fixes." For the same reason, JIRA talks about tickets as its coarse-grained working unit. On this level, a JIRA ticket can be compared to a task in "task-based development."

Going deeper, it's wise to distinguish between types of tasks (and tickets) by dividing and organizing the work into more granular tasks, in a processes that has become known as *slicing*. For example, suppose you're documenting the software requirements in the ticket type requirement (JIRA allows you to configure the ticket types and relationships) or in user stories or use cases,[5] whichever is most appropriate in your context. These tickets have relationships to tickets of type task. In these tasks, the features are documented technically, but at a high level. Tasks have subtasks that contain the specific technical tasks to be implemented. Subtasks are a way to break down high-level tasks into smaller units to be estimated and rolled up into the larger estimate.

Another way to slice the items is to use features (describing the high-level functionality), stories (special use cases), and tasks (the technical face).

4.2.2   *Working on tasks with Eclipse and Mylyn*

The IDE is the place where developers implement the requirements. We're using Eclipse in this toolchain, and we can add further Eclipse plug-ins to this Eclipse configuration to access the VCS. In this toolchain, we want to connect to a Subversion repository. The Subclipse plug-in is a good choice for interacting with the repository, and you can install it via the Eclipse update manager.

Mylyn is an Eclipse-based task framework. It can integrate with ticket and bug-tracking tools such as JIRA, Bugzilla, Trac, and Mantis. After installing Mylyn with the appropriate ticket system connector for JIRA, and configuring it to connect to your task repository by providing the URL and credentials to login, an additional view is added to Eclipse, showing all tasks matching your search criteria, as shown in figure 4.5. Once your tasks are integrated, Mylyn monitors your work activities and synchronizes with the ticket system automatically. You can reference parts of the sources you're working on in Eclipse as the context of a task. This context can be attached to the task or even posted as an attachment to the ticket.

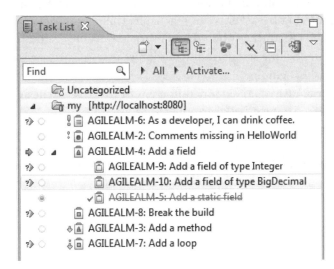

Figure 4.5   Mylyn adds a task-based view in Eclipse. In the Eclipse task view, important information about the tasks (such as issue type, status and priorities) are shown directly, but double-clicking will open the complete ticket in your Eclipse editor. Tickets can be grouped by relationships of subtasks. In the left area, incoming and outgoing changes made by you or other developers are identified with icons. Unread tickets—tickets that haven't been opened yet—are identified with a question mark.

---

[5] For slicing user stories, see Mike Cohn, *User Stories Applied* (Addison-Wesley, 2004). For slicing use cases, see Alistair Cockburn, *Writing Effective Use Cases* (Addison-Wesley, 2001).

NOTE Other IDEs support an ALM approach too. IntelliJ IDEA from Jet-Brains, for example, can integrate with task repositories, including Atlassian's JIRA.

One developer can import into their workbench a context that has been provided by another developer. This helps to standardize views. You can easily switch tasks in Eclipse, getting individual views on the sources. Tasks in your workspace are updated automatically.

These are Mylyn's main features:

- Mylyn accesses and integrates with your task tracker. The integration is in both directions: You import and read tasks in your workspace, and you update and create items in your workspace.
- Mylyn supports filtering, sorting, highlighting, and folding. You can query your tracker for tasks, you can update tasks, you can see change notifications in Eclipse, and you can use contexts to slice and group your sources according to tasks. You can also activate tasks to indicate that you're working on them.
- Mylyn integrates with VCS changesets. A changeset can be linked to a task. A changeset can be checked in as a single atomic transaction.
- Mylyn integrates with build servers, for instance, Hudson/Jenkins.
- Mylyn supports activating tasks. Activating a task removes all those files from the IDE view that are unnecessary to complete the activated task. The workspace and its visible files are aligned with the task.
- Mylyn supports attaching context information to a task and uploading this context information to the ticket in the bug tracker.
- Mylyn allows working offline: Locally cached tasks can still be maintained although the central task tracker is not reachable. Changes to tasks can be synchronized with the task tracker when the network is available again.
- Mylyn is part of the Eclipse standard distribution.
- Mylyn enables task scheduling.
- In addition to Java, Mylyn has extended its support to C/C++, PHP, and Spring Framework–powered enterprise Java applications.
- Additional commercial features are provided by Tasktop (see www.tasktop.com). The commercial product extends task focus to time tracking, web browsing, and desktop documents, and it includes other connectors to integrate with more tools.

Mylyn subprojects include the following:

- Tasks for integrating task and change management
- SCM for integrating source code management
- Build for integrating build management and continuous integration
- Review for collaborative code review

Figure 4.6 Committing changes to VCS in Eclipse. In the commit dialog box, developers add a reference to the tickets they've worked on. In this case, the ticket AGILEALM-10 motivated the code changes that are committed now.

Mylyn has evolved into a unified platform for ALM and ALM vendors. Mylyn embraces the Open Services for Lifecycle Collaboration (OSLC) standards for ALM.

AGILE PLANNER LEVERAGES MYLYN CONNECTORS Tasktop provides a tool called Agile Planner. This tool can manage existing defect and project management systems directly from Eclipse, making it effortless to maintain project status awareness and keep plans up to date. Agile Planner supports planning across multiple vendors' solutions. For more details, see http://tasktop .com/connectors/agile.php.

The developer checks in the code changes to the Subversion repository. In the commit dialog box, the developer extends the commit message (which describes what he has done) with the ticket number. In our case, based on figure 4.6, adding AGILEALM-10 provides the information to JIRA and Bamboo to link this change to the ticket.

4.2.3 *Tracking source changes with FishEye*

Atlassian's FishEye is an advanced source code repository browser. You can view the content of the repository and any changes applied to it. FishEye's features are the following:

- FishEye lets you view user activity and track code changes.
- FishEye enables you to search and navigate through the repository.
- FishEye supports Subversion, CVS, Git, ClearCase, and others, with real-time notifications of changes plus web-based reporting.
- FishEye identifies diffs between versions.

Figure 4.7   The FishEye web application: browsing the repository. Changes (activities) are displayed in a timeline. Revisions with their changes (for instance, how many lines were added) are visualized and can be compared with each other. You can zoom in to see the respective versions of the sources.

- FishEye provides a web application for convenient browsing of the repository (see figure 4.7).
- FishEye enables you to view multiple communication channels, including JIRA issues, Bamboo builds, email alerts, and IDE. This means, you can gain Bamboo's build information from within a couple of tools in a highly integrated manner.

FishEye is a web application that continuously scans the repository. The browser acts in two different ways: It allows you to see which tasks are associated with specific changes, and it allows you to browse the VCS, with its content, and browse the changes of single files. Figure 4.8 shows the FishEye integration with JIRA, illustrating the history of VCS changes referencing this ticket. Important information is displayed: who made the change and what was changed.

After installing the FishEye plug-in in JIRA, a Source tab is added to every JIRA ticket. There, you can see changes associated with each ticket and diffs in a convenient way. The example in figure 4.8 illustrates that changeset 37 in Subversion was triggered by

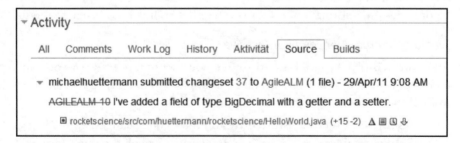

Figure 4.8   FishEye integrated into JIRA: A dedicated tab shows source changes associated with each ticket. One Subversion commit resulted in this entry: 1 file was changed, 15 lines were added in the file, and 2 were removed. Icons provide links to FishEye so you can zoom in if you're interested in more information.

me, and it contains changes in one file. You can browse the file, create version diffs, and so on. The main benefit is that people can trace changes and reference them to tickets, which allows impact analysis. This means you can monitor developers' changes and their consequences on tickets. Also tech leads or senior developers or the team can closely look at commits and what effect they have had on the codebase.

Further integrations are available, such as a plug-in that integrates FishEye functionality into Eclipse.

Creating and updating tasks in JIRA was the first step. Next, you'll view the tasks and work on them from within your IDE. Then you'll build the software and associate the builds with the tasks created.

4.2.4 *Build view with Bamboo*

Bamboo is a continuous integration server that automates your software builds. You can create your own build plans to create your software on a scheduled basis (with Ant or Maven, for example), or a developer's check-in can trigger it. Key features of Bamboo include monitoring build progress, deploying steps, and reviewing the results of static code analysis. Together with JIRA, development activity can be monitored. Bamboo helps to bridge the development phase with delivery and testing.

Continuous integration servers like Bamboo (or CruiseControl, Hudson/Jenkins, TeamCity) support continuous integration and facilitate rapid application development. When used together as a toolchain, Bamboo and JIRA help to do the following:

- Track builds to tasks
- Monitor progress and success on working on tasks
- Trace issues fixed to a specific build

BUILD COMPARISON AND CHANGE TRACKING One major feature Bamboo offers (as do other continuous integration servers) is verbose build comparison. Efficient comparison of different builds (of the same software) delivers answers to questions like "What changes went into the build that might have caused a previously working feature to fail (regression)?" or "What caused the latest build to fail?" Linking a build server to the ticketing system adds even more value. For example, it can answer questions like "What changes does the new release deliver?" or "What problems are fixed for a customer if they upgrade to a new build?"

Bamboo can be integrated with different tools. For JIRA, it can be implemented as a plug-in, or as a separate application that's accessible via a web interface. It can also be integrated into Eclipse by installing the Atlassian Connector for Eclipse. In a dedicated Eclipse view, you can trigger builds from your workspace, monitor builds, or comment on builds.

JIRA AND HUDSON/JENKINS If you're using Hudson or Jenkins as a continuous integration server (instead of Bamboo), you can use a plug-in to integrate either of them with JIRA. The plug-ins can be installed via the administration panel.

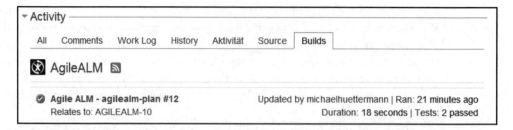

Figure 4.9   Bamboo integration in JIRA: builds associated with this ticket. If you're interested in more information, you can easily navigate to the Bamboo web application by clicking a link.

Connecting JIRA and Bamboo adds an additional Bamboo Builds tab to all of your tickets. In this tab, you'll see all builds referencing this ticket. Figure 4.9 shows that the Bamboo build number 12 provided changes that are responsible for fixing the task AGILEALM-10. You'll also see further information, such as who did the commit that references this ticket and triggered the build, how long the build ran, how many tests passed, and so on. Again, you can zoom in and navigate to Bamboo itself if you're interested in further information, such as by clicking the #12 link, which leads directly to the build detail page in Bamboo.

By using the Bamboo web application, you can gain a lot more information about your builds (see figure 4.10). You can enter the application by using links in Eclipse or JIRA or by entering the start URL and navigating from there.

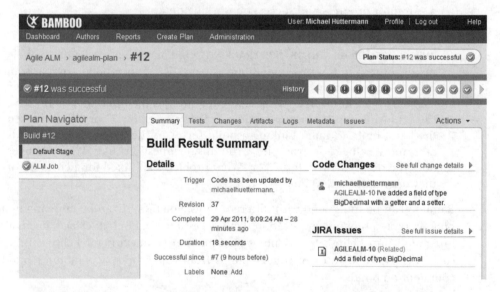

Figure 4.10   The build result summary of the Bamboo web application. The summary page shows details about the build, such as why the build was triggered and what changes were newly integrated with this build. A history feature and further tabs allow you to navigate through builds and to zoom in to respective test results, generated artifacts, logs, and so on. Besides its continuous integration and build server features, it links to issues in the ticketing system.

In the cloud: JIRA Studio with a commit-driven approach

Atlassian offers a full, commercial toolchain named JIRA Studio (www.atlassian.com/hosted/studio/). This hosted and integrated toolchain includes Subversion, JIRA, GreenHopper, Confluence, FishEye, and Bamboo. This toolchain eliminates the installation effort and reduces administration efforts. Integrating the tools yourself will cost you some time, but you would have the advantage of configuring the toolchain in a way that meets your specific requirements.

JIRA Studio also supports interacting with JIRA via commit messages. For example, to add something like "MYPROJ-4711 #time 4h #comment ALM #resolve" to your commit message to log four hours of work against issue MYPROJ-4711, add the comment "ALM" to trigger the state transition of the ticket in JIRA, from open to resolved, finally resolving the issue.

Other comparable tool suites are also available—for instance, ScrumWorks (www.danube.com/scrumworks) and codeBeamer (www.intland.com/products/cb/overview.html).

The official Bamboo documentation explains all the product features in detail, including how to configure and retrieve information about your tests and changes, how to add artifacts to your build plan, and so on. The documentation also explains all the result views provided by Bamboo. Of special interest here is the Issues tab on the Build Result Page. Once you have correctly integrated JIRA and Bamboo, you'll see the issues fixed or referenced in the build.

Another way to closely integrate Bamboo with JIRA is to use the Bamboo Release Management plug-in (https://plugins.atlassian.com/plugin/details/28559). This plug-in triggers different actions in one step, including running a release build, publishing artifacts, tagging a version in the VCS, releasing a version in JIRA, creating a branch for the next version in the VCS, and switching the build to use a new branch.

Bamboo supports even more features for task-based development, and for release management in general: It offers a pipeline feature—a pipeline is composed of stages that contain several subplans. Subplans are like Bamboo plans except they don't have dependencies and notifications, and they can't be run manually. In order for a pipeline to transition from one stage to another, all subplans in the current stage must pass successfully. For the pipeline to complete successfully, all subplans in all stages must pass successfully. The pipeline can pass artifacts between stages so that builds in later stages can consume previously built artifacts produced in the same pipeline. Additionally, there is functionality to promote artifacts.

4.3 *Trac bug tracking and project management*

Trac (http://trac.edgewall.org) is an open source tool developed and maintained by Edgewall Software. Trac is a mixture of a release management and bug-tracking tool as well as a wiki and version-control browser. Trac provides a comprehensive tool to help

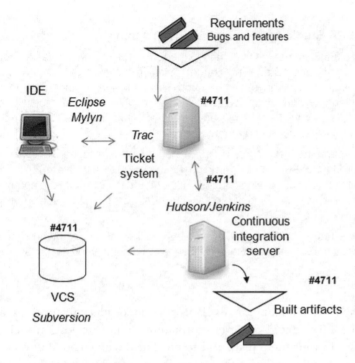

Figure 4.11   A system for task-based development, based on Trac. Trac is the ticket system that integrates with the VCS and CI. Eclipse and Mylyn are used on developers' desktops. This example shows Hudson/Jenkins being used as the CI server.

teams get started with software development. Although it doesn't dictate any special development process to your team, it can be configured to be used in an Agile context. A toolchain for task-based development based on Trac is illustrated in figure 4.11.

> **NOTE**   In the discussion of this Trac toolchain, I won't repeat previous discussions of aspects like build server integration or Eclipse with Mylyn. They are only suggested and mentioned as nodes in the overall toolchain here, because you already know about them from our first toolchain. In this section, we'll discuss new aspects that haven't been mentioned so far, such as the wiki. As a consequence, you can easily include the Atlassian Confluence wiki in the first toolchain to profit from a wiki there, or you can easily integrate a build server like Hudson/Jenkins into this second toolchain in order to link builds to tickets. Remember, driving lightweight toolchains is also about being flexible, adapting to changes, and being able to replace single tools in the overall toolchain without touching the remaining tools.

Trac is a lightweight system that allows Agile planning of projects. Developers use Mylyn to enrich their IDEs (figure 4.5 shows how this can look). Trac connects to a VCS (in our case, Subversion). It allows you to browse source changes and track other changes in the complete system (such as wiki changes). Trac contains its own wiki and can be integrated with a continuous integration server (such as Hudson/Jenkins; section 4.2 discusses what traceability on the build server can look like). Trac uses its wiki markup to semantically link the version-control repository, the wiki, and the issue tracker and to glue wiki pages, changesets, and tickets to each other. Trac's timeline view shows recent activities in all those areas.

Trac is written in Python, and it's available for different platforms such as Windows and Linux derivatives. It can be both extended and configured. Trac's main features include the following:

- Release management support (roadmaps, milestones)
- Ticket system
- Timeline of all recent activities
- Fine-grained permission system
- Wiki, with wiki markup
- Customized reporting
- Web interface for Subversion, including changeset support
- Multiproject support
- Minimalistic approach enabling Agile development
- Plug-ins like the Agile-Trac[6] plug-in to further support Agile development and to add further features to Trac, such as iterations
- Support for task-based development

4.3.1   Installing Trac

To install Trac, you must install a couple of required libraries. Using a prebuilt package provided by BitNami makes it easier (available at http://bitnami.org/stack/trac).

> **REDMINE** The Redmine tool is comparable to Trac. Redmine is based on Ruby on Rails. Its feature set is equal to Trac's, and it can be installed via BitNami as well.

BitNami makes it easy to use and deploy Trac by providing native installers for Windows, Linux, and Mac OS X. Each installer contains all the necessary components to run out of the box. The installed Trac configuration is self-contained and doesn't interfere with other software on your system. After downloading the installer and running it, a wizard guides you through the process. You can also let the wizard create a Trac project for you, which is a space inside your installation that you can use for your release work. The installation takes only a few minutes and installs the following components on your system:

- Apache 2
- Python
- Subversion
- SQLite
- Trac and its required dependencies

---

[6]   See the Agile-Trac plug-in page: http://trac-hacks.org/wiki/AgileTracPlugin.

Native installer, virtual images, and Amazon EC2

Besides the normal Trac stack (and other full-packaged open source tools), BitNami also provides two different distribution formats: virtual machine images and cloud.

The virtual machine image contains a Linux operating system and the fully configured Trac installation. Running the image requires a virtualization host such as VMWare or VirtualBox.

The cloud approach is an image that can be run in the cloud, namely Amazon EC2. You can run BitNami applications on EC2 on a pay-as-you-go basis, programmatically starting and stopping them.

After your package is installed, you may want to configure it for your specific needs. The central point for that is the trac.ini executable installed in the same place as Trac. Here you can configure the Subversion repository you want to use, the layout, and the behavior of the Trac components, such as the wiki, the ticketing system, and the timeline.

Let's look a bit deeper into some of these features. Assuming Trac is running on port 8010 on your central server, you'll see a screen like the one shown in figure 4.12.

Let's go through the main points of interest, including the wiki functionality entry page and the timeline, roadmap, source browser, and ticket manager.

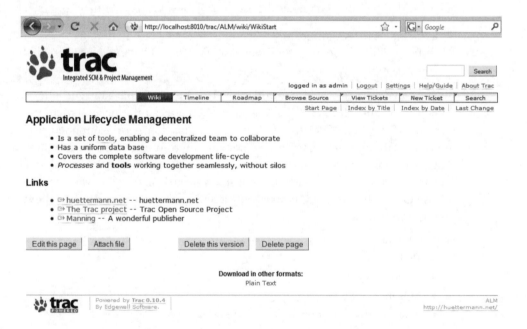

Figure 4.12   The start page of Trac: the edited wiki entry page, including access to the timeline, roadmap, source browser, and ticket viewer

4.3.2   *The wiki*

The Trac entry page shows the wiki, which is one of the major features of Trac. A *wiki* is a system of linked HTML pages that can be edited on an ongoing basis. The wiki is a collaboration platform extended and maintained by users. For example, if you click the "Edit This Page" button for the Trac entry page, you'll get its content. The following listing shows the content in plain text format with the Trac markup notation.

Listing 4.1   The content of the start page (excerpt)

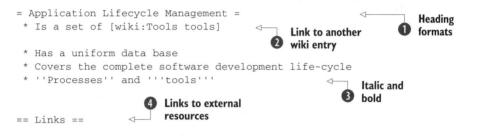

```
= Application Lifecycle Management =
 * Is a set of [wiki:Tools tools]

 * Has a uniform data base
 * Covers the complete software development life-cycle
 * ''Processes'' and '''tools'''

== Links ==

 * [http://www.huettermann.net/ huettermann.net] -- huettermann.net
 * [http://trac.edgewall.org/ The Trac project] -- Trac Open Source Project
 * [http://www.manning.com/ Manning] -- A wonderful publisher
```

You can arrange text and create new pages as needed. The comprehensive formatting support allows you to enter different header styles ❶, link to other pages inside the wiki ❷ or outside the wiki ❹, and emphasize text, such as displaying it in italic or bold ❸.

An interesting feature of Trac's wiki is that you can monitor the changes (including the change history) to the page, line by line. A bit later we'll see a similar display for exploring the source code.

Agilo for Scrum

Agilo for Scrum is an application developed on top of Trac (see www.agile42.com/cms/pages/agilo/). Agilo is an open source tool available through an installer or hosted service. It contains many features that support the daily work of Scrum teams, including a configurable product and sprint backlog, the creation of requirements or user stories, multiteam and distributed team support, a wiki, a roadmap, a dashboard, and real-time burn-down charts. Agilo can be integrated with Subversion, and a ticketing system is also available.

The default Trac installation is more open than Aglio with respect to the development process you choose. With the default Trac installation, you can support Agile projects.

Agilo also ships in a commercial pro version that includes more features, such as an integrated whiteboard.

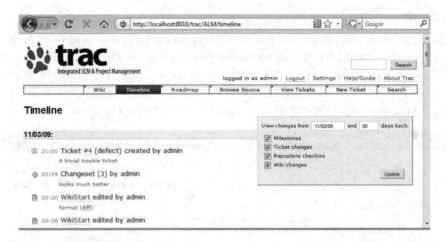

Figure 4.13   The timeline view showing who changed what in the system, including changes on tickets, the subversion repository, wiki pages, and milestone planning

4.3.3   *Timeline and sources*

You can display the timeline by clicking on the Timeline tab. Doing so will display the recent changes made on the system. The attractive feature here is that the changes are displayed across all possible change types including changes to milestone planning, tickets, the repository, and the wiki. This functionality fits well into the ALM environment.

Figure 4.13 shows the changes and who did what at what time. The admin user edited the wiki start page, created a new ticket with the unique number 4, and submitted something into the Subversion repository. Because Trac is monitoring the underly-

Figure 4.14   A changeset, including changes on the code base done in this atomic commit

ing source repository, it detects the change and displays the groups of commits as changesets.

You can configure the view via the options in the box at the right of figure 4.13. You can customize the timeline and the information that should be collected and summarized on this page. If you want more detail, click on the link to go to the next page and view the additional details. For example, if you're interested in the changeset, you can click on the changeset number (3) and view the page shown in figure 4.14.

Continuous integration with Hudson and Bitten

The Hudson Trac Plugin (http://trac-hacks.org/wiki/HudsonTracPlugin) integrates build results delivered by Hudson into the Trac timeline and provides a menu link to jump to the Hudson application.

Bitten (http://bitten.edgewall.org) is a Trac extension for continuous integration, and it joins the Trac ecosystem seamlessly. It uses a distributed build model, where one or more slaves run the tests and a master gathers the results and displays them on a web page.

The touched file is displayed with its differences compared to the older version. Inside the file, lines are colored to express the type of change, such as red for removed and green for added. You also have access to the revision numbers that Subversion increases continuously. In figure 4.14, Trac detects that with Subversion revision 1, the file was initially imported, and this file was changed with Subversion revision 3. You could now also extract the status of the file at those two moments in time (the revisions) by clicking the links provided—r1 and r3, respectively. In addition, you can generate a diff between two revision numbers of a file, and you can enter the two revision numbers freely.

> **PROVIDING OUTLOOK TASKS** Another interesting extension in context task-based development is the bridge to Outlook (http://sites.google.com/site/outlooktrac/). Many teams use Outlook for time management, and this plug-in provides Trac tickets as personal Outlook tasks.

When viewing changesets, Trac's Browse Source tab is opened. If you click on that tab when you're not viewing a changeset, you'll see the complete Subversion repository with its contents, including its individual state (its revision numbers), its age, and the last change. This way, you can browse the complete repository.

4.3.4 *Roadmap and tickets*

By clicking on the Roadmap tab, you see Trac's release management facility, which allows you to create milestones for your development.

Ticket updates are based on Trac's configurable status transition and workflow facility (for example, assigning tickets to other people). Tickets can be assigned to milestones. Milestones also display the ticket status; for instance, which tickets are open and which ones are closed. Besides seeing the ratio of closed to active tickets, you can see the milestone due date and can enter the milestone detail page.

The Trac *roadmap* is a list of future milestones. You can customize ticket grouping and adjust the view by filtering the roadmap to show or hide specific milestones.

> **ECLIPSE AND TRAC** Similar to the first toolchain we discussed in section 4.2, you can integrate Eclipse with your ticketing system. Again, the Eclipse plugin Mylyn is used to integrate Eclipse and Trac. In our first toolchain, we configured Mylyn to use the available JIRA connector; here you have to use the Trac connector that glues Trac to Eclipse.

This concludes our tour of Trac. We saw Trac's main features that support task-based management. The integrated approach lets you link and navigate through different aspects of your daily work across different media and development phases:

- The smart repository browser gives you access to the Subversion repository.
- The roadmap can aggregate tickets to releases.
- The timeline feature aggregates all different change types on one view.
- The wiki function lets you use Trac as a central knowledge base.

All this is linked through wiki markup. Trac is based on plug-ins, and you can extend and configure it according to your requirements.

4.4   *Summary*

In this chapter, we discussed lightweight tools for setting up and driving an Agile ALM process: JIRA, FishEye, and Bamboo are lightweight, commercial tools for planning and tracking tasks. Adding Mylyn to this chain makes it possible for developers to manage a task from their workspaces. GreenHopper is a JIRA extension that adds more visualization features, such as cards.

Trac also offers features for planning and tracking tasks. It's an open source tool that provides a central view on your development activities across development phases. Besides the wiki, it contains release management functionality, including timeline and roadmap features, a ticketing system, and a Subversion repository browser. Trac can be integrated with Mylyn and Hudson/Jenkins. Both Trac and JIRA are highly configurable, feature-rich tools. They can be integrated with other tools, they can aggregate information, and they can serve as one-stop shops for managing your activities by managing tasks. In both toolchains, task-based development is based on the convention of using the ticket number in the check-in comment.

Handling toolchains can be complex. The detailed examples we looked at in this chapter should give you a good idea of how to implement lightweight toolchains to support task-based development.

In the next chapter, we'll discuss integration management and the technical releasing of software, based on Maven.

Part 3

Integration and release management

With part 3 of this book, we leave the functional aspects of Agile ALM and dive into the more technical aspects. This part is about integration management and (technical) releasing. It details strategies and introduces tools to integrate software artifacts and create releases. Additionally, this part covers productive development environments and advanced continuous integration.

In chapter 5, we'll discuss Maven's core features, particularly its dependency management concepts. You'll learn how to orchestrate tools to run component repositories in different flavors. We'll also explore a real-world use case for (technical) releasing of software.

Chapter 6 examines strategies to create productive development environments. Major aspects include strategies and tools for working with artifacts in isolated environments—for example, on developers' desktops. This workspace management involves using congruent build systems in order to provide fast feedback.

Chapter 7 delivers recipes and tools for advanced continuous integration. This chapter reviews the basics and presents scenarios that show how you can integrate different languages and platforms and how to unify toolchains. We'll also look at staging releases without rebuilding, performing continuous inspections, and integrating different version-control systems to enable feature branching.

At the end of this part of the book, we'll have completed our discussion of functional and technical release management, and we can start discovering outside-in development.

Integration and release management

This chapter covers

- Integration and release management basics
- Maven as a comprehensive integration and release management tool
- Different ways to store artifacts and dependencies in a repository
- A real-world use case of releasing with Maven

Integration and release management allow you to produce software artifacts and release those configuration items that perform a function for end users. I refer to the process of building the software and providing a final product to the end user as *technical releasing*.

The first chapters of this book discussed the strategy of using a component repository and the value that a VCS like Subversion adds to the software development process. We've discussed the general requirements for ALM as well as the functional and technical aspects of releasing. Now we'll go one step further: We'll use Maven to release the complete software—to build and store it in a component repository. We'll discuss the relevant basics of Maven, how Maven implements component repositories, and how you can host these component repositories. Finally, we'll work through a real-world use case to illustrate how a complex project can be released with Maven.

In chapter 3, we talked about releasing software and bridging the functional releasing to the technical releasing. Applying a task-based development approach, we've improved the development process to focus on work items and make the development progress visible and traceable. That's what we did in chapter 4. In this chapter, we'll look at more details of technical releasing. We'll now talk about integrating and releasing the software technically.

In this chapter, you'll learn how Maven supports the common tasks of release management in an out-of-the-box way. Aside from building, packaging, and deploying, you'll also want to support automated unit and integration testing with Maven, which we'll discuss later in this chapter. We'll discuss some accompanying tools such as Artifactory which helps to host component repositories and can help streamline your integration and release management tool infrastructure. We'll also review lightweight alternatives to a full-fledged component repository by discussing hosting binaries in Subversion. I refer to the latter approach to be the "poor man's solution" because although using Subversion as a component repository has advantages, using a dedicated product for hosting a component repository is often preferred.

The rest of the book will further detail the release and test management functions. We'll use Maven where appropriate and show other detailed use cases and views on integration and release management. Chapter 6 also contains best practices for using Maven and discusses concepts for setting up productive environments. We'll review how developers can consume, integrate, and test artifacts efficiently. Chapter 7 contains recipes and tools for continuous integration. We'll discuss tools such as Maven, Jenkins, and Artifactory, and talk about staging and audits. Chapter 8 will cover test management in more detail and how it can be bridged to the development of software, also partly based on Maven. Chapter 8 will focus on the QA/tester view of Agile ALM and integrate testing activities with the creation of software.

Now let's start our discussion on the integration and release management function.

5.1   *The integration and release management function*

The integration and release management function is the backbone of your Agile ALM. How your integration and release ecosystem will look depends a lot on your development process and your individual requirements, but in this chapter, I'll explain commonly used practices and implement them with tools.

Developers write the software, checking their sources and build scripts into a VCS (such as Subversion). Developers implement requirements in their workspaces. They check in and update sources to the VCS, as shown in figure 5.1.

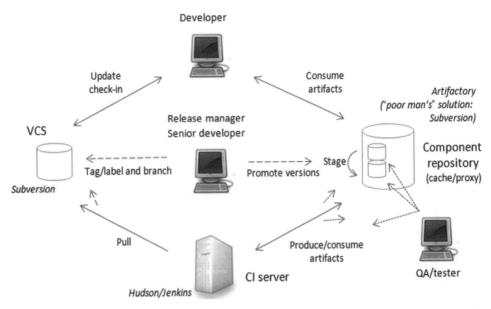

Figure 5.1   Integration and release management system: Sources and build scripts are shared in a VCS; a CI server builds, tests, and deploys versions; and a component repository stores ongoing versions as well as releases of the software (as binaries). Several roles and responsibilities exist; a release manager takes care of creating and staging releases.

Produced and consumed artifacts are stored in the component repository for further usage. You can configure the component repository to act as a cache or proxy for third-party products and as a shared pool where developers continuously deploy versions of their built code.

A *component repository* stores binaries and acts as a cache for artifacts.[1] Binaries can be separated into snapshot versions and released versions. Snapshots express artifacts that are currently under development. Released binaries are final, baselined versions of artifacts that fulfill defined quality requirements. A *release* is a special type of version—either the version after reaching a deadline (in a timeboxed environment, for example) or the version that implements all requirements (tasks) and fulfills the requirements of test management. The release might represent a minor milestone (for instance, the completion of a sprint) or a deployable release candidate that includes all of the requirements expected for delivery to an end user. Typically, the sources that correspond to released binaries and that were produced by the team are labeled in the VCS.

The continuous integration (CI) server (such as Hudson/Jenkins) is set up to automatically trigger a build when the code is committed, using Maven to do the build, packaging, unit tests, and deployment. Ideally, the developers should use the same

---

[1]   In this context, a *component* is a concise collection of software units that has a specific meaning for the team.

Maven build scripts for their private builds as are used for the official builds on the central CI server. Build scripts manage build dependencies and change as the project grows or when sources use other or new parts of the software. These build scripts (such as the Maven POM; more on that a bit later) should be version controlled like any other artifact essential for the release. Once this is set up, the CI server builds, packages, unit tests, and integrates components, and it may deploy the release to an integration test machine. This approach and these tools provide a streamlined approach to continuously building, releasing, and integrating the code.

The CI server pulls sources and build scripts from the VCS and builds the software on a dedicated build machine, continuously. The main task of the CI server is to produce artifacts. The generated artifacts, as well as the build process itself are both often called *build*. Often the CI server integrates and deploys the software on the integration test machine (the developers don't do that themselves!). For producing artifacts, the CI server has to consume artifacts such as artifacts that the produced artifacts depend on to fulfill build-time dependencies. Those consumed artifacts are artifacts that were produced previously, such as artifacts created by a feature team during a release or components developed by a component team. Most of the consumed artifacts are third-party libraries, though, such as testing frameworks or other Java libraries. All these consumed artifacts are fetched from the component repository, which acts as a pool of shared assets.

As we discussed in chapter 3, developers and their workspaces are the first rung on the staging ladder. Developers consume artifacts in well-defined versions, which means that developers integrate necessary binaries into their workspaces to develop the software that was specified and prioritized by the customer.

For testing and releasing software, the built software is staged. This means different logical repositories can be used inside a physical component repository. Typically, for each test environment, a dedicated logical component repository is in place. In many projects, the CI server continuously deploys snapshot versions to an integration test environment. The software is then deployed to other environments, such as the system test environment, without rebuilding the software, but rather by staging and reconfiguring the baselined software.

By using a tag or label in a VCS, the person responsible for the release management function creates releases that are baselined and may create branches. This job may be performed by an independent release management function (for example, a release manager or a developer, depending on how you slice your roles) or a developer tasked with creating the official release. With the help of branches, fixes can be applied on the release (a branch) without affecting the ongoing development (on the head and trunk).

The software is promoted to higher testing environments by a release manager. The release management function is also performed by the expert who deploys the release artifacts to the component repository or promotes existing artifacts. Depending on the process, that person may stage the artifacts (all artifacts belonging to one release) to another (logical) repository inside the component repository. The overall system should be based on clear responsibilities that are implemented by access and authentication security systems and tools; not all developers should be able to deploy (or remove) artifacts to a release component repository or to stage software.

Often, tagging and branching, as well as automatic testing and parts of the staging process, are triggered by the CI server. If the CI server stages software automatically or supports the staging in parts, this is often called *staged builds* or *build pipelines*. The development process and its roles, as well as their activities, are highly integrated. Additionally, the produced artifacts are integrated continuously.

Integration on different levels, meaning integration of software and integration of people and status, directly leads to having synchronization points. The development process consists of implicit synchronization points. This means that aspects like a staged build, automatic testing, or the use of component repositories synchronize people with each other and with the status of the project. By using inherent synchronization points, defects in the process and in the software are discovered early and often and are made visible to the team.

QA (testers or the whole team) are supported by scripts. Many tests can be automated, so test results can be made visible to the team continuously, in an objective and efficient way.[2] QA audits and static analyses are done by scripts. Developers should run those scripts in the developers' workspaces, and they should also be run on the CI server, depending on your personalized staging strategy and your defined quality gates.

Many teams find it difficult to reach consensus when trying to choose a build management tool. Teams that choose Maven usually do so because of Maven's focus on convention over configuration, allowing Maven to do the heavy lifting. What this means is that Maven allows you to assume reasonable defaults and reasonable default behavior. Maven also provides a fully featured project description incorporating automatic binding for project dependencies. Many developers also like Maven's seamless integration with IDEs and the ease of learning another team's build process (which is based upon Maven's standardized build convention). Some developers find Maven to be complex, which isn't surprising because it's both a lifecycle management and an integration tool.

In the next section, we'll first discuss some of Maven's core features, particularly in the context of testing. This basic information will prepare you for the following sections, but it isn't a full Maven guide. Please refer to Maven's online documentation (http://maven.apache.org) or to dedicated books for more information about Maven in general.[3]

---

[2] Tests that can't be automated are exploratory tests, for instance. More on tests in chapter 8.

[3] See the free Maven books by Sonatype (www.sonatype.com) or Brett Porter and Maria Odea Ching, *Apache Maven 2 Effective Implementation* (Packt Publishing, 2009).

5.2   *Maven feature set*

Maven is free and extensible and it's distributed as a small core module. All features are implemented as plug-ins and are loaded on demand. These plug-ins are also stored in repositories. You (or other developers) can easily write plug-ins in Java or other scripting languages. Maven scripts can run Ant scripts and vice versa.

To get Maven running with its default settings (including its default repositories), you must start the standard Maven distribution. I'll show you several examples of running Maven from the command line.

> **TIP** It can be helpful to transition to Maven in steps. You don't need to immediately use m2eclipse to use Maven from within Eclipse. As a first step, you may use only the console interface (although the IDE integration is much more convenient) because IDE integration adds complexity, and command-line commands can help you understand initially what is happening.

Maven provides a simple way to set up projects that follow common best practices, including a default directory structure that makes it easier to understand how a project is structured. A consistent and unified directory structure simplifies software development and provides a standard based on industry best practices. This focus on convention over configuration increases cross-project knowledge and makes it easier to get up to speed on another team's project. Many Maven features, configurations, and settings are provided implicitly. You can change Maven's default behavior at many points and can configure almost everything, but generally it's better to stay with the commonly accepted conventions.

When it runs the first time, Maven creates a local repository for your artifacts and updates it during subsequent runs continuously. Maven requires a settings.xml file that's shipped with default values as part of Maven's standard distribution; for the moment, suppose the location of settings.xml is $M2_REPO. All developers have a settings.xml in their local filesystem. Its location is either "~/.m2/settings.xml" or "$M2_HOME/conf/settings.xml." It contains personal data, such as user credentials, that allows you to access repositories or to route to a private SSH key. This personal data shouldn't be bundled with a specific project in the project object models (POMs).

You can run Maven from the command line or in your favorite IDE. Or you can have the CI server trigger it automatically. Manually configuring classpaths and dependencies in the IDE can be a difficult and error-prone task. With Maven IDE integration in place, the classpath is resolved automatically, so you don't need to manually configure project settings in your IDE. We'll discuss that more in the next chapter.

On centralized build and integration servers, you'll want to run build scripts (such as Ant or Maven scripts) to build your software. Whether you're building from within the IDE or on a centralized server, you should use the same build scripts. Eclipse or other IDEs aren't build tools, and normally you won't run Eclipse on your integration server to build your software. Maven supports this approach of context-free builds, which is what I call *congruent build management* (chapter 6 explains this in more detail).

Now let's take a close look at the Maven project object model (POM).

5.2.1 POMs and dependencies

Each project (in the sense of a module or component) needs one Maven model to be described. This Maven model is called the POM (project object model) and it's written in XML (you can write the meta information that's expressed in the POM with Groovy as well).

A POM is defined by its GAV coordinates: `groupId`, `artifactId`, and `version`, as shown in the following listing. Besides its coordinates, the POM includes sections for defining dependencies (also referenced by its coordinates) and for configuring its complete build processing (including testing). More on this later.

Listing 5.1 Basic POM

```
<project
    xmlns=http://maven.apache.org/POM/4.0.0
    xmlns:xsi=http://www.w3.org/2001/XMLSchema-instance
    xsi:schemaLocation="http://maven.apache.org/POM/4.0.0
          http://maven.apache.org/maven-v4_0_0.xsd">
  <modelVersion>4.0.0</modelVersion>
  <groupId>com.huettermann</groupId>
  <artifactId>myartifact</artifactId>                   GAV coordinates
  <packaging>war</packaging>
  <version>1.0</version>
  <dependencies>                                         Dependencies of
    <dependency>                                    ❶    this module
      <groupId>junit</groupId>
      <artifactId>junit</artifactId>
      <version>3.8.1</version>
      <scope>test</scope>                               Scope restricted
    </dependency>                                   ❷    to "test"
  </dependencies>
  <build>                                      Build
    ...                                   ❸    section
  </build>
  <reporting>                                   Reporting
    ...                                    ❹    section
  </reporting>
  <repositories>                              Repositories for incoming
    <repository>                         ❺    dependencies
     <id>snapshots</id>
     <url>...</url>
    </repository>
  </repositories>
  <distributionManagement>                    Repositories for
    <repository>                         ❻    generated artifacts
     <id>huettermann</id>
     <url>...</url>
    </repository>
  </distributionManagement>
</project>
```

Normally, the `groupId` is unique to a company or a project and classifies the origins of its artifacts. Dots are often used in the `groupId` to form hierarchies, but that's not required (for example, JUnit uses its name as the `groupId`). It's also not mandatory to map the groupId to your package structure, although this is a common best practice. When stored in a directory (or in the repository), the groups act as a separator so that you can distinguish them from the Java packaging structures.

The artifactId is the unique name of the module or project. Consider a project that produces a lot of artifacts. They all share the same groupId and differ in their artifactId. The combination of groupId and artifactId creates a unique key for identifying the artifact. This is also a valid way to address the module in a repository. In our case, the project is located in $M2_REPO/com/huettermann/myartifact.

The combination of groupId and artifactId defines the module, but it doesn't contain information about its versions. The version element defines that. As soon as you update your own sources to work against a new target version of your software or you use a dependency in another version, your POM should reflect these changes. By adding the version information to the groupId and artifactId, you get the full path to your artifact (for a specific version) in your repository. In our case, the full path would be $M2_REPO/com/huettermann/myartifact/1.0.

The packaging adds the artifact type (the architect would say, deployment unit) to the address structure of groupId:artifactId:version. The model-based approach supports standard output types like JAR, WAR, EAR, or OSGi artifacts. One Maven model produces exactly one deployment unit by default; you can add additional ones. Maven knows how to build these types. Unlike Ant, you don't have to write the logic for each step of the build again; instead, you declaratively describe what your project is about.

The dependencies section specifies the modules our module is dependent upon ❶. Maven provides dependency management for all dependencies including transitive dependencies (dependencies of your dependencies). You can also use scopes ❷ to specify resulting classpaths (during compiling or testing) and limit the transitivity of dependencies. Maven looks for these dependencies in the repositories defined in your POM. Dependency management is a core feature of Maven. For further information about dependency management, see the relevant part of the official Maven documentation.[4]

The build section ❸ configures the build (via Maven's build lifecycle) and the reporting section ❹ configures the reporting (via Maven's site lifecycle). The POM also contains information about the repositories to which you need to connect ❺ (to resolve your dependencies) and to which you want to deploy your own artifacts ❻. Dependencies can also be managed in Ant with Ivy.

Dependency management with Ant and Ivy

Another popular build tool is Ant, which has many features. With Ant, you must code your build scripts imperatively, which means that you have to specify each step and assume nothing. This also means you need to write new scripts for each new build project. You must tell Ant how you want to achieve something.

---

[4] http://maven.apache.org/guides/introduction/introduction-to-dependency-mechanism.html

> *(continued)*
>
> In contrast to Ant, Maven runs a declarative approach, based on conventions and best practices. You tell Maven what you want to achieve, and Maven knows how to achieve it.
>
> If you have based your projects on Ant and are interested in advanced dependency management, you can use the Maven–Ant bridge, working with dependencies from inside Ant scripts or Ivy. Ivy is a dependency manager that took many concepts from Maven. Using Ivy, you don't have to leave the Ant ecosystem to gain advanced dependency management (see http://ant.apache.org/ivy/).
>
> You may be driven by requirements or as part of a migration path to use Ant, Ivy, and Maven in parallel or in conjunction.

5.2.2 Inheritance and aggregation

You can use Maven inheritance and aggregation to organize your projects.

Inheritance means your project can define a parent project from which it derives settings. An example of inheritance is that the project POM derives from Maven's Super POM implicitly. The Super POM ships with Maven, and it consists of basic settings that dictate, for example, which artifact repositories to use. If you don't define optional settings in your POM, the default values are taken from the Super POM.

Aggregation is used when you join different projects into a container POM. This is often used in complex multimodule settings where an application consists of, for example, a Java web archive (WAR), a Java enterprise archive (EAR), or Eclipse OSGi bundles aggregated to a feature or a target platform. Another example is where you want to build and test a project with the parent module referencing and managing all of the other modules specified in the POMs.

The following listing shows a POM that specifies an Eclipse bundle.

Listing 5.2   POM referencing a parent POM

```xml
<?xml version="1.0" encoding="UTF-8"?>
<project
  xsi:schemaLocation="http://maven.apache.org/POM/4.0.0
     http://maven.apache.org/xsd/maven-4.0.0.xsd"
  xmlns="http://maven.apache.org/POM/4.0.0"
  xmlns:xsi="http://www.w3.org/2001/XMLSchema-instance">
  <modelVersion>4.0.0</modelVersion>                        ❶ Define module
  <artifactId>com.huettermann.plugin</artifactId>
  <packaging>eclipse-plugin</packaging>                     ❷ Use Eclipse plug-in
  <version>1.0.0</version>                                     packaging
  <parent>                                                  ❸ Reference
   <artifactId>parent</artifactId>                            parent
   <groupId>com.huettermann.parent</groupId>
   <version>1.0.0</version>
   <relativePath>../com.huettermann.parent/pom.xml
   </relativePath>                                         ❹ Specify relative
  </parent>                                                    path to parent
</project>
```

The POM is pretty lean. Besides its coordinates, it only defines itself ❶ as an Eclipse plug-in ❷ and references its parent POM ❸, inheriting the parent's configurations (note that for managing OSGi bundles, you need Maven 3). The scripts are referenced using a relative path addressing the parent ❹. The POM inherits the configurations of its parent. The parent is shown in the following listing.

Listing 5.3   Parent POM with central settings and multiple modules

```xml
<?xml version="1.0" encoding="UTF-8"?>
<project
  xsi:schemaLocation="http://maven.apache.org/POM/4.0.0
     http://maven.apache.org/xsd/maven-4.0.0.xsd"
  xmlns="http://maven.apache.org/POM/4.0.0"
  xmlns:xsi="http://www.w3.org/2001/XMLSchema-instance">
  <modelVersion>4.0.0</modelVersion>
  <groupId>com.huettermann.parent</groupId>
  <artifactId>parent</artifactId>
  <version>1.0.0</version>
  <packaging>pom</packaging>                      ❶ Specify
                                                    packaging

  <modules>
    <module>../com.huettermann.plugin</module>     Include modules in
    <module>../com.huettermann.test</module>    ❷ this container project
  </modules>

  <build> ... </build>
  <distributionManagement>                        Specify distributionManagement
    <repository>                                ❸ configuration
     <id>huettermann</id>
     <url>http://... /libs-releases-local</url>
   </repository>
  </distributionManagement>
</project>
```

The parent POM defines the packaging type pom ❶, and it has two tasks. The first is the parent POM acts as a container by referencing a couple of modules ❷. The second task is to configure the central settings used by the child POMs, for example, to configure the distributionManagement section describing the target to which the artifacts are deployed ❸. In this example, the parent POM includes the OSGi bundle discussed earlier and adds a test bundle to the aggregation. Therefore, if you run the parent POM, all its child POMs will be built successfully.

5.2.3   *Lifecycles, phases, and goals*

Maven requires that you describe what your project is doing. To this end, Maven offers lifecycles and individual phases that you can configure to tell Maven what to do in these phases.

Maven has three lifecycles: *clean* (removing previously built artifacts, like a "tidy up" lifecycle), *build* (which contains the main logic), and *site* (for reporting). The build lifecycle contains the following main phases:

- *Validate*—Validate that the project is correct and all necessary information is available

- *Compile*—Compile the source code of the project
- *Test*—Test the compiled source code using a unit testing framework
- *Package*—Take the compiled code and package it in its distributable format, such as a JAR
- *Integration test*—Do integration tests or process and deploy the package into an environment where integration tests can be run
- *Verify*—Run any checks to verify that the package is valid and that it meets quality criteria
- *Install*—Install the package into the local repository, for use as a dependency in other projects locally
- *Deploy*—Copy the final package to the remote repository for sharing with other developers and projects (done in an integration or release environment)

Based on these standard phases, Maven would perform the following tasks in a real-world use case:

- Download dependencies
- Compile the code
- Run the unit tests
- Package the source code into a WAR archive
- Download the Java container for the integration tests
- Deploy the artifacts in the installed Java container
- Start the Selenium server to run user interface tests
- Start a browser
- Run the integration tests
- Clean up the integration test environment
- Install the artifact in the local repository

Some parts of this process are already covered by entries in the POM (for example, defining WAR as the packaging type). Others are available out of the box (such as testing), and some can be described declaratively with dedicated plug-ins that you can attach to run in Maven's phases.

> **NOTE** Calling one phase (such as running mvn install on the console) does execute the phase, as well as all phases in the Maven lifecycle placed before the called phase.

Plug-ins allow you to configure their behavior. The Surefire plug-in (responsible for testing) provides the property maven.test.skip, which you can use to configure the plug-in to do nothing. You do this by passing the Java parameter to your Maven call:

```
mvn install -Dmaven.test.skip
```

All phases consist of *goals*. Goals offer a more technical view, whereas phases provide a high-level functional entry point. Internally, Maven organizes entry points as *packages*.

Each package maps one or more goals to one or more phases by default—some have more than one, and some have none. Phases often have default goals that are executed automatically based on the project's packaging type. You can also directly trigger a goal by adding it to its phase, separated by a colon. For the install goal, it would be `mvn install:install`.

5.2.4   *Maven and testing*

Maven is ideally suited for running all your tests as part of your normal build setup. You don't need a customized environment for different types of tests. Unit tests run by default, and integration tests are specified as a phase in the Maven build (between the packaging and the install phases). In this way, you can rely upon the previously built package, which can output a WAR file. To run your integration tests, you need to add and configure the dedicated plug-ins.

The Surefire plug-in is responsible for tests. It can be configured inside the POM's `build` element. By default, the plug-in looks for test cases in the src/test/java folder. It runs in the Maven test phase and by default looks for classes with the patterns `**/Test*.java`, `**/*Test.java`, and `**/*TestCase.java`. It's possible to run both unit tests and integration tests with the Surefire plug-in. In most cases, this will meet your requirements right out of the box.

For more complex integration tests, consider using Maven's Failsafe plug-in. It's a fork of the Surefire plug-in and ensures that the post-integration phase runs even if there's an error in the integration tests. In addition to not breaking the build on test failure, the Failsafe plug-in also enables more convenient configuration. For example, it allows you to skip the integration tests but run the unit tests. To create integration tests (instead of unit tests), you can save the tests with names following any of these patterns, which include the letters "IT": `**/IT*.java`, `**/*IT.java`, and `**/*ITCase.java`.

Both plug-ins can run JUnit and TestNG tests. All you need to do is include the dependency of the framework in your project POM.

Maven's plug-ins block further execution until they've completed their tasks. This can be helpful if you start a server for integration tests and want to wait until everything is started, deployed, and ready for testing.

The following listing shows an extract of a typical POM.

Listing 5.4   Maven POM

```
<project
    xmlns="http://maven.apache.org/POM/4.0.0"
    xmlns:xsi="http://www.w3.org/2001/XMLSchema-instance"
    xsi:schemaLocation="http://maven.apache.org/POM/4.0.0
            http://maven.apache.org/maven-v4_0_0.xsd">
  <modelVersion>4.0.0</modelVersion>
```

```
<groupId>group</groupId>                        ◁        Model's project
<artifactId>artifact</artifactId>                ❶       coordinates
<packaging>war</packaging>              ◁        Project built
<version>1.0</version>                   ❷       as WAR
<name>name</name>
<dependencies>                    ◁       Model describing
  <dependency>                    ❸       project dependencies
   <groupId>junit</groupId>                    ◁        JUnit
   <artifactId>junit</artifactId>               ❹       dependency
   <version>3.8.1</version>
  </dependency>
  <dependency>                  ◁        TestNG
   <groupId>org.testng</groupId>          ❺       dependency
   <artifactId>testng</artifactId>
   <version>5.10</version>
   <scope>test</scope>
   <classifier>jdk15</classifier>
  </dependency>
</dependencies>
<build>                        ◁       Build lifecycle
  <plugins>                     ❻       configuration
    <plugin>
      <groupId>org.codehaus.cargo</groupId>
      <artifactId>cargo-maven2-plugin</artifactId>
      <configuration>
        ...
      </configuration>
      <executions>
        ...
      </executions>
    </plugin>
  </plugins>
</build>
...
</project>
```

There are a number of things to note in this POM file. First, each model is described through project coordinates containing groupId, artifactId, and version ❶. The project is built in a WAR file ❷. The model also describes the project dependencies by referencing their project coordinates ❸. JUnit version 3.8.1 is a dependency in this case ❹. Another dependency is TestNG 5.10 ❺. You can define the scope of the dependencies and further parameters. Finally, you can configure Maven's build lifecycle ❻, which also includes testing, compiling, and packaging, by adding and configuring plug-ins.

5.2.5 *Maven ecosystem*

Tycho (http://tycho.sonatype.org/) extends Maven by providing a toolchain and embedded runtime (Equinox) for building OSGi bundles, Eclipse plug-ins, and rich client platform (RCP) apps. OSGi bundles have features similar to Maven, such as providing dependency management. Most OSGi apps were built with Eclipse's plug-in development environment (PDE), which is based on Ant scripts that often lead to complex build scripts. With Maven Tycho, OSGi is a first-class citizen in the Java enterprise build and release management ecosystem. Tycho makes it possible to transparently build OSGi apps with Maven—Maven takes care of the building behind the scenes. OSGi and POMs are synchronized and compatible.

Polyglot Maven (http://polyglot.sonatype.org/) adds yet more flexibility to the Maven core by allowing domain-specific languages (DSLs) access to the core functionality.

Maven Shell (http://shell.sonatype.org/) is a command-line interface for Maven enabling faster builds. With Maven Shell, project information and Maven plug-ins are loaded into a single, always-ready Java Virtual Machine (JVM) instance that can execute a Maven build.

Maven and its comprehensive lifecycle management facility aggregates project information as part of the build, and this data can be published on a Maven-generated website. Because of its first-class dependency management support and its integration with various VCSs, it's able to support automatic release management. All of these features make Maven a compelling choice for many technology professionals.

Another important feature is Maven component repositories.

5.3   *Maven component repositories*

Maven repositories are essential for organizing build artifacts of varying types and their dependencies on each other. Two types of repositories are *remote* and *local*.

A remote repository is any centralized repository that's accessed by a variety of protocols such as file://, scpexe://, and http://. These repositories might be truly remote, set up by a third party. They provide their artifacts for downloading. For example, the official Maven repository is available under http://repo1.maven.org. Artifacts are provided in Maven's central repository, and your Maven installation downloads them on an as-needed base. This type of repository is named a *public repository*, and it's illustrated in figure 5.2.

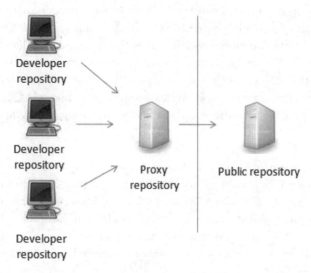

Figure 5.2   Maven repository topology: developer repositories, a central proxy repository, and a remote public repository. The public repository is an external system, normally on the internet. All other repositories are internal systems.

Other remote repositories may be internal repositories located inside your network, or what some IT professionals call a *DMZ* (demilitarized zone). They're set up on a file or HTTP server within your project or company, and they're used to share private artifacts between development teams and for releases. This sort of repository is often called a *proxy repository*. A proxy repository acts as an intermediary for requests from desktop machines seeking or providing binaries.

A key benefit of proxy repositories is that you don't need to download artifacts multiple times from remote sources; rather, you download quality-assured artifacts once and share them across projects and teams via the repository proxy. This way, the developer machines' access to the internet can be restricted, and developers can pull unified artifacts from the proxy repository.

Proxy repositories are essential for managing your dependencies. *Dependencies* are external libraries that are required to compile and run your code and related artifacts. They can be external libraries like Checkstyle and Log4J or internal dependencies like your shared libraries that are deployed to the proxy repository for further reuse.

Local repositories are placed on the developers' machines. They're individual caches of artifacts that have been downloaded from the proxy repository. In addition, they contain build artifacts that haven't yet been released from workspaces and that aren't yet visible to others.

An artifact is stored in a Java-like package structure derived from its `groupId` and `artifactId` data, which also provides version information, as shown in figure 5.3.

Under the repository's root folder, inside the folders named for the `groupId` and `artifactId`, you'll see different version folders containing several JAR files, a POM file, and additional meta information. In figure 5.3, the repository root is located under repository and the folder structure contains checkstyle as the `groupId` and the `artifactId`, followed by the individual folders for versions, in this case 4.1 and 4.4.

I've selected the folder named 4.4, so in the file explorer, the lower part of the window displays its

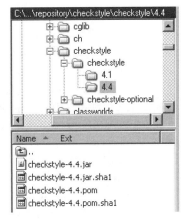

Figure 5.3   Extract of a local developer's repository

contents. JAR is the deployment unit created by this module (and its build), as described in the POM. You can add additional JARs to accomplish tasks such as distributing the sources. The files with the sha1 extensions are files generated with a cryptographic hash function in order to validate their integrity.

Remote and local repositories are structured equally so that scripts can be easily run on either side. They can also be synchronized for offline use, but the layout of the repositories is completely transparent to the Maven user.

An important lifecycle feature is the option to not only consume dependencies, but also to publish the project's artifacts. The published artifacts can then be consumed as dependencies by other developers or projects. Maven provides a standard lifecycle phase called *deploy,* which needs to be configured to specify a repository that publishes artifacts, making them available to the other developers. Once deployed, these artifacts can be added to a project's POM as dependencies.

There are various ways to set up a repository infrastructure:

- Use a shared filesystem and deploy artifacts to it via network mounts, FTP, or SSH-based secure copy. For serving the repository, a web server like Apache HTTP could run on the same machine, exposing the repository for dependency resolution. Alternatively, the web server, if equipped with WebDAV features, could be used to serve the publishing process as well.

- Use a repository manager product such as Apache Archiva, Sonatype Nexus, or JFrog Artifactory. These products must be run in a J2EE/JEE web application container (quick-start versions are also available where the distribution is already bundled with a container), accessible by artifact publishers and consumers. They offer many additional benefits such as security models, search features, permission models, workflows, and so on. Later in this chapter, we'll look at Artifactory to get a basic understanding of the features provided by a repository manager.

Open source projects have the option to deploy to the central Maven repository, and many do so. The central Maven repository is http://repo1.maven.org/maven2 (often mirrored). Therefore, this repository is the source where you can browse and include your dependencies. The process for deploying artifacts to the central repository is described in detail on the Maven website.[5]

Although the central repository is the preferred mechanism for publishing public artifacts, the process requires some administrative effort. Most notably, the recommended way of publishing requires a staging repository that's accessible by secure copy (scp), which means that the team will still have to establish a self-hosted proxy repository in your internal system.

To accelerate development flow and rapidly work on code in an Agile development effort, relying solely on repositories isn't enough. Imagine you have different development teams developing components for your overall application, and the components have interdependencies. In continuous release mode, where you're continuously providing the most recent development state, the output is unreliable. A lot of bugs and unstable developments are released too soon and are included in the development work your colleagues do. But what you want is a productive work environment, with private workspaces that consist of reliable, quality-assured versions of artifacts. You need a way to declare frozen versions of dependencies to other components, so

---

[5] See Maven's "Guide to uploading artifacts to the central repository," http://maven.apache.org/guides/mini/guide-central-repository-upload.html.

Maven enables you to specify dependencies between components. With Maven, one team can continue working on new features, and another can develop against a stable API and version. In your individual project model, you can decide to provide either a versioned artifact of your work or a snapshot.

> **SNAPSHOTS AND SITES** If you have a CI server, such as Hudson or Bamboo, you should configure a `snapshotRepository`, which the CI server uses to store the nightly build results. If you're also building and deploying the project's website with Maven, you need to define the `site` element as well.

A snapshot is a special version that indicates a current development state. Unlike regular versions, Maven will check for a new snapshot version in a remote repository for every build, once a day, or however often you choose to define as the frequency. For normal versions (releases), Maven downloads—once only—the artifacts from a remote repository to your local repository. This artifact bootstrapping (where you download the artifact only once to serve all further requests to it out of the local repository) applies to proxy repositories, too, in terms of their dependencies upon the artifacts in remote repositories. Versioned artifacts and snapshot artifacts are stored in both local and remote repositories. For that, different access paths or folder structures are used.

> **REPOSITORIES AND MIRRORS** Repositories can be defined in POMs. You can set up a parent POM that contains the enterprise settings on which all your individual projects will be based. Alternatively, or in combination, you can define repositories in your private Maven settings file. Using a mirror, you can replace a public repository (such as "central," where Maven connects to when it automatically tries to resolve missing dependencies) with your own proxy repository.

Developers can choose to use either snapshots or versioned artifacts for development, depending on whether they're actively developing or preparing a release of the code. Having a choice between versioned artifacts and snapshots dramatically improves the quality of the software process, purges the workspaces (and avoids workspace clutter), and keeps the component repository clear of duplicate libraries. Developers don't need to check out sources and their references in a manual, error-prone way, nor do they need to build third-party code again from scratch. They only need to include the binaries in their workspaces. This is what they should do to develop their own components. (Sources for debugging can be attached, though.)

5.3.1 *Managing sources and binaries in conjunction*

Source code management, including branching strategies, and management of binaries are used in conjunction with each other. For example, an application and its sources are developed on the VCS head or trunk (see figure 5.4). A continuous build consumes and produces binaries, and it deploys the current snapshots to the component repository. During the process of building a release (for instance, during a *code*

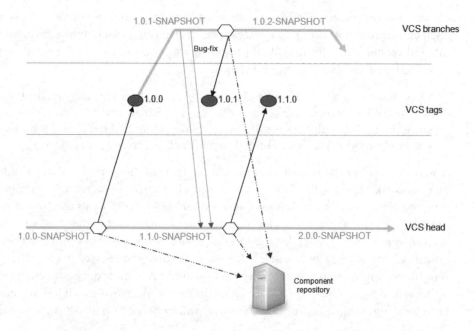

Figure 5.4   Branching strategies and the deployment of binaries (snapshot and release) are used in conjunction with each other. The frozen versions that were tagged from the head are 1.0.0 and 1.1.0. Version 1.0.0 had two bugs, so a branch was created, where the two bugs were fixed; the bug fixes were merged into the head as well. At specific moments (the diamonds in the figure), the versions are frozen. The head is frozen to version 1.1.0 and the branch is frozen to version 1.0.1. Both new versions contain the two new bug fixes.

freeze), a VCS tag is created (for instance, 1.0.0), and its corresponding release binaries are deployed to the component repository.

If you release software continuously, in a timeboxed way, you may not need any branches at all, because you can always work on the most recent head version of the software. But if you want to change a formerly released build without including further development that was already done on the head (such as new features), you'll need to branch.

A branch is an isolated code stream, parallel to the head stream and other branches that are in place already. Changes on the branch are backported to the head: they're committed to the head ideally directly after the commit on the branch. Many projects find it helpful to create branches as part of the releasing process in the *code freeze* interval, or even earlier in the *frozen zone* interval.

It is a good strategy to create VCS branches on demand only. This means that you don't branch prophylactically but only when needed, at the last possible moment—when a new version of the software is required.[6] A new version is then based

---

[6] Using Subversion, you can create branches at any time based on a given tag or a given Subversion revision number. Physically, branches and tags in Subversion are copies of the folder structures in the repository.

on a version that was previously frozen, tagged, and shipped. It's important that you focus only on changes on the branch that are critical and of high value for the customer. Don't fix bugs of lower priority and don't develop new features on a branch, because that counteracts the functional releasing process that was discussed in chapter 3.

The ranges of version numbers are different on branches and heads. Release binaries have unique identifiers and should be deployed to the component repository only once. You should set up the same CI process on the branch that you've already set up for the head. This is important in order to find defects there early and often and to start preparing and training the final release of the branched version early. Like the setup on the head, commits on the branch trigger new builds, trigger tests, and create new binaries that are deployed to the component repository. The CI process on the branch also includes the creation of snapshot versions as well as release binaries.

A branch should be closed. Closing a branch retires it: No further work is done on the branch (no new commits to the branch), and all necessary changes are merged to the head. Closing a branch may be implemented by convention (when the release is finished) and can be supported technically, such as by preventing developers from committing to the branch by using Subversion hooks.

You'll normally want to close a branch soon, because once a branch is created, it's another development line for the team. CI requires you to integrate software and synchronize the team, and having too many branches that must be merged back to the mainline is additional overhead and often slows down the workflow on the head, counteracting the basic idea of CI.

CI is also a communication vehicle that relies on the current, synchronized, most recent version of the software.[7] Although branches also act as communication points, the development flow and its pace is determined on the head, and branches fragment communication. For the same reason, mechanisms such as developer branches, where developers have their own isolated code lines in the repository, should be avoided.

5.3.2 *Artifactory's enterprise component repository*

Artifactory is a component repository manager. It allows you to have full control over your project's binary artifacts, acting as both a secure warehouse for locally hosted artifacts and a smart caching proxy for remotely hosted artifacts. Artifactory provides a few unique management features and some cross-technology integrations that make it compelling to use in environments ranging from a small startup project to large CI setups.

These are the core features of Artifactory:

- Stores artifacts (your own artifacts should be created by a CI server)
- Acts as a proxy for artifacts

---

[7] This is the main reason why people should commit early and often. Investing much time in developing software in the workspace without committing changes to the repository and having the changes integrated with the work of others is a lost opportunity.

- Avoids hitting public remote repositories
- Deploys, manages, and shares local artifacts
- Offers full control over artifacts' resolution and delivery
- Provides a fine-grained security system, including repository administration, and distinguishes between read, write, and delete permissions for working with artifacts

Artifactory's origins

In 2006, Yoav Landman started Artifactory's development with the purpose of providing a better alternative to the existing repository managers at that time (such as Maven-proxy and Proximity) that lacked basic features such as security, filtering, indexed searches, and a user-friendly UI. This was a time when large enterprises were using Maven and managed artifacts. They had no real solution to enterprise needs for artifact management.

The Artifactory project was hosted on SourceForge, where it's still hosted at the time of this writing. In 2008, JFrog (www.jfrog.org) was founded to support the product and its future development.

Artifactory provides support for managing remote repositories. By configuring a public repository (the major ones are already preconfigured), Artifactory creates its own cache out of the box; you don't need to add repositories and link them to public repositories. For example, using the Maven repo1 central public repository, Artifactory sets up a repo1-cache directly, as shown in figure 5.5.

Artifactory also supports *virtual repositories*. Virtual repositories wrap local and remote repositories under a single identifier, acting like a facade, so you can create combinations of repositories and expose them to clients as a single virtual repository. This way, you can decouple the logical repository view for developers from the technical implementation view that a repository admin must have.

Virtual repositories can also wrap around other virtual repositories. Whenever a repository (local, remote, or virtual) is added to, changed, or removed from such a virtual repository, the change is automatically propagated to all virtual repositories.

Artifactory ships with a conveniently embedded virtual repository called repo.

Figure 5.5   Artifacts in the Artifactory repository browser

This means that all you need to get your local workspace connected to Artifactory is a settings.xml file, such as the one shown in the following listing.

Listing 5.5   A settings.xml file with server credentials and repositories

```
<settings xmlns="http://maven.apache.org/settings/1.0.0"
    xmlns:xsi="http://www.w3.org/2001/XMLSchema-instance"
    xsi:schemaLocation="http://maven.apache.org/SETTINGS/1.0.0
          http://maven.apache.org/xsd/settings-1.0.0.xsd">
<servers>
  <server>
   <id>snap</id>                          ❶ Set server elements
   <username>michael</username>             with repository
   <password>secret</password>              credentials
  </server>
  <server>
   <id>rel</id>
   <username>michael</username>
   <password>secret</password>
  </server>
  <server>
   <id>central</id>
   <username>michael</username>
   <password>secret</password>
  </server>
  <server>
   <id>snapshots</id>
   <username>michael</username>
   <password>secret</password>
  </server>
  <server>
   <id>repo</id>
   <username>michael</username>
   <password>secret</password>
  </server>
 </servers>
 <mirrors>
  <mirror>                                  ❷ Mirror unresolved
   <mirrorOf>*</mirrorOf>                      repository requests
   <name>repo</name>
   <url>http://localhost:8081/artifactory/repo</url>
   <id>repo</id>                            ❸ Add ID to
  </mirror>                                    server section
 </mirrors>
 <profiles>
  <profile>                                 ❹ Use default
   <repositories>                             profile
    <repository>
     <snapshots>                            ❺ Specify shadow
      <enabled>false</enabled>                 maven2 repository
     </snapshots>                             central
     <id>central</id>
     <name>libs-releases</name>            ❻ Point to virtual
<url>http://localhost:8081/artifactory/repo</url>  repo repository
```

```
    </repository>
    <repository>
     <snapshots />
     <id>snapshots</id>
     <name>libs-snapshots</name>
     <url>http://localhost:8081/artifactory/repo</url>
    </repository>
   </repositories>
   <pluginRepositories>
...
   </pluginRepositories>
   <id>artifactory</id>
  </profile>
 </profiles>
 <activeProfiles>
  <activeProfile>artifactory</activeProfile>
 </activeProfiles>
</settings>
```

◄── ❼ **Specify plug-in repository, skipped here**

◄── ❽ **Specify ID for profile**

◄── ❾ **Set profile to active**

To enable non-anonymous access, we set up the server elements to contain repository credentials ❶. These include an ID mapping to the id element of a repository
fragment. Next, we mirror all unresolved repository requests ❷; it can also be useful
to hide maven2 central. The ID must be added to the server section with valid credentials ❸. We use a default profile ❹. Next, we shadow the maven2 central repository ❺, overwriting the same entry in the Super POM, and then point to the virtual
repo repository ❻, which automatically maps to repo1-cache. This listing skips over
the plug-in repository ❼, which contains similar entries for managing plug-ins. After
providing an ID for the profile ❽, we set the profile to active ❾. The profile will be
applied without any further preconditions.

You also need a distributionManagement section in your POM, as shown in the
following listing. This can be placed in a parent POM.

Listing 5.6   POM distribution management

```
<distributionManagement>
  <snapshotRepository>
    <id>snap</id>
    <url>http://localhost:8081/artifactory/libs-snapshots-local</url>
  </snapshotRepository>
  <repository>
    <id>rel</id>
    <url>http://localhost:8081/artifactory/libs-releases-local</url>
  </repository>
</distributionManagement>
```

◄── **Specify snapshot artifacts deployed to this repository**

──┘ **Repository ID must match settings.xml**

◄── **Define deployment target**

This example shows the advanced features for mirroring repositories. Here we use
mirroring with a wildcard, a star (*) in the mirrorOf element of the XML file, so all
unresolved repositories will access Artifactory's virtual repository, named repo). The
example also shows advanced permission settings. In the previous listing, Artifactory is
configured to prevent anonymous access, so we have to use valid usernames, as you

can see in the different username elements of the XML file. The default is to allow anonymous access, so you have to disable that via Artifactory's web interface.

On top of Artifactory's open source version, there's a Power Pack set of commercial add-ons targeted at enterprise users. With a little more effort, many of the commercial enterprise features can be utilized in the open source version by using Artifactory's REST API. JFrog also offers a fully hosted Artifactory service—Artifactory Online (www.artifactoryonline.com)—targeted at small to medium-sized organizations. This cloud-based repository manager provides its subscribers with the latest version of Artifactory and the Power Pack.

Artifactory is a generic binaries repository. Although it initially started as a Maven repository manager, Artifactory isn't intended only for Maven users; Grails or Ivy users can use it as well. Artifacts that are deployed to Artifactory with Ivy can be retrieved with Maven, and vice versa. Therefore, the tool offers features that are targeted at other build tools:

- Generic uploading from the UI to any path
- Indexing of any artifact type
- Searching inside the content of Ivy modules (parallel to searching inside Maven POMs)
- Integration with the Gradle (www.gradle.org) and Ivy (http://ant.apache.org/ivy/) build tools
- Encrypted password support

For Maven, Artifactory offers many features:

- Uploading of artifacts with optional POM editing and auto-guess properties
- Special searches
- Auto-generated settings.xml files (derived from repositories configured in Artifactory)
- Centrally controlled snapshot policy and convenient POM views
- Cleanup of POMs from troublesome remote repository references
- Finding and deleting of selected artifact versions under a folder
- Copying and moving of artifacts (single and bulk)

All artifacts in Artifactory are merely pointers to binaries, and binaries can be stored either on the filesystem or in a configurable relational database. Artifactory comes with a built-in Derby database that can be used to store data for production-level repositories (up to hundreds of gigabytes). Artifactory's storage layer supports pluggable storage implementations; this is made possible by the underlying Jackrabbit Java Content Repository (JCR), so you can configure Artifactory to run with almost any JDBC database or even store data completely on the filesystem. The storage used by Artifactory is checksum-based, which means it doesn't matter how many times a file exists in Artifactory; it will still be stored only once. This makes operations such as moving or copying cheap in terms of speed and space. Copying artifacts is unavoidable if, for example, the same binary needs to be exposed to different groups of people who are allowed access to different repositories, and you can't (or it's way too complicated to) do this by sharing one repository and applying fine-grained security rules.

Artifact management and metadata is atomic in Artifactory—moving multiple artifacts, deploying artifacts with their metadata, deleting groups of artifacts, and so on, can all be done in an all-or-nothing fashion.

In Artifactory, all files and folders are candidates for receiving an unlimited amount of metadata that can contain any appropriate information that further describes the artifact. Any XML metadata can be attached using the UI or the REST API and can be managed, created, or deleted. This metadata is also indexed, so it's fully searchable from the UI or REST. The commercial version of Artifactory takes this one step further by offering user-defined, strongly typed custom properties on top of XML metadata that provide a specialized UI according to the property type. For example, if the user has defined a single-value, closed list property for the performance level of an artifact, they will get a single-select dropdown when annotating an artifact with this property.

The user interface is intuitive and easy to understand. Items are displayed clearly on the screen, and all items are either self-descriptive or have decent online help. The UI is mostly Ajax-based and is implemented using Apache Wicket with many custom components and the Dojo JavaScript library. The UI can be branded (from the UI) with a custom logo and footer.

Artifactory puts searches in the center of the user activity and offers the following types:

- Quick search
- Class or archive content (for example, properties file in a JAR) search, with the ability to see the class that was found
- XPath search inside Maven POMs, Ivy modules, or any deployed XML content
- `groupId`, `artifactId`, `version`, and `classifier` search (for Maven artifacts)
- Properties search (in the commercial version; more about properties later in this section)

All searches are exposed through Artifactory's REST API.

Artifactory takes searches one step further by making them the prime vehicle for artifact management. All search results are navigable to the repository tree, where you can annotate, move, remove, view, or download the artifact. Figure 5.6 shows Artifactory's search facility.

The commercial version of Artifactory is even more powerful, offering smart searches. You can save your search results, search again, and add or subtract the results from the saved ones (as many times as you wish), tweak the saved results manually, and operate with them as one unit of work. For example, you can search for all artifacts of a certain group and version in a dev repository, save the results, search again for all the sources with the same group and version, subtract the sources from

Figure 5.6   **Artifactory's search facility: POM/XML search**

the original result, and finally promote (move) the results to another repository accessible to the QA team.

Artifactory provides a simple, yet powerful, security model that allows the assignment of the following four permissions:

- Read
- Write
- Delete (also implies redeploy or overwrite)
- Annotate (with metadata)

Permissions are applied to a target consisting of a group of selected repositories and a set of include or exclude path patterns on these repositories. Permissions are then assigned to either individual users or user groups. This simple model works well in practice and is easy to understand and to control, incurring minimal security management overhead. Permissions of artifacts are viewable by an in-place effective permission page. Artifactory also offers out-of-the-box support for LDAP and Active Directory authentication. Support for highly optimized LDAP groups authorization is part of the commercial add-ons. (Standard LDAP support is freely available.)

Have you experienced situations where colleagues accidentally override artifacts and POMs with older versions or outdated sources by locally running only an `mvn deploy`? Artifactory's Watches notifies you by mail whenever a create or delete operation is run on a certain Artifactory repository, folder, or artifact.

Maven manages a certain amount of metadata by adding it to artifacts. The coordinates (`groupId`, `artifactId`, `version`) provide important value, but Maven has no feature to add more context metadata to artifacts that would be helpful right when they're deployed. Properties, or artifact tagging, is a neat feature that can enrich your build infrastructure. Generally, properties are arbitrary meta-information. For example, a property is a Maven or POM property that will become an Artifactory property—a

Maven build property exposed to Artifactory. You can use these properties to locate and identify the deployed artifacts that originated from the same build so you can promote them later on.

Properties can be attached to artifacts in many ways: via the UI or REST API using PUT requests, or piggybacked on artifacts that are PUT to Artifactory using matrix parameters. To add parameters, you need to configure your POM's distributionMan-agement section; using a good design approach, this configuration should be in one location—in one parent POM. It could look like this:

```
<distributionManagement>
  <repository>
    <id>qa-releases</id>
    <url>http://srv/artifactory/repo;build=${number}</url>
  </repository>
</distributionManagement>
```

This pair of arguments is added to the deployment repo definition. The values are usually taken from regular Maven properties and can be updated by any POM. Technically, they're a set of key-value pairs separated by a semicolon—a standard HTTP communication protocol. Using Maven's native properties approach, this matrix property can be configured and set in a top-level POM or injected by a command-line interface.

Artifactory allows you to search for properties and copy or move the result set to allow sophisticated staging and promoting. Figure 5.7 shows an example of how you

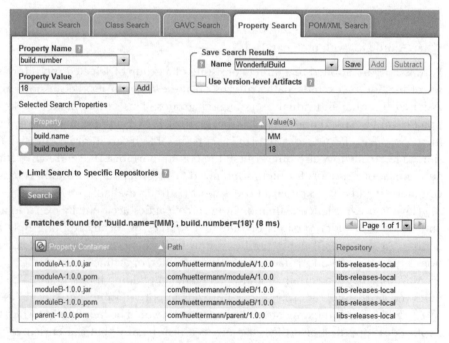

Figure 5.7   Property search: searching repositories for properties. Examples of properties are build.name and build.number.

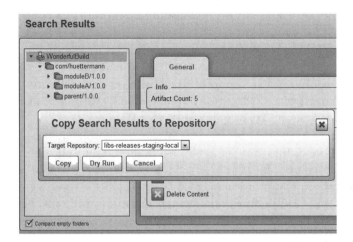

Figure 5.8 Working on search results, and copying an artifact set to a different repository. This allows smart artifact staging and promoting.

can search for artifacts tagged with the properties `build.name` and `build.number` and their values `MM` and `18`. As we'll discuss in chapter 7, the Jenkins/Artifactory integration automatically injects these properties with every build. This way you gain from traceable builds.

Once you've tagged artifacts in your repositories with any set of properties, setting them manually or automatically, you can search for these annotated artifacts. Once they're found, you can save and refine the search results (add or subtract results from the former result) for later reuse. Artifactory acts as a shopping cart of artifacts, making bulk artifact management a lot easier. Once you're done, you can move or copy the results.

One use case for searching and performing bulk operations is to navigate to all saved searches, mark the search results you want to work with, and then copy or move all artifacts belonging to the search result to another repository. Figure 5.8 shows the artifacts found by a save search being copied.

5.3.3 Using Subversion to serve a simple Maven repository

> —*This section contributed by René Gielen*

When you're starting without Maven, additional infrastructure and software is needed to set up a Maven topology, such as a proxy repository on a dedicated machine. This might not be possible in the organization's environment for either technical or political reasons. Open source project teams, on the other hand, might fear some of the administrative overhead involved in publishing to the central repository, and resources such as self-hosted repository managers might be beyond the budget. But any such project team should feel highly encouraged to consider central repository publishing, at least for the early stages of a project.

Often, project teams don't regard central repository publishing as a suitable option, and they lack the ability to establish or access additional infrastructure. The question is, could there be a solution for establishing a repository without the need for extra resources?

Any method of publishing is workable as long as it results in a normalized repository structure tree accessible by the HTTP or HTTPS protocol. Maven's deploy phase publishing mechanism utilizes a transport abstraction layer called Wagon that provides a service provider interface (SPI) to be implemented by various transport plugins, such as Wagon File, Wagon FTP, Wagon WebDAV, or Wagon SSH.

One of the (possibly) less known providers is Wagon SVN, which makes it possible to publish artifacts to the Subversion VCS. Subversion allows you to browse the latest revision of the repository tree via its web server integration using simple HTTP GET requests. Project teams using Subversion over HTTP or HTTPS for version control can utilize Subversion to gain a fully functional Maven repository without needing any additional resources other than those they're already using.

The first step is to choose and create a suitable folder structure in the Subversion repository. My recommendation is to create a Maven folder along with the usual trunk, branches, and tag folders. Another common practice is to differentiate between release and snapshot artifacts, where you create two additional subfolders, one named *snapshots* and the other one *releases* or *staging*. The latter name implies that this folder might later serve as a staging

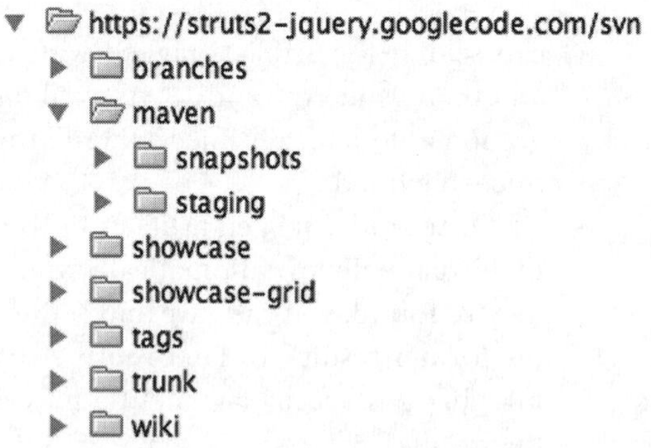

Figure 5.9 Sample Subversion folder layout

repository for publishing to a more general repository, maybe even central. The repository contents will be published in these two folders, depending on whether the artifact you're deploying is a release or a snapshot version, as shown in figure 5.9.

Next, the project's pom.xml has to be extended to configure the target repository locations to which you're going to deploy and that the Wagon provider will use. This is shown in the following listing.

Listing 5.7 POM configuring Wagon

```
<project ... />
  <groupId>com.myorg</groupId>
  <artifactId>myproject</artifactId>
  <version>1.0.0-SNAPSHOT</version>
  ...
  <distributionManagement>
    <repository>
      <id>myproject.staging</id>
      <name>MyProject Staging Repository</name>          ❶ Configure Subversion in
      <url>                                                 distributionManagement
```

```
      svn:https://myorg.com/svn/myproject/maven/staging
    </url>
  </repository>
  <snapshotRepository>
    <id>myproject.snapshots</id>
    <name>MyProject Snapshots Repository</name>
    <url>
     svn:https://myorg.com/svn/myproject/maven/snapshots
    </url>
    <uniqueVersion>false</uniqueVersion>
  </snapshotRepository>
</distributionManagement>
...
<build>
  <extensions>
    <extension>
      <groupId>org.jvnet.wagon-svn</groupId>
      <artifactId>wagon-svn</artifactId>
      <version>1.9</version>
    </extension>
  </extensions>
  ...
</build>
...
</project>
```

2 Add Subversion as snapshot repository

3 Configure wagon-svn extension

In the distributionManagement section, we configure the release repository location within the repository element **1** and the snapshot repository location within the snapshotRepository element **2**. Both elements require a unique ID, which we'll use later to configure the matching private credentials. The name element should contain a handy, human-readable description of the location. The url element defines the transport endpoint for the Wagon mechanism. The configured values for both endpoints **3**, representing the HTTP address of the repository folders created earlier, are prefixed by the svn: pseudo protocol scheme. The standard Wagon mechanism won't know how to deal with that, so we add the wagon-svn plug-in as a build extension dependency, which, after being resolved, will register itself for the handling of the svn: prefix. By setting the uniqueVersion configuration option to false, we ensure that snapshot version numbers for the artifact won't be extended by a timestamp on each deployment.

The next step is to configure the credentials needed to authenticate against Subversion for publishing. These credentials are subject to nondisclosure and should reflect the authorization of the person issuing the Maven deployment, so they won't be configured in the project-wide pom.xml file, but rather in the individual team member's local Maven configuration file, usually found at $HOME/.m2/settings.xml. An example is shown in the following listing.

Listing 5.8 Configuring credentials in settings.xml

```
<settings>
  ...
  <servers>
    <server>
```

```
    <id>myproject.staging</id>
    <username>dave_deployer</username>
    <password>secret</username>
  </server>
  <server>
    <id>myproject.snapshots</id>
    <username>dave_deployer</username>
    <password>secret</username>
  </server>
  ...
 </servers>
 ...
</settings>
```

> **Credentials for staging repo**

> **Credentials for snapshot repo**

Please note that the server ID values have to match those configured in the `distributionManagement` section of the project's pom.xml file. From now on, each authorized team member can publish artifacts to the Subversion-based Maven repository as with any other repository management solution:

```
> mvn deploy
```

Whether the artifact will be published to the snapshot or the staging repository depends on whether the project version found in the pom.xml file at the time of deployment is a snapshot or a release version. An example folder structure also containing snapshot versions is shown in figure 5.10.

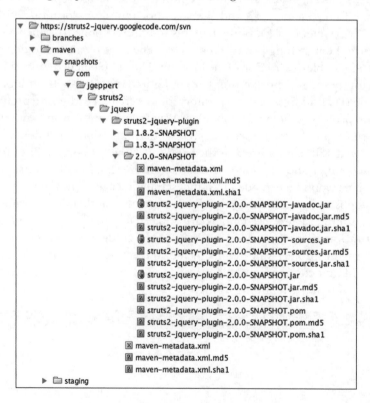

Figure 5.10 This expanded repository tree contains various deployed artifacts.

To consume the deployed artifacts as dependencies in another project, this project's pom.xml file must be modified to recognize the additional custom Maven repository to be used for dependency resolution (see the following listing).

Listing 5.9 Dependency resolution pointing to the repository

```
<project ...>
  ...
  <repositories>
    ...
    <repository>                                          Configuration
      <id>myproject.repository</id>            ◁──────┘  of repository
      <name>Repository for the MyProject artifacts</name>
      <url>http://myorg.com/svn/myproject/maven/staging</url>
    </repository>
    ...
  </repositories>
  ...
  <dependencies>
    ...
    <dependency>
      <groupId>com.myorg</groupId>                 Example dependencies
      <artifactId>myproject</artifactId>    ◁────┘ for project
      <version>1.0.0</version>
    </dependency>
    ...
  </dependencies>
  ...
</project>
```

How you set up the project repository to resolve both the snapshot and the release artifact versions is shown in the following listing.

Listing 5.10 Repository settings with both staging and snapshot

```
<project ...>
...
  <repositories>
    ...
    <repository>                                   Configuration of
      <id>myproject.staging.repository</id>  ◁───┘ release repository
      <name>Staging Repository for MyProject</name>
      <url>http://myorg.com/svn/myproject/maven/staging</url>
      <releases>true</releases>
      <snapshots>false</snapshots>
    </repository>
    <repository>                                   Configuration of
      <id>myproject.snapshot.repository</id> ◁───┘ snapshot repository
      <name>Snapshot Repository for MyProject</name>
      <url>http://myorg.com/svn/myproject/maven/snapshots</url>
      <releases>false</releases>
      <snapshots>true</snapshots>
    </repository>
    ...
```

```
    </repositories>
    ...
    </project>
```

This section described using Subversion as a Maven repository. The next section shows how to create releases with Maven.

5.4   *Releasing with Maven*

—This section contributed by Matthias Weßendorf

The release of software packages is an important phase of the Agile ALM. You should put the source code into a VCS (for example, Subversion) and extract it to be compiled and packaged. In most cases, your customer will require a complete release package (also referred to as a *distribution*) that also contains additional information. In this section, you'll learn how to create a software release and distribute it using Subversion, Maven, and some useful Maven plug-ins. You'll also learn how to leverage additional tools, such as Python scripts, to automate almost all steps of the release process.

Before you start creating your release, you must be clear about what is expected to ship with the software. Typically a release needs a lot more than some compiled Java classes. Common artifacts in a distribution include the following:

- *Executables*—The software itself, such as binaries, property files, database scripts, installers, and so on.
- *Documentation*—Practical user guides, such as installation guides or how-to documents, and API descriptions, created with tools like Javadoc or TagDocs, need to be made available as part of a release.
- *Examples*—Showcase applications, a reference implementation, API usage examples should be included. Most open source releases contain examples, which may be simple or rather complex, showing many features.
- *Distribution of the source code*—This may not only be important for open source projects. Releases for in-house projects or business partners may also distribute the source code, which makes debugging easier.
- *Anything else of value in your individual situation*—For project-specific requirements, you may need to ship additional artifacts.

The location of the release deliverables is also important. For instance, with Maven, JAR files (including sources and JUnit tests) can be deployed to an in-house repository, which is an HTTP or file server (for example, Artifactory or SVN) that follows a defined directory layout. The complete release package is often placed somewhere else. It's common to place these files on your company website or an open source project website. Another option is to deliver the distribution on a network filesystem (such as NFS), which you use to exchange files with your business partners or other in-house teams.

Once it's clear where the distribution will be placed and what it contains, you're faced with what is probably the most important question: How do you deploy the release? Several tools and options are available to get a release out the door. These can be historic make files or Bash or Perl scripts that run the software build and assemble the final release package. On older Java projects, you may still see the use of home-grown Ant tasks to generate the release and its distribution package. Today, the de facto standard for Java-based projects is Maven. This not only manages the build system of a software project, but also helps to manage the project through its entire lifespan. Maven support includes aspects such as the following:

- Creating documentation (like the product website or Javadoc documents)
- Managing source code (the location of the SVN repository)
- Branching and tagging in SVN
- Creating the distribution of the release

BEST PRACTICES IN MAVEN PLUG-INS Commonly established best practices are coded into many of the available plug-ins. This means the Agile development process starts with the choice of a powerful tool belt.

Maven is a framework that executes plug-ins that accomplish a variety of important tasks. The plug-ins can help you perform tasks that are essential for building, packaging, and deploying your software. An example would be to use Maven to post the results of your nightly builds to Twitter (see http://code.google.com/p/maven-twitter -plugin/). Normally, you won't want to publish results to the public via Twitter, but Maven supports you in making the status visible and ensuring the build gets fixed back to green as soon as possible. In this section, we'll look at several major plug-ins (and their required configurations) that are ideal for producing a software release.

Before you start to generate a release, you need to understand that there are several ways to do it. You could start in the SVN trunk folder, which is probably not a good idea, because the main codeline is usually developed on the trunk. It's a common practice to create a separate release branch using a standard naming convention such as "release-version-x.y.z."

In this example, we use a common SVN layout:

```
-myProject/
 -branches/
  -branchA
  -branchB
 -tags/
 -trunk/
  -src
  -pom.xml
...
```

The first task is to include the Maven Release plug-in in your POM as part of the project's Maven build lifecycle:

```
<groupId>org.apache.maven.plugins</groupId>
<artifactId>maven-release-plugin</artifactId>
<version>2.0</version>
```

5.4.1   *Creating the branch and preparing the release*

Creating the entire release from a release branch is a good pattern. Doing so ensures that the main development can continue on the trunk without having any undesired side effects on your release. Imagine if some of the changes weren't ready in time for a scheduled release. In this case, you'd want to revert the changes that aren't complete, and this is much easier if you're using a release branch that contains only the tested and completed features approved for the release.

You can create a branch with the tools provided by SVN, like `svn copy`. Windows has convenient graphical tools (such as TortoiseSVN, see chapter 2) that support creating branches and tags. Even with Maven there are several ways to create a branch, such as with the Maven SCM plug-in or the Maven Release plug-in. You can use the Maven Release plug-in to help automate the release process, including creating a release branch automatically.

Before you can use the Release plug-in for branch creation, you must configure your source control management (which is named SCM in Maven) settings inside the project's pom.xml file. See the following listing.

Listing 5.11   Configuring SCM in project's model (POM)

```
<scm>                                                    ❶ URL to
 <connection>                                               check code
  scm:svn:http://server/svn/path/to/project/trunk/
 </connection>                                           ❷ URL to work
 <developerConnection>                                      on code
  scm:svn:https://server/svn/path/to/project/trunk/
 </developerConnection>                                  ❸ URL for web
 <url>http://www.anexample.com</url>                        interface
</scm>
```

> **MAVEN SITE GENERATION**   The SCM configuration in the preceding listing is used when the Maven Site plug-in creates the project's website. The information about the used source code repository is made available on the generated source-repository.html webpage (see MyFaces, at http://myfaces .apache.org/source-repository.html, or CXF, at http://cxf.apache.org/ source-repository.html).

The `connection` element represents the URL that's used by everybody to check the source code ❶. Usually, the anonymous checkout is done through an unsecured HTTP connection. The `developerConnection` section contains the URL that's used by the project's developers to commit their changes back to the source repository ❷. In almost all cases, this is done through a secured HTTP (HTTPS) connection. The only exception would be when the repository is already hidden by a corporate firewall. The last parameter (`url`) is a "nice to have" setting. Usually, it contains a web interface to the source code stored in the repository ❸. Most Subversion servers have something like ViewVC (www.viewvc.org/) or WebSVN (http://websvn.tigris.org/) installed.

Using GIT as your repository

If you plan to use GIT as your repository, you can use Gitweb (http://git.wiki.kernel.org/index.php/Gitweb) or even host your entire project directly on GitHub (http://github.com/). The benefit of a web interface installation is that you can easily view the annotated source code with additional information: You get a colored overview of the difference between two revisions and some more advanced information about who added or changed the file in which revision.

To get similar information from your source code system, you would need to use the command-line tool, like `git blame`. In SVN you would use the command `svn blame`. You could use TortoiseSVN, or you could benefit from a toolchain that integrates a VCS browser, such as FishEye with SVN.

Once you configure the required settings, it's time to create the first branch:

```
mvn release:branch -DbranchName=myFirstRelease
```

Shortly after executing the plug-in, it asks for the next version number (which is then recorded in the POM) on your trunk. For instance, if your project has the version number 1.0.0-SNAPSHOT (check your pom.xml for its `<version/>` XML element), you'd see the following prompt:

```
What is the new working copy version for "my-tool"? (com.book:my-tool)
    1.0.1-SNAPSHOT:
```

> **MAVEN VERSION SCHEMA**　The Maven Release plug-in requires the version scheme to end with -SNAPSHOT, such as 1.2.4-alpha-4-SNAPSHOT.

Hitting the Enter key accepts the suggested value, or you can specify a different version number. After that, the plug-in updates the version number in pom.xml and commits the change to the SVN trunk. The plug-in also creates the new branching folder in the source repository. The pattern for the myFirstRelease branch would be something like this: https://server/svn/path/to/project/branches/myFirstRelease.

Maven Release plug-in: tools and processes

Tools follow the development process, which means that the process decides about tools; we discussed this in chapter 2. But some people state that the Maven Release plug-in doesn't support the individual release process that exists in their project.

You shouldn't customize your process to map to what Maven suggests with the Release plug-in. If the plug-in works for you and your process, that's fine. If you have the option to personalize your process and align it with commonly accepted best practices, you can also use the Maven Release plug-in. But you can also implement either part or all of the releasing process yourself with other tools than Maven. For instance, it's easy to write a small Ant script that uses a replace function and that scans your POM files and increments version numbers (see http://ant.apache.org/manual/Tasks/replace.html).

The Release plug-in checks whether you have modified files on your project. If this is the case, you'll get a build failure:

```
[ERROR] BUILD FAILURE
[INFO] --------------------------------------------------------------------
[INFO] can't prepare the release because you have local modifications :
[pom.xml:modified]
```

To continue, you need to evaluate the change and commit it to the SVN trunk or revert it if it wasn't intended. Then you need to check the newly created branch:

```
svn checkout
  https://server/svn/path/to/project/branches/myFirstRelease/
  directoryToContainTheBranch
```

If you look at the scm section of the pom.xml file in the version of the code you just checked, you'll notice that the previous branch goal also updated this section. It contains the right URLs to point to the new SVN branch.

Before you can continue with the release preparation, your project's pom.xml file needs some extra configuration (see the following listing).

Listing 5.12   Maven Release plug-in in the project's POM

```
<build>
 <plugins>
  <plugin>
     <groupId>org.apache.maven.plugins</groupId>        ❶ Include
     <artifactId>maven-release-plugin</artifactId>   ◁─┘   Release plug-in
     <version>2.0</version>
     <configuration>                                      Configure
<preparationGoals>clean verify install</preparationGoals> ◁─┘ preparation goals
<tagBase>https://server/svn/path/to/project/tags</tagBase> ◁─
     </configuration>                                     Specify base
    </plugin>                                             location
 </plugins>                                             ❷ of tags
 ...
</build>
```

Inside the build section of your pom.xml file, you must configure the Maven Release plug-in ❶. The important part here is the tagBase element, which tells the plug-in the base location for all of your Subversion tags ❷. By default, the plug-in assumes that you created the release out of the trunk folder. Therefore, it can automatically follow the common pattern to create all tags as subdirectories of the default SVN tag location (the tags/ folder). Because we want to run the release preparation from a branch, we specify that configuration in the pom.xml file.

> **GENERATING OUT OF THE TRUNK**   Generating releases out of the trunk folder is common, but this approach has some risks, because you're modifying the trunk. You should take this approach only if you have some experience with the tools. It's safer to have a separate release branch folder for this step. The good news is that the extra setup isn't too difficult.

Now you can finally start the preparation of your release:

```
mvn release:prepare
```

What does preparation mean? If your branch has some Maven snapshot dependencies, the plug-in asks if you want to continue with the release procedure. Generally it's a bad idea to branch and release a software package that has a dependency on a snapshot, because snapshots are unreleased software or software under development, and they're usually generated every day with a nightly build. If you depend on snapshots, your released project can become unstable. In the worst case, it can mean that some depreciated APIs will be removed from your dependency overnight, making your released software no longer usable. You want to avoid this scenario and should never release software that has a snapshot dependency; instead you want to reference stable versions.

Once the Release plug-in identifies a snapshot dependency in your project, it gives you the following prompt:

```
There are still some remaining snapshot dependencies.: Do you want to _
    resolve them now? (yes/no) no:
```

The default value for the prompt is no, as you should avoid snapshot dependencies. If you continue with the release by entering yes even if there's one or more snapshot dependencies in your project, the plug-in will force you to upgrade to the released version of the dependency.

> **TIP** To avoid any snapshot dependencies in your project, use the Maven Enforcer plug-in, which we'll discuss later in this chapter.

For instance, if your project depends on a 1.0.2-SNAPSHOT dependency, the plug-in wants to use the 1.0.2 released version. If your project depends on a change that was made in 1.0.2-SNAPSHOT and there's no such release yet, you should delay releasing the latest changes and instead use an earlier release version of the dependency.

"But I must release with snapshots!"

Sometimes there are no other options and you must release with a snapshot dependency; perhaps a critical bug was fixed on the dependent project.

One approach to releasing is to build the dependency on your local desktop and add the dependency to your local repository. Then you can manually change the version to something that would never be picked by the original project team (in order to prevent the situation where an officially released version of that third-party library has the version number you've used). For example, using a version string like 1.0.2-modified-by-MyCompany-for-iteration-1 makes it clear that you (or your team) provided the modified (or hacked) dependency. This special dependency is also a candidate for your distribution, as it's not available elsewhere. Note that this approach is only a valid option if the license of the open source dependency fits into your own schema.

(continued)

Another option for dealing with snapshots is the versions:lock-snapshots plug-in. It inspects all POMs and replaces all snapshot versions with the current timestamp version of that -SNAPSHOT (for instance, -20100320.172301-4). You can release with this modified code base. You could also switch back to regular snapshots via the versions:unlock-snapshots plug-in. Maven's Versions plug-in also provides some other interesting goals for working with versions (see http://mojo.codehaus.org/versions -maven-plugin/).

To continue with the preparation, let's assume there's a release, but you haven't picked up the released version yet. You could manually update the version and commit the change to SVN or let the Release plug-in do it for you. During the execution of the `release:prepare` goal, the plug-in asks you for the release's version number:

```
What is the release version for "my-tool"? (com.book:my-tool) 1.0.0: : _
    1.0.0-alpha

What is SCM release tag or label for "my-tool"? (com.book:my-tool) _
    my-tool-1.0.0-alpha: :

What is the new development version for "my-tool"? (com.book:my-tool) _
    1.0.1-alpha-SNAPSHOT: :
```

For the version number, you could accept the suggested 1.0.0 value, or you could specify a different version ID. It's always good to have some alpha, beta, or release-candidate releases before shipping a final release, so let's imagine there's a demand for an alpha release. At the prompt, type in `1.0.0-alpha` and accept the suggested defaults for the Subversion tag and the next version number increment. After you have specified the version number, the plug-in triggers the regular project build and executes some SVN tasks. Under the hood, it creates the tag (the URL would be http://server/svn/path/to/project/tags/my-tool-1.0.0-alpha) and updates and commits the new version number (1.0.1-alpha-SNAPSHOT) to your previously created branch.

SVN TAG A tag inside the Subversion repository is, by convention, a folder that's never updated. Tag folders are a single source of truth because they identify the exact version of the source code that was used to create a baselined release. Later, if you have to patch an existing release—for instance, due to a critical security bug—you usually create a branch by copying the corresponding tag folder to make sure that you're patching the correct baseline of the code. By committing changes to the tag (which is possible by default), the tag automatically becomes a branch (by convention), which can be confusing. If you want to be sure that this doesn't happen, restrict the access to tag folders by using SVN hooks.

If problems occur during the `release:prepare` goal, execution could lead to a build failure. In such cases, you need to solve the failures. For instance, if your SVN server is down, you need your admin to get it back up. Once the problems are fixed, you can continue from where the Maven Release plug-in exited the job by entering this command:

```
mvn release:prepare -Dresume
```

Another option would be to run `mvn release:clean release:prepare` after first deleting all temporary files created by the plug-in, and then rerun the entire release preparation again. If the Release plug-in has already changed some of your files, like the `version` in the pom.xml files, you can roll back these changes (before re-running `prepare`):

```
mvn release:rollback
```

The Release plug-in has built-in safety features, so you won't spend extra hours reassembling the release again and again. This is part of the Agile strategy behind Maven and similar tools.

5.4.2 Creating the release

Before you can perform the last steps on your release—the creation of the release—configure your pom.xml file's `distributionManagement` section. Here's an example of what this might look like:

```
<distributionManagement>
 <repository>
  <id>local-repository</id>
  <name>My staging component repo</name>
  <url>file:///m2_repo</url>
 </repository>
</distributionManagement>
```

Inside the `distributionManagement` section, you specify the Maven repository to which the release should be deployed. Usually the Maven repository is a remote (HTTP) server, via SSH. For now, we'll use a folder on the local filesystem, because it works just as well. Later in the chapter, we'll discuss uploading to a remote Maven repository and the required configuration.

To finish the release procedure, you need to invoke the `release:perform` goal:

```
mvn release:perform
```

The plug-in creates a target/checkout directory and checks the previously created Subversion tagged version of your project. Next, it executes the normal build process. With the `release:perform` goal, you not only generate the normal JAR file (or whatever deployment unit your project delivers); the plug-in also generates the matching javadoc-jar and source-jar files:

```
my-tool-1.0.0-alpha-javadoc.jar
my-tool-1.0.0-alpha-sources.jar
my-tool-1.0.0-alpha.jar
```

During the execution of the `release:perform` goal, the Maven Release plug-in uses the Deploy plug-in and handles the upload to the Maven repository, which has been configured in the `distributionManagement` section of your project's pom.xml file. If no error occurs, the Release plug-in cleans up its temporary files by internally calling the following:

```
mvn release:clean
```

This erases the backup POM files (pom.xml.releaseBackup) and the release.properties file, which store information about the ongoing release process. Congratulations! Your release is complete.

You saw many useful Maven features implemented through its plug-ins. But there's still some room for improving this release process. By configuring a remote repository (the component repository), the invocation of `mvn release:perform` will deploy the artifacts to the server. But you don't always want to directly deploy the newly generated Maven artifacts to a production Maven repository. In a case like that, use `release:stage` goal:

```
mvn release:stage
-DstagingRepository=remote-repo::default::scpexe://URL_TO_DIR
```

The `release:stage` goal doesn't require a repository URL to be present in the pom.xml file, but the same settings.xml configuration is still needed. Note that the `stagingRepository` parameter starts with the ID of the specified server.

5.4.3   *Testing the release*

A software release requires more than merely compiling sources from a Subversion tag. The QA team must review and test the generated artifacts (such as documentation and binary JAR files). Every project has many JUnit tests, and the entire development starts with a test case. The final testing is done by the QA team that eventually approves the release.

The QA team gets the released artifacts from a staging Maven repository. The best solution would be that the QA and the customer get exactly those files that the QA team has tested and verified. Sometimes, you need to make the exact JAR files that you used for testing available. Imagine that your project is implementing some (Java) standard (such as part of the Java Community Process, JCP) and that executing a TCK (technology compatibility kit) is part of the required test plan.

The staging repository could be the previously specified file:///m2_repo directory, which could be mounted as a network device. The QA test plan is executed against the previously created release artifacts.

Once the QA team gives its approval, you should deploy the Maven artifacts to a production or release Maven repository. Here are a few options for automating the deployment:

- Rebuild the bits from the Subversion tag. Once you build the code, you'll need to use the Maven Deploy plug-in to deploy the artifacts. This plug-in reruns the important parts of the previous release procedure, without having QA test the generated bits. Testing is important, because mistakes can happen while rebuilding the release from the TAG folder.

- Copy the artifacts to the final repository. Use secure copy `scp` (or copy `cp`) to manually copy the artifacts. This ensures the exact JAR files are made available through the Maven repository, but doing so will destroy the Maven metadata.
- Use the Maven Stage plug-in with the `stage:copy` goal: `mvn stage:copy`

```
-Dsource="file:///m2_local_staging_repo/" \
-Dtarget="scp://maven_repository_server/path/to/repo" \
-Dversion=1.2.3
```

This plug-in is a smarter version of the copy process, because it honors the Maven metadata. The plug-in creates a zip file of everything in the local staging repository and uses `scp` to upload it to the specified remote server. Then, the zip is extracted and removed. This means that the artifacts are now correctly deployed to your Maven repository.

The Stage plug-in is useful, particularly when you care about keeping Maven metadata files intact. But the plug-in itself has some small issues. You have to specify a meaningless version parameter, and it's not possible to download from a remote server to your local folder. Additionally, your current user account needs to exist on the server, and you're required to have `write` access rights for the remote directory. Finally, the password entered for the remote account is displayed in plain text. These are significant limitations, but the overall benefits outweigh the extra effort.

- Copy the artifact via a repository manager feature set. Artifactory provides a context menu for all artifacts in your repositories (see figure 5.11). You can mark artifacts and copy or move them to another repository (such as a special staging repository). Artifactory provides a dry-run feature, so you can first try to execute the command without any commit to keep a consistent state, even if something goes wrong. If your check is successful, you can then execute the

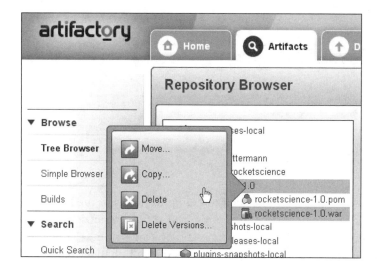

Figure 5.11 Copy artifacts to a staging repository with Artifactory

command. You can also use advanced staging strategies by applying matrix parameters and smart searches. For more details on this, see chapter 7.

5.4.4   *Useful Maven plug-ins for releasing*

Previously, we talked about the undesired effect of introducing a snapshot dependency into your project. In most commercial software projects, the code is released only after it has successfully completed a formal release process. The Maven Release plug-in can help catch snapshot dependencies, but there are better options. Catching unreleased dependencies is something that needs to happen as soon as possible, not a few days before the release deadline.

One way to ensure that you never introduce snapshot dependencies is to use the Maven Enforcer plug-in. This plug-in evaluates a given set of rules to make sure they're honored on every build of your project. It not only helps to prevent dependencies on unreleased software (and force that no snapshots are included as dependencies), but you can also require a specific version of the JDK, as shown in the following listing.

Listing 5.13   Maven Enforcer plug-in ensuring no snapshots are used

```
<plugin>
  <groupId>org.apache.maven.plugins</groupId>
  <artifactId>maven-enforcer-plugin</artifactId>
  <version>1.0-beta-1</version>
  <executions>
   <execution>
    <id>enforce-versions</id>
    <goals>
     <goal>enforce</goal>
    </goals>
    <configuration>
     <rules>                                        ❶ Bans
      <requireReleaseDeps>                             snapshots
       <message>
        You need management approval before you use SNAPSHOTS
       </message>
      </requireReleaseDeps>>                         ❷ Requires
      <requireJavaVersion>                             Java version I.6
       <message>
        Project needs to be compiled with Java 6
       </message>
       <version>1.6</version>
      </requireJavaVersion>
     </rules>
    </configuration>
   </execution>
  </executions>
</plugin>
```

In order to use the plug-in, you need to configure it inside the `build` section of your project. The `enforce` goal runs the configured rule set against every module of your build. This is important for the `requireReleaseDeps` rule ❶. For the JDK rule ❷, you could use the `enforce-once` goal, as this doesn't change for the submodules of your multimodule project. Violating the rules will cause a build error, so no code is compiled.

It's recommended that you specify `message` for each rule to provide information on why the build failed. If you don't configure the custom message, the Enforcer plug-in will use a default one. For instance, executing our project with Java 5 will display the following warning:

```
[WARNING] Rule 0: org.apache.maven.plugins.enforcer.RequireJavaVersion _
    failed with message:
Project needs to be compiled with Java 6
```

The warning message for dependencies that have been disallowed looks similar:

```
[WARNING] Rule 0: org.apache.maven.plugins.enforcer.RequireReleaseDeps _
    failed with message:
You need approval before you use SNAPSHOTS
Found Banned Dependency: org.project.foo.:jar:1.0-SNAPSHOT
```

The Enforcer plug-in helps to ascertain which JAR files have caused the problem.

More rules can be used with the Enforcer plug-in. For instance, you could enforce the existence and values of properties, or you can restrict the execution of the build to Linux-based systems (see http://maven.apache.org/enforcer/enforcer-rules/). It's important to note that the plug-in isn't limited to its built-in rules: It offers a rich API for creating custom rules (see the documentation at http://maven.apache.org/enforcer/enforcer-api/writing-a-custom-rule.html).

5.4.5 *Using cryptography with Maven*

Another helpful plug-in is Maven GPG. Security is essential. If your company makes the generated release artifacts available to the wider public, it's important to sign the release with a cryptographic key. Doing so assures potential users that the package is tamperproof and comes from a legitimate source. The same is true for open source projects. Potential users (or customers) downloading the files from your website or a Maven repository assume that your release manager created those files and that they won't cause problems. To deliver on the trust you have built, you must sign all generated artifacts of the release by using GPG (GNU Privacy Guard).

The GnuPG project (http://gnupg.org) is a popular implementation of the Open-PGP standard, which is defined in RFC 4880 (OpenPGP Message Format). Merely signing the artifacts isn't enough. You need to make your public keys for the release managers available. Open source projects usually offer some information on how to verify the distributed files[8]. If something is wrong with the JAR file, the verification will give you an error message:

```
$ gpg --verify my-tool-1.2.3.jar.asc my-tool-1.2.3.jar
gpg: Signature made Fri 12 Feb 2010 12:33:38 PM CET using DSA key ID 1CE17EDC
gpg: BAD signature from "Your name <you@company.de>"
```

---

[8] See Apache-MyFaces at http://myfaces.apache.org.

In order to sign the release artifacts, you must install GPG and create your own key pair. GnuPG has instructions on how to install the software on different operating systems. On Ubuntu, the software is usually already on your machine. A good quick introduction is available here: http://wiki.wsmoak.net/cgi-bin/wiki.pl?ReleaseSigning.

Once you have your key pair, you need to sign all the files that you're uploading to the public:

```
gpg --armor --output my-tool-1.2.3.jar.asc --detach-sig my-tool-1.2.3.jar
```

This can be time-consuming on projects with many artifacts. Thankfully, in the Maven ecosystem, the Maven GPG plug-in does the job for you, as shown in the following listing.

> **Listing 5.14   Maven GPG plug-in signing files on every build**

```
<plugin>
  <groupId>org.apache.maven.plugins</groupId>
  <artifactId>maven-gpg-plugin</artifactId>
  <version>1.0</version>
  <executions>
   <execution>
    <id>sign-artifacts</id>
    <phase>verify</phase>
    <goals>
     <goal>sign</goal>
    </goals>
   </execution>
  </executions>
 </plugin>
```

This configuration prompts for the private key and then creates a cryptographic signature on every build. Usually, you won't want to sign the files all the time. It's only needed when you build the release. A common practice is to put this plug-in into a special release profile. We'll discuss the definition of profiles in the next section.

5.4.6   *Maven assembly*

Another helpful plug-in is Maven Assembly. Your project's JAR files (including -javadoc.jar and -sources.jar files) are usually deployed to a Maven repository. But when your project generates many different artifacts besides the JAR files, such as documentation or WAR files, you'll generally also want a binary distribution that ships all the artifacts. (Note that the distribution has to contain the JAR files as well, because obviously the Maven repository may not be accessible to a potential user.)

The Assembly plug-in assists you with the creation of distributions. A simple configuration is shown in the following listing.

> **Listing 5.15   Maven Assembly plug-in**

```
<project ...>
<plugin>
  <artifactId>maven-assembly-plugin</artifactId>
  <version>2.2-beta-5</version>
```

```
  <configuration>
   <descriptorRefs>
    <descriptorRef>jar-with-dependencies</descriptorRef>
    <descriptorRef>bin</descriptorRef>
    <descriptorRef>src</descriptorRef>
    <descriptorRef>project</descriptorRef>
   </descriptorRefs>
  </configuration>
</plugin>
```

You can invoke the Assembly plug-in with the following command:

```
mvn assembly:assembly
```

This starts the regular build and creates a few standard distributions:

- *Dependency JAR*—Creates a JAR file that contains all classes of your module and those that it depends on. For instance, if your project has a dependency against Apache Log4j, the plug-in extracts its classes into your my-tool-1.2.3-jar-with-dependencies.jar file. That means that you can ship your application and all its dependencies in a single (huge) JAR file.
- *bin*—Contains all JAR files of the module.
- *src*—Contains the content of the src folder, including the module's pom.xml file.
- *Project*—Contains the source code of the embedding module (not all modules).

The formats for the distributions are different. Although the Dependency JAR distribution is created as a JAR file, the other distributions (BIN, SRC, and Project) come in different formats, such as these:

- .zip
- .tar.gz
- .tar.bz2
- .jar* (only used for the "Dependency JAR")

The four default distribution options are convenient for small projects that have only one module. In most cases, though, they aren't enough because a typical Maven project consists of multiple modules:

```
/API
/Implementation
/web-app-spring
/web-app-simple
...
```

This means that your distribution needs to ship multiple JAR files and all example applications along with the source code for all modules.

To deliver the source code, you can use the built-in `project` descriptor. For the binary part of the distribution, you need to create a custom description file that you place under the src/assembly of the root directory (see the following listing).

Listing 5.16   Assembly description file

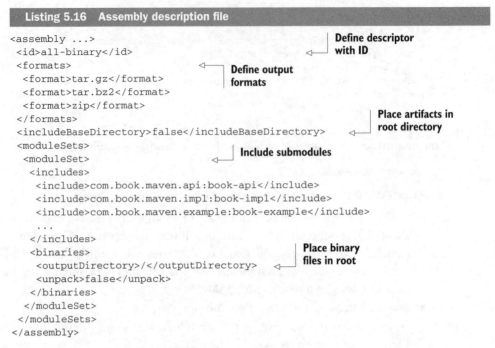

```
<assembly ...>                                    Define descriptor
 <id>all-binary</id>                              with ID
 <formats>                          Define output
  <format>tar.gz</format>          formats
  <format>tar.bz2</format>
  <format>zip</format>
 </formats>                                       Place artifacts in
 <includeBaseDirectory>false</includeBaseDirectory>  root directory
 <moduleSets>                       Include submodules
  <moduleSet>
   <includes>
    <include>com.book.maven.api:book-api</include>
    <include>com.book.maven.impl:book-impl</include>
    <include>com.book.maven.example:book-example</include>
    ...
   </includes>
   <binaries>                                     Place binary
    <outputDirectory>/</outputDirectory>          files in root
    <unpack>false</unpack>
   </binaries>
  </moduleSet>
 </moduleSets>
</assembly>
```

To use the preceding XML file, you must register it with the Assembly plug-in. Because the complete assembly process takes quite some time, you shouldn't execute it on the regular build. Instead, you can define a special profile (see the following listing).

Listing 5.17   Configuring Assembly as a profile

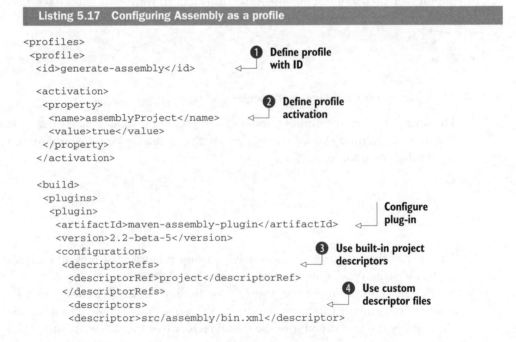

```
<profiles>
 <profile>                          ❶ Define profile
  <id>generate-assembly</id>          with ID

  <activation>
   <property>                       ❷ Define profile
    <name>assemblyProject</name>      activation
    <value>true</value>
   </property>
  </activation>

  <build>
   <plugins>
    <plugin>                                      Configure
     <artifactId>maven-assembly-plugin</artifactId>  plug-in
     <version>2.2-beta-5</version>
     <configuration>                ❸ Use built-in project
      <descriptorRefs>                descriptors
       <descriptorRef>project</descriptorRef>
      </descriptorRefs>             ❹ Use custom
      <descriptors>                   descriptor files
       <descriptor>src/assembly/bin.xml</descriptor>
```

```
      </descriptors>
    </configuration>
   </plugin>
  </plugins>
 </build>
 </profile>
</profiles>
```

The new profile with the ID `generate-assembly` ❶ is invoked when the `assembly-Project` is set to `true` ❷. The complete command for this profile is as follows:

```
mvn -DassemblyProject=true package assembly:assembly
```

Executing the command runs the build process and then creates all the archive files. The configuration is quite simple. The `descriptorRefs` section reuses the built-in `project` descriptor ❸, and within the `descriptors` element ❹, point the Assembly plug-in to your custom assembly file. The result of the archive looks like this:

```
ARCHIVE-FILE:
/book-api-version.jar
/book-impl-version.jar
/book-web-app-spring-version.war
/book-web-app-simple-version.war
```

Even with these results, you aren't done yet. A complete distribution needs more than the binary deliverables. Most projects also make the generated Javadoc files available as well.

To make this happen, you must use the Maven Dependency plug-in, because you need to copy the desired artifacts. The Dependency plug-in provides the capability to manipulate artifacts—it can copy or unpack artifacts from local or remote repositories to a specified location. Inside the `generate-assembly` profile, you need to configure the Maven Dependency plug-in, as shown in the following listing.

Listing 5.18 Maven Dependency plug-in to include Javadoc

```
<plugin>
 <groupId>org.apache.maven.plugins</groupId>
 <artifactId>maven-dependency-plugin</artifactId>          ⟵  Use Maven
 <version>2.1</version>                                        Dependency plug-in
 <executions>
  <execution>                                              Configure execution
   <id>copy-javadoc</id>                            ⟵      to copy Javadoc
   <phase>generate-resources</phase>
   <goals>
    <goal>copy</goal>
   </goals>
   <configuration>
    <artifactItems>                                        Define
     <artifactItem>                             ⟵          artifact
      <groupId>com.book.maven.api</groupId>
      <artifactId>book-api</artifactId>
      <version>${project.version}</version>
```

```
    <classifier>javadoc</classifier>
   </artifactItem>
   ...
  </artifactItems>
  <outputDirectory>                      Target
   ${project.build.directory}/javadoc    directory
  </outputDirectory>
 </configuration>
</execution>
</executions>
</plugin>
```

Inside the plug-in, you can define multiple `execution` elements. You could define a global `copy-everything` execution ID, but don't because doing so would mix different artifacts, such as sources-jar and javadoc-jar files in the same folder of the package. To keep things more organized, make sure every artifact `classifier` has an `execution` element, like `copy-javadoc` or `copy-sources`. In the preceding configuration, the specified `copy` goal copies all nested `artifactItems` to the javadoc folder inside the Target directory. If you want to make the -sources-jar files available, you should place them, through their own `execution` element, into a sources folder in the Target directory.

Next. you need to tell the assembly process to pick up the `javadoc` artifacts. To do so, add the following `fileSet` element to your custom assembly descriptor, the bin.xml file:

```
<fileSets>
 <fileSet>
  <directory>target/javadoc</directory>
  <outputDirectory>javadoc</outputDirectory>
 </fileSet>
</fileSets>
```

Last but not least, it's commonly required that you make your dependencies available. If your customer gets your artifact from a repository, you don't need to worry about this, because Maven resolves their dependencies and downloads them along with your files. But for those without a Maven project, you need to ship the dependencies as part of the distribution:

```
<dependencySets>
 <dependencySet>
  <outputDirectory>lib</outputDirectory>
  <scope>compile</scope>
 </dependencySet>
</dependencySets>
```

You must add the preceding configuration to your custom assembly descriptor. It adds all compile-time dependencies of your root pom.xml file to the final distribution, inside its lib folder. You can use different Maven scopes to bind the operation to the defined phase, such as `compile` in the preceding example. Dependencies of a different Maven scope require a separate `dependencySet` element.

The preceding distribution process defines a profile inside of the root pom.xml file to generate the different archives. Consequently, the pom.xml grows hard to read. To keep pom.xml files small, create a separate assembly module as part of the project. As before with the `generate-assembly` profile, you shouldn't execute this module as part of the regular build, which means you won't list this module inside the `modules` section:

```
<modules>
 <module>book-api<module>
 <module>book-impl<module>
 . . .
</modules>
```

To generate the distribution, you must navigate into the assembly module and run the `mvn package assembly:assembly` command from there.

In section 5.4.1, you saw that executing `mvn release:prepare` increases the version numbers for all (sub)module pom.xml files. Because you're excluding the assembly module from the `modules` section, you need to ensure the `version` of the assembly module gets updated as well. To archive this, introduce a `prepare-release` profile, as shown in the following listing.

Listing 5.19 Include the assembly as part of a release to update its version

```
<profiles>
 <profile>
  <id>prepare-release</id>
  <activation>
   <property>
    <name>prepareRelease</name>
    <value>true</value>
   </property>
  </activation>
  <modules>
   <module>my-assembly</module>
  </modules>
 </profile>
```

The profile is invoked when the `prepareRelease` parameter is set to `true`. In addition to the `release:prepare` goal, specify the parameter:

```
mvn release:prepare -DprepareRelease=true
```

This statement applies the command to all (default) modules and to those that are listed in the `prepare-release` profile.

5.4.7 *Tooling beyond Maven and outlook*

The plug-ins we've discussed help to generate a Maven release with a complete distribution. The Release (or Stage) plug-in also deploys the Maven artifacts to a given Maven repository, but the final distribution should also be made available on your website. Because your release process already signs all generated JAR files, the final distribution should be signed too.

To make this procedure simple and easy for all team members to use, you could create a Python script that automates the distribution signing and uploading. The script should also combine the various `mvn` commands, such as `mvn -Dassembly-Project=true package assembly:assembly` or `mvn release:stage...` The Apache MyFaces project uses a Python script for this: http://svn.apache.org/repos/asf/myfaces/trinidad/trunk/scripts/trinidad-build-release.py. You can download and customize it as needed. The script is executed as follows:

```
./script.py passpharse /folder/to/the/source
```

Most plug-ins are configured in the root pom.xml file, because they're visible for the submodules as well. But because a software company has several products or projects, and all have similar requirements, like a release or the configuration of the source code management, it's recommended that you create a master POM that contains the most common plug-ins and dependencies. On each project, your root pom.xml will point to your master POM file as its parent:

```
<project ...>
 <modelVersion>4.0.0</modelVersion>
 <parent>
  <groupId>com.company.devision</groupId>
  <artifactId>devision</artifactId>
  <version>2</version>
 </parent>
 <groupId>com.company.devision.current-project</groupId>
 ...
```

This is a common pattern in a big organization, such as the Apache Software Foundation (ASF). The ASF releases a master POM (see https://svn.apache.org/repos/asf/maven/pom/trunk/asf/pom.xml) that contains fundamental dependencies and profiles, and each Maven-based Apache project inherits from this POM. Following this pattern makes sense. Over time the master POM evolves and includes more convenient settings that the subprojects inherit.

The Apache Maven project doesn't only maintain the master POM—it also outlines the release guidelines for every project within Apache (http://maven.apache.org/developers/release/apache-release.html). In companies with different development teams, defining a similar guide makes perfect sense. It's also important to maintain both the release guide and the master POM, because a build environment (including the release process) isn't static. Things change over time.

As a final note, it's recommended that you document the entire process for every release on your company's wiki. This helps to document any potential problems and workarounds, resulting in a repeatable process whether you release your code monthly, nightly, or hourly, via a CI server.

5.5   *Summary*

This chapter introduced integration and release management, as well as Maven and its major release tools and plug-ins. We looked at where Maven stores its artifacts and which tooling options you have for hosting a component repository. You learned that it's also possible to host Maven artifacts in Subversion, although using a dedicated repository manager like Artifactory adds much more value and results in a better solution. Additionally, you saw how Maven can be used for management integration and release management.

This chapter also serves as preparation for the advanced use cases that we'll discuss later in this book. In the next chapter, we'll talk about productive working environments, where Maven plays yet another important role.

Creating a productive
development environment

6

This chapter covers

- Approaches to accelerating development on the developer's desktop
- Strategies and tools for streamlining the development and build process
- Tools like Mockito and Cargo that help with testing and deployment

This chapter illustrates strategies and tools for setting up controllable and highly maintainable environments that are isolated from those of other developers and production systems, and that include private workspaces (sometimes called *sandboxes*). But what does *isolation* have to do with collaborative team play? In fact, being able to work in isolation is essential for effective software development and team collaboration. Management has the obligation to foster reusability and protect investments, but it's important for all stakeholders, such as developers, to be familiar with strategies for creating a productive development environment.

In this chapter, we'll first look at what makes productive workspaces and review concepts from earlier chapters, including how to build code in sandboxes. Next, we'll take a deeper look at a technique for creating testing stubs called *mocking*, which uses substitutes for real objects in tests. We'll discuss mocking in general, and Mockito—a leading Java mocking framework—in particular. Lastly, we'll talk about Cargo, which is a smart interface to application containers, and we'll discuss TeamCity for running private builds on a remote build machine. We'll also cover the importance of having consistent builds whether they're triggered in a private workspace or on the official build server. I call this capability a *congruent build*.

6.1 Congruent builds and workspace management

Developers need consistent environments and private workspaces that are controlled and isolated from unexpected changes. This helps developers reproduce and detect bugs. Components include versioning the IDE configuration in version-control systems (VCSs) and checking in all dependencies, not only for code or components, but also for tools like Tomcat and Ant.

6.1.1 Workspace management and the VCS

As a rule, put as much into your VCS as you can, and give control to the relevant stakeholders, where it makes sense. This makes it much easier to rebuild a development environment or to switch to another machine quickly. Additionally, workspaces that can be reproducibly set up from the VCS help to maintain consistent standards across the team. Because the workspace is the first rung of the staging ladder, it's important to have workspaces in a defined state that can be reproduced automatically. You should also commit the default configuration settings of your developed software or of the tools you use to the VCS. These settings are valid for all developers and can be used by all developers to test and run the application from inside their workspaces. Personalized configuration settings, such as individual usernames or individual database schemes, shouldn't be kept in the VCS as part of the developed software, because they can't be shared across the team.

Many teams find it helpful to put the Jenkins configuration settings to the VCS. They're stored on hard disk and can be easily added to version control. It's also convenient to use snippets that are stored in the VCS to trigger builds. For example, having a CruiseControl build server running suggests that you'll have a build machine automating builds for different components or projects. You could put the CruiseControl control script (config.xml) into a VCS, or this container script could be stored outside of any specific project that has to be built with CruiseControl. You could put project-specific, build-related code snippets into the VCS folders belonging to the project, or put these snippets on the build server while checking them out of VCS and including them with native XML entities. Another solution could be to use CruiseControl's `include.projects` element, which includes different build projects.

Another important aspect of productive environments is the ability to check a version of the complete project and run all automated tests quickly. Among other things, this approach allows you to check sources from VCS and run tests in one step, without having to manually start servers or similar items. This ability is often associated with a *headless* running mode—running tests without having to start a complete environment, IDE, or user interface. This gains even more significance with complicated technologies such as JBoss, Tomcat, and others. It's also important to use the API and any related tool support where available, particularly in the context of testing. For instance, while using Spring, get acquainted with the Spring support for JUnit.

6.1.2 Workspace management and integrating code

Integrating code can be difficult. Developers must work on their code in isolation and must keep up with the functions completed by other developers. As a centralized synchronization point, the VCS and the continuous integration (CI) server help with this effort. The VCS contains the successfully integrated code; think of it as being the authoritative single source of truth. During development, developers are continuously committing to and updating from the codebase in the VCS. A typical sequence of activities can look like this:

1 Get up to date by synchronizing with the VCS and updating changes.
2 Make your own changes in alignment with the tasks.
3 Prior to each check-in, run a local build with all tests.
4 Update the workspace with the latest version in the VCS.
5 Rebuild and retest.
6 If everything looks good, then check in or commit your changes to the VCS.

A merging conflict can result from synchronizing your changes with the most recent version in the VCS, but most of the time you can easily resolve the conflict and check in your changes to produce a new, consistent version of the software.

Although these kinds of merging conflicts can be painful, there are other conflicts that are even worse: Given that you only check merged code into the VCS when it's free of compile errors, the other category of errors concerns *semantic* correctness. Developers implement customers' requirements, and the source code expresses functionality and semantic behavior. Merging different versions of the sources leads to one version that contains all interdependencies between the components and their functionality. Merging code and checking in the new version to VCS can lead to a new software version that's free of compile errors but that no longer implements the customer's requirements.

How can you minimize the probability as well as the risks of merge conflicts? When you check in small changes frequently, you minimize the chances of a conflict and ensure that any conflicts will be minor and easily resolved. Semantic changes can be detected early and often by writing automated tests and running them continuously. These tests compare the current behavior of the application with the expected one. We'll look more at tests in chapter 8.

The more throughput your Agile team has, the more important it is to take care of finding bugs early, which means that you want to integrate early and often and to work in a private, isolated sandbox. To achieve excellent speed in delivering as much software in as short iterations as possible, you need workspaces isolated from outside changes—places where developers can work on their code and concentrate on finishing their individual tasks.

> **ISOLATION AND DATABASE SYSTEMS**   Isolation is a core feature in database systems. It defines how and when changes made by one operation become visible to other concurrent operations. Isolation is one of the ACID (Atomicity, Consistency, Isolation, and Durability) properties of database management systems. Because the term isolation suggests a noncollaborative approach, I prefer to talk about *productive* workspaces.

In the normal course of development, the work your colleagues do results in changes being committed to the VCS that could potentially impact your environment, and it's difficult to get any work done if the code in your sandbox is changing constantly. For example, if you regularly refresh your sandbox by pulling the latest changes from the VCS, you'll never have a reliable workspace, because integrating each atomic change into your workspace impacts the stability of your environment. Constant updates lead to churn and waste a lot of time. It also prevents you from reliably tracking the results of merging changes with your coding (which hasn't yet been transferred to the VCS).

Agile teams do integrate, but integration can be done differently in different contexts:

- On a central build server, teams integrate continuously. This may lead to broken builds and crashed versions, but this is tolerated in order to identify bugs and integration issues early.
- Developers work in their private workspaces and they have control over the version of the code that they're working on. They control when and how their own isolated environment changes. Developers need to set up an environment and a flow that enables them to keep up with the code line, which is changing continuously, while empowering them to make progress without being distracted by changes made by others.

The build system on your local workspace should be as close as possible to the integration build system, with at least the same compiler and versions of external components that are required for the build. Typical features that may not be included locally are comprehensive test coverage and integration with or connection to all external resources, such as databases.

6.1.3   *Workspace management and running tests*

Besides source code and build scripts, all tests and the source code for integrating to remote resources, are maintained in the developers' workspaces as well. But the developers don't run all of those tests locally and often don't connect to remote resources from their workspaces. Typically, functional tests run exclusively on a CI system where remote resources are connected.

These differences are a good reason to keep up the development flow: Waiting too long for test feedback or to run a full-fledged infrastructure slows you down. Instead of running the full bunch of tests as a single group, you should categorize your tests.

By categorizing tests according to type, your builds become more Agile and tests run more focused and more frequently.

TestNG[1] is a popular Java testing framework that was created with the intent of improving upon the earlier testing frameworks (such as JUnit). TestNG allows you to use test groups, and you can determine which groups of tests run where and when (see the following listing).

Listing 6.1 Different test groups with TestNG

```
package com.huettermann.testng;

import org.testng.annotations.*;

public class SampleTest {
    @Test(groups = { "groupA" })          ← First test
    public void methodA() {                  group
        System.out.println("groupA");
    }
    @Test(groups = { "groupB" })          ← Second test
    public void methodB() {                  group
        System.out.println("groupB");
    }
}
```

Test groups allow you to run smoke tests or sanity checks locally. Then, you can run a full set of tests on the centralized build server. We'll discuss TestNG in more detail in chapter 8.

6.1.4 *Workspace management and dependencies*

Many developers find that it's difficult to manage isolation in a development workspace, and without isolation, you can have unexpected problems with other build dependencies. Managing your code and isolation around your workspace is essential. Automated build scripts can help to build your code and all required dependencies. If something isn't part of your workspace, you must ensure that it can't impact the work that you're doing. Sometimes you may find that other developers have private copies of artifacts that, if left uncontrolled, can impact your build.

Ideally, your workspace should be isolated so that it contains only code that you've built locally. Source code of components built by other departments or third-party libraries shouldn't be included in your workspace. In fact, having unnecessary parts of software in your workspace leads to less reusability and more possible variations, and both can prevent you from improving the whole development process. Sources of third-party libraries can be used to debug, but it's not your job to build them. Remember, the component vendor or provider is responsible for the build script that constructs the reproducible component.

This is one reason why the Maven approach is appealing. It includes dependent artifacts as binaries and sources in the local workspace are optional. This way you can rely

---

[1] See Cédric Beust and Hani Suleiman, *Next Generation Java Testing, TestNG and Advanced Concepts* (Addison-Wesley, 2008).

upon stable versions of the component dependencies. Maven describes components through coordinates consisting of a collection of attributes (`groupId`, `artifactId`, and version):

```
<dependency>
    <groupId>junit</groupId>
    <artifactId>junit</artifactId>
    <version>4.0</version>
    <type>jar</type>
    <scope>test</scope>
</dependency>
```

You can include dependencies by documenting the dependency to another artifact via XML. The rest is done by Maven, eliminating manual and error-prone copying of JARs. The build system shouldn't depend on where it's started or how it's used. For instance, you shouldn't natively rely upon an IDE to build your system. Instead, use build scripts that you can execute from the command line, or even better, from a CI server.

These build scripts can be triggered from the console (with Ant or Maven commands) or from inside the IDE or from an application (like a build server). Ant has been integrated into IDEs for years and the Maven integration is mature as well. For Eclipse, Sonatype offers the free m2eclipse Eclipse plug-in, which offers dependency management and the ability to use Maven archetypes to search and browse Maven repositories, automatically download dependencies, and edit POMs conveniently, among other features (see http://m2eclipse.sonatype.org/).

> **MAVEN AND IDES** All major Java IDEs have native Maven support, including Eclipse, NetBeans, and IntelliJ IDEA.

Dependency management, including the illustration of the dependencies, is a big benefit of Maven and m2eclipse. Figure 6.1 shows an example from a workspace.

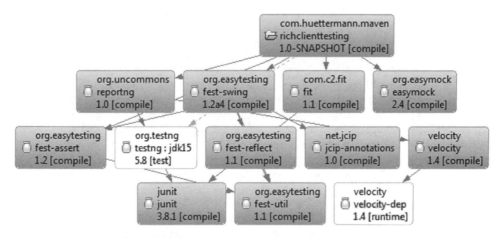

Figure 6.1 Dependencies visualized in real time by Maven and m2eclipse. The color of the background expresses the scope. Dependencies with `compile` scope are displayed with a darker background. Dependencies with a white background have other scopes, such as `test` or `runtime`.

All artifacts have dependencies on other artifacts, including transitive dependencies (dependencies of their dependencies)—this is part of the Java classpath approach. Using Maven and m2eclipse, all dependencies are described as part of the POM. M2eclipse fetches this information and provides POM editing support in your IDE, as well as a dependency visualization feature. This allows you to immediately see which artifact (identified through `groupId`, `artifactId`) depends upon which other specific artifact. The transitive dependencies are of special interest, as are the conflicts. (A conflict can occur, for example, when two artifacts depend on different versions of the same third artifact.)

> **SONATYPE PROFESSIONAL** Sonatype Professional (www.sonatype.com) is a commercial product that ties together open source products like Hudson, Nexus, m2eclipse, and Eclipse, making it easy to install and support out-of-the-box solution.

In order to manage projects in the workspace, m2eclipse must use classpaths, and you can configure the classpath to enable compiling and development. POMs and their specified dependencies provide another mechanism that contains information needed to set up the classpath (and related dependencies). But often you don't want to (or you can't) work with classpaths on a central build system in an elegant way. M2eclipse manages the Eclipse classpaths for you simultaneously. Add a dependency in your POM, and then m2eclipse automatically downloads the artifact and adds it to the classpath.

This approach is efficient. To accomplish it, m2eclipse uses a Maven classpath container (see figure 6.2). All artifacts (in binary format) are referenced automatically, and they're stored in your individual local repository. Consequently, you don't need to repeatedly check the JARs as part of the project; you only manage the meta model

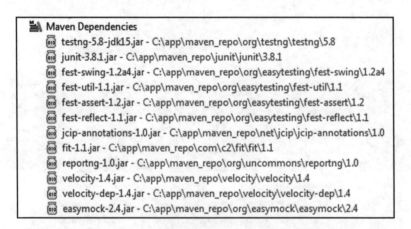

Figure 6.2   M2eclipse manages the Eclipse Maven classpath container. In your Eclipse project, all JARs are referenced as binary dependencies. No manual referencing or checking of artifacts is needed, and the approach is congruent, both in your workspace (IDE) and in your build script.

(the POM) and put this document into the VCS. In the figure, the local repository is located under C:\app\maven_repo.

6.1.5 *Workspace management and bootstrapping the development*

M2eclipse also supports using Maven archetypes, which is a feature that helps to enable productive environments. The Archetype plug-in allows you to create a Maven project from an existing template called an *archetype*. As a result, you get a basic build script skeleton derived from the common template. You can also create an archetype from an existing project.

Archetypes can be described, built, and delivered with Maven. An archetype project has a special structure—the main difference from a normal Maven project is its archetype-resources and META-INF folders. The META-INF folder contains an archetype.xml file that decides which resources are put into a new project created by this archetype. It typically consists of references to source and test folders and files:

```
<archetype>
  <id>archetype</id>
  <sources>
    <source>src/main/java/App.java</source>
  </sources>
  <testSources>
    <source>src/test/java/AppTest.java</source>
  </testSources>
</archetype>
```

The folders and files are put into the archetype-resources folder, which also contains a template for a resulting POM. You can use parameters while executing the archetype by calling the `archetype:generate` goal. Parameters can be set for filling placeholders in your resulting POM. For many open source projects, archetypes already exist, offering you a smart, quick start. Additionally, archetypes are great for organizations that want to provide a set of standard builds on a central, parent POM, which helps new products set up their environments quickly and consistently.

Another great way to work more efficiently is to use a technique known as mocking, which sets a placeholder for functions that aren't yet completed.

6.2 *Using Mockito to isolate systems*

  —*This section contributed by Szczepan Faber*

Mocking is a technique of using substitutes for real objects in tests. Mocking lets you test code that's ready and leave a test stub in place for other functions as they become ready. Additionally, mocks are helpful for executing tests more quickly, because they can use mocked-out infrastructure. Mocks allow you to isolate the code under test so that a test case can fail only for the reason intended.

Gerard Meszaros (in his book, *xUnit Test Patterns*) defines the following types of objects that simulate behavior:

- *Dummy object*—Keeps the compiler happy. Dummy objects are placeholder objects passed to the system under test but that are never used.

- *Test stub*—Can be configured to return predictable, canned values. In Meszaros's terms, test stubs provide the indirect input.
- *Test spy*—Can be asked what happened; for instance, "Was this method called on a spy?" Spies are helpful because they can also be stubbed (akin to a spy's disguise). Officially, the test spy provides a way to verify that the system under test performed the correct indirect output.
- *Mock object*—Can be configured to receive expected method calls. Mock objects can also return canned values if needed. Mock objects provide the system under test with both indirect input and a way to verify indirect output.

The main reason to use mocks is to isolate the code under test so that the test case can fail only for the reason intended, and not because a collaborator has a defect or because an external resource is in an unexpected state. If the code under test has dependencies on collaborating classes, environmental configuration settings, or external resources, then the test is fragile and can't reliably tell you whether the asserted behavior is occurring. Depending on the scope of the code under test, you might isolate larger or smaller subsets of the application code. The purpose of isolation in this context is to guarantee that the test tells you what it's intended to tell you, and not to merely work around difficulties in using real objects.

It's useful to know the official language that experts in the mocking world speak. But often I adjust the language for the sake of simplicity and use the mock term, as it's fairly easy to grasp. As a friend once said, "At the end of the day, a mock is a mock."

The differences between Mockito and conventional mocking frameworks revolve around the use of the terms *spy* versus *mock*, but there are a couple of interesting developer-friendly Mockito features. Some of these aren't unique to Mockito—other tools might do something similar, and if they don't, I encourage their authors to implement it! I am certain that when Mockito was developed, I couldn't find those features in other tools:

- Clean stack trace
- Clickable locations in failure information to optimize debugging (debugging is necessary, although debugging time should be reduced to a minimum)
- Handy annotations that make tests more readable and DRY (*Don't Repeat Yourself*, which means that your tests should be made modular to avoid repetition errors)
- Feedback on what you did wrong if you misuse the API, and how to fix it

Let's start by discussing the importance of isolation in the testing process.

6.2.1   *Isolation and dependency injection*

Mocks enable you to test certain pieces of your system in isolation, but it's wise to remember that *isolation* itself isn't a goal. The underlying principle is to write readable and maintainable tests and to gain from fast feedback cycles. That's it. Isolating is one of the ways to achieve highly maintainable tests.

The fundamental use case for mock objects is a situation where using real objects is impractical. For a trivial example, consider the following listing.

Listing 6.2　Code to be tested with mocks

```
public class SmartDictionary {

  private final Translator translator =
    new OnlineTranslator();
  private final History history = new DatabaseHistory();

  public String search(String word) {
    String translated = translator.translate(word);
    history.rememberSearch(word, translated);
    return translated;
  }
}
```

❶ Creating instance can be time-consuming

❷ Time-consuming database access

When testing `SmartDictionary`, you have to take care of its collaborators: `Online-Translator` ❶ and `DatabaseHistory` ❷. Both are problematic from the standpoint of testing. `OnlineTranslator` uses a remote service, so managing this external source that you can't control may be problematic. The `DatabaseHistory` talks to the database: It makes the test cumbersome and slow and forces you to consider the leftover and initial database state. To test `SmartDictionary`, it's impractical to use real `Translator` and `History` objects.

Let's refactor the code so we can replace instances of collaborators. This is shown in the following listing.

Listing 6.3　Code with dependency injection enabled

```
public class SmartDictionary {

  private final Translator translator;
  private final History history;

  public SmartDictionary(Translator translator,
      History history) {
    this.translator = translator;
    this.history = history;
  }

  public SmartDictionary() {
    this(new OnlineTranslator(), new DatabaseHistory());
  }

  public String search(String word) {
    String translated = translator.translate(word);
    history.rememberSearch(word);
    return translated;
  }
}
```

❶ New constructor allows passing objects to SmartDictionary

Default constructor, existing API isn't broken

The new constructor enables you to inject dependencies into SmartDictionary **❶**. In general, dependency injection pretty much enables mocking. You need to be able to inject mocked instances into the system under test.

Given that the API now allows injecting dependencies, the test looks like this:

Listing 6.4   Your first sip of Mockito

```
import static org.Mockito.*;                              ⟵  Imports
                                                          ❶  Mockito
public class SmartDictionaryTest {
                                                          ❷  Sets up
  Translator translator = mock(Translator.class);         ⟵    test
  History history = mock(History.class);
  SmartDictionary dictionary = new SmartDictionary(translator, history);

  @Test
  public void shouldFindWord() throws Exception {

    when(translator.translate("mock")).
      thenReturn("substitute");                        ⟵  Provides given
                                                       ❸  information
    String result = dictionary.search("mock");

    assertEquals("substitute", result);
  }

  @Test
  public void shouldKeepHistory() throws Exception {
    dictionary.search("I want to mock");
                                                       ❹  Ensures particular
    verify(history).rememberSearch("I want to mock");  ⟵    method was called
  }
}
```

The static import of Mockito **❶** makes it easy to access the entire Mockito API. To maximize clarity, the test setup **❷** is placed outside the test method. Our givens **❸** are that the mock is stubbed to return a canned result when a particular method with a particular argument is called using the stubbing API. We ensure that a particular method with particular arguments **❹** was called on the collaborator (verification API).

6.2.2   *Mocks in test-driven development*

I can't imagine test-driven development (TDD) without mocks. The use of mock objects comes from extreme programming (XP), so no wonder there's a bond between TDD and mocks. Mockito's implementation was test-driven from day one. The API and error handling had been continuously optimized for TDD.

I've already mentioned that the fundamental use case for mocks is substituting unwieldy objects. But mocks do more than that. Mocks in TDD play a crucial role in interface discovery, a technique that allows you to design the communication between the collaborators *from* the test. It sounds difficult but it's not, unless you don't know yet which collaborators your tested object needs. As you continue implementing a test, you gradually figure out what collaborating roles are required. You can learn more about this in an interesting book called *Growing Object-Oriented Software, Guided by Tests* by Steve Freeman and Nat Pryce.

> **TEST-DRIVEN DEVELOPMENT**   TDD is a technique that relies on the repetition of a short development cycle: The developer first writes a failing test that defines a functionality, then produces code to pass that test, and finally refactors the new code. *Refactoring* means changing the code without modifying its external functional behavior, in order to improve its internal quality. TDD, initially defined by Kent Beck, encourages simple designs.[2]

Let's do a TDD exercise that I like to call "ping-pong programming:" I write a test, and you write the code that makes the test pass. The test for the first feature is shown in the following listing.

Listing 6.5   The test for finding word feature

```
public class SmartDictionaryTest {

  @Test
  public void shouldFindWord() throws Exception {
    Translator translator = mock(Translator.class);          Given
    SmartDictionary dictionary = new SmartDictionary(translator);
    when(translator.translate("mock")).
      thenReturn("substitute");
                                                       When

    String result = dictionary.search("mock");

                                                        Then
    assertEquals("substitute", result);
  }
```

Now running the test, the test will fail. It's pretty easy to implement the code so that the test passes.

Here's another test method, this time for a different feature that starts with a test method that initially fails:

Listing 6.6   The test for keeping history feature

```
@Test
public void shouldKeepHistory() throws Exception {
  Translator translator = mock(Translator.class);
  History history = mock(History.class);
  SmartDictionary dictionary = new SmartDictionary(translator, history);

  dictionary.search("i want to mock");
                                                  When
                                                          Then
  verify(history).rememberSearch("i want to mock");
}
```

---

[2] See Kent Beck, *Test-Driven Development* (Addison-Wesley, 2002).

It's your turn to make this test green—go ahead and implement the missing code.

Once you see the green bar, you can do some refactoring. You should watch for duplication in the complete test and then remove it to get the test DRY (Don't Repeat Yourself). You should make your tests modular to avoid repetition errors and so you have less code to maintain.

6.2.3   *The flavor of behavior-driven development*

Did you notice the *given, when,* and *then* comments in the preceding examples? Those comments are the simplest possible technique for increasing the quality of your tests. Start writing them in your tests for one month, and you'll never go back. Every test should consist of those three components: *given, when,* and *then* to clearly describe the setup, the test, and the result.

Behavior-driven development (BDD) is so much more than those three comments, but this chapter is too short to fully describe the BDD technique. Suffice to say (quoting J. B. Rainsberger), "BDD is TDD done correctly, nothing else." We'll get into a detailed discussion of BDD in chapter 8.

Explicit *given, when,* and *then* comments are great, but unfortunately, the Mockito stubbing API doesn't play nicely with them. Mockito stubbing starts with `when()`, but stubbing is a part of the *given* component of the test. Mocking rookies often become confused, so Mockito added aliases for stubbing:

```
//note the different static import
import static org.BDDMockito.*;
//given
given(translator.translate("mock")).willReturn("substitute");
```

BDDMockito is a base class from the Mockito framework that allows you to work easily with *given, when,* and *then* comments. Many other helpful features are available, including a powerful API.

6.2.4   *Other handy features of Mockito*

Most of the Mockito API is available via static methods. To take the most advantage of static imports, you can apply two configuration tweaks to your IDE:

- *Favorite static imports*—Some IDEs (for example, Eclipse) can't figure out the static import if you type the method name (for instance, `verify`, `mock`). It's useful to instruct your IDE about the static methods you often use. Search in your Eclipse preferences for "favorite static imports" and you'll be able to add `org.Mockito.*;` as one of your favorites.
- *Organize static imports smartly*—It's useful to configure your IDE to always use a wildcard (`*`) for static imports. Decent IDEs allow you to configure the number of imports before a wildcard is used. I usually configure the number to 1 for static imports. This way, `import static org.Mockito.*` is always at the top

of my tests; and I can take advantage of intelligent features (such as IDE auto-completion).

Often, interaction with collaborators means passing specific method arguments. It's easy to verify and stub interactions that take simple arguments like primitives or strings. The trouble occurs when complex types are parameters of interactions. In that situation, you have the following options:

- Make sure the complex type implements the `equals()` method. This method is used by Mockito to match arguments passed to collaborators. This technique is the most natural, but in some cases it may be impractical to set up expected parameters in the test (for example, there may be too much irrelevant setup).

- Use the `ArgumentCaptor` to store the arguments of an interaction. This way, you can explicitly and selectively assert certain properties of the argument. It's a useful technique, as it may provide a more readable and focused test. Here's an example:

```
ArgumentCaptor<Person> argument = ArgumentCaptor.forClass(Person.class);
verify(registry).delete(argument.capture());
assertEquals("John", argument.getValue().getName());
```

Bear in mind that it doesn't make sense to use `ArgumentCaptor` for stubbing.

- Implement an `ArgumentMatcher`. It's a Boolean function that will match the arguments for the purposes of stubbing or verification. `ArgumentMatcher` is mostly useful for stubbing or when an argument is repetitively matched the same way across many tests.

The `@Mock` annotation helps you to DRY the test and clarify what's being mocked in a given test. Using annotations has additional benefits: The field name is used in verification failures, making them more descriptive. That's shown in the following listing.

Listing 6.7   Using the `@Mock` annotation

```
public class SmartDictionaryTest {

  @Mock Translator translator;          ❶ Specify @Mock
  @Mock History history;                   annotations

  @Before public void before() {                    ❷ Initiate fields marked
    MockitoAnnotations.initMocks(this);      ◀──┘      by annotation
    SmartDictionary dictionary = new SmartDictionary(translator, history);
  }
```

You can see the clarity in the `@Mock` annotations that mark class fields that are mocked ❶. The `initMocks` method initiates those fields marked by an annotation ❷. Alternatively, you can use `MockitoJUnitRunner` for this task.

Now that we've covered a number of helpful tips and use cases, let's discuss some antipatterns that you should avoid.

6.2.5 *Antipatterns*

Although the Mockito API is fairly straightforward, some users may find it difficult to use unless they read the Javadocs carefully. I've also noticed that users who come from other mocking tools tend to occasionally misuse the API.

ASK and TELL (verifying stubs) are the first antipatterns we'll look at. Mockito makes a clear distinction between ASK-style (in `translator.translate(word)`) and TELL-style (`history.rememberSearch(word)`) interactions:

```
public String search(String word) {
    String translated = translator.translate(word);
    history.rememberSearch(word);
    return translated;
}
```

The API is designed this way in order to improve test readability and to make the process of writing tests more natural. In object-oriented design, we usually prefer TELL interactions because they promote pushing the responsibilities and complexities into separate objects. We tell the collaborator to do something and we forget about it. It's their responsibility to deal with it. This leads to better design and more single-responsibility objects. If you write a lot of tests, you already know that TELL interactions are more convenient from the standpoint of testing with mocks. If you're interested in the subject, you can look up more information on the "Tell don't ask" principle in object-oriented design.[3]

Verifying all surrounding interactions is the second antipattern. Mockito enables you to verify interactions explicitly and selectively. You can verify exactly what you want, which means you can write readable, maintainable, and focused tests. Occasionally, though, you might be interested in verifying all surrounding interactions:

```
verify(listener).notify(event);
verifyNoMoreInteractions(listener);
```

This ensures that no other interaction was made with the `listener` collaborator. Some users tend to exercise `verifyNoMoreInteractions()` often, even in every test method, but this isn't recommended; `verifyNoMoreInteractions()` is a handy assertion from the interaction testing toolkit. Use it only when it's relevant. Abusing it leads to overspecified, less maintainable tests.

The third antipattern is unnecessary verification in order. Mockito supports verifying interactions in a specific order, and this might be useful on occasion, but it's certainly not a way to implement all your tests. You can create the `inOrder` object to pass any mocks that need to be verified in order:

```
InOrder inOrder = inOrder(firstMock, secondMock);
inOrder.verify(firstMock).add("was called first");
inOrder.verify(secondMock).add("was called second");
```

---

[3] On their website, Cunningham and Cunningham provide an article about the "tell don't ask" principle: http://c2.com/cgi/wiki?TellDontAsk.

Just because you can doesn't mean you should. Developers tend to test implementation details rather than behavior; I've observed that some developers feel better writing more defensive tests, overusing in order verification. In the majority of cases, it doesn't make sense to verify the order of calls. It makes the test overspecified because the reader feels the order is relevant. It also makes the test less maintainable, as it can break for invalid reasons (such as refactoring of code).

Mockito assumes a lenient mock definition by default, which makes it easier for you to take a behavior-oriented approach to TDD (which is an accepted good practice). If unit tests "know" too much about the internal operations of the code's interaction with collaborators, the tests become fragile when the application code is refactored. Refactoring shouldn't break tests, because the behavior of the application shouldn't change. When refactoring breaks a test, you must be able to depend on the test to tell you that you made a mistake when refactoring. Otherwise, you'll ignore test failures, and that leads to the creation of defects. Tests that "know too much" make it harder to refactor the application code, and when it becomes harder, developers tend to stop doing it.

Cargo is often used to manage application deployment to containers in a standard way, and we'll discuss it in the next section.

6.3   *Interfacing application containers with Cargo*

Cargo, in combination with Maven, provides a multipurpose utility to help manage Java containers in a build environment. You can download, start, stop, and configure Java containers, and you can deploy modules into them. Because there are so many different containers (for example, JBoss, Jetty, Tomcat, WebLogic), Cargo sees itself as a thin standard wrapper around them.

Suppose we need a clean Tomcat server to deploy our web archive (WAR) file and run our tests against this server. The Cargo Maven2 plug-in is a good integration of Cargo into the Maven lifecycle. The plug-in can easily be included in the build section of your POM.

The following listing shows the configuration of Cargo to use Tomcat. We configure the download of Tomcat and where it should be unzipped in the build.

Listing 6.8   Configuration of Cargo to use Tomcat

```
<build>
   <plugins>
      <plugin>
<groupId>org.codehaus.cargo</groupId>
<artifactId>cargo-maven2-plugin</artifactId>
<configuration>
   <wait>false</wait>
   <container>
      <containerId>tomcat6x</containerId>        ◁──┐ Use Tomcat to configure
      <zipUrlInstaller>                               download URL
         <url>
            http://www.apache.org/dist/tomcat/
               tomcat-6/v6.0.32/bin/apache-tomcat-6.0.32.zip
         </url>
```

```
            </zipUrlInstaller>
        </container>                          Configure usage, home
        <configuration>            ◄─┐       directory, port
          <home>
             ${project.build.directory}/tomcat6x/container
          </home>
          <properties>
             <cargo.servlet.port>${webserver-port}</cargo.servlet.port>
          </properties>
        </configuration>
</configuration>
...
```

Now that we have Tomcat in place, we can start it in the preintegration test phase of
Maven and deploy the artifact. In the following listing, Cargo starts Tomcat, deploys
the WAR, and blocks the execution until it can ping the URL of the deployed artifact.

Listing 6.9 Configuration of execution

```
<build>
   <plugins>
      <plugin>
<groupId>org.codehaus.cargo</groupId>
<artifactId>cargo-maven2-plugin</artifactId>
<configuration>
...
</configuration>
<executions>
   <execution>
      <id>start-container</id>
      <phase>pre-integration-test</phase>    ◄─┐  Trigger
      <goals>                                ◄─   plug-in
         <goal>start</goal>                   Start Tomcat,
         <goal>deploy</goal>                  deploy WAR
      </goals>
      <configuration>
         <deployer>
            <deployables>
               <deployable>
                  <groupId>${project.groupId}</groupId>
                  <artifactId>myartifact</artifactId>
                  <type>war</type>                       Block execution until
<pingURL>                                      ◄─        ping successful
   http://localhost:${webserver-port}/mycontext/index.jsp
</pingURL>
                  <pingTimeout>300000</pingTimeout>
                  <properties>
                     <context>mycontext</context>
                  </properties>
               </deployable>
            </deployables>
         </deployer>
      </configuration>
   </execution>
   <execution>
```

```
        <id>stop-container</id>
        <phase>post-integration-test</phase>          Stop
        <goals>                                        container
            <goal>stop</goal>
        </goals>
    </execution>
</executions>
...
```

As you see in the listing, Cargo provides an API that allows you to easily use and configure your application server. You can deploy your application into the container and run your tests. This dramatically increases your productivity, and it can be integrated into your continuous build script.

Cargo helps to manage containers. In the next section, we'll discuss another integration server called TeamCity, which has several helpful features, particularly for running remote builds.

6.4   *Remote builds with TeamCity*

In section 6.1, I mentioned that you should use the same build scripts locally that you use for the central build, but running builds and tests locally has drawbacks. One major drawback is that the procedure allocates your local desktop to this task—you can't work on other things, or your work is at least delayed until the build is finished. Another drawback is that your private environment probably isn't equal to the central one that hosts the build server. But you don't want to trigger the central build server during your development because you don't know whether your software contains bugs or doesn't integrate. Besides that, the central build server normally pulls sources out of the VCS that are already committed to VCS. You don't want to commit your untested changes to the VCS merely to see if they'll build successfully. One solution is to run your private build using a centralized build server.

To test how successful your changes are, you can create personal builds in JetBrains' TeamCity (www.jetbrains.com/teamcity/) using its remote run feature. The modified files are submitted to the server, bypassing the VCS. In addition, using the pretested commit feature, the project codebase always stays clean: If the tests fail, the code isn't integrated into the codebase, the developer can safely work on a fix, and the team's work isn't interrupted. If the build is successful, the changes are committed to the VCS automatically (this

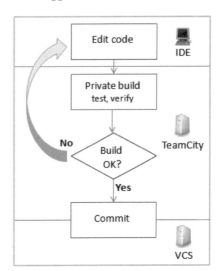

Figure 6.3   Continuous integration with remote run and delayed commit. A build doesn't block the IDE, because it runs on the central build server. If the private build passes, the underlying code changes are committed to the VCS. If the build fails, the central VCS isn't affected.

is an opt-in request). From there, the changes will be automatically integrated into the next regular integration build (see figure 6.3).

Like other continuous integration servers, TeamCity is based on a central job that starts builds and a web application for managing build plans. You must enrich your IDE to support the remote run feature. For Eclipse, you must download the dedicated Eclipse plug-in if it's not part of the TeamCity standard distribution you may have already downloaded. Support for IntelliJ IDEA and Microsoft Visual Studio are similar to the Eclipse support.

> **YOUTRACK BUG-TRACKING INTEGRATION** Because JetBrains' bug tracker, You-Track, integrates with TeamCity, you can easily see how your code changes align with your bug-fixing activity, and you can determine which bugs have been fixed in a particular product build.

What does it look like when you use TeamCity's remote run feature? Figure 6.4 shows Eclipse's TeamCity Remote Run dialog box, which is opened by selecting Team > Remote Run in a project's context menu. You can enter the username and password for connecting TeamCity and Subversion, if necessary.

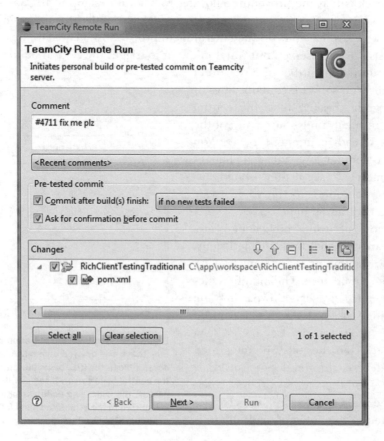

Figure 6.4 Eclipse's TeamCity Remote Run dialog box: Although you see all your local changes (compared to the central VCS) and you can commit your changes (both when a build runs and after it succeeds), the changes are committed to the VCS and not the other way around.

After the build is finished and special post conditions are met, you can enter a commit message and decide whether you want to commit your changes to the VCS or not. Besides the traditional condition that no test failed, you can also configure the changes that are put into the VCS if no *new* tests failed. In figure 6.4, we'll also be asked if we want to commit, after the build runs.

The Changes pane at the bottom of the dialog box lists all local changes compared to the central VCS. In this example, we changed one file (the POM). In a subsequent dialog box (not displayed here), you must specify which TeamCity build configuration you want to link to your build request. TeamCity lists the existing build plans and anticipates which ones have applicable configurations. Your selection is saved locally, so you must do this linking only once.

After starting the private build on the remote server, TeamCity documents its activity on its web interface. Figure 6.5 shows the UI, illustrating that personal changes are transferred and the remote build will start soon. Although the TeamCity dashboard does show the current activities (including personal builds), the personal build isn't added to the public build history. You must go into the build's detail page (by clicking on Build Me) to see a full list of all builds (regular builds and private builds). They're differentiated by the icons there.

— ⓘ **Build Me** ˅			
#55	🗪 Personal changes transferred: 10.45Kb total ˅	No artifacts	admin (1) ˅	22s left ▮▮▮
#54	● Tests failed: 4, passed: 76, ignored: 2 ˅	Artifacts ˅	michael (1) ˅	01 Mar 10 23:32 (1m:06s)

Figure 6.5   The TeamCity web interface, documenting that a personal build has started

When the private build completes successfully (according to the configured metrics), a new dialog box opens in the Eclipse IDE and asks if you want to commit(see figure 6.6). If you confirm at this point, a commit is executed: Your changes will be checked into the VCS. This may motivate a new central build, if you've configured new builds to run after VCS changes occur.

Delayed Commit

❓ Remote Run completed succesfully, would you like to commit changes?

Commit comment: "#4711 fix me"

[Yes]   [No]

Figure 6.6   In Eclipse, TeamCity asks you to commit your changes to the VCS. The remote run of your build completed successfully, and you must now click Yes to commit the changes. All information (changes, commit messages) should already be known.

TeamCity provides several useful features and is the preferred CI server for many development teams. Remote runs (together with delayed commits) are another practice that will help your team enjoy a productive development environment.

6.5   *Summary*

In this chapter, we talked about productive environments. You learned what it means to work in isolated developer workspaces and which strategies and tools you can use. We talked about general strategies and best practices and how they're covered by Maven. We talked about mocking with Mockito, using DRY tests, wrapping application servers with Cargo, and running private builds with delayed VCS commit using Team-City. This chapter provided a number of helpful examples and use cases to explain what it means to have a productive environment and how to implement productive environments.

In the next chapter, we'll focus on CI recipes and tools.

Advanced CI tools and recipes

This chapter covers

- Tools and recipes for continuous integration
- Approaches for integrating different artifact types
- Strategies and tooling for staging artifacts

This chapter provides techniques to help you implement advanced continuous integration (CI). As you learned in earlier chapters, CI is the backbone of an Agile ALM. But why do we need to discuss *advanced* CI? CI is a widespread discipline. Its basic concepts are widely understood and supported by all build servers (such as Jenkins, Bamboo, TeamCity, Continuum, and CruiseControl), but advanced topics, such as those I cover in this chapter, are rarely covered elsewhere. This chapter explains how to implement Agile ALM in the context of CI, as illustrated in figure 7.1.

> **NOTE** If you're interested in CI basics that we don't cover in this book, consider reading *Continuous Integration: Improving Software Quality and Reducing Risk* by Paul. M. Duvall (Addison-Wesley, 2007) or Martin Fowler's free online resources (http://martinfowler.com/articles/continuousIntegration.html).

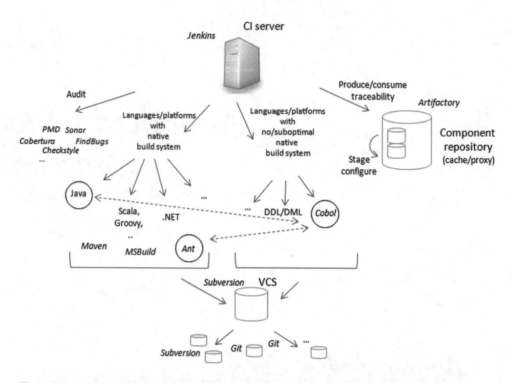

Figure 7.1 Advanced CI scenarios for Agile ALM that are covered in this chapter: building and integrating platforms or languages (.NET and integrating Cobol by using Java and Ant), enabling traceable deployment of artifacts, building artifacts for multiple target environments (staging these artifacts by configuration, without rebuilding them), bridging different VCSs, and performing audits.

This chapter starts with examples of integrating different artifact types into a comprehensive CI ecosystem. The first approach is to use a platform or language (such as Java), and the build systems it offers, to drive and manage the builds of other languages or platforms (such as Cobol). This approach is helpful in situations where languages and platforms don't have their own native build systems (or have only support for integrating with an enterprise integration system). The examples we'll look at will deal with those languages and platforms (specifically, integrating Cobol by using Java and Ant).

Where possible, we'll use the tools available for the platform and then integrate the native build scripts on the common build servers. We'll also cover .NET and look at how to build and integrate source code using lightweight (open and flexible) tools, such as Subversion and TeamCity, without having to use proprietary products like Microsoft's Team Foundation Server.

After discussing builds (spanning different artifact types), we'll talk about creating builds for multiple target environments. This is a good example of *staging*, discussed in chapters 2 and 3. We'll cover strategies and solutions for promoting artifacts to other target environments, merely by configuring them (without rebuilding).

Then, we'll discuss bridging different VCSs. As you already know, all artifact types (Java, Cobol, and so on) should be stored in a VCS, but sometimes you might need to work with different VCSs in a complex project setup. You may need to view this effort as a soft migration from one VCS tool to another, where you don't try to replace the entire VCS in one step. These are all common scenarios, and I'll explain how to deal with them in an Agile ALM context. We'll look at an example of how to bridge a widespread enterprise VCS (Subversion) to another one (Git, a distributed VCS) to implement feature branching.

We'll look at builds and audits with Jenkins. Checkstyle, FindBugs, PMD, Cobertura, and Sonar perform code audits. Then, you'll learn strategies for building specific facets of your builds depending on where the build is running, and for injecting version numbers into the built applications. Another important aspect of this discussion will be deploying and staging artifacts or builds with Jenkins and Artifactory. In this section, I'll show you how to deploy and stage a Maven based project to the component repository in a consistent and traceable way. By default, deploying a multi-module Maven project (a project that consists of multiple modules) results in deploying each module isolated from each other. This approach will illustrate how to deploy the complete application in a single downstream step, but only after each module build (including successful compiles and tests) has already succeeded.

All these views and issues are important facets of running a comprehensive, uniform Agile ALM infrastructure. This chapter explains strategies, and it shows by example how you can orchestrate tool chains in a cohesive and integrated way. Strategies and specific tool examples will show you how to set up an open Agile ALM infrastructure.

Let's start by looking at how to integrate legacy Cobol applications.

7.1   *Integrating other artifact types: Cobol*

Integrating Java artifacts is a common task. All you need to get started is a build server and a build script. Compiling, packaging, and deploying Java artifacts are routine jobs. But Agile ALM comprises more than operating on only Java and derived artifacts compiled to Java bytecode (like Groovy, Scala, JRuby, and more). In this book, I can't possibly illustrate how to integrate all the different artifact types and programming languages. In this section, though, we'll look at how to prototype the processing of Cobol host sources. *Host* refers to IBM System/360 compatible product lines with operating systems like OS/390, MVS, and z/OS.

In this section, we'll also look at an example of how to set up a CI environment to support Cobol development and how to control the processing using Java. We'll integrate building Cobol artifacts into our CI ecosystem. This real-world solution also shows a strategy for continuously integrating and building non-Java artifact types. This approach shows how to use a platform or language (like Java) to drive and manage the build of other languages or platforms.

7.1.1   *Preconditions and basic thoughts*

Traditionally, Cobol development is done in a mainframe-based environment: Cobol sources are written and compiled on the host. Compiled Cobol sources are called "load modules," or "modules." After compiling sources, the generated modules are loaded to host libraries. This mainframe-based approach is different from how other applications are developed, such as Java applications, where you don't develop sources on a host or transfer sources to a central host in order to compile them.

Different approaches often lead to silos, but that need not be the case. There are ways to bring those two worlds—developing Java and Cobol applications—together, and to foster a comprehensive Agile ALM approach. Bridging the two platform ecosystems is possible by using the same IDE for developing software in Java and Cobol and using CI in both cases. Feature-rich, commercial tools (such as products of the IBM Rational product family) nowadays enable developing and even compiling Cobol sources on the developer's desktop workspaces.

Many projects find it helpful to transfer Cobol sources from the developer's workspace to the host manually, such as via FTP, in order to compile the sources on the host. As this section will show, you can also develop Cobol sources on the desktop and use the host compiler to compile the sources, in an automatic, lightweight, and convenient way.

A basic precondition for processing Cobol sources is that the sources must be imported and managed in a VCS. We've already discussed the importance of managing sources in a VCS, and Cobol source code should be stored in a VCS as is the source code of any other programming language. Some people may suggest that this isn't necessary because Cobol is a mainframe host language, and there have been mainframe facilities (such as libraries) in which both source and compiled binaries have been managed for some time. But the advantages of putting Cobol sources into a VCS include benefiting from all the features of a modern VCS and being able to add Cobol processing to a CI system. The CI system can trigger Cobol processing on the host continuously. Compiled Cobol sources (binaries, load modules) can be stored in a VCS or a component repository so they can be reused later by other CI build jobs that stage those modules to other test environments on the host.

During software development, a repetitive activity is using an IDE, such as Eclipse (with its Cobol support), and synchronizing the sources to a VCS with Eclipse's excellent support for all common types of VCSs. But after editing sources, how do we compile them, and how do we put them onto the host? By using Cobol compilers, the compiling can be done on the developer's desktop. But it's much more common to upload the sources to the host for compiling, and not upload binaries into libraries.

Developing Cobol applications in an IDE on the desktop and offloading the build onto the mainframe further improves the quality, reduces the risk of late bug detection, accelerates feedback cycles, and prevents the desktop from being blocked by long processing times. Offloading the build to the host fosters productive workspaces (discussed in chapter 5). Besides that, when developing Cobol applications, desktop and workspace Cobol compilers may differ in functionality and handling. But how can we transfer sources to the host?

You can use FTP for communication between a developer's desktop and the host. To do this, you need the following:

- A host machine that runs an FTP server.
- An authorized user with a valid user account.

Once you have the FTP server and the authorized user up and running, you can set up FTP-based processing. In general, the FTP server can address and communicate with the host's job entry subsystem (JES). The JES is part of the operating system used to schedule and run jobs and control their output. On a mainframe, the job control language (JCL) controls the jobs. For instance, a JCL script may contain commands to compile a Cobol source. JCL scripts consist of steps (that are commands for the host) and programming features to implement conditional statements and workflow. If you submit JCL scripts into the JES, the resulting jobs are processed immediately, depending on job priorities. Here is a small JCL example:

```
//XXXXXXXJ JOB (ACCTCODE),'ABCDEF',NOTIFY=D123456,CLASS=I,
//          MSGLEVEL=(1,1),MSGCLASS=C
//*
//STEP1    EXEC PGM=ABCDE99
```

As you can see, it's a simple file with only one step. An FTP server provides access to JES functions, including submitting and deleting jobs, displaying the status of jobs, and receiving the output of JCL messages.

There are many possible ways to manage your FTP communication. We'll discuss the two main ones here, using either Ant or the Java API. We'll start with the pragmatic approach, which uses Ant.

7.1.2   *FTP communication with Ant*

The Ant approach is pragmatic, in that it helps you handle the processing of JCL jobs in a straightforward way. This approach has two benefits. One, it's lightweight, and, two, it's mainly scripted in a native build scripting language (Ant) and can be directly included in a CI process. You don't need to write a full-featured program to set up the communication between the build server or the developers' machines and the host.

In brief, the approach of processing the Cobol sources is as follows:

- The CI server checks out Cobol sources from the VCS and generates signal files, as well as JCL files (one signal file and one JCL file for each Cobol source), and a bash script (see figure 7.2).
- The bash script is triggered by CI and transfers the Cobol and JCL files to the host.
- On the host, the JCL files kick off host jobs that process the Cobol files according to the type of processing defined in the JCL files. Typically, processing means that Cobol sources are compiled, and generated libraries are loaded on the host. The host runs the JCL jobs asynchronously, so we use signal files on the CI server to monitor the process.

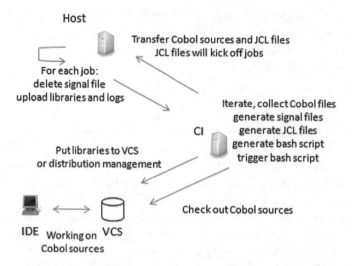

Figure 7.2   The processing of Cobol sources is based on Ant scripts that are dynamically generated and triggered by the CI server. Files are transferred from the CI server to the host and vice versa via FTP. CI with Cobol is similar to how we integrate Java applications: Cobol sources are managed by the VCS. The CI server checks Cobol sources and triggers and then monitors the success of Cobol compilation on the host. Compiled Cobol sources can be loaded into libraries on the host and transferred back to the CI server to store them in the VCS or a component repository for further reuse.

- FTP commands inside the JCL files trigger the transfer of generated libraries (the compiled Cobol sources) and log files back to the CI server.
- In each JCL job, an FTP command removes the signal files from the CI server to indicate that the processing of this specific Cobol source is finished. The CI server can put the libraries into the VCS or distribution management in order to reuse these binaries for other test environments without again compiling them (*compile once, run everywhere*).

This lightweight process is based on a sequence of dynamically created Ant scripts that check sources from the VCS, generate files, run a bash[1] script to upload them to the host, wait for the host to process all the files, and collect the returned files.

Here are the steps of the solution in more detail:

1 Check out all Cobol sources from the VCS. Use Ant for this.

NOTE   This is a generic solution (which will work regardless of the names of the Cobol sources), so the following steps include the generation of generic scripts.

---

[1]   Bash, or a Windows equivalent. Although Java is platform-independent, I've assumed Linux or Unix to be the test and production environments in this section. This won't necessarily be the case, though.

2   Iterate over the Cobol sources to identify the filenames and store them in a Java collection. Do this in a Java class that's called by your Ant script. You can also write your own Ant task that wraps the functionality and can be used directly from outside your Ant script.

3   In the same Java class, generate a bash script to transport the files (the Cobol sources and the to-be-generated JCL files that will include logic about what to do with the Cobol source on the host) via FTP directly. This means you'll use FTP commands in your bash script. The script starts with #!/bin/sh and it's essential to specify the FTP site correctly in the JCL: filetype=jes for the jobs and filetype=seq for the artifacts, as shown in listing 7.1. You can use variables for environment-specific configuration settings. The specific values for these placeholders are held in a Java properties file and can be injected into Ant scripts by filter-chaining at execution time (more on Ant's filtering feature in section 7.3).

Listing 7.1   Generating bash script for uploading files

```
for (Iterator<FileHandler> iterator = cics.iterator(); iterator
                        .hasNext();) {              ◁──┐ Iterate all files
    FileHandler fh = (FileHandler) iterator.next();    │ to be processed
    if (fh != null) {
        print += "quote SITE FILETYPE=SEQ"        ◁──┐ Generate script
  + System.getProperty("line.separator") + "put "     │ to upload artifacts
  + path + fh.getNameWithExtension()
  + " '${cics.sourcelib}(" + fh.getName() + ")'"   ◁──┐ Use Ant variables,
  + System.getProperty("line.separator")              │ to be filtered later
  + "quote SITE FILETYPE=JES"                    ◁──── Generate JCL files
  + System.getProperty("line.separator") + "put "
  + path + fh.getName() + ".jcl" + " "
  + fh.getName() + ".jcl"
  + System.getProperty("line.separator");
    }
}
```

4   In the Java class, you also generate an Ant script that uses the Ant touch task.[2] Using it once touches every source and generates *signal* files: one use of this command impacts each Cobol source you checked out from the VCS and creates an empty file for each Cobol source. These empty files can be called *barriers* or *signal* files. The reason for creating these files is that once you put JCL files on the host, they are processed by the host asynchronously. By introducing these barriers, the transferring system (the CI server) can monitor the asynchronous processing and it will be informed when the processing on the host is completed. You call the generated Ant script dynamically to create these empty files; you can place these barrier files into an inbox folder.

---

[2]   See the Ant documentation of the touch task: http://ant.apache.org/manual/Tasks/touch.html.

The use case of this section shows that you can upload the Cobol artifacts and the corresponding JCL files in pairs to control processing of the Cobol artifacts. All files (Cobol sources as well as the JCL files) must be in place for the script to find them. You can configure where to place the files. It's good practice to copy all Cobol sources to an outbox folder where you've also placed the corresponding JCL files. The following listing shows an example touch script snippet that generates Ant script.

Listing 7.2   Generating touch script

```
private String getTouchScript(){
    int countCics =                                          Retrieve number
      ((ArrayList<FileHandler>) cics).size();         ◁──┐   of sources
                                                          └── to be processed
    String touchScript = "<?xml version=\"1.0\" encoding=\"ISO-8859-1\"?>"
        + System.getProperty("line.separator")
        + "<project name=\"waitfor\" default=\"wait\" basedir=\".\">"
        + System.getProperty("line.separator")
        + "<target name=\"wait\">";
    for (int i = 0; i < countCics; i++) {
        FileHandler fc = cics.get(i);
        touchScript = touchScript
      + System.getProperty("line.separator")            Create empty file
      + "<touch file=\""                          ◁──┘   with Ant touch task
            + inbox + "${myuniqueprefix}." + fc.getName()   ◁──┐ Prefix filenames
            + ".running\"/>";                                  └─ with unique IDs
    }

    touchScript=touchScript +
    System.getProperty("line.separator")+"</target>" +
    System.getProperty("line.separator")+"</project>";
    return touchScript;
}
```

5 In the Java class, you dynamically generate one JCL file for each Cobol source. This JCL contains the JCL steps for processing the individual Cobol resources on the host. The JCL can vary, depending on the type of Cobol file (for instance, online or batch) and will include different JCL steps or Cobol compiling options. You can also include FTP commands in your JCL snippets. Firing these into the JES results in host jobs uploading log files or load libraries to the build server. You must add an FTP command to your JCL to remove the signal file that monitors the processing for this JCL.

Executing the bash script transports the files to the host. You don't need to manually call the script, as it can be part of your build logic. For example, a sequence of Ant scripts can start by generating the files and then running them. In the script, you must include logic to pause until the host removes all signals. You can, for instance, write a small Java class, creating threads monitoring the inbox folder and its entries. When the folder is empty, the host has processed all jobs. Afterward, you can collect possible return files (like load modules) and store them in the VCS.

MAVEN AND ANT Ant scripts can be integrated with Maven scripts by using Maven's AntRun plug-in for Ant: http://maven.apache.org/plugins/maven-antrun-plugin/.

We've reviewed automating common tasks, such as FTP, using Ant and scripting. Next we'll examine how to use Java for FTP communication.

7.1.3 FTP communication with Java

Instead of using Ant to handle communication with the host, you can code it with Java. You can work with sockets yourself, or you can use the Commons Net library (http://commons.apache.org/net/). This library is an easy-to-use abstraction for handling different protocols, including FTP.

> **NOTE** Wherever possible, you should use common abstractions for communication, which means using higher levels of the Open Systems Interconnection (OSI) model (such as the application layer). FTP and HTTP are examples of such common abstractions.

Let's transfer the JCL file shown earlier onto the host and execute it in the JES. The following listing shows how to achieve this with Java.

Listing 7.3   Uploading artifacts by using FTP

```
public class FileTransferProtocol {
    public static void main (String [ ] args)  {
    String serverName ="my.zos.mainframe";
    String userName ="userid";
    String password ="********";
    FTPClient ftp = new FTPClient();
    try {                                                ❶ Connect to
        ftp.connect (serverName);                          FTP server
        String replyText =ftp.getReplyString();
        System.out.println (replyText) ;
    }
    catch (Exception  e)  {
            e.printStackTrace ();
    }
    try {                                                ❷ Log into
            ftp.login (userName, password);                FTP server
            String replyText = ftp.getReplyString();
            System.out.println (replyText);
    } catch (Exception e) {
            e.printStackTrace();
    }
    try {                                                ❸ Configure
            ftp.site ("filetype=jes");                     file type
            String replyText = ftp.getReplyString();     ❹ Retrieve
            System.out.println (replyText);                result
    }
    catch (Exception e) {
            e.printStackTrace() ;
```

```
        }
        try {
                FileInputStream inputStream =
                  new FileInputStream ("C:\\job.jcl") ;
                ftp.storeFile (serverName,inputStream) ;         Read file,
                String replyText = ftp.getReplyString() ;    5   submit to host
                System.out.println (replyText);
        }
        catch (Exception e) {
                e.printStackTrace() ;
        }
        try {
                ftp.quit() ;
        }
        catch (Exception e) {
                e.printStackTrace();
        }
    }
}
```

For more details on how to manage host jobs with Java, see the IBM documentation.[3]

Listing 7.3 starts by connecting ❶ and logging in ❷ to the remote FTP server. Commons Net provides an FTP client; you don't need to work with sockets on your own. We then configure the file type ❸, which outputs "200" if it all worked successfully, retrieves the result ❹, confirms that "200 SITE Command was accepted", and reads the file to submit it to the host ❺.

Please keep in mind that those are the most important high-level points. In addition, we handle exceptions (but only on a basic level, in order to avoid long code listings and an overly complex example).

For uploading JCL and generating jobs, it's essential to set the file type to jes so the jobs get executed. On the other hand, for uploading Cobol sources, you need to set the file type to seq. This way they're stored in a library instead of in the job queue.

Afterward, you can access the results of your operation and wait for the host to execute the job. The API is powerful: You can monitor the host job queue and scan for your jobs. You can also configure your FTP client by assigning a custom parser to work on the results in a more convenient way.

You can integrate the compiled Java class into a CI process depending on your requirements. For example, the Java class can be called by an Ant script or be included as an Ant task.

Java is powerful, but Microsoft .NET also has many helpful features, which we'll cover next.

---

[3] For instance, see "Submit batch jobs from Java on z/OS" by Nagesh Subrahmanyam (www.ibm.com/developerworks/systems/library/es-batch-zos.html) and "Access z/OS batch jobs from Java" by Evan Williams (www.ibm.com/developerworks/systems/library/es-zosbatchjavav/index.html).

7.2   *Integrating other artifact types: .NET*

>   —*This section contributed by Hadi Hariri*

This section will show you how easy it is to use a build framework such as MSBuild to build .NET software. Additionally, it will demonstrate how to add CI with .NET applications to an Agile ALM CI ecosystem that can also integrate other artifact types, such as Java.

To demonstrate using CI with .NET, we'll use TeamCity as the build server, but build frameworks like MSBuild are agnostic regarding build servers, so you can add your build scripts to other build servers as well. TeamCity is a powerful build server that can be used to integrate different platforms and languages, including Java and Microsoft-related ones, in parallel.

The strategy presented in this section is to orchestrate best-of-breed tools and integrate them into a configured, personalized toolchain (as discussed in chapter 1). You don't need to stick to proprietary Microsoft tooling, such as Visual Studio, to build your .NET software; rather, you can use lightweight tools instead. Additionally, it's not necessary to use Microsoft Team Foundation Server to manage your .NET sources; you can manage the sources in parallel with other project artifacts in the same tool, such as Subversion, in order to foster an Agile ALM approach. Finally, this section shows an example implementation of the service-oriented approach that you learned about in chapter 1. You'll see how easy it is to temporarily add additional build machines to your CI system by running builds in the cloud.

Like many other tools and practices in .NET, CI originated from the world of Java. But despite its relative newcomer status, .NET has certainly gained maturity in terms of adoption of best practices that evolved in the Java world. Much of this is impacted by the number of tools in .NET that support the key elements required for successful CI.

> ### Ted Neward on integrating .NET and Java systems
>
> I once asked Ted Neward, .NET and Java expert, "What's your opinion about adding .NET artifacts to continuous integration processes and systems that are based on open source or lightweight tools, in the case that projects don't want to use TFS, Visual Studio, or other Microsoft products?" This was his answer:
>
> "In general, as much as I spend time handling integration between .NET and Java systems, I'm not a huge fan of mixing the developer tools across those two platforms—trying to get Maven to build .NET artifacts, for example, can be a royal pain to get right. In general, the best success I've had with this is to fall back to MSBuild, and kick it off as you would any other command-line tool. The build results can be captured to a text file and examined later, or if a more fine-grained control is needed, a shell around MSBuild can be built (probably with PowerShell, depending on the complexity of the problem) to capture events during the build. This doesn't mean I'm going to tell .NET developers to stick with plain-vanilla Visual Studio or TFS, mind you. Better tools definitely exist for handling continuous integration builds than what comes out of the box. Pick one of those CI tools, figure out how to invoke a command-line tool from the CI infrastructure, use that to kick off MSBuild, and call it a day."

When talking about build tools in the .NET space, there are two main contenders. On one side there's NAnt, which is a port of Java's Ant, and on the other there's MSBuild, which is the .NET framework's native build system from Microsoft. The core principles behind MSBuild are the same as those for NAnt.

7.2.1   Using MSBuild to build .NET projects

MSBuild provides a series of targets, each of which defines one or more tasks to be carried out. Targets are a sequence of grouped steps; this is similar to Ant, where targets are a sequence of Ant tasks. The following listing shows a sample build script.

Listing 7.4   A simple build script for .NET with MSBuild

```xml
<?xml version="1.0" encoding="utf-8" ?>
<Project
xmlns="http://schemas.microsoft.com/developer/msbuild/2003"
DefaultTargets="Build">
  <ItemGroup>                                               ◁──┐  Custom item
    <Compile Include="*.cs"/>                                   │  group
  </ItemGroup>
  <PropertyGroup Condition="'$(BuildType)'=='Release'">    ◁──┐
    <OutputPath>Bin\</OutputPath>                              │  Property groups
    <OutputAssembly>Example.exe</OutputAssembly>               │  using conditions
  </PropertyGroup>
  <PropertyGroup Condition="'$(BuildType)'=='Debug'">
    <OutputPath>Debug\</OutputPath>
    <OutputAssembly>Example.exe</OutputAssembly>
    <Optimize>false</Optimize>
    <DebugType>full</DebugType>
  </PropertyGroup>
  <Target Name="Clean">                                     ◁──┐  Targets
    <RemoveDir Directories="$(OutputPath)"                      │
       Condition="Exists('$(OutputPath)')"/>
  </Target>
  <Target Name="Build">
    <MakeDir Condition="!Exists('$(OutputPath)')"
       Directories="$(OutputPath)"/>
    <Csc Optimize="$(Optimize)" DebugType="$(DebugType)"
      Sources="@(Compile)"
      OutputAssembly="$(OutputPath)$(OutputAssembly)"/>
  </Target>
  <Target Name="Rebuild" DependsOnTargets="Clean;Build"/>
</Project>
```

As you can see, there's support for concepts such as multiple targets (that is, one script being able to run different tasks and operations), property definitions, and conditions. Like NAnt, MSBuild is also extensible. You can create new tasks by implementing an interface and referencing it as an external assembly.[4]

---

[4] A complete reference on all possible commands can be found at Microsoft's ".NET Development" site (http://msdn.microsoft.com/en-us/library/aa139615.aspx).

TeamCity, from JetBrains, supports CI for both Java and .NET projects and has become one of the most popular CI servers.

7.2.2   *Using TeamCity to trigger .NET builds*

TeamCity ((see http://www.jetbrains.com/teamcity/) is available in two flavors: Professional, which is free, and Enterprise. It has quickly gained popularity over other tools, such as CruiseControl, due to its ease of use and rich feature set. In this section, we're going to look at some of the features that TeamCity provides, starting with visual configuration of the environment.

VISUAL CONFIGURATION ENVIRONMENT

One of the more painful issues with CruiseControl is the requirement to set up the configuration through XML files and having to make these changes on the production CI server. With TeamCity, rather than requiring users to have permission to access folders on the server, all access control is handled via a web interface, allowing different levels of permissions. All project configurations are carried out using this interface, making setup easier and less error-prone.

Figure 7.3 shows how you can configure a build runner to choose between Ant, Maven2, MSBuild, NAnt, and many others.

Ease of configuration is a main feature of TeamCity, although its ability to facilitate integration with other tools is also essential.

INTEGRATION IS CORE

TeamCity was built with the goal of being integrated with other tools and frameworks. Each developer or company has its own policies and ways of working. Some prefer to use tools such as MSTest for testing and MSBuild for build automation, whereas others

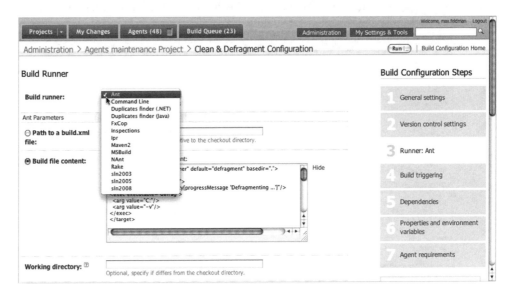

Figure 7.3   Configuration in TeamCity: selecting a build runner (such as MSBuild or NAnt)

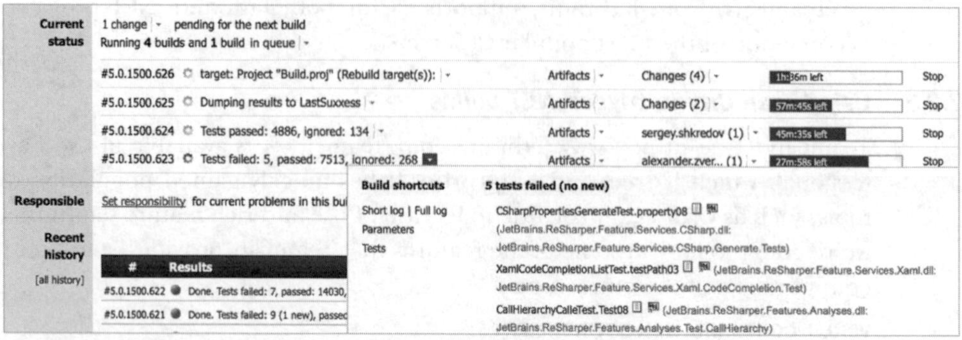

Current status	1 change ⌄ pending for the next build
	Running 4 builds and 1 build in queue ⌄

#5.0.1500.626	○ target: Project "Build.proj" (Rebuild target(s)): ⌄	Artifacts ⌄	Changes (4) ⌄	1h:36m left	Stop
#5.0.1500.625	○ Dumping results to LastSuxxess ⌄	Artifacts ⌄	Changes (2) ⌄	57m:45s left	Stop
#5.0.1500.624	○ Tests passed: 4886, ignored: 134 ⌄	Artifacts ⌄	sergey.shkredov (1) ⌄	45m:35s left	Stop
#5.0.1500.623	○ Tests failed: 5, passed: 7513, ignored: 268 ◨	Artifacts ⌄	alexander.zver... (1) ⌄	27m:58s left	Stop

Responsible: Set responsibility for current problems in this bu...

Build shortcuts

Short log | Full log
Parameters
Tests

5 tests failed (no new)

CSharpPropertiesGenerateTest.property08 ▤ ◫
(JetBrains.ReSharper.Feature.Services.CSharp.dll:
JetBrains.ReSharper.Feature.Services.CSharp.Generate.Tests)

XamlCodeCompletionListTest.testPath03 ▤ ◫ (JetBrains.ReSharper.Feature.Services.Xaml.dll:
JetBrains.ReSharper.Feature.Services.Xaml.CodeCompletion.Test)

CallHierarchyCalleTest.Test08 ▤ ◫ (JetBrains.ReSharper.Features.Analyses.dll:
JetBrains.ReSharper.Features.Analyses.Test.CallHierarchy)

Recent history
[all history]

#	Results
#5.0.1500.622	● Done. Tests failed: 7, passed: 14030,
#5.0.1500.621	● Done. Tests failed: 9 (1 new), passed

Figure 7.4   Example TeamCity output screen showing test results

prefer to use open source tools such as NUnit and NAnt. TeamCity tries to accommodate as many frameworks as possible by providing support for a variety of them. This is a key feature when it comes to having a productive CI environment.

One of the core benefits of CI is immediate feedback. When you break the build, you need to know why, to see test results, and so on. All this needs to be easily accessible and viewable without requiring a lot of effort. By supporting different testing and code coverage frameworks, TeamCity allows this seamless integration.

Figure 7.4 shows a sample output screen of build results with relevant information that allows you to investigate further if required.

Apart from the more traditional build tools, TeamCity also supports some newer tools that are starting to gain interest among developers, such as Ruby's Rake for build automation or Cucumber for testing. In addition to integrating with unit testing, code coverage, and automation tools, TeamCity also works with various types of source

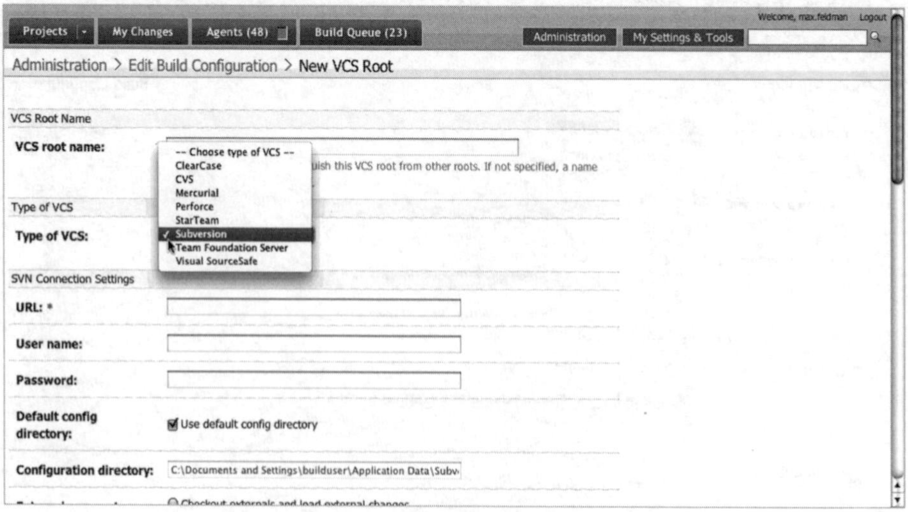

Figure 7.5   Selecting a VCS for the .NET project build (with Subversion)

control management, including Team Foundation Server, Subversion, and some more popular distributed VCSs such as Git and Mercurial, as shown in figure 7.5.

Another important aspect when it comes to integration is issue tracking systems. Again, TeamCity allows integration with common tools such as JIRA as well as Jet-Brains' own issue tracker called YouTrack.

CI with .NET, but without Microsoft

Although you can use Microsoft tools (like the Team Foundation Server) to store your artifacts and run builds, this isn't necessary. Tools like TeamCity or Jenkins are popular for building .NET projects (using MSBuild or NBuild), and you can store the artifacts in a common VCS, like Subversion.

What's different when comparing CI with .NET to CI with Java is that you must use the specific .NET tools, such as MSBuild or NAnt, for building (and testing) the .NET components in what's known as a *managed environment*. The most important point here is that you can host your .NET projects on the same VCS where you host projects for other languages and platforms (such as Java) and integrate them on the same build server where you also integrate other projects (such as Java projects).

There are also other approaches to integrating different platforms and languages and using a common, unified tool infrastructure, such as hosting your sources in TFS and building them with Jenkins (with the help of Jenkins's TFS plug-in).

The flexibility of building and storing sources makes Agile ALM effective. Using remote build agents and cloud computing are also popular practices.

BUILD AGENTS AND CLOUD COMPUTING

Many CI tools, including Jenkins, support the concept of build agents. The idea is to have one machine that handles the process and delegates the computing to other machines. As such, the main CI server would handle the configuring, reporting, and other non–CPU intensive processes, and one or more machines (called *agents*) would handle the compiling, building, and testing of the code. Figure 7.6 shows a build matrix that indicates the status of all agents and their utilization.

TeamCity has supported the concept of build agents from the beginning, but what's new in the recent releases is its integration with cloud computing. Amazon's EC2 cloud computing infrastructure is a pay-per-use concept where you pay for machines based on the number of hours they're on—if your machine is running for, say, five hours, you would be charged for five hours of use. TeamCity uses EC2 via virtual build agents, which are similar to standard ones except that they run on virtual instances on the Amazon EC2. This means that TeamCity can dynamically start as many instances of agents as needed in order to keep the build queue under control during high loads. Additionally, TeamCity can shut down virtual build agents when they aren't needed anymore; this minimizes EC2 consumption of uptime.

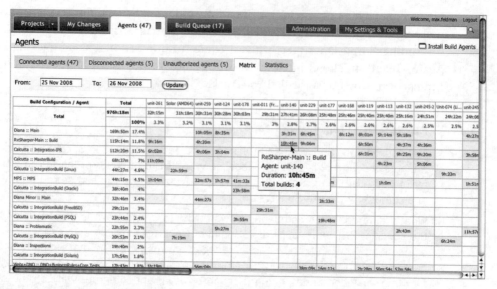

Figure 7.6   TeamCity showing agents

Figure 7.7 shows how to create an EC2 cloud profile in TeamCity.

CI is the same, whether it's in Java, Ruby, or .NET. What's important when it comes to implementing CI is having the correct tools to make the whole process efficient and fast. Spending time to integrate multiple products for every project is cumbersome

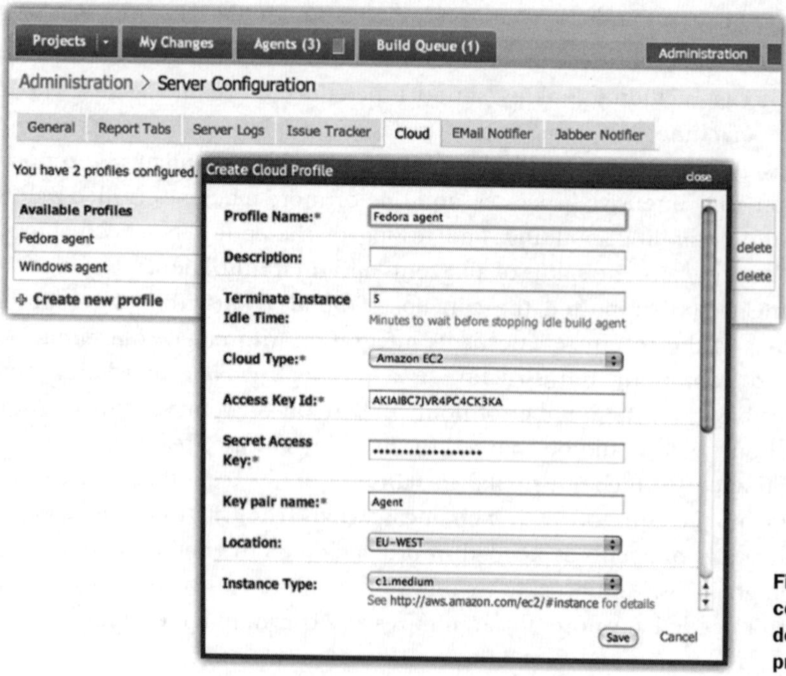

Figure 7.7   Server configuration, defining a cloud profile for EC2

and a waste of resources, and that's why it's important to have tools that can seamlessly work with multiple frameworks, platforms, and tools, such as Jenkins and TeamCity. This leads to an effective toolchain that consists of one central CI server that integrates and works with different platforms and tools, such as Java and .NET.

7.3   Configure: building (web) apps for multiple environments

—This section contributed by Max Antoni

Java applications consist of artifacts such as EAR, WAR, or JAR packages. When developing an application, you might want to do some integration tests and then deploy the application onto a test environment and into production. Deploying the application on one specific machine may require that you configure environment-specific application properties. But you often won't want to run the script on each environment individually because it takes too long and you want to rely on one specific version of the software.

How can you support multiple environments and cope with runtime configurations? Generally, you have many options:

- Use the artifacts and manually configure them for each environment (bad!).
- Aggregate environment-specific data in Java properties, replacing them manually for each environment.
- Write a script that scans configuration files, automatically replacing specific entries with other values.
- Write scripts that check on which server the build is running, the target environment, and where tools are installed, to detect the configuration parameters for the output.
- Use dependency injection, based on the technology you're using.[5]

It's more elegant to use the features your build tool offers. If you use Ant, you can apply its filter-chaining feature. For instance, by embedding a filter chain together with an `expandproperties` command in a `copy` task, Ant will replace placeholders with values of property files. A basic template looks like this:

```
<copy todir="targetDir">
<fileset dir="templates" />
<filterchain>
<expandproperties/>
</filterchain>
</copy>
```

This section will show an elegant solution that uses Maven.

---

[5] One example of using dependency injection with Java EE 6 can be found in Juliano Viana's "Application configuration in Java EE 6 using CDI—a simple example" blog entry on java.net: http://weblogs.java.net/blog/jjviana/archive/2010/05/18/applicaction-configuration-java-ee-6-using-cdi-simple-example.

When people start using Maven, one of the first things they discover is that it always produces a single artifact per POM. This is good for identifying dependencies and avoiding circular dependency issues or duplicated class files in the classpath. In Maven, a specific artifact (that is, a specific version of your artifact) is defined by its `groupId`, `artifactId`, and `version` number (its GAV coordinates, in short). These coordinates shouldn't be changed, even when the artifact is deployed to a different target environment. Let's look at how Maven helps with this configuration using profiles.

A common solution to this configuration problem is to run the build with a different *profile* for each environment (profiles are discussed in section 7.3.3). This has the advantage of keeping the build simple. But the disadvantage is that you can't use the results of the same build in multiple environments. This might be a critical issue if you have to meet common compliance or audit requirements. Besides governance issues, there may be technical reasons to avoid this approach. If you're using the Maven Release plug-in to establish a full-fledged release based on Maven, it becomes a critical limitation because you create the release (that is, the output of the Release plug-in) only once. You would have to check out the sources from the created tag, and then build and deploy it again with the corresponding profiles activated. It's much easier to have a single build that produces all artifacts for all environments.

You should try to keep your configuration data separated from your binaries. With Maven, you can create separate artifacts for each environment by using classifiers, different profiles, or projects.[6] In your build process, by default, you should build all artifacts for all possible target environments.

Another typical way is using assemblies, discussed next.

7.3.1 *Multiple artifacts with assemblies*

Maven has assemblies that let you create multiple distributions of your application. Artifacts may produce a zip file with the source code, a JAR with all dependencies, and much more.

Let's look at an example of a perfect approach for a web application. In this case, we want to produce a WAR file, which we do in a standard POM by specifying war in the packaging tag: `<packaging>war</packaging>`. You can add an assembly to your build's `plugin` section, as shown in the following listing.

Listing 7.5 Maven assembly plug-ins

```
<plugin>
    <artifactId>maven-assembly-plugin</artifactId>
    <configuration>
        <descriptors>
        <descriptor>src/main/assembly/prod.xml</descriptor>    ◁─┐  ❶ Descriptor from
        </descriptors>                                              dedicated
    </configuration>                                                XML file
```

---

[6] See the official documentation on the Maven web page: http://maven.apache.org/guides/mini/guide-building-for-different-environments.html.

```
<executions>
    <execution>                              ❷ Assembly is part of
        <phase>package</phase>                 Maven's package phase
        <goals><goal>attached</goal></goals>  ⟵
    </execution>
</executions>
</plugin>
```

This next example in listing 7.6 produces the assembly ❶ as part of the package phase ❷. By convention, assembly descriptors are placed in src/main/assembly. The assembly descriptor will produce another WAR file next to the one that the POM creates by default. The assembly ID that's specified gets attached to the filename, so you end up with something like this in your target directory:

```
webapp-1.0-SNAPSHOT.war
webapp-1.0-SNAPSHOT-prod.war
```

The referenced assembly descriptor is shown in the following listing.

Listing 7.6 Assembly for production (prod.xml)

```
<assembly>
    <id>prod</id>                          ⟵⎤ Specifies
    <formats                                  ⎦ descriptor
        <format>war</format>
    </formats>

    <includeBaseDirectory>false</includeBaseDirectory>

    <dependencySets>
        <dependencySet>
            <outputDirectory>/</outputDirectory>
            <includes>
                <include>net.huettermann:webapp:war
                </include>
            </includes>                          ⎤ Unpacks
            <unpack>true</unpack>            ⟵ ⎦ generated WAR
            <unpackOptions>                          ⟵⎤ Allows overwriting
                <excludes>                              ⎦ newer files
                    <exclude>**/filtered.properties</exclude>
                </excludes>
            </unpackOptions>
            <scope>runtime</scope>
        </dependencySet>
    </dependencySets>

    <fileSets>
        <fileSet>
            <directory>src/main/config/prod</directory>
            <outputDirectory>WEB-INF/classes</outputDirectory>
            <includes>
                <include>**/*.properties</include>
            </includes>                          ⎤ Specifies environment
            <filtered>true</filtered>        ⟵ ⎦ properties
```

```
          </fileSet>
      </fileSets>
  </assembly>
```

We configure the assembly to produce the same WAR as the normal development version. To do so, we add a dependency set that unpacks the dev WAR file. The production WAR file gets patched with the properties file in the dist directory by configuring a file set in the prod assembly.

7.3.2   *Applying different configurations*

You don't want to hardcode specific data values in your application. Instead, it's good practice to have environment-specific information grouped together in one or two configuration files. Assuming the configuration of our web application lives in Java property files, we can now have a basic configuration for development and additional configurations for each assembly being created (for example, production). In addition to that, a development team might need different configurations for their environments.

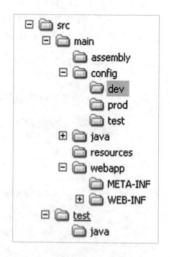

Figure 7.8   Directory structure, including configuration for different environments (dev, prod, test)

To achieve this, we'll first separate the configuration files from other resources and place them into src/main/config/dev and src/main/config/prod. The resulting directory structure is shown in figure 7.8.

The production version of the property files might contain information like database connections, but the development version could use placeholders that are filtered by Maven to contain values for the individual developers' profiles. This can be done by overriding Maven's default configuration for resources in the POM. The following listing shows how to configure the resources folder.

Listing 7.7   Overriding default configuration in the POM

```
<properties>
    <variant>dev</variant>
</properties>

<build>
    <resources>                                        ❶ Platform-specific
        <resource>                                       resource folder
            <directory>src/main/config/dev</directory>
            <targetPath>${project.build.outputDirectory}</targetPath>
            <filtering>true</filtering>
        </resource>                                    ❷ Platform-opaque
        <resource>                                       resource folder
            <directory>src/main/resources</directory>
```

```
            <targetPath>${project.build.outputDirectory}</targetPath>
        </resource>
    </resources>
</build>
```

First we define the platform-specific resource folder ❶ and configure it to allow filtering. Next, we define the resource folder ❷ containing the platform-opaque content.

By setting up the resources correctly, accessing the content is transparent. The next listing shows a major part of our example web application.

Listing 7.8   Accessing configuration properties

```
public class HelloWorldServlet extends HttpServlet {
    private static final long serialVersionUID = 8689617527304514864L;
    private Properties filteredProperties;    ❶ Set environment-dependent properties
    private Properties staticProperties;         ⯇┐ Set environmentally
                                                 ❷ opaque properties

    protected void doGet(HttpServletRequest req, HttpServletResponse resp)
                                 throws ServletException, IOException {
        resp.setStatus(HttpServletResponse.SC_OK);
        String text =
          staticProperties.getProperty("text");     ⯇┐ Access
        PrintWriter writer = resp.getWriter();       │ properties
        writer.append("<html><head><title>");
        writer.append(text);
        writer.append("</title></head><body><h3>");
        writer.append(text);
        writer.append(" ");
        writer.append
          (filteredProperties.getProperty("version"));  ⯇┐ Choose correct
        writer.append("</h3></body></html>");            │ environment
        writer.flush();
    }

    public void init() throws ServletException {
        filteredProperties = new Properties();
        staticProperties = new Properties();
        try {
    filteredProperties.load
      (HelloWorldServlet.class.getResourceAsStream
      ("/filtered.properties"));                        ⯇┐
    staticProperties.load                               ┊  Load
      (HelloWorldServlet.class.getResourceAsStream   ❸ │ properties
      ("/static.properties"));                          ⯇┘
        }
        catch (IOException e) {
        throw new ServletException(e);
        }
        super.init();
    }
}
```

We read the properties content in the `init` method of our servlet. To demonstrate the two ways of accessing content (content that's dependent on the environment ❶ and content that's platform-independent ❷), we specify two properties files. In the Java class, the approach is the same. In both cases we load the resource as a stream ❸. Maven puts the properties into the correct folders.

Running `mvn clean package` now produces two WAR files with different configurations. But we might not want to create all versions for all environments on each build. In the next section, I'll show you how to use a distribution profile to handle multiple environments.

7.3.3   *Using a distribution profile and executing the example*

To optimize the current POM, the entire assembly plug-in configuration in the build section can be wrapped into a `dist` profile. This has the advantage that a developer can choose when to produce the WAR files for all target environments. You can also use this approach to automate this step when producing a release. The following listing shows the profile.

Listing 7.9   Profiles

```
<profiles>
   <profile>
      <id>dist</id>                                    ⟵ Define profile
      <build>                                            dist
         <plugins>
            <plugin>
               <artifactId>maven-assembly-plugin</artifactId>
               <inherited>false</inherited>
               <configuration>
                  <descriptors>
<descriptor>src/main/assembly/test.xml</descriptor>    Define test and
<descriptor>src/main/assembly/prod.xml</descriptor>    prod assemblies
                  </descriptors>
               </configuration>
               <executions>
                  <execution>
                     <phase>package</phase>            ⟵ Execute in
                     <goals>                             package phase
                        <goal>attached</goal>
                     </goals>
                  </execution>
               </executions>
            </plugin>
         </plugins>
      </build>
   </profile>
</profiles>
```

Maven's Release plug-in offers a convenient way to work with profiles during releasing. By configuring the `releaseProfiles` element, the defined profiles are activated automatically. Here's an example:

```
<plugin>
   <artifactId>maven-release-plugin</artifactId>
```

```
  <configuration>
    <releaseProfiles>dist</releaseProfiles>
    <goals>install</goals>
  </configuration>
</plugin>
```

You can now run the example with `mvn clean package -Pdist`. Maven will compile and package the web application, putting three WARs into your target folder:

```
webapp-1.0-SNAPSHOT.war
webapp-1.0-SNAPSHOT-prod.war
webapp-1.0-SNAPSHOT-test.war
```

Accelerating development with the Maven Jetty plug-in

Sooner or later, you'll want to deploy your coded and packaged web application to a servlet container for development testing purposes. Usually, you would download a servlet container such as Tomcat, and then copy and unpack your WAR file to the container's webapps folder. But with Maven, you profit from a much faster feedback loop by using the Maven Jetty plug-in to run your web application within Maven. You have to configure the Jetty plug-in in your POM and run special Maven Jetty goals to deploy and run the WAR file.

Using the Maven Jetty plug-in, the dev build can be created and tested in one single step. Add this to the plug-ins section of your POM:

```
<plugin>
   <groupId>org.mortbay.jetty</groupId>
   <artifactId>maven-jetty-plugin</artifactId>
</plugin>
```

Now run `mvn clean jetty:run` and then open http://localhost:8080/webapp/ in your browser. The test and prod environments can be tested by deploying the respective WAR files into a servlet container and then opening http://localhost:8080/webapp-1.0-SNAPSHOT-test/ and http://localhost:8080/webapp-1.0-SNAPSHOT-prod/ in your browser.

In summary, Maven offers functionality to configure artifacts for different target environments. By using assemblies, a build produces multiple artifacts for your specified environments. This way it's easy to maintain the application and it encourages a clean separation of environment-specific configuration files. Combined with Maven's releasing facilities, creating a release for multiple environments is done in a single step.

7.4 *Building, auditing, and staging with Jenkins*

Kohsuke Kawaguchi is currently lead developer on the Jenkins project, an open source CI server that was originally released in February of 2005 (under the name Hudson). Many developers find Jenkins easy to install and configure with its web interface written in Ajax (instead of using XML configuration files, as is required by

Cruise Control). With Jenkins, many different artifact types can be built, such as .NET and Java.[7]

JENKINS AND HUDSON Hudson split into two different products: Hudson (http://hudson-ci.org) and Jenkins (http://jenkins-ci.org). The original founder and core contributor, Kawaguchi, along with others, works on the open source product Jenkins. Hudson development is led by Oracle, together with Sonatype and others. Jenkins and Hudson follow different strategies regarding releasing and licensing—for details, please refer to the respective product sites. I used Jenkins in writing this book, but all discussions apply to both products. it's possible, though, that divergent developments and incompatibilities may result in the future.

It's recommended that you run Jenkins in a servlet container such as Tomcat or JBoss, but you can also start by executing `java -jar Jenkins.war` on the command line. Jenkins has a component architecture, so it supports a large library of plug-ins that extend its functionality. Using plug-ins, you can, for example, add different build types to your system, like .NET projects; add further reporting or auditing facilities; or add different communication channels, like posting build results on Twitter.

Discussing Jenkins could fill a whole book. Here, we'll focus on introducing Jenkins and looking at it in the context of audits and its Artifactory integration.

7.4.1 Jenkins and triggering jobs

Jenkins jobs allow you to specify *what* you want Jenkins to build and to schedule *when* they should be built. Jenkins also specifies which artifacts should be procured as a result of the build. It also provides reporting on channels and a definition of what to do after the build has run.

Jenkins is a build server, so it doesn't know how to build your project. You need build scripts, such as Maven, Ant, Ivy, MSBuild, and so on, to build your project,. Jenkins allows you to manage these build scripts (inside a Jenkins job) and run builds, depending on specific criteria.

These are the typical approaches to triggering a build:

- A developer checks something into your VCS, and Jenkins then builds a new version of your software including these recent changes, because it's monitoring changes to the VCS. This is a nice approach for setting up a continuous build. You can align this with your individual needs in many ways. For example, by configuring when Jenkins checks for changes. You could require that Jenkins checks the VCS once every hour by using a cron-like syntax in the Jenkins job configuration panel.

  Some projects use postcommit hooks inside their VCS to start a new build after a check-in. This is also a valid and effective approach. You can do this by

---

[7] For further details on Jenkins, see John Ferguson Smart, *Jenkins: The Definitive Guide* (O'Reilly, 2011).

referencing a shell script as a postcommit hook containing a single `wget` call to your build URL. This fosters a task-based approach, but it also has drawbacks. If you have many local changes to be synchronized with your central VCS, starting a build directly may lead to code in the VCS that's inconsistent. This makes it difficult to check in your changes frequently, even if the changes don't have any interdependency with each other. In this case, you should rely on the Jenkins feature. Letting Jenkins check the VCS for changes is more elegant and is often done on an hourly basis. Don't be afraid of performance bottlenecks here. Jenkins doesn't check out the entire source tree. For example, for Subversion, Jenkins checks the revision number to detect any changes.

■ Configure the job to start a scheduled build. This is often used to run nightly builds that may contain more complex logic, may do more testing, and so on. These builds are done once a day, typically overnight, to deliver the results in the morning when developers can then react to them.

■ Use dependency builds, which means a build job is dependent on the run of another job. This allows complex build chaining (often also called a *staged build*). One such scenario is to have a simple build job that compiles, packages, and does some basic sanity checks. Only if this is successful is a second downstream job run to complete the test coverage. This allows much better feedback loops than putting the complete build and test logic into one monolithic build job. On the success of the previous build, another Jenkins downstream job could be triggered to deploy the created artifact to a test environment. For instance, Jenkins' Deploy plug-in can deploy artifacts to common application servers; build dependencies can also be configured by using Jenkins' Build Pipeline plug-in.[8] You can also configure dependency builds across build tools. Using the Bamboo plug-in for Jenkins, for example, you can trigger a Bamboo build as the postbuild action in Jenkins. Besides that, Jenkins offers you features that aggregate build results for dependant builds. As an example, you can configure Jenkins to aggregate test results across different jobs.

■ Push the build start button manually.

Jenkins organizes builds with build jobs that are aggregated on Jenkins' dashboard.

7.4.2 *Jenkins dashboard and Jenkins jobs*

Jenkins provides intuitive navigation, starting with the Jenkins dashboard, which lists your build jobs. There, you can click on one job to see more details on a particular build job (for example, the workspace consisting of all sources checked out by Jenkins). Finally, you can go into one of the job runs to check its individual result.

What does this look like in detail? Figure 7.9 shows the dashboard listing a couple of jobs—you can see the status of the different jobs.

---

[8] Jenkins' Deploy plug-in can be found at https://wiki.jenkins-ci.org/display/JENKINS/Deploy+Plugin. The Build Pipeline plug-in is at https://wiki.jenkins-ci.org/display/JENKINS/Build+Pipeline+Plugin.

S	W	Job ↓	Last Success	Last Failure	Last Duration	
●	🌦	ALM-BuildMe	1 hr 32 min (#14)	7 hr 36 min (#6)	2 min 40 sec	🔄
●	⛅	CrazyProject	22 hr (#53)	22 hr (#52)	3 min 2 sec	🔄
●	☁	MM	2 hr 46 min (#18)	5 hr 20 min (#15)	25 sec	🔄
●	⛅	OSGi	N/A	7 hr 41 min (#8)	29 sec	🔄

Figure 7.9   Jenkins dashboard listing the configured jobs and information about them (result of the last build, trend, duration). You can also start new builds by clicking the buttons at the far right.

The balls in the first column indicate whether the last job run was successful or not. Here, green indicates success (but the green must be configured by installing another plug-in; success in Jenkins is traditionally indicated with blue balls). Other possible indicators are red balls (for failed builds, due to compile errors, for example) and yellow balls (pointing to unstable builds, due to failed tests, for instance). You can configure what fails a build. For example, you can define when a build is considered to be unstable, based on the results of audits, tests, and test coverage.

The trend is displayed in the second (weather) column, which analyzes the last builds, and the subsequent columns provide pointers to the times of the last builds and their durations. You can also start new builds by clicking the button on the right. Rolling the mouse over a visual UI item delivers more detailed context information.

Proceeding from the dashboard to a specific build job, you'll see the following (depending upon how you've configured Jenkins and what Jenkins plug-ins you've installed):

- Links to a change history that shows the build history and the VCS changes new in this build (and identifying who did this change). This can be linked with a repository browser like FishEye and an issue tracker like JIRA.
- Links to associated tools (like Trac or Sonar), if configured.
- Links to the coverage report showing test coverage and its trend across builds—for example, measured by the Cobertura coverage tool (if you configure the Cobertura plug-in as part of your Maven build). For example, a display of code coverage on package, file, class, method, line, and conditional levels.
- Exposed and stored artifacts, like a JAR built by the job. This can't replace more sophisticated storage, like in a VCS or in a component repository like Artifactory. Depending on your context, you could provide a zip file that's generated by your Maven build (via the Maven Assembly plug-in); for example, you could generate a target platform for your OSGi project or any similar package of artifacts you want to provide.
- Links to the latest test results, which include pages containing a list of test modules and the test results (for instance, test failures new with this build).
- Aggregated data about audits and tests and the trends across builds (if you configure the audit tools as part of your Maven build and reference the audit XML results in Jenkins).

- Dedicated trend illustrations for tests and static code auditing (FindBugs, PMD, Checkstyle), as well as a handy overview of all violations detected by a specific tool (if you configure the audit tools as part of your Maven build).

- The Javadocs delivered by the build (if they're part of the Maven project description).

- A link to the generated Maven site.

- Links to Maven modules showing fine-grained information on the module level (such as audit violations).

- A link to the Jenkins workspace showing the current sandbox checked out of VCS (by VCS *checkout* or *update*, according to what you've configured).

- Links to configuration pages to configure what you see.

When a job runs, it adds the results of a specific build to the history. Whereas the job overview page aggregates information or shows the last results, each job build occurrence has its individual information. This is important, because with Jenkins you can also inspect older builds in addition to the most current one. Each build shows the information illustrated in figure 7.10, as part of the build detail page.

> **JENKINS AND ITS MATRIX PROJECT JOB TYPE** Jenkins comes with a job type called matrix project (see the official plugin page: http://wiki.Jenkins-ci.org/display/JENKINS/Aboutncysa). This job type expands a freestyle software

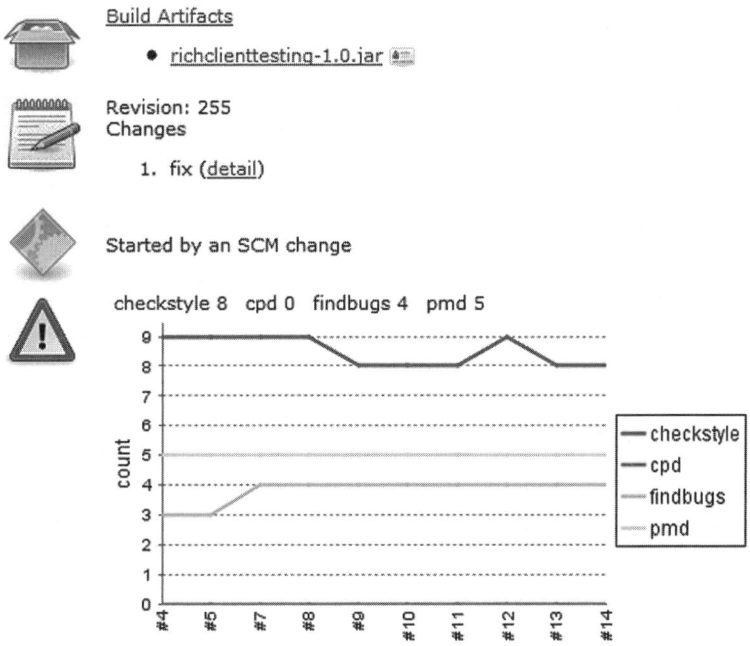

Build Artifacts

- richclienttesting-1.0.jar

Revision: 255
Changes

1. fix (detail)

Started by an SCM change

checkstyle 8   cpd 0   findbugs 4   pmd 5

Figure 7.10   On the build detail pages, Jenkins provides more information, including build artifacts, details on why the build was triggered (here a change in Subversion, revision 255, detected by Jenkins), and an overview of static code analysis violations.

project to a large number of parameterized build configurations. Matrix project lets you set up a single configuration with user-defined parameters. When you tell Jenkins to build it, it will build all the possible combinations of parameters and then aggregate the results. In addition to testing, this job type can also be useful for building a project for multiple target platforms. The plug-in is extended with further functionality continuously.

Figure 7.11 shows another excerpt of the build detail page with links to test results, audits, Artifactory, and built modules.

In the next section, we'll discuss using Sonar with Jenkins. Sonar is an open source code analysis tool that helps to improve code quality.

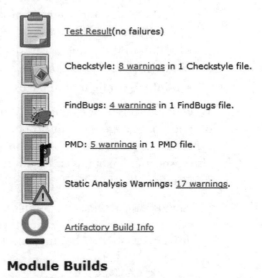

Test Result(no failures)

Checkstyle: 8 warnings in 1 Checkstyle file.

FindBugs: 4 warnings in 1 FindBugs file.

PMD: 5 warnings in 1 PMD file.

Static Analysis Warnings: 17 warnings.

Artifactory Build Info

Figure 7.11   On the build detail pages, Jenkins links to test results, dedicated reporting pages according to code violations (here Checkstyle, FindBugs, and PMD), an aggregation page of violations (static analysis warnings), and to Artifactory and individual modules of the Maven build.

Module Builds

RichClientTesting

7.4.3   *Auditing with Jenkins and Sonar*

Jenkins and Sonar both deliver reporting and data-aggregation support for auditing your software development. Auditing with Jenkins relies on configured build scripts, whereas Sonar doesn't require your build scripts to be changed. Sonar can be integrated with Jenkins. Let's start auditing with Jenkins.

AUDITING WITH JENKINS

As a precondition for using your chosen auditing tools, you must configure your build project appropriately. This way, you can run the build script without Jenkins, for instance locally in the developer's workspace, and get the result of those audits as well. Jenkins triggers the builds and aggregates and visualizes audit results. The following POM snippet shows what this can look like.

> **Listing 7.10   POM with Cobertura, FindBugs, Checkstyle, and PMD configuration**

```
<reporting>
  <plugins>
    <plugin>
      <groupId>org.codehaus.mojo</groupId>
      <artifactId>cobertura-maven-plugin</artifactId>        ◁──┤ Add
                                                                 Cobertura
```

```
        <configuration>                        ◁─┐  Configure output
            <formats>                             │  formats
                <format>html</format>
                <format>xml</format>
            </formats>
        </configuration>
    </plugin>
    <plugin>
        <groupId>org.apache.maven.plugins</groupId>    ─┐  Add Checkstyle
        <artifactId>maven-checkstyle-plugin</artifactId>  ◁─  functionality
        <configuration>                            ◁─  Reference config file,
            <configLocation>checkstyle.xml</configLocation>  exclude special files
            <excludes>**/package-info.java</excludes>
        </configuration>
    </plugin>
    <plugin>
        <groupId>org.apache.maven.plugins</groupId>    │  Add PMD
        <artifactId>maven-pmd-plugin</artifactId>    ◁─┘  to build
        <configuration>                            ◁─┐  Reference rule set, exclude
            <rulesets>                                │  files from processing
                <ruleset>pmd.xml</ruleset>
            </rulesets>
            <excludes>
                <exclude>**/package-info.java</exclude>
            </excludes>
        </configuration>
    </plugin>
    <plugin>
        <groupId>org.codehaus.mojo</groupId>        │  Add
        <artifactId>findbugs-maven-plugin</artifactId>  ◁─  FindBugs
        <configuration>                            ◁─  Configure
            <effort>Max</effort>                        FindBugs
            <threshold>Low</threshold>
            <includeFilterFile>include.xml</includeFilterFile>
            <excludeFilterFile>exclude.xml</excludeFilterFile>
        </configuration>
    </plugin>
    </plugins>
</reporting>
```

You can place your auditing plug-ins into the POM's `build` and `reporting` sections. In the `reporting` section, shown in listing 7.10, Maven inspects your code and reports the result. This has an informal character only because the build itself isn't influenced by the result of the audits. You can configure Jenkins to influence the reported project health, or even break the build. There are limitations, though, in handling the granularity and criticality of violations. Jenkins counts only the violations.

In the `build` section, auditing results can influence the build directly. This is handy for implementing quality gates, if, say, you want to break the build when defined requirements aren't met. Another use case for including audits in the `build` section (and not in the `site` section) is if you don't want or need to use Maven's site lifecycle to generate these reports.

> **CONTINUOUS INSPECTION VERSUS ONE-TIME INSPECTION**   Some projects experience good results with a single one-time inspection instead of continuous inspections. These projects claim that it's enough to include specific inspections for a particular instance, and then not run them again afterward. In these cases, this approach will point to possible design defects that result in a learning opportunity for the team. This is a task-based approach that allows developers to focus on their work instead of constantly focusing on passing audits.

Audit tools support the configuration of rules in dedicated configuration files. If you choose to use detailed files for configuring rules, you may place these files into a dedicated Maven project. You *must* place these files in a dedicated project if you run a multimodule Maven build. Then, in your parent POM `build` section, you add an `extension` element that adds only artifacts to the Maven compile classpath. This section extends the compile classpath, adding the audit rules:

```
<extensions>
   <extension>
      <groupId>net.huettermann</groupId>
      <artifactId>resource</artifactId>
      <version>1.0.0</version>
   </extension>
</extensions>
```

The `resource` project consists of only the configuration files for the audit tools, placed in the default file structure where Maven expects general resources: src/main/resources/. Be aware that you can't use the `extensions` construct in a POM's `reporting` section.

Figure 7.10 showed an aggregation of static code violations that can be detected by various audit tools (such as Checkstyle, FindBugs, PMD).

> **FALSE POSITIVES**   Remember that you have to align audits with your individual context. In part, this involves placing a value on the auditing rules you include. A valuable rule for one project can be misleading and of no value for another project. For example, consider FindBugs' `UWF_FIELD_NOT_INITIALIZED_IN_CONSTRUCTOR` rule, which rule checks whether you've initialized fields in the constructor. If you use any kind of Java injection mechanism, this may lead to a lot of false positives because the injection system takes care of initializing properties. Other rules are debatable; one person may state it's perfect and a good design to have only one return statement at the end of your block. Another person may state that using multiple return statements improves clarity and reduces the overhead.

Figure 7.12 provides an example of using Checkstyle for code audits.

```
31    /**
32     * Example service method reading something out of the DB
33     * working on the return value.
34     */
35    public String getSomething() {
```

Figure 7.12 Checkstyle found an antipattern: this method isn't designed for extension.

In figure 7.12, Checkstyle analyzed the code and found a design antipattern. According to Checkstyle, the method isn't designed for extension—the method should be abstract or final. Checkstyle knows this rule as `DesignForExtensionCheck`. Jenkins reports this with a special colored background.

The example in figure 7.13 shows PMD in action. PMD detected an empty catch block (an unhandled exception), which is considered to be an antipattern.

```
133   private void newFilter() {
134       try {
135           sorter.setRowFilter(RowFilter.regexFilter("^"+myFilter.getText(), 0));
136       } catch (java.util.regex.PatternSyntaxException e) {
137           /* swallow */
138       }
139   }
```

Figure 7.13 PMD detects an empty catch block.

The last auditing example is shown in figure 7.14. FindBugs detected a code fragment that was obviously a coding defect. By accident, the developer repeated a conditional test. The developer wanted to add a different condition but made a mistake while doing so.

```
40    int i = 0;
41    if (i==0 || i==0) {
42        System.err.println("hu");
43    }
```

Figure 7.14 FindBugs points to a repeated conditional test, which is most likely a coding defect.

Discussing all tools or even all rules in detail is beyond the scope of this book. The lesson here is that you should include audits in your build and let Jenkins report and aggregate the results. For more information on the individual rules (and how to configure them), please consult the available documentation for these free tools:

- *FindBugs*—http://findbugs.sourceforge.net/
- *Checkstyle*—http://checkstyle.sourceforge.net/
- *PMD*—http://pmd.sourceforge.net/

What makes Checkstyle, PMD, and FindBugs complementary?

Although there's some overlap, all three tools have different usage scopes and individual strengths.

Checkstyle focuses on conventions. For instance, does the code correspond to a defined format, are Javadocs set correctly, and are the Sun/Oracle naming conventions followed?

PMD focuses on bad practices, such as well-known antipatterns—code fragments that will lead to difficulties over time. Typical examples are having dead (unreached) code, too many complex methods, and direct use of implementations instead of interfaces.

Finally, FindBugs focuses on potential bugs. These are code statements or sequences that aren't immediately clear but that will lead to terribly bad situations. Multiple parameters must be taken into account to detect such a circumstance. Examples include a code change that uses a conditional statement twice or that returns references to mutable objects while exposing internal representations.

SUN/ORACLE CODE CONVENTIONS The Sun/Oracle code conventions usually don't target project requirements (they're too restrictive and too fine-grained), but you can use them as a template to customize your own conventions. Conventions are important for a team to follow, in order to collaborate with the greatest efficiency and to maintain a common standard while sharing code.

As mentioned, you can configure a failed build based on the results of your audits. Although you can directly configure the auditing tools and plug-ins in Maven (for example, to automatically break a build completely as soon as the test coverage is ascertained to be insufficient), Jenkins's configuration helps to control operational efficiency. Although developers can use Jenkins, too, the build scripts aren't usually supported by the build manager: Instead, project developers write and maintain build scripts as part of the application development effort. Depending on how you slice project roles, a central build manager may use Jenkins to apply centralized quality gates, but they probably won't change the scripts themselves (because of organizational restrictions or because they don't have the skills to do so).

JENKINS, AUDITS, AND IDES Jenkins integrations for IDEs are available, too, and there's support for auditing in the IDE. For example, it can be wise to use the Checkstyle plug-in for Eclipse, but this should be integrated with the build stream. It's more important to include audits (and only the audits that add value in your individual situation) in your build system than in your IDE.

Coverage Breakdown by Package

Name	Files		Classes		Methods	
com.huettermann.mock	100%	0/0	100%	0/0	N/A	
com.huettermann.fit.framework	100%	1/1	100%	1/1	100%	2/2
com.huettermann.fit.application	100%	1/1	100%	4/4	75%	9/12
com.huettermann.mock.connector	0%	0/1	0%	0/1	0%	0/2
com.huettermann.fit.util	33%	1/3	33%	1/3	40%	2/5
com.huettermann.mock.service	100%	1/1	100%	1/1	67%	2/3

Figure 7.15   Code coverage breakdown by package, showing packages and their files, classes, and methods coverage

Many IDEs also provide auditing rules or apply conventions. You can configure Eclipse, for example, to apply rules, such as organizing imports, when you save. If you use this configuration, you check in your configurations to your VCS and provide them to others, but you can't force colleagues to use them (which is a good reason for integrating audits with a build run on the central build server).

Finally, let's look at test coverage. We added Cobertura to our Maven POM; figure 7.15 shows the test coverage of the project built via Jenkins, on the package level. You can navigate further into files, classes, and methods, inspecting which tests passed (and how often) and which didn't. Please keep in mind that Jenkins is a tool that provides reporting and aggregating; it doesn't measure or inspect code.

AUDITING WITH SONAR

Although Jenkins provides a centralized view of your build results (including reporting of audits), there are other common tools for tracking code quality. Sonar (http://sonar.codehaus.org/) is one such application. It's self-contained and isn't dependent on build scripts or Jenkins. If you reference your Sonar installation in Jenkins, Sonar will examine the quality of the builds Jenkins performs.

Sonar can be configured to apply FindBugs, Checkstyle, and PMD, among other tools, and it can apply code coverage for your project without having to configure the tools in the Maven POMs. Because it doesn't require any POM modifications, it can be executed on every Maven project. The benefit of this is that it allows Maven to do its core job (build the project) and it keeps the POMs lean. But this can be a drawback too, because you lose early feedback on simple compliance errors in your builds. Another benefit is that you can easily analyze projects. SonarSource (commercial support for Sonar) added reporting on many open source projects to their audit server hosted under their *nemo* subdomain: http://nemo.sonarsource.org.

Figure 7.16 shows the results of a build in the Sonar dashboard.

Figure 7.16 A project inspected by Sonar, showing the results of FindBugs, Checkstyle, and PMD inspections, and the results of code coverage

Continuous inspection, by Simon Brandhof (SonarSource founder and technical lead)

More than ten years ago, the concept of continuous integration was introduced. Its ultimate goal was to become capable of firing a release of any type at any time with minimal risk. To reach this objective, continuous integration has introduced new quality requirements on projects:

- Anybody must be able to build the project from any place and at any time.
- All unit tests must be executed during the continuous integration build.
- All unit tests must pass during the continuous integration build.
- The output of the continuous integration build is a package ready to ship.
- When one of the preceding requirements are violated, nothing is more important for the team than fixing it.

This is a good starting point, but it isn't sufficient to ensure total quality. What about other source code quality requirements? Requirements could be

- Any new code should come with corresponding unit tests (regardless of previous state in code coverage).
- New methods must not have a complexity higher than a defined threshold.

(continued)

- No cycle between packages must be added.
- No duplication blocks must be added.
- No violation to coding standard must be added.
- No call to deprecated methods should be added.
- More generally, how to keep overall technical debt under control and only let it increase consciously: this is the concept of continuous inspection.

A continuous inspection process can be seen as an information radiator dedicated to making the source code quality information available at any time to every stakeholder. Transparency is certainly one of the main reasons open source software is usually of better quality than closed source software is. A developer writing a new piece of code should always think about the next person or team who will maintain it. Continuous inspection ensures this golden rule is not forgotten.

Sonar enables you to navigate through components and provides appealing visualizations. You can also zoom in on individual class statements. An in-depth discussion of Sonar is beyond the scope of this book, but it's worth taking a closer look at this technology. This is particularly true if you're interested in audits and are looking for a one-stop solution that eliminates the need to integrate different tools into your build scripts.

For projects based on Maven, Sonar permits you to visualize artifact dependencies (for example, libraries cartography, which specifies the project and library in use). Sonar supports analyzing project sources to identify what project is using a specific version of a library. You can also use the functionality provided by Maven's Dependency plug-in (http://maven.apache.org/plugins/maven-dependency-plugin) by running the dedicated commands on the console or by binding the functionality to a Maven phase, but Sonar's reporting is much more convenient. Besides the improved convenience, questions like "Which projects are using commons-logging or any other specific library?" aren't possible to answer when you use Maven's Dependency plug-in directly.

But keep in mind that Sonar isn't a substitution for a repository manager, like Artifactory, and Maven's site lifecycle can read POMs and visualize dependencies as well.

7.4.4 *Running build fragments in Jenkins only*

It can be handy to run parts of your build scripts using Jenkins (that is, on a central integration server), but it's also useful to have fast-running builds on developers' machines, so developers can run their build scripts before code check-in. But build scripts should be the same whatever their running context is—how can build scripts know if they're running in Jenkins or not? To resolve this, we need a special configuration or another mechanism to detect the runtime environment.

> **NOTE** Many developers don't want to wait until test coverage (or other audits) are measured before each VCS commit. They only want to do a smoke test

consisting of compiling and packaging artifacts. Other developers would like to run test coverage and other audits in their workspace, but they value fast builds and fast feedback, and many builds aren't quick enough. Audits (or other similar advanced practices) can be run on the central build machine.

One solution is to configure Jenkins to inject specific Java properties into your build. While running the build script, it detects which specific parameters are or are not available if you start your build script on a developer's desktop. Another solution is to use one of the implicit parameters that Jenkins automatically injects into every build (for instance, BUILD_NUMBER). In either case, you'll need to use Maven profiles to handle the different build behaviors.

The next listing shows an example where we define a profile inside a parent POM. Using Maven profiles enables you to create different configurations, depending on where the script runs.

Listing 7.11   A Maven profile activated by Jenkins

```
<profiles>
    <profile>
        <id>Jenkins</id>
        <activation>                              ❶ Activate
            <property>                               the profile
                <name>BUILD_NUMBER</name>
            </property>
        </activation>                             ❷ Customize
        <build>                                     the script
            <plugins>
                <plugin>
                    <groupId>org.codehaus.mojo</groupId>
                    <artifactId>cobertura-maven-plugin</artifactId>
                </plugin>
            </plugins>
        </build>
    </profile>
</profiles>
```

Each profile has a unique identifier and contains information specifying when it will be activated. Many options for activating a profile are available, such as activating a default profile on particular operating systems, or Java versions, or if properties are set. In this case, we activate the profile ❶ when the property BUILD_NUMBER is set. The value of the property isn't important in this example, only that it exists. Next, we configure the Maven logic ❷ by adding the Cobertura plug-in to the build phase. Many areas of your POM can be customized with profiles.[9]

Because <property file="${user.name}.properties"/> is a commonly seen pattern, it could be useful to provide a properties file named Jenkins.properties. If

---

[9] For a comprehensive discussion, see the Maven "Introduction to Build Profiles" (http://maven.apache.org/guides/introduction/introduction-to-profiles.html).

Jenkins runs as user `Jenkins`, it will run without further intervention. In other cases, you have to start your build script with `-Duser.name=Jenkins`, which is equal to setting `user.name=Jenkins` somewhere in the properties, although you probably don't want to do this.

> ### Advanced Maven pluginManagement
>
> Besides adding a Maven plug-in to your build or reporting section, you can also use Maven's `pluginManagement` section. There, you can define and fully configure a plug-in inside a parent POM for further flexible reuse. Once a plug-in has been defined and configured in the `pluginManagement` section, child POMs can reference the plug-in for usage without repeating the full configuration. This enables you to centrally provide default plug-in settings so that child projects don't have to repeat the configuration settings again and again.
>
> This feature allows you to configure project builds that inherit from the current one, but this configures only those plug-ins that are referenced within the `plugins` element in the children. The children have every right to override `pluginManagement` definitions.

Jenkins allows you to pass arbitrary use data as a key/value pair to the build script. You can evaluate this data to activate a Maven profile, for example by checking whether the parameter (the key) is set and passed to the build script, or whether the key has a specific value. Another use case for processing passed data is that you can process the build number in the build script.

7.4.5 *Injecting build numbers into applications*

A developed and delivered application should have a visible version number. Often different version numbers are used: a version number that is primarily used by domain experts and users of the applications, and a version number that is used by the development team. A shared version number improves communication between the stakeholders (developers, testers, and users) by linking bug fixes and features to delivered versions of the software.

Agile ALM encourages communication between stakeholders, so many Agile ALM projects inject a technical version number into the applications. One commonly used version number is the build number that is incremented by Jenkins because this build number is unique for each build project.

A typical setup to inject the build number into an application built with Maven may look like this: In your Jenkins build project, you can configure parameters to be passed to your build script. Parameters are key/value pairs, and in your build script you can access the key and read the passed value. In this case, we'll assign Jenkins' implicit variable `$BUILD_NUMBER` to the key `jenkins.build_number`. An *implicit variable* is not a user-defined variable, rather this variable has a specific meaning for

Jenkins: Jenkins replaces the variable with the concrete build number whenever the build job runs. The resulting key/value pair looks like this:

```
jenkins.build_number=$BUILD_NUMBER
```

Jenkins triggers the project's Maven build system. In the Maven POM, you can access the parameter and further process it, as shown in the following listing.

Listing 7.12   A Maven profile activated by Jenkins

```
<build>
  <plugins>
    <plugin>
      <artifactId>maven-antrun-plugin</artifactId>
      <executions>
        <execution>
          <id>write-version-file</id>
          <phase>process-resources</phase>
          <configuration>
        <target>
          <echo file="${dist.version.ui.filename}"      ❶ Parameterized
            append="false">                                 filename
           build_number=${jenkins.build_number}         ❷ Jenkins' build number,
          </echo>                                           written to file
        </target>
          </configuration>
          <goals>
            <goal>run</goal>
          </goals>
        </execution>
      </executions>
    </plugin>
  </plugins>
</build>
```

The Maven POM uses Maven's Ant plug-in to call Ant's echo task. The echo task writes the build number to a file ❷. The name and the location of the file are parameterized. This means that in the central parent POM (our master POM, not shown in this example), we configured the variable as a Maven property so we can access the property later where we want to use it (as we did at ❶).

The remaining aspect of integrating the version number into the application is to read the previously written version number file in the developed application, as you can see in this listing.

Listing 7.13   Reading the version file

```
public static String getVersionNumber() {
  Properties properties = new Properties();
  try {
    InputStream stream =
  MyClazz.class.getResourceAsStream("/version.txt");   ❶ Access the file
    if (stream != null) {                                  via Java
```

```
      try {
        properties.load(stream);
      } finally {
        stream.close();
      }
    }
  } catch (IOException e) {
    ;  //NOOPT
  }
  return properties.getProperty("build_number");
}
```

❷ Return the build number

In the application, the file can be read ❶ and the retrieved version number can be put into a semantic context, such as by displaying it in the user interface. The convenience method encapsulates the reading of the version number and has the version number as its return value ❷.

Now that we've discussed different approaches to integrating Jenkins with your build system, we'll talk about integrating Jenkins with the component repository, Artifactory.

7.4.6 *Jenkins, Artifactory, staging, and atomic deployment of Maven artifacts*

Integrating Jenkins with Artifactory has many appealing benefits. The most obvious advantage is that your CI server should deploy artifacts to a component repository, such as to Artifactory. But there are more advantages.

By integrating those two tools, you profit from atomic deployments of build artifacts. Additionally, the integration better links built and deployed artifacts to build jobs. Linking artifacts to builds enables Artifactory to semantically group binaries so that you can operate commands on the semantic group of artifacts, instead of operating commands on single, loosely coupled artifacts. A common command that you'll want to apply on a group is staging the group of artifacts.

But first, let's start with setting up the integration of Jenkins with Artifactory.

INSTALLING AND CONFIGURING THE JENKINS/ARTIFACTORY BRIDGE

The Jenkins/Artifactory communication is done with Artifactory's REST API, and the Artifactory UI shows convenient views of this data as part of the Power Pack commercial add-ons. To install and configure the integration with Jenkins, here is what you need to do:[10]

1 Get Jenkins running.
2 Get Artifactory running (with the commercial Build Integration Jenkins add-on).
3 Install the Jenkins Artifactory plug-in (available through the Jenkins plug-in manager).
4 In Jenkins, configure your Artifactory server and user credentials in the Jenkins configuration panel.

---

[10] For further information about the Jenkins/Artifactory integration, see the plug-in's web page: https://wiki.jenkins-ci.org/display/JENKINS/Artifactory+Plugin.

5 In your build job in Jenkins, configure your build section to run `mvn clean install`. This will install the artifacts to a Jenkins repository, from which Jenkins deploys the artifacts to Artifactory.

6 In your build job in Jenkins, configure a postbuild action to deploy artifacts to Artifactory (after the full build goes through successfully).

7 In your build job in Jenkins, in the Artifactory Configuration section, select the Artifactory server, the target repositories for releases and snapshots, and check boxes to deploy Maven artifacts and capture and publish build info (see figure 7.17). Jenkins offers a drop-down list for scanning all available repositories. Double-check that you have the deployment permissions on the target repository (in Artifactory) and that the credentials are set correctly (in Jenkins). The Artifactory plug-in for Jenkins also includes a link on the Jenkins user interface to redeploy artifacts to Artifactory at any time.

Artifactory Configuration

Artifactory server	http://huttermann.artifactoryonline.com/huttermann ▼
Target releases repository	libs-releases-local ▼ ⑦
Target snapshots repository	libs-snapshots-local ▼ ⑦

☐ Override default deployer credentials ⑦

☐ Deploy even if the build is unstable ⑦

☑ Deploy maven artifacts ⑦

Include Patterns [   ] ⑦

Exclude Patterns [   ] ⑦

Deployment properties [   ] ⑦

☑ Capture and publish build info ⑦

  ☐ Include all environment variables ⑦

☐ Run license checks (requires Artifactory Pro) ⑦

☐ Discard old builds from Artifactory (requires Artifactory Pro) ⑦

☐ Enable isolated resolution for downstream builds (requires Artifactory Pro) ⑦

Figure 7.17 Configuring the integration of Jenkins with Artifactory. Jenkins resolves the central settings that you've set on the Jenkins configuration page and suggests valid entries for Artifactory server and target repositories. In this example, Jenkins will deploy artifacts to Artifactory after all single Maven modules are built successfully. It will also capture build information and pass it to the Artifactory server. Help texts are available on demand for all configuration settings (by clicking the question marks).

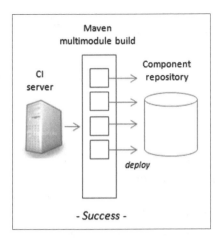 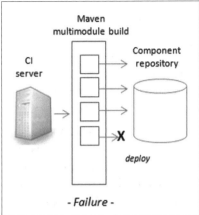

Figure 7.18 The default way of deploying Maven artifacts in a multimodule project: All single Maven projects are deployed one by one. If the multimodule build fails, some artifacts are deployed to the component repository, and others aren't. The result is an inconsistent state.

ATOMIC DEPLOYMENTS WITH JENKINS/ARTIFACTORY

Jenkins is a build server that can trigger Maven goals. If you configure Jenkins to *deploy* a Maven multimodule build project, the deployment is executed on all POMs, including parent and children.

If one Maven module deployment fails due to a build error, this may leave the build in an inconsistent state, with some artifacts being deployed into your component repository and others not, as shown in figure 7.18.

Using Artifactory, together with Jenkins, the deployment is done as one atomic operation only at the end, after every single module has been processed successfully.

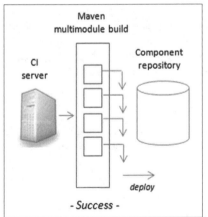 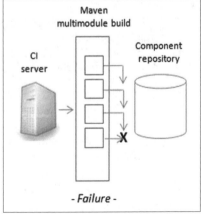

Figure 7.19 Deploying Maven artifacts in a multimodule project, with Artifactory and Jenkins: All single Maven projects are installed locally. If the complete multimodule build succeeds, all artifacts are deployed to the component repository. In the case of a build failure, no single module is deployed. This result is a consistent state.

This is a big step forward and solves the problem with Maven deploying each module separately as part of the deploy phase, which can leave your repository with partial deployments and inconsistent builds (see figure 7.19).

Based on this *atomic deployment* feature, you can set up a sophisticated build system to ensure high-quality and state-of-the-art releasing. For instance, one Jenkins job does some essential tasks like compiling and packaging, and a second downstream job does comprehensive testing. Only if all the tests pass are the artifacts published to Artifactory.

STAGING ARTIFACTS IN ARTIFACTORY

Another common requirement is identifying (and semantically grouping) artifacts deployed to your component repository. The process of staging software involves picking artifacts and promoting them as a single unit. For staging, you must identify and reference all artifacts built by a Jenkins build job. And identifying them isn't enough—you must change their locations (or their visibility) in one atomic step. These are common challenges, and Jenkins, in conjunction with Artifactory, provides a viable solution.

> **STAGING VERSUS PROMOTING IN ARTIFACTORY** This book doesn't distinguish between the staging and promoting of artifacts. Both terms refer to moving artifacts from one rung of the staging ladder to a higher rung. Artifactory does distinguish between staging and promoting. Given a Maven-based build, *staging* in Artifactory involves replacing the snapshot version numbers in the sources of the modules to released version numbers before the released modules are built again and put into a different target repository. Promoting artifacts doesn't change the sources; it moves (or copies) the artifacts to another logical repository, without rebuilding.

Staging artifacts

Regardless of what scripts you use (such as Ant, Maven, or shell build scripts), you'll probably consider some kind of *promotion build*; there are just as many ways to implement a *staging build*. In a staging build, you'll specify all of the individual requirements for the environment that will be used to run the release.

Some general pieces of advice, already discussed in this book, apply to many projects:

- All your sources should be put into a VCS.
- Releasing means applying tags or labels to the baselined version (the release).
- Promoting has the precondition of being able to access the results of former builds again.

The artifacts that are built during releasing should be stored in such a way that you can promote them, so you should store the generated artifacts (at least the artifacts identified as being part of a release) in a component repository. This can be a VCS (like Subversion), a tool like Artifactory, or the build archive where Jenkins stores its

(continued)
build results. Once this is done, promoting means pulling these stored artifacts and putting them, by hand or by script, into another context (often deploying to another environment, without rebuilding). A script can pick up the artifacts from your component repository and deploy them accordingly.

This process can have many variations and can be supported by additional tools. One example is using Artifactory's features to stage artifacts, as discussed in this chapter. Another option is using Jenkins's build promotion plug-in. Once you install it, you can configure your individual promotion as part of the build job description. Parts of this description are the criteria for when a build is qualified to be promoted and what happens when it's promoted. Concerning qualification criteria in Jenkins, you can manually mark builds as being promoted or note whether any downstream jobs (for example, running special tests) run successfully. Then the build is marked with a star in the build job history. The promotion action triggered by Jenkins afterward could run a different script.

In a nutshell, the principle is simple: Your CI server is the entity having the most complete knowledge about the project. This information is captured during build time and is sent to Artifactory upon deployment at the end of the build process (as a JSON object). The information contains the produced modules, their published artifacts and dependencies, and data about the build environment (server version, JVM version, properties, and so on). Once you have all this information inside Artifactory, you can do the following:

- You can collect the data required to reproduce the build.
- You can see the builds' artifacts and dependencies.
- You can see the builds each artifact belongs to.
- You can get warnings when you try to delete artifacts used in builds.
- You can export the whole set of artifacts or dependencies for a build as an archive to deploy or reuse elsewhere.
- You can operate on the whole set of artifacts or dependencies for a build as one unit (promote, remove, and so on).
- You can navigate to the build information in Jenkins and from the Jenkins build page to the Artifactory build info.

In Artifactory you can click on the Builds panel. This will display all build projects (corresponding to the name of the build job in Jenkins) that deployed artifacts to Artifactory (see figure 7.20).

You can select the build project of interest, and on the next page you'll see a list of all builds sorted by the Jenkins build number. For each build job item, you can now use the context menu to jump directly to Jenkins (to the corresponding job detail page) or you go into Artifactory's build detail page.

Build Browser

All Builds ▸ Task-based

History for Build 'Task-based'

Build Number	Time Built	Release Status
16	16-05-11 17:37:33 UTC	
15	14-05-11 17:13:30 UTC	
14	14-05-11 17:11:37 UTC	Released
13	13-05-11 16:38:09 UTC	
12	13-05-11 16:36:25 UTC	Released
11	13-05-11 16:32:56 UTC	
10	13-05-11 16:31:56 UTC	
9	13-05-11 16:30:56 UTC	
8	13-05-11 16:29:56 UTC	
7	13-05-11 16:28:56 UTC	
6	13-05-11 16:27:56 UTC	
5	13-05-11 16:26:56 UTC	
4	13-05-11 16:25:56 UTC	

Figure 7.20   Artifactory's Build Browser lists all builds for a specific build name (in this case, Task-based). The build name corresponds with the name of the Jenkins job that produced the builds. You can click on one specific build to get more information about it.

Artifactory's build detail page provides many pieces of information about the build, including general build information (for example, who performed the deployment and when) and what the published modules are. In figure 7.21, two Maven modules belonging to build #14 are listed: a JAR and the corresponding POM.

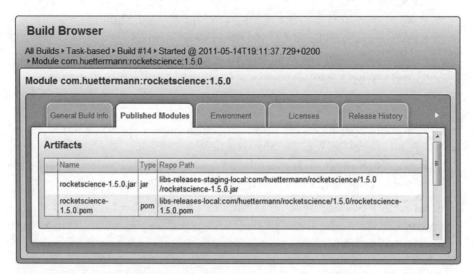

Figure 7.21   Artifactory shows published modules for all builds, including in which repositories the artifacts are located (in the Repo Path column).

Clicking on an artifact in the Published Modules tab (see figure 7.21), opens the repository browser showing that artifact (valid for build artifacts and their dependencies). You can do this, too, by opening Artifactory's repository browser (where you can browse all repositories and their artifacts in their versions) and navigating to and marking the artifact of interest.

When you display an artifact in Artifactory's repository browser, you can see which build produced the artifact (the Produced By section in figure 7.22), with the build name and build number referencing the information from Jenkins. Artifactory also lists artifacts built using this artifact (the Used By section in figure 7.22). In this case, another Jenkins build job named `Multi project` references the artifact.

Promoting all artifacts belonging to a specific build is easy. Jenkins injects the two parameters (or properties) into Artifactory: `build.name` and `build.number`. You already learned in chapter 5 how to proceed from here. You perform a property search to find all artifacts belonging to this build, and save the search. Alternatively, you can save the search in the General Build Info tab in the Builds browser. Finally, you perform a bulk operation (such as copying artifacts to a special staging repository), as shown in chapter 5.

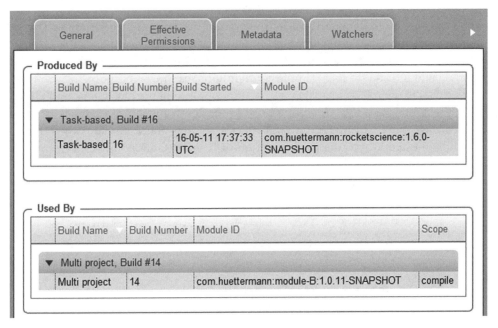

Figure 7.22   Artifactory shows the producers and consumers of artifacts built by Jenkins.

Injecting arbitrary properties into Artifactory

You can submit arbitrary properties from Jenkins to Artifactory through your Maven build. Your POM's deployment sections are ignored when you deploy via Jenkins, so you must specify the properties in the Jenkins Artifactory plug-in, configuring the target Artifactory server.

As of this writing, this approach is less than completely reliable. A workaround is to edit the config.xml file (in .Jenkins/jobs/jobName/config.xml) of your Jenkins job to extend the `repositoryKey` by the property in the publisher's section:

`<repositoryKey>path;myProperty=${myProperty}</repositoryKey>`

In Jenkins, you must reload the configuration from disk afterward.

You now have traceable information about all jobs that deployed artifacts. This is good, because you know now how each artifact ended up being in Artifactory, who put it there, and when. You have information about the job created, and you know what else was published by each job. This is a great deal more information than you have in the traditional Maven approach.

STAGING/PROMOTING ARTIFACTS IN JENKINS

Using the Jenkins/Artifactory integration, it's possible to trigger both stagings and promotions out of Jenkins conveniently.[11]

To use this integration feature, you need to activate it in the respective Jenkins build job and do some simple configuration, as shown in figure 7.23. You need to first enable the release management feature by clicking the check box, and then configure a VCS tag base URL. You don't need to configure any VCS credentials, because the Jenkins/Artifactory integration will take the settings that you've already configured in the dedicated VCS configuration section of Jenkins. Optionally, you can force Jenkins to

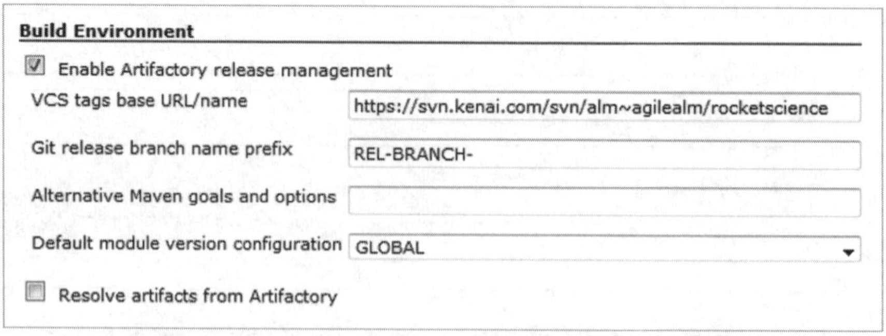

Figure 7.23   Configuring the Jenkins build job to use the Jenkins/Artifactory release management functionality. The VCS base URL for this Jenkins build job must be specified. Among other options, you can force Jenkins to resolve all artifacts from Artifactory during builds.

---

[11] You'll need the commercial Artifactory Pro in order to use all the features.

resolve all artifacts from Artifactory, which can further improve the quality of your builds, because you ensure that all artifacts (such as compile dependencies) are pulled from Artifactory, not from any other location. As a result, this quality gate overwrites any other settings developers may use in their individual workspaces.

For Maven projects, the Jenkins/Artifactory combination performs the following steps to stage a project:

1 Change the POM version from snapshot to release (this also applies to multi-module builds).
2 Trigger the Maven build.
3 Commit the changed sources to VCS. This will trigger a new build in Jenkins, the release build, which will deploy the released modules to Artifactory.
4 Change the POM version to the next development version (which is again a snapshot version).
5 Commit the changes to VCS. This will trigger a new build in Jenkins, the next development build, which will deploy the new snapshot versions to Artifactory.

After activating and configuring the release management facility, an Artifactory release management staging link appears in the left panel of your Jenkins build job page. Clicking the link opens a new page in Jenkins to configure and trigger the staging process, as shown in figure 7.24. To stage the artifacts that were produced by a past

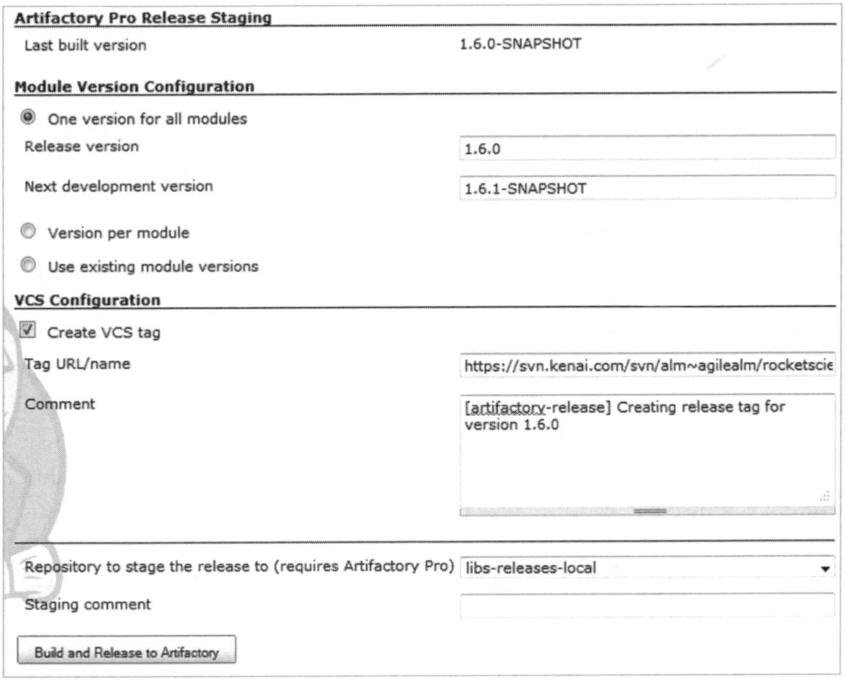

Figure 7.24 Staging the artifacts that were produced by a past Jenkins build. Before starting the staging process, you must configure versions and a target repository.

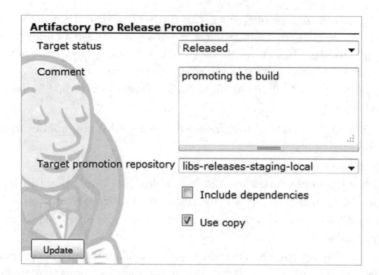

Figure 7.25   Promoting a build from inside Jenkins requires selecting a target promotion repository. You can configure it to include dependencies and specify whether you want to copy the artifacts in Artifactory or move them.

Jenkins build, specify the last built version that will be the base for staging, configure the new versions for your Maven modules, and optionally create a tag in VCS. Finally, configure the target repository where you want to stage the release to. The target repository is a logical repository inside Artifactory. Clicking the Build and Release to Artifactory button starts the staging process.

Staging is wrapped as Jenkins builds, so you can open the Jenkins console for these builds and read the output of these job interactively and after the fact. In Jenkins, a successful release build is marked with a special icon beside the job in the job history.

After the staging is done and a release build has been finished successfully, you can promote the build. Promoting the build means that the build is moved (or copied, depending on how you configure the staging process) to another logical repository in Artifactory, without rebuilding (see figure 7.25).

Promoting built artifacts from inside Jenkins is a convenient way to put artifacts into a different repository location while still gaining from traceability. As part of this traceability, the Build Browser (see figure 7.20) is updated to show staged or released as the release status of Jenkins builds that were deployed as artifacts to Artifactory. Additional information can be found in the Release History tab of Artifactory's build detail page (see figure 7.21).

Jenkins, Artifactory, and Maven provide considerable functionality. Another approach is to use Git and the git-svn bridge for feature branch–driven CI.

7.5   *Using Git and git-svn bridge for feature branch–driven CI*

—*This section contributed by René Gielen*

The mainline of a feature development phase—also called *trunk* or *head* if the development isn't taking place on a branch of the source code—is the unique line of development in the VCS. The mainline often also contains the latest revisions of the software's features.

USING BOTH SUBVERSION AND GIT The git-svn bridge is often used to enable the use of both the Git and Subversion VCSs in parallel. This can be a good approach if you want to softly migrate from one tool to the other, or if your organizational structure requires you to use one tool for managing source code centrally (for instance, Subversion) but where developers have the freedom to use other tools in addition (such as Git).

In almost every case, a central CI job is set up to be triggered by check-ins to the mainline. Developers work on the mainline; they check out code, change code, and commit changes. They are notified by the central CI job about the results of their and their colleagues' commits. Figure 7.26 illustrates the standard workflow (without feature branching).

This is a good approach, because you always want to ensure that the mainline integrates properly, unless you're willing to sacrifice the benefit of having a continuous line of release candidates. Nevertheless, a number of problems might arise when the mainline CI is the only build and test automation is taking place:

- Although a feature that a developer is currently working on might be far from complete and still subject to heavy changes and refactoring, their solution steps related to commits will continuously be integrated against other developers' work. There's a good chance that more integration problems will have to be resolved, as compared to an approach where the developer's work wouldn't have to be integrated against the team's work until their feature is completed.

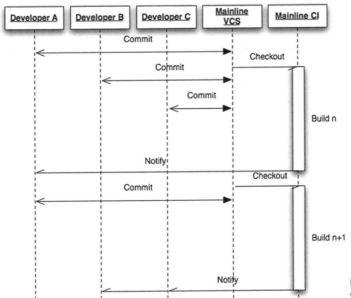

Figure 7.26 Mainline CI without feature branching

- If the team embraces the "commit early, commit often" policy, the triggered CI builds will often include changes from more than a single commit, given the common case where the next build job isn't allowed to fire unless the previous CI job is completed. Therefore, the features of the various change-sets that are committed, while the previous build blocks the following CI's turn, might bleed into each other. If a build fails, each developer who committed during the previous build will be notified by the CI system as potentially having caused the problem. Even though only one or two of them would be to blame, each of these developers—maybe most of the team, for complex and long-running CI cycles—will have to interrupt their work to check whether they're at fault for the broken build. This approach will often require updating and merging the local working copy of the code with the code in the VCS mainline, and this loss of focus might decrease the team's productivity.

- Forcing the CI system to fork build jobs unconditionally on any commit doesn't solve the previous problem either. It will make it harder to investigate the last successful build and determine whether it has been completed, and it will be harder to determine the appropriate cumulated change-set that's the target for investigation to find the problem and create a solution. In addition, if Developer A is to blame (or partly to blame) for an integration problem, which a later commit of Developer B reveals by breaking a CI build, then Developer B—as the only team member being notified—has to investigate the full problem and the cumulated change-set in doubt. This may potentially result in them having to notify developer A to check whether their commit may have broken the build. This process foils the idea of automatic detection of problematic change-sets and automatic and well-targeted developer notification.

- Unless the developers in charge of fixing a broken CI have succeeded, the CI system will be useless to the rest of the team because their commits will always result in broken builds due to previous errors. Meanwhile, the change-sets that need to be investigated for a possible consecutive CI break might pile up significantly.

- Being blamed for breaking the team's CI is something a developer will try to avoid, particularly when their commit causes the project build to break; this means that each team member fetching their changes won't be able to build the project locally until the fix is applied. Consequently, developers might be tempted to double-check that their upcoming commits won't break the build, resulting in a process of updating and merging the local repository with the latest mainline revision followed by issuing a full project build. Doing this immediately wipes out the advantage of shortened turnaround cycles by shifting long-running tasks to the build server.

- A common side effect of the team dealing with the previously described problems is that the individual developer will tend to pile up their work results and not commit to the VCS until they regard the feature they are focusing on as being completed. This clearly violates the "commit early, commit often" policy, leading to implications such as change-sets that are huge, poorly documented, and lacking safe rollback points during the feature development process.

This is an impressive list of possible problems. Teams need to see positive results in the form of improved build processes or enhanced productivity in order to maintain the acceptance and support for implementing improved practices such as CI. Without visible results, support for CI will drop dramatically over time.

7.5.1 Feature branching comes to the rescue

The concept of feature branching addresses most of the problems previously mentioned. The idea is pretty simple: Each developer is given an isolated branch in the VCS to use for their changes for as long as is necessary to implement a specific feature. Reaching this milestone, they would then merge the cumulated changes on their feature branch back to the project's VCS mainline, which will then trigger the mainline CI job to check for proper integration.

> **Feature branching and CI**
>
> Some people claim that feature branching strictly conflicts with CI, because CI suggests that you should focus on a single VCS mainline (the head) and you shouldn't branch in VCS (or at least should minimize branching). Too many branches can lead to delays in the development flow, big merging efforts, and overall communication fragmenting; having a single code line in the VCS means that you have a central, single synchronization point.
>
> Depending on your specific requirements, feature branches can be the best approach for a given problem. If your task is to migrate major parts of the software to another solution, Martin Fowler suggests applying an approach named *branch by abstraction* instead of feature branching. See his "Feature Branch" discussion at http://martinfowler.com/bliki/FeatureBranch.html.

In an environment that uses Subversion as the VCS, which I have found to be common, the process would be similar to the following. First the developer starts work on a feature by creating a feature branch. They then switch their working copy to that branch:

```
> svn copy http://svn.myorg/ourproject/trunk \
     http://svn.myorg/ourproject/branches/myfeature \
     -m "Starting work on feature myfeature"
> cd checkout/ourproject
> svn switch http://svn.myorg/ourproject/branches/myfeature .
```

The developer starts working on the feature, issuing commits early and often. When finished, they reintegrate their work back to the trunk:

```
> svn switch -r HEAD http://svn.myorg/ourproject/trunk .
> svn merge --reintegrate \
```

```
      http://svn.myorg/ourproject/branches/myfeature
> svn commit -m "Merged myfeature into trunk"
```

Although working with Subversion for feature branching is possible nowadays, it hasn't always been ideal. The reintegration of the full commit history when merging a branch into the mainline wasn't available before Subversion 1.5, and support for managing conflicting merges is historically not considered a forte of Subversion.

Here's where one would argue that this is a perfect use case for a distributed VCS, such as Git. In contrast to a server-based VCS such as Subversion, the concept of a local working copy is replaced by forking a central master repository as a fully featured local repository on which changes will be done directly. Commits always affect only the local repository. To reintegrate the changes, the Git user pushes a chosen change-set, which consists of various commits and their commit messages, back to the master repository.

The developer starts their work by cloning the master repository locally:

```
> git clone git://git.myorg/ourproject .
```

The developer starts working on the feature, issuing commits early and often. When finished, they reintegrate their work back to the master repository:

```
> git push
```

Given that this is the native and recommended way to work with Git, it should be used as a solution for establishing a feature branch–driven process, because Git has a good reputation for automatic conflict resolution—even in the case of complicated conflicting changes.

Regardless of whether the team decides to use Subversion or Git for a feature-branching process, in both cases, the CI setup can be configured to define additional build jobs for each feature branch. An ongoing discussion is occurring about whether these jobs should be called *continuous building* instead of *continuous integration*, which reflects the conviction that "real" integration checks can happen only against the mainline.[12] In my opinion, running feature-branch build jobs with a CI server can still be considered CI, because in such a setup, the change-sets of an individual developer are continuously integrated against a frozen state of the overall project, given that the feature-build job will incorporate automatic testing and validation. Combined with mainline CI, it might be seen as a staged CI. Figure 7.27 illustrates this setup.

The advantages of this approach are quite obvious:

- The problem of having the integration of unstable code happen too early, causing more integration problems than necessary, is addressed by a process in which only complete features are integrated back into the mainline.
- A commit-triggered feature-branch CI build will always cover minimal change-sets by having only the one developer working on that branch, making it easy to focus notifications and investigate problems in the case of breaking integration.

---

[12] See Martin Fowler on feature branching at http://martinfowler.com/bliki/FeatureBranch.html.

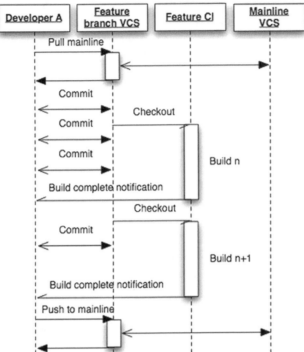

Figure 7.27 Feature-branching CI

- Breaking feature-branch CI won't affect any other team members, even if the project build breaks. The developer won't be blamed for holding up the team, and they can be truly confident in delegating full project builds and testing to the build server without causing harm. The individual developer can take full advantage of partial build and isolated testing features in their development environment and increase productivity and focus.
- The "commit early, commit often" policy won't negatively impact team productivity and developer reputation as described earlier, highly motivating the individual team member to embrace this policy.
- A well-organized feature-branching setup allows for cherry-picking features in the deliverable product.
- Build server job setups can easily be extended to do automatic deployments to, say, a testing environment, after successfully accomplished CI builds. This enables the developer to manually test the outcome without having to wait for a local build and deployment.

7.5.2 *The Lone Ranger problem and how the git-svn bridge can fix it*

Having a convincing concept isn't enough—it has to stand up to a reality check. If you try to move to a feature branch–driven process that includes CI, you might encounter some unexpected obstacles.

Let's imagine a senior developer with a rather progressive mindset, maybe even a contractor working on a rather traditional company's project as part of the team. Let's call him the Lone Ranger, fighting for a better world where software craftsmanship is regarded highly. He wants to take advantage of the described benefits but suddenly must face one or more of the following problems:

- The company refuses to provide a CI infrastructure. Whether this is reasonable or not, the contractor has to accept it as a political decision.
- The company, the infrastructure team, or the development team refuses to establish a Subversion branching policy, maybe because they fear the increased complexity of the VCS setup and handling.
- Switching to Git isn't an option. Maybe the infrastructure team doesn't have the knowledge or resources to set up a suitable Git infrastructure, or maybe the company recently switched from CVS to Subversion and refuses to reverse this decision, preferring to switch to a better product when it comes along. Maybe the Lone Ranger was the one who convinced them to switch to Subversion, and his reputation would be damaged if he now suggested switching to yet another product so soon after making his initial recommendation.
- The provided CI infrastructure isn't able to deal with the increased load of many parallel builds when defining jobs per feature branch in addition to the mainline CI.

It seems like there's no chance for a happy ending. But the Lone Ranger always has to win in the end, doesn't he? Let's see if we can manage to help him with that.

Both main problems—the lack of a CI infrastructure and the lack of a suitable VCS setup—can be addressed. Today's software development workstations are, in most cases, comparable to small servers, with multicore CPUs and a good amount of main memory. Such a workstation is astonishingly well suited to run a background CI build server, IDE, and whatever else a developer needs. In addition, the developer having a CI system in the background can ditch the time and resource-consuming full project foreground builds for the sake of partial builds and isolated tests. Setting up a local build server for CI takes only minutes using free products such as Jenkins or TeamCity. We would have to configure a proper build job. Doing so requires a repository we can watch for commit triggering and checking the working copy of the CI build.

Here is where the *git-svn bridge* comes in handy. The bridge makes it possible to work with a local Git repository as if it were in a full Git-based working environment. The only change is that the role of the master repository is assigned to the conventional central Subversion repository. The git-svn bridge translates (transparently) most of the Git push and pull operations to the Subversion repository instead of to a Git master repository.

Let's see how it works: Initialize a local Git repository to act as a Subversion repository clone, assuming that the repository has a standard layout as recommended by Subversion:

```
> git svn init -s
http://svn.myorg/ourproject/http://svn.myorg/ourproject/trunk
```

Fetch the Subversion change history into the local Git repository:

```
> git svn fetch
```

For Subversion repositories containing a rather small amount of changes, this will work quickly. For larger repositories, you would want to delimit the number of historical changes to fetch, which can be accomplished with the poorly documented but functional `--log-window-size` option:

```
> git svn fetch --log-window-size 1000
```

Configure the local CI job to watch and check out from the local Git repository. Start working on the feature in focus, issuing commits early and often:

```
> git commit -a \
-m "Refactored foo to separate interface and implementation"
```

When the feature is completed, push the changes to the central Subversion repository:

```
> git svn dcommit
```

Pull the latest changes from the Subversion repository to start working on the next feature:

```
> git svn rebase
```

Although the cleanroom process doesn't recommend fetching changes from the central repository during a local, uncompleted feature development cycle, you might nevertheless face the real-world requirement to do so. Because Git doesn't let you rebase the local repository if it has local-only changes in place, you'll have to decide how to move those changes out of the way. Obviously, you could push the local changes to the master repository, but the developer wouldn't want to do so unless they consider their feature to be completed. To perform a probably more desirable local merge similar to the behavior of `svn update` instead, you would utilize the stashing feature of Git as follows:

1 Move your local commits to a safe hidden place to prepare for pulling changes from the central repository:
2 `> git stash`
3 Fetch the changes from Subversion into your local Git repository:

    ```
    > git svn rebase
    ```

4 Apply the hidden local changes by merging them back to your local repository, which now represents the updated state from Subversion:

    ```
    > git stash pop
    ```

With this in place, the happy ending for the Lone Ranger's mission is within reach.

This was a focused introduction to a set of Git's features, enabling you to deal with a specific use case without diving too deeply into a complex tool and its implied workflows. Whenever the word branch is used in conjunction with Git, most users with Git experience will have Git's extremely powerful native branching and merging features in mind, which is intentionally not used in the workflow that this section describes. Nevertheless, if a developer is new to Git and starts to embrace it, we recommend that they learn about Git's branching and other advanced features.

7.6   *Summary*

In this chapter, we discussed CI, tooling, and strategies. You learned how to integrate all artifact types even with legacy technologies such as Cobol. You saw how an approach using a platform or language, such as Java, can be used to drive and manage the build of other languages or platforms. Where available, you can follow the second approach: use what exists for this platform and integrate the native build scripts with common build servers.

We discussed using .NET without all of the associated Microsoft tools. Although it's a proprietary platform, .NET can be handled with common tools. You don't have to use a complete proprietary toolchain; you can use lightweight tools (such as Subversion) to store your artifacts and to manage your builds. In one case, we dropped an Ant script into a CI server. In a second case, we dropped the MSBuild script into TeamCity.

We also discussed advanced configuration and staging recipes. One strategy involved building applications for different environments, and you saw that you should build your artifacts once and promote them to higher environments by plain configuration without rebuilding. It's also possible to use handmade scripts to scan your data-driven application configurations and automatically replace context-sensitive data, or to use standard approaches like Java properties. But these strategies have limits and aren't always the most efficient. In the other strategy, you learned how to use Maven to generate builds that run on multiple environments.

Two major CI servers, Jenkins and TeamCity, were part of our discussion. In general, both tools are similar. With Jenkins, you saw how to build, audit, and stage your Maven-based software. Here, the bridge to Artifactory was of special interest. TeamCity can also manage build scripts in a sophisticated way. We briefly prototyped how to drop .NET builds into a CI server and visualized how a build farm and an EC2 profile are connected.

We also talked about using feature branches with Git and Subversion. With this approach, you can use Subversion for version control and can also profit (or softly migrate) by using Git for feature branches.

In the next chapter, I'll describe strategies and tools for collaborative and barrier-free development and testing. Starting with a data-driven approach, we'll prototype acceptance tests and move on to behavior-driven development.

Part 4

Outside-in and barrier-free development

This last part of the book is about outside-in development. It discusses collaborative development and shows approaches to integrating different languages and tools for barrier-free development and testing.

Chapter 8 discusses Agile ALM approaches to requirements and test management. Here you'll learn collaborative approaches to development and testing. We'll discuss data-driven tests, acceptance tests, and behavior-driven development, and we'll go through example use cases with lightweight toolchains.

Chapter 9 continues to discuss barrier-free development. This chapter deals with polyglot platforms and covers Groovy and BDD with Scala/specs2. By the end of this part of the book, we'll have completed our thorough tour of Agile ALM.

Requirements and test management

In this chapter, we'll discuss how to implement collaborative and barrier-free development. We've already discussed tools that support release management, connecting the roles and artifacts in a task-based way. We also looked at how you can integrate the software delivery step into this process chain by integrating Mylyn with build engines. But build engines such as Jenkins, Bamboo, and TeamCity are only the infrastructure—they call your scripts, compile and test your application, and then package and deploy it. These steps don't say anything about the quality of the software in terms of how (and *if*) it implements customers' requirements.

In this chapter, we'll focus on the requirements and test management, and on integrating them with the coding phase.[1] Solid requirements management is essential for project success. "Studies of factors on challenged projects revealed that 37% of factors related to problems with requirements," such as poor user inputs.[2] As you have already learned, the development phases are highly integrated. Requirements management, development, and delivery are all part of the development lifecycle.

The integrated Agile ALM approach focuses on the customer's needs. In chapter 1 (section 1.3.4) we discussed what outside-in development comprises and that it's an essential part of Agile ALM to archive exactly that: a focus on satisfying the needs of the customer.[3] In this chapter, we'll discuss outside-in development in more detail, and I'll explain how to host it using integrated toolchains. We'll look at some use cases in the context of acceptance tests and behavior-driven development, and we'll focus on satisfying the needs of stakeholders. We'll start with a data-driven approach, continue with acceptance testing, and finish with behavior-driven development.

Integrated toolchains are recommended, and we'll introduce them with the help of some example use cases. The seamless characteristic of seamlessly integrated toolchains and programming languages is what I call barrier-free because you don't need to be concerned that there are different programming languages, different project roles, or different test types. (In chapter 9 we'll discuss polyglot programming—the aspect of the barrier-free approach that focuses on programming languages—in more detail.) All stakeholders use the same infrastructure and frameworks for the entire development process. As discussed in chapter 1, the Agile ALM approach provides a single view of the truth—a single view of the project, its processes, data, and status—as opposed to multiple and confusing versions, such as when you have organizational or technical silos across your project. The project infrastructure is collaborative because different project roles work together while writing and managing tests. Running collaborative tests frequently, as part of your continuous integration ecosystem, leads to early feedback and a living software documentation

Because I don't like to read overly academic stuff myself, I won't inflict it on you. This chapter focuses on specific and applied use cases. You may develop SWT applications rather than Swing applications, or you may prefer a specific tool in the discussed toolchains to another, but the strategies are the same. In this section, you'll gain further insight into what Agile ALM is and what it means to develop in an outside-in and barrier-free way.[4]

---

[1] Many people think that coding and testing aren't two distinct phases; rather, they belong to one project phase called "development."

[2] See Craig Larman, *Applying UML and Patterns* (Prentice Hall, 2002), pg. 42.

[3] For more information on outside-in, I recommend Carl Kessler and John Sweitzer, *Outside-in Software Development* (IBM Press, 2007).

[4] For more details on Agile requirements and test management, I recommend Lisa Crispin and Janet Gregory, *Agile Testing* (Addison-Wesley, 2009), and Dean Leffingwell, *Agile Software Requirements* (Addison-Wesley, 2011).

8.1   *Collaborative tests*

Software should be developed in a collaborative way. All roles, particularly developers, testers, and domain experts, should work closely to create the best software possible. But the barrier-free approach can also be supported by collaborative processes and tools.

Essential aspects of writing tests collaboratively include writing good acceptance tests, using the language of the domain expert, keeping the tests in an executable form, and considering behavior-driven development (BDD). Acceptance tests define the expectations of the customer (the person with the money) or the user (the person who is affected by or affects the product), or both. Writing acceptance tests in a ubiquitous language and in an executable way fosters outside-in development, further improves collaboration, and leads to better and more meaningful feedback loops. BDD is another way to apply outside-in development.

In 2003, Brian Marick defined an Agile testing matrix that was further refined by Lisa Crispin.[5] The matrix distinguishes between business-facing tests and technology-facing tests (see figure 8.1). A business-facing test is one that's understandable by a domain expert, whereas a technology-facing test is one written by and for developers only. Additionally, the matrix groups tests that support the team and tests that critique the product.

Supportive tests directly help during the process of developing the software, whereas tests that critique the product are after-the-fact tests that validate the completed product (or a reasonable increment of it) in order to find defects. The matrix in figure 8.1 consists of four quadrants, Q1–Q4.

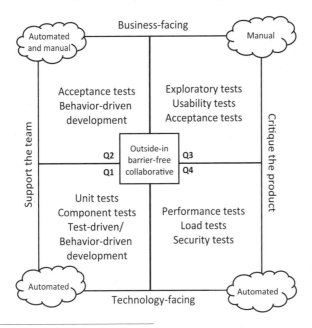

Figure 8.1   A test matrix (a skeletal based on Lisa Crispin's version of Brian Marick's diagram) that arranges acceptance tests and BDD in quadrants. Tests can be divided into business-facing and technology-facing as well as those that support the team and those that critique the product.

---

[5]   Brian Marick's original blog post, from August 21, 2003, can be found here: http://www.exampler.com/ old-blog/2003/08/21/. Lisa Crispin's refinements can be found in her book, *Agile Testing* (Addison Wesley, 2009), pg. 98.

The lower-left quadrant (Q1) represents technical tests (often provided with the help of tools from the xUnit family). This quadrant commonly includes unit tests and component tests, where a component is more coarse-grained than a unit is and often spans different artifacts or architectural layers. These tests help to improve the design of the code and improve the internal quality of the software. These *white box* tests address how a specific task is solved.

Another aspect that relates to Q1 is test-driven development (TDD).[6] TDD is a widely accepted concept that includes writing tests first and refactoring the code continuously. The goal is to focus on the specific task, while eliminating waste, improving the design of the code, and setting up and maintaining adequate test coverage. In his book *Clean Code, A Handbook of Agile Software Craftsmanship*, Robert C. Martin lists "Three Laws of Test-Driven Development":

- You may not write production code until you have written a failing unit test.
- You may not write more of a unit test than is sufficient to fail, and not compiling is failing.
- You may not write more production code than is sufficient to pass the currently failing test.

BDD often touches Q1 too. Within the context of Q1, BDD is similar to TDD, but with more focus on specifications that lead to low-level specifications for the code.

The tests in Q2 are often highly automated as well, but they drive the development at a higher, functional level and target the external quality of the software. There, tests define functional requirements and run as *black box* tests. They address the question of what the specific task is. "Design itself is the process of converting a black box to a white (or transparent) box—one in which we can clearly see all the details of *how*."[7] This quadrant includes acceptance tests and BDD.

Acceptance tests are also used in Q3 after the software is developed (development milestones can be provided frequently). These manual tests address aspects that are hard to automate, such as usability.

Finally, Q4 includes tests that critique the product on a technical level. This area often addresses nonfunctional requirements.

Acceptance tests are business-facing tests. They represent functional requirements for software that's under construction (coordinating what's developed) or already completed, ensuring that changes don't break existing functionality. Tests that validate that changes don't break existing functionality are often called regression tests.

Acceptance tests should be executed automatically in order to reduce the cycle time and to deliver objective results. The technique of BDD, which we'll look at a bit later, also supports the team while developing the software. Acceptance tests and BDD foster outside-in, barrier-free, and collaborative development. Implemented and integrated

---

[6] See Kent Beck, *Test-Driven Development* (Addison-Wesley, 2002) and Lasse Koskela, *Test Driven* (Manning, 2008).

[7] Donald C. Gause and Gerald M. Weinberg, *Exploring Requirements, Quality before Design* (Dorset House, 1989), pg. 249.

with the right tools, these strategies are powerful vehicles for requirements and test management. By integrating different quadrants of the matrix with each other, all the different test categories can be run in conjunction with one step, and the results can be aggregated.

Let's start by looking at the basics of writing good data-driven tests. Data-driven tests are the prerequisite for any further advanced strategy.

8.1.1 Data-driven tests

An important aspect of testing is how you generate and manage the physical test data. Data-driven testing means testing with test data that's decoupled from the test scripts. You write data-driven tests before (or while) developing the application. Using data-driven testing only for after-the-fact functional testing is often considered an antipattern.

There are many advantages to separating the data from the tests, including the following:[8]

- It makes test data easy to edit.
- It makes adding new test cases easier.
- It helps reduce failures caused by invalid data.

The data-driven testing approach focuses on the separation of concerns instead of the hardcoded data, and it allows you to change data easily. You can distinguish between input data and output data; in an approach that's fully data-driven, both types of data should be excluded from the code. Therefore, both types of data can be managed without touching the test classes. Where you need to reference the data in test classes, solutions must support variables inside these test classes and generate verifications dynamically. Examples of mediums for input and output data are flat files, HTML files, and Excel documents.

For user interface (UI) testing, you can use a capture and replay (CR) tool to collect input data (and user interactions) for test input. CR tools for UI testing can add value, but you shouldn't rely on them solely. Captured and saved interactions result in scripts that are like source code: You must maintain these tests scripts, refactor them, and optimize them. This optimization includes isolating tests after recording them, and making them robust for future changes. For example, you should identify UI controls relatively, not by an absolute position that directly depends on other controls. Software changes, and input scripts must be flexible enough to evolve along with the software.

Depending on the context, having a small set of automatic UI tests can be a good start. You could use a small set of automatic UI tests as a sanity check that runs after every build or as a first quality gate in a staged build environment. Many projects use several UI tests, and they find it helpful; some even automate all their acceptance tests as UI tests. But testing via the UI is often slow and brittle. Not everything should be tested via the UI; only a subset of all existing tests of different test types should be. You should always take care to slice your tests adequately. For example, if you must start a

---

[8] See Thomas Hammell, *Test-Driven Development* (Apress, 2005), pg. 169.

UI test in order to test a database operation or business logic, something can be improved for sure.

Collecting and using data for tests has been a common practice for quite some time now. But what differentiates good tests from simple data-driven tests? The answer is that good tests should be acceptance tests, which is what we'll discuss next.

8.1.2   Acceptance tests

Acceptance tests determine whether a system satisfies its specified acceptance criteria. This helps the customer to decide whether to accept the software: "Acceptance tests allow the customer to know when the system works and tell the programmers what needs to be done."[9] This means that acceptance tests also tell the programmers what the customer doesn't want them to do.

Using acceptance tests to determine what has to be delivered to the customer is sometimes called *acceptance test-driven development* (ATDD). The name suggests an analogy to traditional TDD, but the latter is more focused on improving the design of the software and delivering the right thing correctly, whereas ATDD has the goal of ensuring that the right thing is delivered and that it's delivered when it's supposed to be delivered. The goals and concepts of these two approaches are similar though.

Compared to a subjective "look and approve" approach, acceptance criteria is measurable and objective. In the worst-case scenario, the acceptance criteria aren't known, or the approval is done by the client in a capricious way.

Setting up acceptance criteria the Agile way means that the specification is neither calculated precisely (in a mathematical sense) nor complete. Rather, the criteria consist of example interactions. That's why this approach is often referred to as *specification by example*.[10] The general process is compatible with traditional requirements management, where you write use cases (or user stories) that also contain scenarios.

Acceptance tests can be used on different specification levels, from coarse-grained to fine-grained, starting with tests for features and stories or scenarios up to tests for tasks. Because each acceptance test examines functionality, they're *functional tests*.

Acceptance tests are another example of focusing on meeting the stakeholder's requirements as advocated by the outside-in approach. You can introduce critical requirements into the test, distinguishing between must-have features and other less important ones. Acceptance tests assess whether the application is doing the right thing; they approach the project from the macro level. Unit tests (or component tests, depending on how you slice them) technically assess the classes and modules; they focus on the micro level. Unit tests validate whether the right thing (according to the acceptance criteria) is done correctly. Acceptance and unit tests should be used in conjunction with each other.

---

[9] See Ron Jeffries, Ann Anderson, and Chet Hendrickson, *Extreme Programming Installed* (Addison-Wesley, 2001), pg. 31.

[10] Gojko Adzic, *Specification by Example* (Manning, 2011).

Although it's strongly recommended that you write acceptance tests before (or while) developing the application, acceptance tests can also be created after the application is written in special cases—for instance, in a migration scenario accessing legacy code. Acceptance criteria should be specified before starting the acceptance routine that's approving the software.

Although you use an incremental and iterative development process, you must know the goal that you're trying to achieve. If your work isn't defined by concrete requirements, you won't be effective. Whether you do it the Agile way or not, clear requirements are essential for achieving measurable and objective success. In the best case, the requirements can be executed and validated automatically, for instance, through triggering by the CI system (like those shown in this chapter). They're part of the release and are put into the VCS along with the other coding artifacts.

Let's now discuss the importance of ubiquitous language in testing.

8.1.3 *Ubiquitous language*

Who can describe the customer's expectations better than the customers can? The domain expert has the deepest domain knowledge. This is the approach taken in the book *Domain-Driven Design*, where Eric Evans defines *ubiquitous language* as being "structured around the domain model and used by all team members to connect all the activities of the team with software."[11] This ubiquitous language breaks down barriers between different roles and organizational units. Where other approaches use different vehicles for stakeholder communication (such as the software architecture[12]), writing acceptance tests in an ubiquitous language is a common Agile practice for stakeholder communication and asking the right questions while moving from the problem domain to the solution domain.

A ubiquitous language keeps you aligned with business values and goals. Information technology is a means to the end of achieving those business goals, so you don't align the communication with the technical language of developers, but rather with the language of the subject area you're working in. Consequently, it's important for the entire team to communicate in the domain language, without having silos.

A common challenge is that customers, domain experts, and the technical crew don't interact often enough and they don't speak the same language. Agile tries to solve that, particularly by writing tests iteratively, focused on functionality and requirements to help overcome any barriers and clarify communication. This is a major difference compared to unit tests that are written by and for developers.

The barrier-free approach of using an ubiquitous language must respect the fact that customers often don't have a detailed technical understanding (nor do they need to). The process should also be efficient, which means the requirements should be documented in a form that the customer can work with. Teamwork is also essential:

---

[11] Eric Evans, *Domain-Driven Design: Tackling Complexity in the Heart of Software* (Addison-Wesley, 2003), pg. 514.

[12] See Len Bass, Paul Clements, and Rick Kazman, *Software Architecture in Practice*, 2nd ed. (Addison-Wesley, 2003), pg. 27.

You must help the customer and support them if they have problems, such as writing tests, or if the customer asks for implementation details.

It can also be good to have a technical person (or business analyst) stand in as a proxy for the customer, to document the requirements in this executable form. This can be helpful if the real customer isn't available, or if the customer doesn't want to write tests in an executable form. The proxy should be installed before a release starts; all project roles (and their responsibilities) should be fixed and assigned to people before the release starts. Clearly communicated project roles and responsibilities are essential for open and direct team communication.

Using a common and relatively unambiguous language is essential. Acceptance tests that are written in the language of the domain expert can be validated continuously if the tests are executable.

8.1.4   *Executable specifications*

Executable specifications allow you to use tools that read the specifications automatically (either after manually starting the process, or continuously as part of a CI process), process them against the system under testing, and output the results in an objectively measurable, efficient, and readable way. The domain expert specifies the tests in simple formats, and the program writes the results after running the tests against the system under test.

Traditional Word documents aren't executable and they're problematic in Agile teams where you want to run tests iteratively and often. Someone must read the specs in Word documents, apply them to the system undergoing the test, verify the results, and document them manually, in isolated manual and error-prone steps. Describing requirements in an executable way fosters the barrier-free approach. Executable requirements help to minimize the number of different artifact types that express the same information about the software. Merging different mediums for documentation (single-sourcing product information) reduces the amount of traditional documentation, because the specification *is* the system's functional documentation and therefore can be efficiently validated against the current software state. Executable specifications lead to living (always up-to-date) software documentation, more efficient code changes, higher product quality and less rework, and a better alignment of activities of different roles on a project (see Adzic, *Specification by Example*, pg. 6).

By combining different test strategies, you can profit from the best results of each. Customer-centric acceptance tests are based on data-driven tests and are written in the language of the domain expert. These specifications test the application "by example" by applying test scenarios to the system under test. Acceptance tests (in the Agile sense) are executable, just as BDD fosters executable specs, as discussed next.

8.1.5   *Behavior-driven development*

Behavior-driven development (BDD) promotes a special approach to writing and applying acceptance tests that's different from the traditional TDD, although BDD also promotes writing tests first. BDD was first defined in Dan North's article, "Introducing

BDD" (http://dannorth.net/introducing-bdd), in which the tests are like (functional) stories in a *given/when/then* format. This specification-oriented technique also uses a natural language to ensure cross-functional communication and to understand business concepts. BDD provides a ubiquitous language for analysis and emphasizes application behavior over testing. BDD fosters writing tests from a domain perspective rather than a technical perspective.

In BDD, user stories are input to test scenarios that specify what the system does. The programmer codes the test scenarios directly in the test tool.[13] BDD is a new Agile software development technique that helps software developers collaborate with businesspeople. But this isn't its only benefit. It also simplifies and clarifies the test code.

Let's discuss the benefits and principles of using BDD in your projects. First, and most importantly, BDD is a specification-oriented technique. This implies that you, as a BDD developer, will be focused on specifications as the main concept. But you're also going to leverage BDD for verifying and writing your code. BDD is a different approach than traditional TDD, focusing more on code verification than on the functionality the code should provide.

Why does BDD matter? Because well-defined specifications help developers write tests that cover all major aspects of system functionality. They also provide a good overview of how everything should work. BDD uses a natural language for specifying interactions and functionality, which is the easiest way to ensure good communication and understanding of business concepts by all members of the project, whether they're developers, project managers, or domain experts.

> **GIVEN/WHEN/THEN AND OTHER STRUCTURES** Don't equate BDD with given/when/then. You can use other ways to structure specifications, like "As a" (which expresses the type of user), "In order to" (which expresses the goal), "I can" (which expresses the task), and "And then" (which expresses the result). Even though BDD has been popularized with the given/when/then structure, the Fit tool (which we'll look at later in this chapter) has been around for much longer than BDD, and it was used by people doing BDD before the BDD name came into use.

I'm sure you have been in situations where you start writing tests and only after some time passes does it become apparent exactly what needs to be tested and how the testing needs to be done. BDD solves this issue by defining in the first step the name of the test method that will describe your business case. Only after that do you start developing your test.

BDD requires names for test methods that describe the functionality each test is supposed to check within the method. The name of the method clarifies what should be tested and how the code should work. This is extremely useful for other developers, because they only need to take one look at your test to get an idea of what it tests and how it works. You might even say that the behavior specification defines your test methods, which defines your application code.

---

[13] James O. Coplien and Gertrud Bjornvig, *Lean Architecture* (Wiley, 2010), pg. 175.

Consider the following example. You're writing code to calculate the sum of two values. You might start by creating the `CalculatorTest` class, which will contain the `testAdd()` method. Then you create the `Calculator` class with an `add()` method that will take two parameters and return their sum. This approach works fine, but you could do that in a better way by defining the behavior, creating tests with appropriate test methods (with well-defined names), and finally creating the `Calculator` class with the `add()` method. The test class might look like this:

```
class CalculatorTest {
  public void addsTwoAndThreeAndReturnsFive() {
    ...
  }
  public void addsMinusOneAndThreeAndReturnsTwo() {
    ...
  }
}
```

BDD can easily be combined with traditional approaches like TDD. All you need to care about is defining your specifications (which should represent the business behavior of your system) before developing the test and then implementing tests directly associated with appropriate specifications.

To write a BDD specification, focus on the three most important BDD phrases:

- *Given*—Defines the initial state of the scenario
- *When*—Defines an event (something that should happen)
- *Then*—Defines the final state of the scenario

The initial state of the scenario is the beginning of your business case. It also serves as the input for the event represented by the term when. The final state should represent the end of your business case. It describes what you want to reach as a consequence of the preceding event.

Suppose a child wants to buy one can of Coca-Cola from a vending machine. We'll consider three main scenarios:

- The machine has enough cans of Coca-Cola; the child pays for one and receives it.
- The machine has enough cans of Coca-Cola; the child pays an insufficient amount of money for one can and receives all the money back.
- The machine is out of cans; the child pays for one can but the machine returns all of the money.

Here's what the BDD approach would look like for the first scenario:

- *Given* that there are enough cans of Coca-Cola.
- *When* the child pays enough money.
- *Then* ensure the child receives one can of Coca-Cola.
- *And* ensure the child receives change.

The first line reads, "There are enough cans of Coca-Cola." This describes the initial state of the scenario (that is, it sets an initial context) and ensures that a sufficient number of cans are available in the machine. Then the "child pays enough money" event occurred. This event represents our business logic. As a result, we should receive two outcomes, which will define the final state of the scenario. These outcomes are "receives one can of Coca-Cola" and "receives change."

The second scenario is defined here:

- *Given* that there are enough cans of Coca-Cola.
- *When* the child pays an insufficient amount of money.
- *Then* ensure the child will not receive a can.
- *And* ensure the child receives all money back.

And here is the third scenario:

- *Given* that there aren't enough cans of Coca-Cola.
- *When* the child pays enough money.
- *Then* ensure the child receives all money back.

These scenarios are described in natural language that can be understood by all project members. They directly represent the business flow and business expectations by describing the initial state, the events, and the final state that should be reached.

BDD is effective, as is the use of test tools such as TestNG, Selenium, and Excel.

8.2 Acceptance testing with TestNG, Selenium, XStream, and Excel

> —*This section contributed by Simon Tiffert*

In this section, we'll test a rich internet application (RIA) with Selenium as the web driver and TestNG as our backbone for data-driven tests. The test data is serialized by XStream. Maven supports all these tools.

Before we start integrating the tools in our example use case, let's briefly discuss the underlying technologies.

8.2.1 TestNG and the data-driven approach

TestNG (http://testng.org) is a testing framework inspired by JUnit and NUnit. It's flexible and perfectly suited for normal unit tests as well as more complex tests of different types: unit tests, integration tests, and acceptance tests. It's supported by all major Java IDEs and build systems. Features like test groups, support for data-driven testing by enabling parameterized tests with complex objects (`@DataProvider`), and test dependencies make TestNG a unique tool.[14]

Test groups can be used to group tests for different setups, and they can be used to prioritize your tests. The first group would be the most important tests; you must run them to ensure that the main system is working. The second group is smoke tests; these should run quickly enough for you to be able to trigger them several times a day. With a smoke test, various areas of the system are analyzed but not in full detail. The

---

[14] See Cédric Beust and Hani Suleiman, *Next Generation Java Testing: TestNG and Advanced Concepts* (Addison-Wesley, 2008).

last test group includes every test and tests in more detail; it should be triggered only once a day, such as in a nightly build.

A test can belong to zero, one, or multiple test groups. This is defined in an annotation at the method or class level. A group definition on the test class is inherited for every test method inside the class. A simple test assigned to the test group smoke-test could look like this:

```
@Test(groups = {"smoke-test"})
public void testToString() {
    User user = new User("Albert", "Einstein");
    Assert.assertEquals(user.toString(), "User: Albert Einstein");
}
```

Implementing the tests from a Maven script is pretty easy. The Surefire plug-in is included in Maven's default configuration and searches test cases in the src/test/java folder. It runs in the Maven test phase and looks for class names that follow these patterns: **/Test*.java, **/*Test.java, and **/*TestCase.java. You can run both unit tests and integration tests with the Surefire plug-in, but this configuration gets more complicated, and there's no way to skip the integration tests.

The Failsafe plug-in is designed to run integration tests. It's a fork of the Surefire plug-in, and it ensures that the postintegration phase runs even if there's an error in the integration tests. To differentiate the tests, you can store the integration tests with any of the following patterns: **/IT*.java, **/*IT.java, and **/*ITCase.java.

Both plug-ins can run JUnit and TestNG tests. All you need to do is include the dependency of the framework. In our example, it's this:

```
<dependency>
    <groupId>org.testng</groupId>
    <artifactId>testng</artifactId>
    <version>5.10</version>
    <scope>test</scope>
    <classifier>jdk15</classifier>
</dependency>
```

If you want to run all the tests, there's nothing else to configure. With the help of different testng.xml files, you can set up finely grained tests. You can define parameters for each test suite and include or exclude Java packages and files or the previously defined test groups. An example TestNG test suite is illustrated in the following listing.

Listing 8.1   TestNG test suite

```
<suite name="smoke" verbose="1">
    <parameter name="PARAMETER_NAME"           ⟵  Parameters passed
        value="PARAMETER_VALUE"/>                   to suite
    <test name="smokeTest">
        <groups>
            <run>
                <include name="smoke-test"/>       Includes/excludes
                <exclude name="broken"/>           used on group level
            </run>
        </groups>
```

```
            <packages>                                   Test defined by
                <package name="PACKAGENAME"/>            specifying package
            </packages>
            <classes>                                    Individual methods
                <class name="A_CLASS">                   assigned to suite
                    <methods>
                        <include name="SMOKE_TEST"/>
                        <exclude name="FUNCTIONAL_TEST"/>
                    </methods>
                </class>
            </classes>
        </test>
</suite>
```

One important feature of TestNG is the separation of test logic and test data. To catch as many error situations and corner cases as possible, you should define them in the most compact form. In the following listing, TestNG's DataProvider is used to inject an array of arrays into the test method.

Listing 8.2   Using data-driven tests with TestNG and its DataProvider

```
import org.testng.Assert;
import org.testng.annotations.DataProvider;
import org.testng.annotations.Test;

public class UserTest {                                  Use DataProvider
    @Test(dataProvider = "users")                        named "users"
    public void testToString(String firstName,
                             String lastName, String result) {
        User user = new User(firstName, lastName);
        Assert.assertEquals(user.toString(), result);   Run tests for
    }                                                    each data set

    @DataProvider(name = "users")                        Annotate method
    public Object[][] createData() {                     as DataProvider
        return new Object[][]{
                {"Paul", "Breitner", "User: Paul Breitner"},
                {null, "Breitner", "User: Breitner"},
                {"", "Breitner", "User: Breitner"},
                {"Paul", null, "User: Paul"},
                {"Paul", "", "User: Paul"},
                {null, null, "no user"},
                {"", null, "no user"}};
    }
}
```

As you can see, we've extracted the data out of the test logic. TestNG expects an array of objects for each test run, and each entry of that array is matched to a parameter of the test method.

Often, you will need the same data for different tests. To reuse the data, you must define the DataProvider to the @Test annotation—that's good. The data is hardcoded inside the test class—that's bad. The next step is to define the test data outside of the class; then other nondevelopers can manage the data, too. You shouldn't do this for unit tests, but in functional tests, you can predefine the test data and program against this data.

The data needs to be defined in a more user-friendly format, such as XML, Excel, or whatever format best suits your needs. Let's first look at an approach based on object trees and XML. Using test tools with a data-driven approach is important. XStream helps makes this effort easier by serializing the XML data.

8.2.2   *Data-driven testing with XStream*

XStream is an XML serializer and deserializer. You'll use it when you need an object from an XML structure or vice versa. It's easy to use and the XML is clean.

If you're defining test data of flat objects in Java, you need to write some glue code. If you need to define object trees, you'll soon realize that Java is the wrong language—it's time-consuming to initialize every child object, set the values, and assign them to the parent object. This would be fine if you needed it at a few points in your application, but if there are predefined object hierarchies, you should extract them. An XML structure is a common way to describe object hierarchies; there are a lot of tools available, and you don't need to worry about using the wrong character sets.

Let's start with a simple example. First, we'll add the XStream dependency to the pom.xml file:

```
<dependency>
   <groupId>com.thoughtworks.xstream</groupId>
   <artifactId>xstream</artifactId>
   <version>1.3.1</version>
</dependency>
```

Now let's write a simple Java bean:

```
public class User {
    private String firstName;
    private String lastName;
    public User(String firstName, String lastName) {
        this.lastName = lastName;
        this.firstName = firstName;
    }
    ...
}
```

To serialize User with XStream, we can use XStream's API as follows:

```
XStream xstream = new XStream();
User user = new User("Paul", "Breitner");
String xml = xstream.toXML(user);
```

Depending on the package name you use in your Java class, the result should look similar to this:

```
<org.agile.alm.entities.User>
  <firstName>Paul</firstName>
  <lastName>Breitner</lastName>
</org.agile.alm.entities.User>
```

As you can see, there are some package definitions in the XML file.

If you want a cleaner XML structure, you can define aliases in XStream. You can define an alias either as an annotation or as a special definition. If you can control your objects, annotations are a handy way to write and forget about the aliases if you use that object multiple times in different code positions. Serializing with a defined alias looks like this:

```
XStream xstream = new XStream();
xstream.alias("user",User.class);
User user = new User("Paul", "Breitner");
String xml = xstream.toXML(user);
```

Working with XStream annotations looks like this:

```
import com.thoughtworks.xstream.annotations.XStreamAlias;

@XStreamAlias("user")
public class User {
    private String firstName;
    private String lastName;
    ...
}
```

In the Java code, serializing based on annotations looks like this:

```
XStream xstream = new XStream();
xstream.processAnnotations(User.class);
User user = new User("Paul", "Breitner");
String xml = xstream.toXML(user);
```

The results are the following XML:

```
<user>
  <firstName>Paul</firstName>
  <lastName>Breitner</lastName>
</user>
```

For deserializing objects back from XML, you must go the following way:

```
String xml = "<user><firstName>Paul</firstName>
<lastName>Breitner</lastName></user>";
XStream xstream = new XStream();
xstream.processAnnotations(User.class);
User user = (User) xstream.fromXML(xml);
```

XStream is even more helpful if you have larger object trees for deserialization. Normally, the objects of your model are already defined, and with XStream, you can easily reuse complex objects to drive your `DataProvider` in TestNG.

Now let's go back to TestNG. To use your list of objects as a `DataProvider` there, you can use a helper function that transforms it into an array of arrays, as shown in the following listing.

Listing 8.3   TestNG test class reading data from XML via XStream

```
import org.agile.alm.entities.User;
import com.thoughtworks.xstream.XStream;
import org.testng.Assert;
```

```
import org.testng.annotations.DataProvider;
import org.testng.annotations.Test;
import java.io.IOException;
import java.io.InputStream;
import java.util.List;

public class TestMe {
    ...
    protected <T> List<T> readListData(String filename) {        Read XML
        return (List<T>) xstream.fromXML(this.getClass().getClassLoader().    with XStream
                getResourceAsStream(filename));
    }

    public static <T> Object[][]                              ❶ Transform list
        getObjectArray(List<T> elements) {                       into array of arrays
        Object[][] values = new Object[elements.size()][1];
        int counter = 0;
        for (T t : elements) {
            values[counter][0] = t;
            counter++;
        }
        return values;
    }

    @DataProvider(name = "users")
    public Object[][] createData() {                          Return data
        List<User> users = readListData("users.xml");;        for tests
        return getObjectArray(users);
    }
    ...
}
```

Transforming the list into an array of arrays ❶ allows it to fit into TestNG's data-Provider format.

The reuse of your model can be handy in data-driven functional tests. If you have ten or more parameters in your user interface that you want to check, the parameter list becomes even more complicated and results in a lot of work. Building your user interface around your model using XStream is the way to go. XStream makes it easy to fill in the important parts of your model.

To further explain this use case, let's talk about using Selenium to test web apps.

8.2.3   *Testing the web UI with Selenium, TestNG, and XStream*

Selenium is a web test framework that drives the user interfaces with JavaScript. It has direct access to the full web page and its DOM. Different types of locators are available that tell Selenium which HTML element a command refers to on the page.

If you're testing in the Java world, you'll normally be faced with Selenium Remote Control (Selenium RC). Selenium RC acts as a small server that gets execution commands. It can start and stop browsers on different platforms; after the browser is started, it communicates with the injected Selenium Core, which is based on JavaScript. Different client libraries are available for different platforms to drive Selenium.

Selenium fits perfectly in a Maven and TestNG setup. The Selenium Maven plug-in starts Selenium RC on the local machine in the preintegration test phase (see the following listing).

Listing 8.4 Starting and stopping the Selenium server via Maven

```
<plugin>
    <groupId>org.codehaus.mojo</groupId>
    <artifactId>selenium-maven-plugin</artifactId>
    <executions>
        <execution>
            <id>start</id>
            <phase>pre-integration-test</phase>          ◁──┐ Start
            <goals>                                           test
                <goal>start-server</goal>
            </goals>
            <configuration>
                <background>true</background>
            </configuration>
        </execution>

        <execution>
            <id>stop</id>
            <phase>post-integration-test</phase>        ◁──┐ Stop
            <goals>                                          test
                <goal>stop-server</goal>
            </goals>
        </execution>
    </executions>
</plugin>
```

The TestNG test suites are defined in XML, and you can tell Maven which test suite to take. Instead of using the Surefire plug-in directly (which is responsible for testing with Maven), you can use the Failsafe plug-in, which is a fork of the Surefire plug-in for running integration tests, as was discussed earlier in this chapter. The Surefire plug-in stops the build when a test failure occurs, with the result that the test environment isn't released correctly. The Failsafe plug-in won't fail the build during the integration-test phase, enabling the postintegration-test phase to execute.

The following listing shows the part of the POM where you define that the testng-firefox-minimal.xml test suite is taken for test definition.

Listing 8.5 Defining the tests in the POM

```
<plugin>
    <groupId>org.apache.maven.plugins </groupId>      ◁──┐ Use failsafe-
    <artifactId>maven-failsafe-plugin</artifactId>      ❶ maven-plugin
    <version>2.8.1</version>
    <executions>
        <execution>
            <id>integration-test</id>
            <goals>
                <goal>integration-test</goal>
```

```
        </goals>
        <configuration>                          ❷ Define TestNG
            <suiteXmlFiles>                         test suite
                <suiteXmlFile>src/test/resources/
                    testng-firefox-minimal.xml</suiteXmlFile>
            </suiteXmlFiles>
        </configuration>
    </execution>
    <execution>
        <id>verify</id>
        <goals>
            <goal>verify</goal>
        </goals>
    </execution>
    </executions>
</plugin>
```

By using the `failsafe-maven-plugin` ❶, the build won't break even if tests fail. The TestNG test suite ❷ is a collection of include and exclude patterns and packages. Generally, for setting up Selenium tests, you need the following:

- A system under test, accessible on the server where Selenium RC runs
- A configuration to access Selenium RC
- Selenium tests to verify that the web user interface is working as expected

Locally, you can start the application with the Maven Cargo plug-in. The application is running on a port you need for test configuration. You additionally need the port of Selenium RC, which is port 4444 by default. The host is `localhost` in this example (as you will see in listing 8.6).

You can prepare test servers with different operating systems and browsers installed. The servers can run Selenium RC as a service, and you only need to point your tests to run against these servers. The application that you want to test could be complex and so large that it's deployed only once a day to an external location. In this case, you could run the tests on different operating systems and browsers against this external location. Be aware that parallel tests get more complicated in such a setup.

Let's go back to the Selenium test setup. The easiest way to get started with Selenium is to use the Selenium IDE until you're familiar with the most recently used commands. Selenium IDE is a Firefox plug-in that can record tests while you use the application under test. This allows you to replay the tests inside the Selenium IDE and export tests in various languages like Java. Once you understand the common commands, you can dig deeper into your DOM, your application, and your tests.

Recorded tests are fragile. The tests may suggest that nothing has changed, but if things like layout or template do change, your tests shouldn't break. Tests should rely on the base of your application, like HTML elements that are marked with a unique ID. This is why we rely on tests written in a higher programming language like Java with the TestNG framework—we can include those test sequences in continuous integration easily. Furthermore, hosting the tests in TestNG enables barrier-free testing: We can aggregate functional tests with other test categories.

To add the compile and classpath dependency to the Selenium Java library, add the following entry to your Maven POM:

```
<dependency>
    <groupId>org.seleniumhq.selenium.client-drivers</groupId>
    <artifactId>selenium-java-client-driver</artifactId>
    <version>1.0.1</version>
</dependency>
```

The following listing shows a simple TestNG test class. It uses the Selenium API provided by selenium-java-client-driver.

Listing 8.6 A simple TestNG test class, including Selenium

```
import com.thoughtworks.selenium.DefaultSelenium;
import com.thoughtworks.selenium.Selenium;
import org.testng.annotations.AfterClass;
import org.testng.annotations.BeforeClass;
import org.testng.annotations.Test;

public class SimpleSeleniumIT {
    private Selenium selenium;

    @BeforeClass
    private void init() throws Exception {
        selenium = new DefaultSelenium("localhost", 4444, "*safari",
                    "http://localhost:8000/");
        selenium.start();                          ◁─┐ Launch browser
    }                                                 │ window

    @Test
    public void testPage() throws Exception {
        selenium.open(
          "http://localhost:8000/webtest/index.jsp");
        selenium.waitForPageToLoad("10000");          │ Perform test
        Assert.assertTrue(
          selenium.isTextPresent("Hello World"));
    }

    @AfterClass
    private void stop() throws Exception {
        selenium.stop();
    }
}
```

The browser is started with TestNG's `@BeforeClass` annotation. You could also use `@BeforeSuite` or `@BeforeTest`. Keep in mind that the browser start process can take a pretty long time, so you should avoid restarts if possible.

With the initialization of the `DefaultSelenium` class, you need four parameters:

- `serverHost`—The host name of the Selenium RC server
- `serverPort`—The port of the Selenium RC server
- `browser`—A Selenium-specific browser string (such as, `*iexplore` for Internet Explorer)
- `browserURL`—The URL of your application

The test in listing 8.6 uses the `@Test` annotation. It first opens the website, waits for the page to load (for a length of time specified in milliseconds), and then verifies whether the text appears.

Let's now complete the data-driven web testing scenario by integrating TestNG, Selenium, and XStream. The following listing is the missing piece.

Listing 8.7   Integrating TestNG, Selenium, and XStream

```
@Test
public void testPage() throws Exception {
    selenium.open("http://localhost:8000/webtest/index.jsp");
    selenium.waitForPageToLoad("10000");
    selenium.isTextPresent("Hello World");
}

@Test(dataProvider = "users")                       ❶ Receive data
public void testDataTable(User user) throws Exception {   by XStream
    selenium.open("http://localhost:8000/webtest/index.jsp");
    selenium.waitForPageToLoad("10000");
    Assert.assertTrue(selenium.isElementPresent
        ("xpath=//table/tbody/tr/td[1][text()='" +      Run tests
        user.getFirstName() + "']"));               ❷ on the data
    Assert.assertTrue(selenium.isElementPresent
        ("xpath=//table/tbody/tr/td[2][text()='" +
        user.getLastName() + "']"));
}
```

This listing shows the remaining details of the TestNG test class that runs a data-driven test. The `testDataTable` method gets its test data from the XStream `DataProvider` ❶ that we discussed earlier in this chapter, and then it runs the test ❷.

It can be more convenient to use Maven profiles to manage which kinds of tests you want to run. The following listing shows such an example.

Listing 8.8   Using profiles to decide which tests to run

```
<profiles>                          ❶ Define first
    <profile>                          profile
        <id>daily</id>                       Set unique
        <activation>                         profile ID
            <property>
                <name>!nightly</name>          Define when profile
            </property>                        will be activated
        </activation>
        <build>                        Derive build
            <plugins>                  phase for profile
                <plugin>
                    <groupId>org.apache.maven.plugins </groupId>
                    <artifactId>maven-failsafe -plugin</artifactId>
                    <version>2.8.11</version>
                    <executions>
                        <execution>
                            <id>integration-test</id>
```

```
                              <goals>
                                  <goal>integration-test</goal>
                              </goals>
                              <configuration>
                                  <suiteXmlFiles>
                                    <suiteXmlFile>PATH/minimal.xml
                                    </suiteXmlFile>
                                  </suiteXmlFiles>
                              </configuration>
                          </execution>
                          <execution>
                              <id>verify</id>
                              <goals>
                                  <goal>verify</goal>
                              </goals>
                          </execution>
                      </executions>
                  </plugin>
              </plugins>
          </build>
      </profile>
      <profile>                             ❷ Define second
          <id>nightly</id>                    profile
          <activation>
              <property>
                  <name>nightly</name>
              </property>
          </activation>
          <build>
              ...
          </build>
      </profile>
</profiles>
```

The `daily` profile ❶ runs the integration test with the Maven Failsafe plug-in. The second profile ❷ has the ID `nightly`. It can look completely different and will run if `nightly` is passed as the parameter. The idea is to define the plug-in in two different profiles and then script the Failsafe plug-in with different TestNG XML configurations. You can use this pattern for various situations.

To activate the profile, you use system properties. This is handy if you need to run different profiles on the same computer. If you need different profiles—for example, for the development computer versus the build server—you had better activate the profiles in the settings.xml file.

To run the normal tests, type the following in your command shell console:

```
mvn clean install
```

To run the nightly tests, you can use your newly created profile:

```
mvn clean install -Dnightly
```

Selenium, TestNG, and XStream are popular testing tools and they integrate with build tools such as Maven and Ant. But many test engineers are successful with running data-driven tests using Excel, too.

8.2.4   *Data-driven testing with Excel*

XStream-based tests inject one object for each test run. If you're dealing with flat structures or using Excel for other project tasks, XML can look like a too-complex, too-technical, developer-centric solution. There are some Excel libraries for Java available, so it's easy to define test data within Excel sheets. This section shows you how to do that. This solution extends the infrastructure we set up for the XStream processing.

Order the Excel columns to match the parameters in your test method, with each row representing a test run. Table 8.1 shows an example Excel sheet.

Table 8.1   Example Excel sheet containing two rows, two columns, and a header

First name	Last name
Paul	Breiter
Bernd	Müller

As in the XStream solution, you need a TestNG host to host the tests and read the test data. The TestNG test method gets data from a TestNG data provider. The logic that converts the Excel sheet into an array of arrays is simple (it's shown shortly in listing 8.9). You also need to choose an Excel library to read the sheets: the Apache POI library (http://poi.apache.org/) or the Java Excel API (http://jexcelapi.source-forge.net/) are both good choices.

The following example uses the Apache POI library, which is added to the pom.xml file:

```
<dependency>
    <groupId>org.apache.poi</groupId>
    <artifactId>poi</artifactId>
    <version>3.6</version>
</dependency>
```

A helper method reads a file that's located in the resources folder of your Maven project. It reads the first sheet and uses Apache POI to find the filled data range. The first line should be excluded because it contains the column headings. The following listing shows this basic example; you can extend this to more specific formats as necessary.

Listing 8.9   Reading from Excel with POI

```
@Test(dataProvider = "xls-users")
public void testXlsDataTable(String firstName, String lastName)     ◁─┐ Get test
throws Exception {                                                     │ data
    ...}


@DataProvider(name = "xls-users")
public Object[][] readXlsData() throws IOException {                ◁─┐ Define data
    return readXlsToArray(userXlsFile);                               │ provider
}
```

```
private String[][] readXlsToArray(String userXlsFile) throws IOException {
    InputStream inputStream = this.getClass().
        getClassLoader().getResourceAsStream(userXlsFile);

    HSSFWorkbook wb = new HSSFWorkbook(inputStream);
    HSSFSheet sheet = wb.getSheetAt(0);

    int rowNumber = sheet.getPhysicalNumberOfRows();
    int cellNumber = sheet.getRow(0).getPhysicalNumberOfCells();

    String [][] xlsArray = new String[rowNumber-1][cellNumber];

    for(int i=1; i < rowNumber; i++) {
        for(int j=0; j < cellNumber; j++ ) {
            try {
                xlsArray[i-1][j] =
                    sheet.getRow(i).getCell(j).getStringCellValue();
            }
            catch(Exception e) {
                xlsArray[i-1][j] = "";
            }
        }
    }

    return xlsArray;
}
```

◁── **Read Excel file as stream**

◁── **Use POI API**

As you have seen, it's easy to use Excel as the source for your tests. If you want to use a different flat data database, you can use CSV with a `StringTokenizer` or fixed-length formats. It's up to you to choose your weapons.

Because the user (domain expert) can specify the application and can help with maintaining tests (test data), data-driven tests with Excel are considered to be acceptance tests, in a narrow sense.

Using Maven, TestNG, and Selenium 2 for web interface testing

Web interfaces are no longer simple forms where you enter data and click Next to reach the next page. We're confronted with more interaction and dynamic interfaces implemented through JavaScript and Ajax. Different browsers have different features, so it's important to test the real usage as closely as possible. On the other hand, you may have limited time for testing. Tests in real browsers are slow. You need to start the browser environment, and the (Selenium) locators are sometimes slow because you need to use the native methods.

HtmlUnit is a browser emulator written in Java that's ideally suited for fast and reliable tests. With the Selenium 2 release, we now have a merge of Selenium 1 and WebDriver, so you can now run the same tests in real browser environments or in HtmlUnit. Which environment you choose depends on your needs.

If you're working with a lot of JavaScript, you should test in real browser environments. But because real browser tests could easily exceed an hour, they aren't suited to run

> **(continued)**
>
> with every check-in on the CI server. Instead, you can run them in the HtmlUnit envi-
> ronment and run the real browser tests nightly. In this way, you can get fast feedback
> for normal errors and then also detect browser differences once a day. The combination
> of Maven, TestNG, and Selenium 2 is a perfect setup for this solution.

Excel and TestNG make an effective test toolchain. Fit, TestNG, and FEST (Fixtures for
Easy Software Testing) also help with creating effective acceptance tests.

8.3 Acceptance testing with Fit, TestNG, and FEST

The example of outside-in development and barrier-free testing with a chain of integrated tools that we'll look at in this section is based on specifying, developing, and
testing a Java Swing application. We'll functionally test the application with our UI testing framework, FEST, automatically validate the acceptance criteria with the test
framework, Fit. The framework that hosts the tests is TestNG. We'll also embed the
tests in both Ant and Maven. We'll integrate both the tests (functional tests and unit
tests) and the build results.

We'll discuss the individual tools and their integration as we come to them. Let's
start with the application under test.

8.3.1 The application

In this section, we'll test a small Swing application. It contains an editable table of two
columns, an input text field, and a button. A document listener is added to the input
field. When entering or removing text, the table is updated accordingly. Table rows
are displayed, and the first column value starts with the pattern entered in the input
field. For example, entering M will display the four result sets that start with *M*, filtering
out others (assuming there are other rows in the table). Under the hood, a table is
associated with a `TableRowSorter` (see figure 8.2).

Let's specify and test this functionality (and develop the code). As you can see,
we need a functional test to verify this user interface behavior. Because Java 1.6, the
sorter functionality is available as part of the standard distribution, so you don't have
to implement it again yourself. Generally, it's an antipattern to test a standard API,

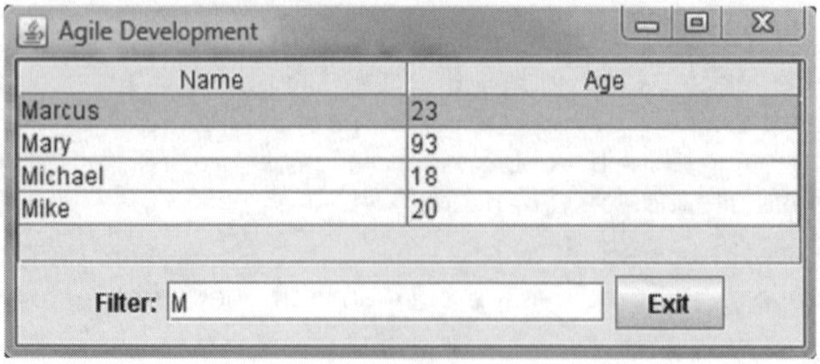

**Figure 8.2 Swing application
with a table and a corresponding
`TableRowSorter`**

but it offers a simple isolated use case for explaining the integration of Fit, TestNG, and FEST.

You can also extend your testing capabilities with Fit.

8.3.2 The specification

Fit (http://fit.c2.com), the Framework for Integrated Test, is a popular, free tool.[15] This tool perfectly meets our need to specify user interactions on the application and to specify expected behavior. Interactions and expected behavior are defined in HTML syntax (see figure 8.3). This is an easy-to-use interface, because customers can edit HTML using any number of tools, including Word.

Fit can process the specification automatically, and it generates another HTML file containing the result of the approval. This new file consists of the same structure and content as the specification and adds the check results to it in the form of colors. We'll talk about the result page in the next section.

fit.ActionFixture		
start	com.huettermann.fit.FitTestActionFixture	
enter	insertRow1Column1	Peter
enter	insertRow1Column2	31
enter	insertRow2Column1	Frank
enter	insertRow2Column2	28
enter	insertRow3Column1	Kurt
enter	insertRow3Column2	12
enter	insertRow4Column1	Felix
enter	insertRow4Column2	66
enter	insertRow5Column1	Friedrich
enter	insertRow5Column2	71
check	checkRow1Column1	Peter
enter	insertFilterText	F
check	countRows	3
check	checkRow1Column1StartsWith	F
check	checkRow2Column1StartsWith	F
check	checkRow3Column1StartsWith	F
press	closeApplication	

Figure 8.3 The HTML specification in the Fit format, viewed in a browser

> **FITNESSE** FitNesse (http://www.fitnesse.org/) is a free, standalone wiki-based tool that integrates with Fit (and with another test system called SLIM). FitNesse allows you to write your tests in a wiki syntax instead of plain HTML tables. More about FitNesse in section 8.4.

By writing `fit.ActionFixture` in the first table row, you specify that you'll use Fit's `ActionFixture`. An action fixture interprets rows as a sequence of commands to be performed in order. The `ActionFixture` knows four Fit commands, and they must be written in the first column:

- `start`—Subsequent commands are directed to an instance of the class that's written in that row of the table (in this case, `com.huettermann.fit.FitTest-ActionFixture`).
- `enter`—Invokes the method of the class with an argument. This command takes values from the Fit specification and enters them in fields on the UI.

---

[15] See Rick Mugridge and Ward Cunningham, *Fit* (Prentice Hall, 2005).

- press—Invokes a method of the class with no arguments. This clicks (or presses) a button on the UI.
- check—Invokes a method of the class with no arguments, and compares the returned value of that method with the given value in the table cell. This reads and validates values from the UI.

REFACTORING FIT TESTS   The FITpro project (http://www.luxoft.com/fit/) provides functionality to integrate Fit into Eclipse, and it offers reporting and refactoring features. This has the benefit of working on Fit tests directly inside Eclipse. You can include Fit into a build script and use this script in your IDE too. Refactoring tests is appealing because you don't need to worry about changes not being applied to all corresponding artifact types (HTML, Java fixtures, and so on).

The Fit specification is associated with the system under test by a Java class (named a *fixture*). You have to develop this Java class by extending Fit's `ActionFixture` base class (see the following listing).

Listing 8.10   The Java fixture associated with the Fit HTML table (extract)

```java
package com.huettermann.fit;

import static org.fest.swing.fixture.TableCell.row;
import org.fest.swing.cell.JTableCellReader;
import org.fest.swing.fixture.FrameFixture;
import org.fest.swing.fixture.TableCell;
import com.huettermann.fit.application.TableFilter;
import com.huettermann.fit.util.BasicJTableCellReader;
import fit.ActionFixture;

public class FitTestActionFixture                          Extends Fit's
        extends ActionFixture {                            base class
    private static String TABLE_NAME = "myTable";
    private static String FILTERTEXT_NAME = "myFilter";

    private FrameFixture window;
    private TableFilter table;
    private JTableCellReader cr;

    public FitTestActionFixture() {
        table = new TableFilter(TABLE_NAME);
        cr = new BasicJTableCellReader();
        window = new FrameFixture(table);          Starts Swing
        window.show();                             application
    }
                                                        Inserts "7l"
    public void insertRow5Column2(int param) {          into cell
        window.table(TABLE_NAME).cell(row(4).
                column(1)).enterValue(String.valueOf(param));
    }
                                                   Checks if cell
    public String checkRow1Column1() {             contains "Peter"
        return window.table(TABLE_NAME).cell(row(0).column(0)).value();
    }
```

```
public void insertFilterText(String param) {
    window.textBox(FILTERTEXT_NAME).enterText(param);
}

public String checkRow1Column1StartsWith() {
    return window.table(TABLE_NAME).cellReader(cr).
            cell(row(0).column(0)).value().substring(0,1);
}

public int countRows() {
    return window.table(TABLE_NAME).contents().length;
}

public void closeApplication() throws InterruptedException {
    window.button().click();
    window.cleanUp();
}
```

Inserts filter text "F"

Checks if cell value starts with "F"

Counts number of rows

Closes application with click

Java reflection has methods that are linked (and later called) according to the names in the table (see figure 8.3) and their signatures.

To find the visual controls on the UI, drive them, and retrieve content, you can use FEST (Fixtures for Easy Software Testing; http://easytesting.org). FEST is free and is technically based on the AWT robot. As you can see in listing 8.10, you can use FEST's fluent interface notation to navigate through the object hierarchy.

NOTE A *fluent interface* is an object-oriented API leading to more readable code. It's normally implemented by method chaining to relay the instruction context of a subsequent call. The approach was widely spread by Eric Evans and Martin Fowler.

Before you can call the Fit test to process a HTML document, you need to write a small adapter, like that shown in the following listing.

Listing 8.11 Calling the Fit application passing parameters (extract)

```
public String runFitTest() throws IOException {
    String result = null;
    FileRunner runner = new FileRunner();
    runner.args(new String[]
        {inputFileName, outputFileName});
    runner.process();
    runner.output.close();
    if (runner.fixture.counts.wrong +
        runner.fixture.counts.exceptions > 0) {
        result = "" + runner.fixture.counts.wrong + " errors and" +
        " " + runner.fixture.counts.exceptions + " exceptions for "
        + this.fitTestName + ". See output " + this.outputFileName;
    }

    return result;
}
```

❶ Use FileRunner to execute HTML document

Pass input HTML format and result page

This adapter receives the HTML Fit spec and calls Fit with it. You can now execute the HTML specification ❶ and compare the defined specification with the current application functionality.

In order to process the spec, you need to glue the tests, which we'll discuss next.

8.3.3   *Gluing the tests and processing the document*

To run the test, you can use the free TestNG, which you saw earlier in section 8.2.1. TestNG and its tests are the entry point for executing the Fit tests. Because we're using unit tests in this example too (for example, with TestNG), we can integrate those tests, profit from aggregated reporting, and minimize barriers and overhead.

Additional glue code?

In some situations, dedicated testers use feature-rich tools to write acceptance tests in specific scripts. The problem with these types of tools is that they generally use some kind of scripting language that's different from what the team is using for production code. Sometimes they use something like JavaScript, and other times a proprietary scripting language. Programmers on the team don't want to switch gears and have to use a different language for writing test scripts.

An Agile team should take a whole team approach, where everyone, regardless of their main role, is responsible for quality and making sure all testing activities are completed for each user story and release, so the whole team needs to choose test tools by consensus so that everyone can use the tool.

An advantage of the Fit/FitNesse model for tools is that if you have testers writing test cases and programmers writing the fixtures that automate them, these two groups are forced to collaborate, which is a big advantage![a]

a. Special thanks to Lisa Crispin for discussing this with me and providing her opinion.

TestNG can not only run tests (as you can see in the example), but it can also host different types (groups) in parallel, enabling you to call groups of tests or all tests. A group can be *all unit tests* or an *integration test*. TestNG and its tests are our entry point for executing the Fit tests. Because you use unit tests, too (for example, with TestNG), you can integrate those tests, profit from the aggregated reporting, and minimize barriers and overhead. The following listing shows how you can set up a TestNG class that hosts different groups.

Listing 8.12   Integrating the Fit test into TestNG

```
package com.huettermann.fit;

import org.testng.Assert;
import org.testng.annotations.Test;
import com.huettermann.fit.framework.FitRunner;

public class AllFitTests_Integration {
```

❶ Append "_Integration" to test class

```
private static final String
   FIT_SPEC_FOLDER = "fit_spec";
private static final String
   FIT_RESULT_FOLDER = "fit_result";
private FitRunner runner;


@Test(groups={"gui"})
public void testTable() throws Exception {
    runner = new FitRunner(FIT_SPEC_FOLDER,
                        FIT_RESULT_FOLDER,
                        "FitTestActionFixture.html");
    String result = runner.runFitTest();
    if (result != null){
       Assert.fail(result);
    }
}


@Test(groups={"backend"})
public void testProcess() throws Exception {
    runner = new FitRunner(FIT_SPEC_FOLDER,
                        FIT_RESULT_FOLDER,
                        "FitTestColumnFixture.html");
    String result = runner.runFitTest();
    if (result != null) {
       Assert.fail(result);
    }a
   }
}
```

② Specify input, output folders

④ Assign test method for group gui

③ Use runner to access framework

⑤ Run Fit runner with parameters

⑥ Introduce second test method for dummy group

First, you append `_Integration` to your test class **①** to indicate that you have integration tests. If you want, you could access classes with this suffix by reflection. Next, you specify **②** the input folder where the HTML spec is located and the output folder where Fit puts the result file. You use `FitRunner` **③** to encapsulate the access to the Fit framework and set up the test method **④** for the first group, gui. You then run the Fit runner **⑤** with parameters to process the HTML document. The second test method for the backend group **⑥** is a dummy in this example to simulate another group.

In this example, one group expresses all GUI tests; the others

fit.ActionFixture		
start	com.huettermann.fit.FitTestActionFixture	
enter	insertRow1Column1	Peter
enter	insertRow1Column2	31
enter	insertRow2Column1	Frank
enter	insertRow2Column2	28
enter	insertRow3Column1	Kurt
enter	insertRow3Column2	12
enter	insertRow4Column1	Felix
enter	insertRow4Column2	66
enter	insertRow5Column1	Friedrich
enter	insertRow5Column2	71
check	checkRow1Column1	Peter
enter	insertFilterText	F
check	countRows	3
check	checkRow1Column1StartsWith	F
check	checkRow2Column1StartsWith	F
check	checkRow3Column1StartsWith	F
press	closeApplication	

Figure 8.4 The Fit result document shows successful checks with a green background.

are backend tests. Running only the tests of type gui will run the functional tests. More about running the tests a bit later.

Running the TestNG test will process the Fit table. FEST will start and drive the Swing application. Executing Fit will create a result table (see figure 8.4).

The content of the result table is exactly the same as the spec file, with one difference: The cell of a check row containing the expected result has a background color. The color is green when the expected result is identical to the actual one (as in the four cases in figure 8.4) and red if it isn't.

8.3.4   Running tests with Ant

You won't want to always trigger the test cycle via an IDE or even manually on the console. You can also use Ant to call the tests automatically. To do that, call TestNG inside the Ant script. The following listing shows an example of how to do that.

Listing 8.13   Running TestNG with Ant (excerpt)

```
<target name="test" depends="ini,compile">          Introduce Ant
    <taskdef name="testng" classpathref="cp"   ◁     target executing
        classname="org.testng.TestNGAntTask"/>     ❶ TestNG
                                                   Define
                                                   TestNG
                                                   task

    <testng classpathref="cp"   ◁       Execute
        haltOnFailure="false"         ❷ TestNG
        useDefaultListeners="false"
        suitename="Agile Development"
        testname="Some agile tests"
        outputdir="${report.dir}"
          listeners=
            "com.huettermann.prio.PriorityInterceptor,  ◁   Add
            org.uncommons.reportng.HTMLReporter,           listeners
            org.uncommons.reportng.JUnitXMLReporter">
            <xmlfileset dir="."
                file="mastersuite.xml"/>            ◁
                <sysproperty key="org.uncommons.reportng.title"   Tell TestNG
                    value="Barrier-free testing"/>             which tests
    </testng>                                        ❸ to process
</target>
```

In the Ant script ❶, you use the embedded TestNG ❷ Ant task xmlfileset to define which tests to process ❸. Using this TestNG feature, you can configure the tests you want to run without hardcoding the test classes in the script.

The referenced mastersuite.xml file is illustrated in the following listing.

Listing 8.14   The TestNG mastersuite.xml defines which tests to run

```
<!DOCTYPE suite SYSTEM "http://testng.org/testng-1.0.dtd" >
<suite name="Master Suite" verbose="1">       Ant target
    <suite-files>                   ◁          executes TestNG
        <suite-file
```

```
            path="./priority-testsuite.xml"></suite-file>
        <suite-file
          path="./mock-testsuite.xml"></suite-file>
        <suite-file
          path="./common-testsuite.xml"></suite-file>
    </suite-files>
</suite>
```

TestNG suite ❶ aggregates three files

This script aggregates different scripts. This way, you can further group the tests. In this example, there are some priority tests, some mocked tests, and a common test suite ❶.

If you investigate the common-testsuite.xml file, you'll see the following listing.

Listing 8.15   TestNG test suite defining which tests to run

```
<!DOCTYPE suite SYSTEM "http://testng.org/testng-1.0.dtd" >
<suite name="Common Test Suite" verbose="1">
    <test name="Component Tests">
        <groups>
            <run>
                <include name="backend" />
                <exclude name="gui" />
            </run>
        </groups>
        <packages>
            <package name="com.huettermann.unittest" />
        </packages>
    </test>
    <test name="Functional Tests">
        <groups>
            <run>
                <include name="backend" />
                <include name="gui" />
            </run>
        </groups>
        <classes>
          <class
            name=
  "com.huettermann.fit.AllFitTests_Integration" />
        </classes>
    </test>
</suite>
```

❶ **Define test collection containing groups, packages**

❷ **Define includes, excludes**

Include pattern, run tests

Test collection for functional tests

Include test groups for functional tests

Define class, including tests

This listing is an XML document that follows the TestNG schema. You can see further hierarchies and collections of tests ❶, and you include and exclude groups to run ❷. The groups in the XML, reference the TestNG groups in the TestNG test class's annotated test methods. The example also demonstrates the flexibility you have to address tests in your Java classes. Besides include and export patterns, you can also reference the artifacts by their package names or class names.

Now it's time to run the script. By calling the Ant script, you compile and package your system and test. Then Fit runs the acceptance tests by starting the application

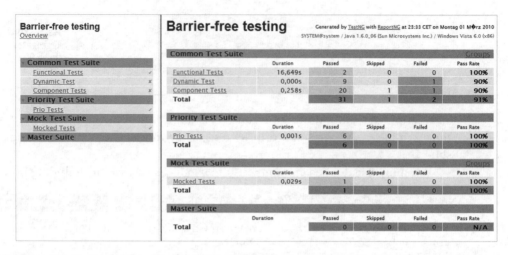

Figure 8.5   ReportNG aggregating TestNG tests, including the functional tests in the common test suite

and driving the UI. Afterward, the output document is written and the system undergoing the test is stopped.

Effective reporting is essential. To validate the success of the test, you don't need to validate all the results. We have one single entry point to the test results because we embedded the acceptance tests into the TestNG suite. Therefore, we have a reporting document that shows the results of all the test types. Figure 8.5 shows the resulting document, which is a bit different from the standard TestNG report.

As you can see in figure 8.5, we integrated ReportNG (freely available at the official project website, http://reportng.uncommons.org) to further facilitate the reporting. ReportNG is a simple report plug-in for TestNG that provides a nicely colored view of the test results. It also produces JUnit format XML output for further integration into CI engines.

You can also integrate these features into the Maven run.

8.3.5   *Running tests with Maven and adding to a Maven site*

Depending on your overall strategy and project conditions, it can be helpful to integrate the Fit tests into Maven, but setting this up can be a bit tricky. This section shows how you can integrate Fit tests into Maven.

Fit tests are stored in files in the directory system. You need to prepare the Fit specs so they're found in the Maven build lifecycle while executing the tests. This means you need to copy them into the target folder before the tests run. You also need to prepare a target folder where the Fit results will be placed. Ant is efficient at copying files and creating folders, but Maven, like Java, lacks an easy way to handle files, so you can use the Maven AntRun plug-in to embed an Ant script in your Maven build file.

The use of this Maven–Ant bridge should be kept to a minimum. It's possible to insert the complete Ant script in the Maven file, but doing this would probably rob you of the Maven features, which were the reason that you chose to use Maven in the first place. (But note that fully integrating bigger Ant scripts with Maven as a first step to migrating the Ant script to Maven could be a valuable migration strategy.) In this example, we'll focus on inserting Ant tasks to copy Fit files.

The code that copies the Fit spec and creates the result folder can look like the following listing.

Listing 8.16   Providing Fit tests

```
<plugin>
    <artifactId>maven-antrun-plugin</artifactId>          ◁──┐  Specify Maven–Ant
    <executions>                                             ❶ bridge
        <execution>
            <phase>generate-sources</phase>             ◁──┐  Enable execution
            <configuration>                                │  before sources
                <tasks>                                   ❷ are processed
                 <copy todir="target/classes/fit_spec">
                     <fileset dir="src/java/fit_spec" />  ◁──┐  Copy Fit specs
                 </copy>                                    ❸ to target folder
                 <mkdir dir="target/classes/fit_result" /> ◁──┐
                </tasks>                                        Prepare result
            </configuration>                                ❹ folder
            <goals>
                <goal>run</goal>
            </goals>
        </execution>
    </executions>
</plugin>
```

First, you add the Maven–Ant bridge for integrating Ant scripts into Maven in the build lifecycle ❶. Next, gluing the Ant processing to the generate-sources phase ❷ enables execution of the Ant tasks before sources are processed. You then copy the Fit specs to the target folder ❸. Finally, you prepare a result folder for the Fit results ❹.

Now we have to configure Maven to find and execute the TestNG tests. The following listing configures Maven's Surefire plug-in for this.

Listing 8.17   Configuring Maven to include the Fit tests

```
<plugin>
    <groupId>org.apache.maven.plugins</groupId>           ┐  Specify plug-in
    <artifactId>maven-surefire-plugin</artifactId>    ◁──┘  for testing
    <version>2.4.3</version>
    <configuration>
        <forkMode>always</forkMode>
        <testFailureIgnore>true</testFailureIgnore>
        <suiteXmlFiles>                                       Reference TestNG
            <suiteXmlFile>mastersuite.xml</suiteXmlFile> ◁──┐ mastersuite.xml
        </suiteXmlFiles>
        <parallel>false</parallel>                        ┐  Specify
        <groups>gui,backend</groups>                   ◁──┘  groups
        <properties>
            <property><name>usedefaultlisteners</name>
```

```
            <value>true</value>
        </property>
        <property><name>listener</name>              <--| Add
            <value>com.huettermann.prio.PriorityInterceptor,    listeners
                org.uncommons.reportng.HTMLReporter,
                org.uncommons.reportng.JUnitXMLReporter</value>
        </property>
        <property><name>reporter</name>
            <value>listenReport.Reporter</value>      <--| Configure
        </property>                                      reporter
    </properties>
</configuration>
</plugin>
```

In the notation of this Maven plug-in, you configure the Surefire plug-in to use your test suite and your listeners. Running the tests with Maven leads to the same test reports you already know (see figure 8.5). But by using Maven and providing the Fit files in their target folders, you also gain from Maven's reporting facility, particularly the Maven website.

The Maven command `mvn clean install site`, entered on the console shell prompt, runs Maven, cleans up Maven's working area, compiles the application under test and runs the tests, and generates a Maven website for your Maven project. The generated Maven website contains all the information about your build, and the site is highly configurable to fit your individual needs. Figure 8.6 shows the website, configured to provide links to the Fit spec and results page.

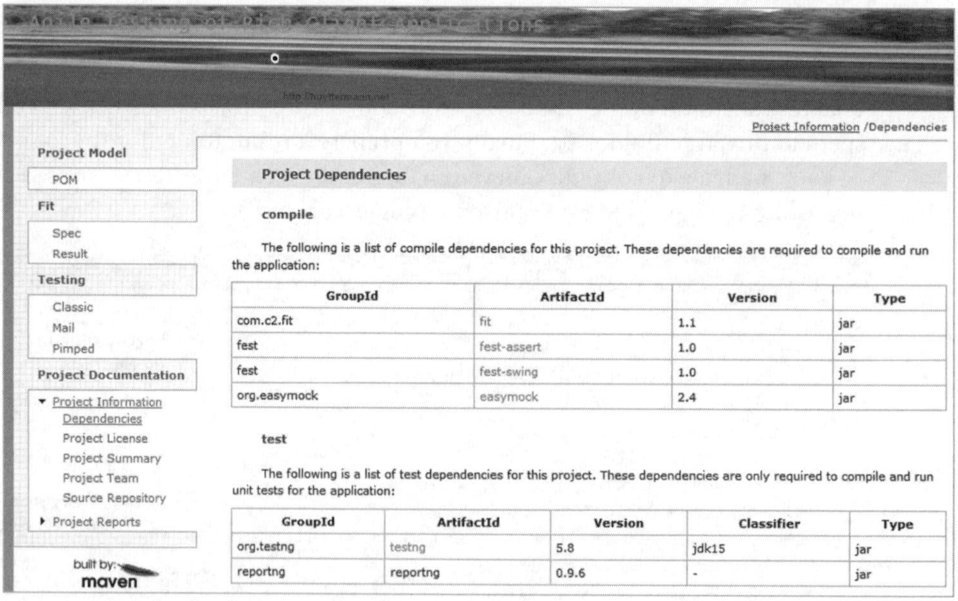

Figure 8.6   The Maven site configured to include the Fit specifications and results page as links in the left sidebar

The Maven Surefire plug-in makes the TestNG test results accessible in the Project Reports area of the site. This is a good example of what I have been calling the barrier-free, integrated approach. The TestNG test tool and Surefire plug-in are useful in implementing an effective approach.

Using BDD in FitNesse with GivWenZen is also an effective approach.

8.4   BDD in FitNesse with GivWenZen

—This section contributed by Wes Williams

FitNesse started as a tool to make Fit more accessible by adding a wiki frontend to it. It's implemented as a simple web server and wiki with a page editor and wiki syntax that's easy and quick to learn. It also provides a runtime environment for the tests.

New wiki pages are created as they are in many wikis—by typing the name of the new page in WikiWord (camel case) style in the URL. To tell FitNesse that this page is a test, click the Properties button in the left menu of the page and select the Test page type.

Installing and running FitNesse with GivWenZen

To get started with FitNesse and GivWenZen, download the latest zip file from the official web site (http://code.google.com/p/givwenzen/downloads/list), unzip the file into a folder, and run the command `java -jar ./lib/fitnesse.jar`.

Once the FitNesse server is running, you can start viewing, creating, and editing wiki pages and creating tests via a simple browser interface. Point your browser to http://localhost/ and you'll see links to the GivWenZen documentation on the Google code site, example test pages, and the tests for GivWenZen.

For more information about using GivWenZen, consult the website at http://code.google.com/p/givwenzen/.

All of the wiki content is saved in the FitNesseRoot folder; this is in the same folder from which you started the FitNesse server. You'll see a hierarchy that represents your URL path in which every ParentPage is located. ChildPage will have a ParentPage folder that contains a ChildPage folder. In each directory, you'll find a content.txt file that contains the wiki markup for the page and a properties.xml file that holds the properties, such as the page type. It's a good practice to put the FitNesseRoot directory under version control, along with the code it describes and tests.

Automated acceptance testing with FitNesse

If you're creating automated acceptance tests, you should be including them in your automated build. This is also true for tests based on FitNesse.

(continued)

Here are a few options for including FitNesse in an automated build:

- Use the set of Ant tasks that come with FitNesse to integrate FitNesse into your build system.
- Include FitNesse in your Maven-based build with the Maven FitNesse Plug-in.
- Use the Hudson/Jenkins plug-in for FitNesse to integrate FitNesse in Hudson/ Jenkins directly.
- Use JUnit to run the FitNesse tests by using the JUnitHelper class that ships with FitNesse. This way you can create JUnit XML result files that can be reported by any build server.

FitNesse will need to know where to find the code that will run the tests and the application code that the tests will verify. This is done with a special wiki syntax: `!path ./ myclasses`. Multiple paths can be created on separate lines, as shown here:

```
!path ./target/classes/main
!path ./target/classes/examples
!path ./lib/commons-logging.jar
!path ./lib/fitnesse.jar
!path ./lib/log4j-1.2.9.jar
!path ./lib/slf4j-simple-1.5.6.jar
!path ./lib/slf4j-api-1.5.6.jar
!path ./lib/javassist.jar
!path ./lib/google-collect-1.0-rc4.jar
!path ./lib/dom4j-1.6.1.jar
!path ./lib/commons-vfs-1.0.jar
```

The path is relative to the working directory in which the FitNesse server was started. Child pages inherit the path of parent pages and can add to the path.

FitNesse originally sat on top of the Fit test system, but Fit has been stagnant since reaching a mature feature set. Additionally, Fit isn't always easy to translate to other languages. This isn't an issue if you don't want to translate the existing library to other languages. But the FitNesse team decided to implement a new test system that they named SLIM. FitNesse can be used with either the Fit or the SLIM test system. If you're just starting with FitNesse, consider choosing SLIM. SLIM is what we'll use in all the following examples; the previous sections of this chapter already demonstrated the use of Fit.

To use SLIM, you must tell FitNesse that you wish to use that test system. You can do this with more special wiki syntax:

```
!define TEST_SYSTEM (slim)
```

This should go in the top-level wiki page of your suite of tests, and then all child pages will inherit this property.

FITLIBRARY FitLibrary is another option in addition to SLIM. Most people who are using the Fit test system use the FitLibrary, which is still maintained and which has a lot of useful features. Unfortunately, the FitNesse team doesn't verify FitLibrary is still working with each release, and occasionally FitLibrary stops working with the latest version of FitNesse.

8.4.1 Testing with GivWenZen

Every SLIM test needs a *fixture*. A fixture is code—Java in this case—that executes a test. SLIM has several built-in table or fixture types: script tables, decision tables, query tables, and so on. We'll be using a simple script table because with GivWenZen the majority of the code required to execute the tests goes into Java classes, which are referred to as *step classes*.

GivWenZen comes with a simple fixture, which we'll start with: org.givwenzen .GivWenZenForSlim. To tell a test page where to find the fixture, you use a special import table:

```
|import|
|org.givwenzen|
```

Now you can tell SLIM to use the fixture with a script table `start` command:

```
-|script|
|start|giv wen zen for slim|
```

Notice the - before the |script| code. This will hide the first row of a table in SLIM. The |script| row is purely technical and adds no value to understanding the test. If you're writing a test, it's needed. But it's not needed when reading the test, so it's better to hide it (so it's not shown in the reporting—more on that a bit later).

Our first page could look like this:

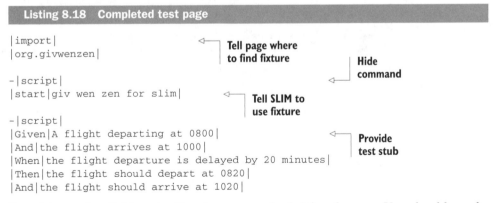

Listing 8.18   Completed test page

```
|import|
|org.givwenzen|                          Tell page where
                                         to find fixture
                                                              Hide
-|script|                                                     command
|start|giv wen zen for slim|
                                         Tell SLIM to
                                         use fixture
-|script|
|Given|A flight departing at 0800|                            Provide
|And|the flight arrives at 1000|                              test stub
|When|the flight departure is delayed by 20 minutes|
|Then|the flight should depart at 0820|
|And|the flight should arrive at 1020|
```

Run this test by clicking the Test button on the left-hand menu. You should results similar to those shown in figure 8.7.

The test will fail, but the fixture should start successfully. We're working in a TDD style at the story level, so its failure is expected. As mentioned earlier, BDD is a nice extension of TDD, when done correctly.

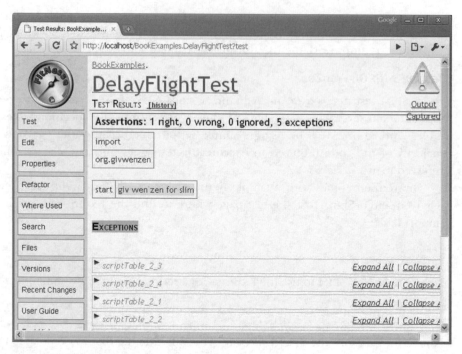

Figure 8.7 Our first, simple test setup, including a fixture

What has happened here is that FitNesse has found the fixture and called the methods given, when, then, and and, passing in the step text as the first parameter. Because we've not defined these steps anywhere, GivWenZen is throwing an exception. Let's take a quick look at the fixture we're using:

Listing 8.19   GivWenZenForSlim script fixture

```
public class GivWenZenForSlim implements GivWenZen {
    private GivWenZenExecutor executor;

    public GivWenZenForSlim() {
        this(GivWenZenExecutorCreator.instance().create());
    }

    public GivWenZenForSlim(GivWenZenExecutor executor) {
        this.executor = executor;
    }

    public Object given(String methodString)
            throws Exception {
        return executor.given(methodString);
    }

    public Object when(String methodString) throws Exception {
        return executor.when(methodString);
    }
```

1 Name of fixture class

2 Rows in wiki mapped to methods in fixture

```
    public Object then(String methodString) throws Exception {
        return executor.then(methodString);
    }

    public Object and(String methodString) throws Exception {
        return executor.and(methodString);
    }

    public GivWenZenExecutor getExecutor() {
        return executor;
    }

    public Object Given(String methodString)
            throws Exception {
        return given(methodString);
    }

    public Object When(String methodString) throws Exception {
        return when(methodString);
    }

    public Object Then(String methodString) throws Exception {
        return then(methodString);
    }

    public Object And(String methodString) throws Exception {
        return and(methodString);
    }
}
```

> ❸ **SLIM methods are case sensitive**

The name of the fixture class ❶ maps to the |start| command on the wiki page. Notice that the given, when, then, and and methods all take a single string parameter. The SLIM script fixture ❷ turns rows into method calls. The method name is determined by taking the value in the first column in a row and every other column after that and concatenating them. The other columns are expected to be parameters to the method.

A test specification written as |Given|...| calls the method public Object Given(String methodString). A test specification written as |given|...| calls the method public Object given(String methodString). This is because SLIM uses a case-sensitive matching for methods. To demonstrate this, our example fixture has two of each method: one beginning with a lowercase letter and one beginning with an uppercase letter. Writing both versions of methods can be convenient if you want to be free in which initial letters you use while writing the test specification ❸.

Our fixture is simple, so the first column in the test is given, when, then, or and. We have no additional method columns, and we have one parameter column that gets passed in to the given, when, then, and and methods. It's a fairly easy concept, and that's all you need to understand about fixtures to use GivWenZen. Now let's implement the steps of the test.

At present, our tests are failing with an error because the steps aren't implemented. See the following sample error output:

```
__EXCEPTION__:org.givwenzen.DomainStepNotFoundException:
You need a step class with an annotated method matching this pattern:
    'A flight departing at 0800'
The step class should be placed in the package or sub-package of bdd.steps or
    your custom package if defined.
Example:
  @DomainSteps
  public class StepClass {
    @DomainStep("A flight departing at 0800")
    public void domainStep() {
      // TODO implement step
    } }
```

The exceptions are listed at the top of the wiki page. SLIM doesn't put them in order, but it's easy to figure out which one belongs to which row in most cases. The error for the first row in the table states we need a step class that has a method with an annotation that matches our step text. The first thing we need to do is create a step class.

By default, GivWenZen looks for step classes in the bdd.steps package, and the class should be annotated with @DomainSteps:

```
package bdd.steps;
import org.givwenzen.annotations.DomainSteps;
@DomainSteps
public class FlightSteps {
}
```

Now that we have the step class, we can start by copying the example method from the error message and adding it to the class. Then we should fix the name of the method, because domainStep isn't descriptive. Let's call it createFlight and make the method return a Boolean and return false for now.

When we run the test again, the former error is gone and the first row has a red background in the first column, indicating that the row executed but failed. Returning false for a row causes SLIM to display it as a failure.

I recommend starting each BDD cycle by getting all your tests to a failure state, with no exceptions. Once there are no exceptions, make the tests pass. Go ahead and create all the methods you need; it's easiest to start with the example methods in the exceptions GivWenZen throws. After you're done, your step class should look similar to the following listing.

Listing 8.20 FlightSteps with default failing steps

```
package bdd.steps;

import org.givwenzen.annotations.DomainStep;
import org.givwenzen.annotations.DomainSteps;                 Define class
                                                              implementing
@DomainSteps                                              ◁── test steps
```

```java
public class FlightSteps {
    @DomainStep("A flight departing at 0800")    ◁─┐  Map wiki row
    public boolean createFlight() {                  │  to test method
        return false;                             ◁──┘
    }

    @DomainStep("the flight arrives at 1000")
    public boolean flightArrivesAt() {
        return false;                             ◁──
    }

    @DomainStep("the flight departure is delayed by 20 minutes")
    public boolean delayFlightBy() {                         Return false
        return false;                             ◁──        from test
    }

    @DomainStep("the flight should depart at 0820")
    public boolean verifyFlightDepartsAt() {
        return false;                             ◁──
    }

    @DomainStep("the flight should arrive at 1020")
    public boolean verifyFlightArrivesAt() {
        return false;                             ◁──
    }
}
```

Your test should look like the one in figure 8.8.

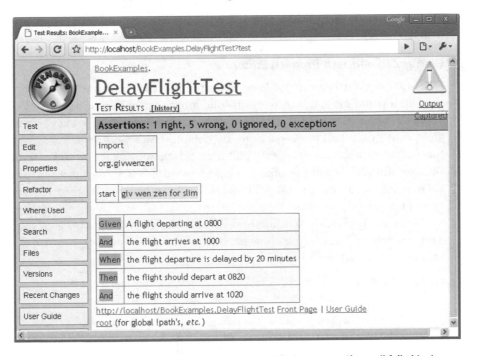

Figure 8.8 Steps implemented (with default method bodies), no exceptions; all failed tests

Finally, you can make your test pass by implementing the methods. Step method parameters are created with regular expression captures that use a regular expression syntax in parentheses: (.*). We'll change 0800 in the annotation for the createFlight method to the value (.*). Next, we'll add a string parameter to the method signature called departureTime. We'll also create a calendar object; this isn't a good object for scheduling, but it will work for our simple examples. We'll set the hour of the day and minutes based on the string passed in. Finally, we'll set the time on the flight object and change the return from false to true.

This should result in a method similar to the following:

```
@DomainStep("A flight departing at (.*)")
public boolean createFlight(String departureTime) {
    Calendar departureCal = Calendar.getInstance();
    departureCal.set(Calendar.HOUR_OF_DAY,
        Integer.valueOf(departureTime.substring(0,2)));
    departureCal.set(Calendar.MINUTE,
        Integer.valueOf(departureTime.substring(2)));
    flight = new Flight();
    flight.departsAt(departureCal);
    return false;
}
```

You can run the test now, and the first row should turn green to indicate that the test is passing. I normally have only the then steps of my tests turn green because these are the real confirmations of completeness.

When you start the next step, you'll see that you need the same exact conversion to a calendar for the arrival time. We'll use the GivWenZen and Java property editors to manage these types.

8.4.2   *GivWenZen and Java PropertyEditors*

Like SLIM, GivWenZen can use Java property editors to convert to a specific type. Let's do that now and move the conversion code into the property editor.

Let's create a class named CalendarEditor that extends PropertyEditorSupport and put it in the bdd.parse package. By default, Java's java.beans.PropertyEditor functionality looks for a property editor in the same package as the class it creates. Because this is the calendar object, we probably don't want to put it in that package. GivWenZen has another package that it looks for in PropertyEditor and that is, you guessed it, the bdd.parse package.

We need to override one method in the CalendarEditor and that's setAsText. This is where we'll move the conversion from string to calendar, too. We should end up with a class that looks like this:

```
public class CalendarEditor extends PropertyEditorSupport {
    @Override
    public void setAsText(String departureTime {
        Calendar departureCal = Calendar.getInstance();
        departureCal.set(Calendar.HOUR_OF_DAY,
            Integer.valueOf(departureTime.substring(0,2)));
        departureCal.set(Calendar.MINUTE,
```

```
        Integer.valueOf(departureTime.substring(2)));
    setValue(departureCal);
    }
}
```

Now we can change the parameter in `FlightSteps#createFlight` to a calendar, greatly simplifying the method. The new method signature is `public   boolean createFlight(Calendar departureTime)`.

The implementation of our next method, `flightArrivesAt`, should be simple now. Change the `1000` value to `(.*)` in the annotation and add a calendar parameter called `arrivalTime`. Implement a new method on the flight that accepts the arrival time, and change the return statement to `true`. Now the first and second step should pass the test.

You don't need a property editor for converting to native types such as `int`, double, and so on, or for converting to a string. Everything we've done in code, including the fixture, should be driven with TDD. The step classes and methods and the editors we create should all follow good coding practices.

The test currently looks a bit like a unit test, and this isn't the sweet spot for FitNesse or GivWenZen. GivWenZen is best used for functional and acceptance testing of a story. In the real world, we would already have some type of domain created, and it would need to be instantiated and interacted with. In between making each step pass, we would be writing unit tests and creating classes to integrate them into real functionality. Moving ahead and finishing the implementation of the remaining steps leads us to the following listing.

Listing 8.21   Steps and flight

```
@DomainSteps
public class FlightSteps {                          ⟵──┐  Fully implemented
    private Flight flight;                              │  flight steps

    @DomainStep("A flight departing at (.*)")
    public boolean createFlight(Calendar departureTime) {
        flight = new Flight();
        flight.departsAt(departureTime);
        return true;
    }

    @DomainStep("the flight arrives at (.*)")
    public boolean flightArrivesAt(Calendar arrivalTime) {
        flight.arrivesAt(arrivalTime);
        return true;
    }

    @DomainStep("the flight departure is delayed by (\\d+) minutes")
    public boolean delayFlightBy(int delayBy) {
        return flight.delayBy(delayBy);
    }

    @DomainStep("the flight should depart at (.*)")
    public boolean verifyFlightDepartsAt(Calendar expectedDepartureTime) {
```

```
      return expectedDepartureTime.get(Calendar.HOUR_OF_DAY) ==
      flight.getDepartureHour() &&
        expectedDepartureTime.get(Calendar.MINUTE) ==
        flight.getDepartureMinute();
  }

  @DomainStep("the flight should arrive at (.*)")
  public boolean verifyFlightArrivesAt(Calendar expectedArrivalTime) {
     return expectedArrivalTime.get(Calendar.HOUR_OF_DAY) ==
        flight.getArrivalHour() &&
     expectedArrivalTime.get(Calendar.MINUTE) ==
        flight.getArrivalMinute();
  }
}

public class Flight {                        ◁──┐ Fully implemented
  private Calendar arrivalTime;                  │ flight object
  private Calendar departureTime;

  public void departsAt(Calendar departureTime) {
     this.departureTime = departureTime;
  }

  public void arrivesAt(Calendar arrivalTime) {
     this.arrivalTime = arrivalTime;
  }

  public boolean delayBy(int delayBy) {
     arrivalTime.add(Calendar.MINUTE, delayBy);
     departureTime.add(Calendar.MINUTE, delayBy);
     return true;
  }

  public int getDepartureHour() {
     return departureTime.get(Calendar.HOUR_OF_DAY);
  }

  public int getDepartureMinute() {
     return departureTime.get(Calendar.MINUTE);
  }

  public int getArrivalHour() {
     return arrivalTime.get(Calendar.HOUR_OF_DAY);
  }

  public int getArrivalMinute() {
     return arrivalTime.get(Calendar.MINUTE);
  }
}
```

We now have a first passing test. Quite often your tests will have steps that touch multiple parts of your domain. Because we put steps related to each separate domain aggregate or service in different step classes in this example, we'll probably need to share states with them. GivWenZen allows this by telling the GivWenZenExecutor, which was created in our fixture, what the shared state is. In the next section, we'll look at adding some additional scenarios.

8.4.3   *Adding further scenarios*

In the flight-scheduling program, what we might have is some additional functionality related to airports and their behavior. We might also have some scenarios related to choosing to delay a flight depending on which airport we are departing from:

```
As a flight scheduler
In order to see the effect that taxi time has on the departure time at an
    airport
When I delay a flight the departure time should be adjusted by the delay time
    plus the taxi time of the airport
```

Our next test, which we can call `DelayFlightWithAirportTaxiTimeTest` could look like this:

```
|Given|airport XXX|
|And|airport XXX has a taxi time of 15 minutes|
|And|A flight departing at 0800|
|And|the flight departs from airport XXX|
|And|the flight arrives at 1000|
|When|the flight departure is delayed by 15 minutes|
|Then|the flight should depart at 0830|
|And|the flight should arrive at 1030|
```

You can give this a try: Create this test and run it. It should fail on the first three `given` statements, with exceptions, and the `when` statements should fail because of invalid values.

Let's create a new `AirportSteps` class and implement the airport steps such that they fail without an exception and the new flight step:

```
@DomainSteps
public class AirportSteps {
   @DomainStep("airport XXX")
    public boolean createAirport() {
      return false;    }
   @DomainStep("airport XXX has a taxi time of 15 minutes")
    public boolean airportTaxiTimeIs() {
      return false;
    }
}
```

For this example, let's create an `Airport` class and for the tests an `AirportSteps` class. We'll create an `AirportService` class to give our `FlightSteps` and `AirportSteps` access to airports.

Next, we'll create a fixture that uses an instance of the `GivWenZenExecutor` that knows about our `AirportService`. To do this, we can extend `GivWenZenForSlim` and override the default no-parameter constructor. In the constructor, we'll create an instance of the `GivWenZenExecutor` using the `GivWenZenExecutorCreator`:

```
public class BookExampleGivWenZenFixture extends GivWenZenForSlim {
   public BookExampleGivWenZenFixture() {
      super(GivWenZenExecutorCreator.instance().
        customStepState(new AirportService()).
```

```
        create()
    );
  }
}
```

At this point, we need to change two places that use the `GivWenZenForSlimFixture` to our new `BookExampleGivWenZenFixture`. Ugh! FitNesse offers us a way around this. Let's create a special wiki page called `SetUp` as a child of the `BookExamples` suite page. In this page, let's put the import table and the table that starts our new fixture, as shown here:

```
|import|
|org.givwenzen|
-|script|
|start|Book Example Giv Wen Zen Fixture|
```

This is a special wiki page that will be included at the top of every page under `BookExamples`. Let's remove the import and start tables from both of our current tests. After changing the properties of the `BookExamples` page to set the `Page` type to `Suite`, we'll save the properties. Running the tests from the `BookExamples` page again results in the original test still passing but the new test fails.

The `AirportService` can now be passed to any of our step classes. Create a constructor in the `FlightSteps` and `AirportSteps` classes that takes an `AirportService` as a parameter:

```
@DomainSteps
public class FlightSteps {
    private Flight flight;
    private AirportService airportService;
    public FlightSteps(AirportService airportService) {
        this.airportService = airportService;
    } ...
```

Now that we have both step classes with access to the `AirportService`, we can implement the new steps. Go ahead and do so; I won't show that here because these are simple methods.

Some comments before we finish this section. I would probably not have implemented the `state` object in this case. The domain would probably have a real service for finding and creating airports, and I would have used that from an `AirportEditor`. This would have allowed me to have airport parameters instead of strings, but this example did show that you can share states between the steps.

It's good practice to break the new test when it's first coded and implements a new story. Tests, fixtures, and step classes are code, and they should be treated like all code. Your tests must be maintainable or they will stop being used and become useless.

SLICING FIXTURES An issue I have seen is fixtures that become too big or have an inheritance hierarchy that's too deep. This makes them difficult to reuse and definitely more difficult to understand. Your fixtures, step classes, and tests should have a logical organization that matches that of your application.

For me, it seems like the step class idea helps with this, but it sure doesn't guarantee it. As you refactor your application, your domain reorganizes your tests and the code that goes with these tests to match the current organization or structure of your domain. Not doing so will lead to confusion and will increase the difficulty of maintaining the tests.

8.4.4   *Creating scenarios*

Scenarios allow steps to be grouped and parameterized so you can use them multiple times with different parameters. A parameter table starts with a row that defines the table as a scenario table by putting the word scenario in the first column. The remaining columns work similarly to the method lookup of a script table. Start with the second column and use every other column after that to build the scenario name. In between the columns are the names of parameters.

The following listing shows an example scenario for the delay flight tests.

> **Listing 8.22   Delay flight with airport taxi time scenario**

```
|scenario|delayed|delayBy|flight|origDepartTime||origArriveTime|with taxi
    time|taxiTime|should adjust departure|newDepartTime|and
    arrival|newArriveTime|times|
|Given|airport XXX|
|And|airport XXX has a taxi time of @taxiTime minutes|
|And|A flight departing at @origDepartTime|
|And|the flight departs from airport XXX|
|And|the flight arrives at @origArriveTime|
|When|the flight departure is delayed by @delayBy minutes|
|Then|the flight should depart at @newDepartTime|
|And|the flight should arrive at @newArriveTime|
```

The name of the scenario in this example is "delayed flight with taxi time should adjust departure and arrival times." See how this is similar to the script table? But notice one strange thing: There's an empty column between origDepartTime and origArriveTime. I left this blank in order to have the scenario name read well. This is better, but the blank column is needed because of the "every other column" rule.

The parameters for the scenario are the values delayBy, origDepartTime, origArriveTime, newDepartTime, and newArriveTime. Looking down through the steps, notice that we replaced exact values with the parameter names appended with an @ symbol.

You can include scenario pages by inserting the following line at the top:

```
!include DelayFlightWithAirportTaxiTimeScenario
|delayed flight with taxi time should adjust departure and arrival times|
|orig depart time|orig arrive time|taxi time|delay by|new depart time|new
    arrive time|
|0800|1000|0|20|0820|1020|
|0800|1000|15|15|0830|1030|
```

The include feature is a nice option to give reusability and remove duplication. It's also possible to have the scenarios automatically included in the page by putting them

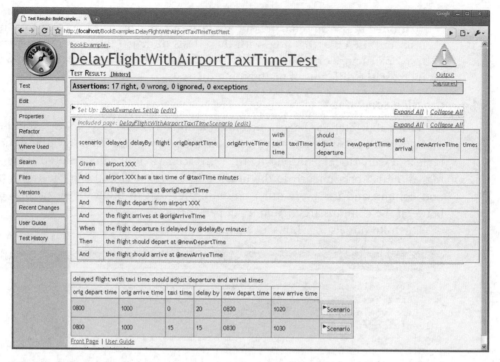

Figure 8.9 Passing scenario tests

in a page called `ScenarioLibrary`. Figure 8.9 shows a more complex example, also using scenarios.

To sum up, we have FitNesse up and running with GivWenZen. We have created a couple of tests in the BDD style with GivWenZen, a fixture, and a couple of step classes.

Automated acceptance tests add a lot of value to a project. Like unit tests, they increase the confidence you have in changes you're making to the application. They describe the application to the whole team and are a meaningful way to collaborate on adding value to your application. But there's a cost: You must maintain these tests.

8.5 Summary

In this chapter, we discussed requirements management and testing, and integrating these phases with the coding phase. Requirements management, development, and delivery are all part of the development lifecycle. This chapter introduced collaborative and barrier-free testing. We talked about data-driven tests, acceptance tests, and behavior-driven development. By discussing real-world examples, we learned how to integrate tools seamlessly.

The next chapter will explore another aspect of collaborative and barrier-free development and testing. With Groovy and Scala, we'll talk about languages other than Java, also running on the JVM. they're part of the polyglot development movement and bridge different technologies, including tools and languages.

Collaborative and barrier-free development with Groovy and Scala

9

This chapter covers

- Approaches for integrating different languages and tools for barrier-free testing
- Agile and polyglot, with Groovy
- Scala and BDD, with specs2

In this chapter, we'll continue to discuss collaborative development and testing. We'll talk about approaches to integrating different languages for barrier-free programming and testing. In our discussion, I'll use the term "polyglot," which means *multilingual*, to refer to using different languages for software engineering, in conjunction, to solve a given problem.

> **POLYGLOT PROGRAMMING** "Polyglot programming refers to leveraging existing platforms by solving problems via solutions that compose special purpose languages." —Neal Ford[1]

---

[1] Neal Ford, "Polyglot Programming: Building Solutions by Composing Languages", www.devx.com/codemag/Article/39419/1763.

We'll discuss Groovy and Scala, both of which are major languages that run on the JVM. Groovy and Scala, used together with Java, bridge different languages, technologies, and tools, providing many valuable features throughout the development lifecycle. As a consequence, Groovy and Scala enable the development of software without any barriers, which makes software development a "barrier-free" experience. Both languages offer interesting features for setting up a polyglot ecosystem, leveraging existing platforms by providing solutions that involve special purpose languages. With Groovy and Scala, you can also write tests and use behavior-driven development, which helps to overcome various barriers:

- Barriers between project phases and project activities (because coding and testing move together more closely)
- Barriers between artifact types (because code and executable specifications are written on the same unified infrastructure)
- Barriers between project roles (because tests are written collaboratively, with mechanisms to use terms close to the problem domain)
- Barriers between tools (because the same tools are used for programming and testing)

In summary, barrier-free development accelerates feedback loops and removes the sources of many potential problems that are barriers to quality.

We've already looked at strategies for avoiding many common problems, and we've discussed integrated approaches. Now let's start to discuss Agile and polyglot programming with Groovy.

9.1 Agile and polyglot with Groovy

—This section contributed by Vaclav Pech

When talking about Agile practices and barrier-free development and testing, we should discuss the Groovy programming language. Due to its features, Groovy is destined to enrich ALM and overcome barriers between testing, development, and operations.

Groovy is an object-oriented programming language, and it's the major language on the JVM besides Java and Scala. It's a dynamic language that can also be used for scripting. Groovy is compiled to the JVM bytecode and works seamlessly with other bytecode that originates from Java sources.

Groovy is well positioned to be used for testing Java code. These are the most noteworthy features that prove this:

- Groovy has the built-in Power Assert command (`assert`), which provides detailed error reports on what went wrong during the running of assertions.
- Groovy has built-in support for JUnit, so you can script JUnit tests in Groovy for your Groovy and Java classes.

- Groovy has relaxed rules for typing that increase test versatility and reduce the verbosity of tests.
- Groovy has relaxed accessibility rules that give tests the freedom to access pretty much any field, method, or class without having to raise the access permission level in the target code.
- Groovy allows easy stubbing and mocking of Java classes thanks to the dynamic nature of Groovy meta-programming.
- Groovy allows scripts to run Groovy tests against an already running application. For example, a web application administrator can log in and type in Groovy code to verify the internal state of the application with a few asserts, getting back immediate feedback about the health of the system.

Thanks to its tight relationship with Java, Groovy can leverage the Java infrastructure completely. All Java libraries can be used as-is in Groovy code. And vice versa, all Groovy-written code is fully accessible from Java or any other JVM-based programming language, such as Scala or Clojure. The power of Java and Groovy code's seamless integration can lead to fancy constructs. For example, consider a Groovy class that implements a Java interface and that will be extended by a Java class. In this construct, a modern editor would not distinguish between the origins of methods, be it a Java artifact or a Groovy artifact (see the following listing).

Listing 9.1   Mixing Java and Groovy

```
package com.huettermann.polyglot;

import polyglot2.IWriter
import javax.swing.JLabel

class Book implements IWriter {          Groovy class
    private String m_title = "Title"     implementing
    private String m_author = "Author"   Java interface

    public String getTitle() {
        return m_title
    }

    public String getAuthor(){
        return m_author
    }

def returning() {
    JLabel entityName='Result:'
    if (valueB==0) return
        return valueA/valueB
    if (a<b) {
        return a
    } else {
        return a
    }
}}
```

```
package com.huettermann.polyglot;

public class Comics extends Book {          ◁─┐ Java class extending
    String character;                             Groovy class

    public static void main(String[] args){
        System.err.println(new Comics().getTitle());
    }

    public String getTitle() {
        return super.getTitle();
    }

    public String getCharacter(){
        return character;
    }
}


package com.huettermann.polyglot;

public interface IWriter {                  ◁─┐ Java
    String getTitle();                            interface
    String getAuthor();
}
```

In recent years, the Groovy community has generated numerous frameworks, the impact of which often extends beyond the boundaries of the Groovy world. Let's look at some of them.

- Gradle (http://gradle.org) is a universal, enterprise-grade build system aiming to compete with and replace Maven. Although implemented in Java, Gradle chose a Groovy-based DSL as the language in which to write build scripts and configuration.
- Grails (http://grails.org) is a rapid web application development framework that adopts many of the Ruby on Rails ideas, such as easy prototyping, scaffolding, configuration-by-exception, DRY[2] or DSL-based MVC architecture, as well as proven, enterprise-scale, Java-based technologies. Groovy serves as the glue language, connecting all the technologies, and a family of Groovy-based DSLs enables developers to create their applications quickly and easily.
- Griffon (http://griffon.codehaus.org), like Grails, adopts many of the Agile principles discussed in this book to rapid desktop application development and uses Groovy as the glue and DSL language.
- Gaelyk (http://groovy.codehaus.org/Gaelyk) is a lightweight Groovy toolkit for developing and deploying Groovy applications on Google's App Engine. It provides a set of DSLs to define the MVC structure of an application and access GAE APIs, like data management, email service, and others.

---

[2] Don't Repeat Yourself.

Groovy's ALM features include built-in testing and mocking capabilities, low-ceremony language constructs, the flexibility to create intuitive yet powerful domain-specific languages (DSLs), a rich ecosystem of innovative frameworks, and the ability to alter code at runtime through scripting or meta-programming. Add in Groovy's Java-like syntax, seamless Java-to-Groovy and Groovy-to-Java interoperability, mature IDE support, and build tool integration, and you'll see Groovy as the powerful vehicle that it is, with the potential to attract and serve well many of the approximately 9 million Java developers worldwide. Several aspects in particular are worth discussing in more depth.

Typing on the Java Virtual Machine

Groovy is a dynamically typed programming language, whereas Java and Scala are statically typed. Generally, a language is said to use static typing when type checking is performed at compile time as opposed to runtime (which is dynamic typing). With JSR 223, version 6 of the Java Standard Edition can also execute scripting languages.

Java 6 comes with its own exemplary language—the Rhino JavaScript engine. Besides that, languages like JRuby, Jython, Groovy, and Scala produce Java bytecode that runs on the JVM. Nowadays, the JVM is more a deployment system and runtime environment that can run many languages other than Java. With JSR 292 (and its new invoked dynamic bytecode), the VM offers support for other languages out of the box. Running something other than Java source compiled code on the JVM is a generational advancement in the technology.

First, Agile development refers to light processes as being "low ceremony," which many developers find more effective and productive than verbose processes that require a great deal of "ceremony." Groovy can help to reduce the ceremony involved with scripting.

9.1.1 *Low ceremony and scripting*

Compared to Java, Groovy reduces the implied ceremony in code, often by a factor of two or more. A dedicated syntax for lists, maps, or functions; an enhanced closure-based API for the JDK classes, called GDK (Groovy Development Toolkit); powerful operators; properties; named parameters; dynamic typing; and many other features all help express programmers' ideas concisely.

Look at the following snippet, for example. You can see that the dedicated syntax for collections plus all the collection-processing methods added to collections, lists, and maps by Groovy reduce verbosity and clearly express the programmer's intent:

```
['Java', 'Groovy']*.toUpperCase()
def cities = [
'Germany' : 'Berlin'
'United Kingdom' : 'London'
'France' : 'Paris'
]
[
```

```
'http://groovy.codehaus.com',
'http://www.dzone.com',
'http://www.infoq.com'
].collect {it.toURL().text}.findAll{it.contains 'groovy'}
```

As a dynamic language, Groovy can accept new code at runtime. A running application could receive new source code as text from the user or as a file, a URL, a database, or any other location, and then compile and use it. Putting aside the security concerns, which should certainly be considered and handled (perhaps by leveraging the standard Java mechanisms of security managers), being able to add code to a live application opens new possibilities. Think of an administration console allowing the administrator to fire ad hoc queries or tests against a server-side application. Imagine a business rule engine offering the ability to alter the rules on the server without any downtime.

Groovy scripting, particularly when combined with the DSL aspect of the language, can also implement macro support, allowing users to customize or automate functionality of off-the-shelf software.

9.1.2 Domain-specific languages

Domain-specific languages (DSLs) are valued for allowing developers to express their ideas in terms close to the problem domain. The smaller the gap is between the language and the domain, the less code is needed (because the code is written in a special purpose language focused on the given problem area) and the fewer bugs that are likely to occur in the program. As a convenient side effect, a nonprogrammer domain expert can often understand and verify the code written by a programmer.

Groovy offers a whole set of tools for creating DSLs. The first feature is the relaxed syntax regarding parentheses, semicolons, and the return keyword, which helps reduce boilerplate code. The ability to override standard operators is also handy in this context. The principles of categories and mix-ins enable classes to take on methods and properties of other classes. And we must not forget about the ability to alter the definition of any class or object at runtime.

To give you a taste of what's possible, in the micro-DSL shown in the following snippet the left shift (>>) operator is overridden to indicate a request to transfer money between two accounts. I defined dynamic properties to convert numbers to money or dates, respectively, and I altered the behavior of the toUpperCase method on the string 'Joe' to add an exclamation mark at the end of the string, hiding the original functionality.

```
'Account1' >> 350.eur >> 'Account2'
(3.days + 5.hours).ago
'Joe'.metaClass.toUpperCase = {-> delegate + '!'}
```

In addition to runtime modifications, the recent addition of AST Transformations to Groovy enables greater flexibility at compile time, with all the benefits of higher performance and potential assistance from IDEs or other tools when compared to the runtime code modifications. In the following code, you can see the Registrations class defines a field named items. Thanks to the @Delegate annotation, all public methods of java.util.List are added at compile-time to the Registrations class, so users can invoke List-specific methods on Registrations instances (people in this case) directly.

```
class Registrations {
    @Delegate List items = []
}

def people = new Registrations()
people.addAll(["Joe", "Dave"])
assert ["Dave", "Joe"] == people.reverse()
```

This, combined with no restrictions (whether the enhanced class has been defined in Java or Groovy), puts explosive power at the developer's fingertips. No wonder frameworks such as Grails or Griffon, the success of which depends on the flexibility and power of their DSLs, have been created around Groovy and enjoy a rapidly increasing adoption rate.

Check out the following examples of DSLs used to build Grails applications. The first example shows the ease of creating simple database queries:

```
def recentBooks = Book.findByReleaseDateBetween now - 5, now
```

Defining constraints for a domain class is also intuitive, isn't it?

```
country nullable:false, unique:true, inList:['de', 'uk', 'cz', 'at']
```

Another DSL is ready to make your life easy whenever you need to explicitly define the mapping of your domain classes to database tables:

```
static mapping = {
table 'CONFERENSES'
if (current == PRODUCTION) {
country column:'COUNTRY_CODE'
age type:'integer'
}
participants fetch:'join', sort:'name'
}
```

DSLs help create tools that solve problems in a specific domain. Spock and easyb are two BDD testing tools implemented as DSLs in Groovy.

9.1.3 *Testing with easyb and Spock*

Writing good tests is an important aspect of Agile development. Groovy comes with built-in support for testing and mocking and can be used to test both Java and Groovy code. IDE support for Groovy is quickly improving and now allows for efficient TDD practices, such as the ability to define or alter class or method definitions for a specific usage or to refactor and generate code. Two BDD frameworks have emerged from the Groovy community—easyb and Spock. Thanks to the close Groovy and Java relationship, they can both be used to implement BDD on pure Java projects.

easyb (www.easyb.org) is a BDD framework for the Java platform. By using a specification-based DSL, easyb aims to enable executable, yet readable, documentation. Its specifications are written in Groovy and run via a Java runner that can be invoked with the command line, with Maven, or with Ant. What's more, easyb supports a few different styles of specifications that range from RSpec's to a story-based DSL with givens, whens, and thens. The following example shows a test case where we invoke the `zipvalidate` function using an invalid zip code, and we confirm that it appropriately returns the value of `false`:

```
given "an invalid zip code", {
    invalidzipcode = "221o1"
}
and "given the zipcodevalidator is initialized", {
    zipvalidate = new ZipCodeValidator()
}
when "validate is invoked with the invalid zip code", {
    value = zipvalidate.validate(invalidzipcode)
}

then "the validator instance should return false", {
    value.shouldBe false
}
```

easyb stories provide an easy way to capture user requirements in natural language, making requirements closely match normal conversations between people. The plain text story DSL is separated from the behavior DSL and implementation. At the early stages of gathering requirements, empty or "pending" stories will typically be created. Pending stories are not yet implemented and leave the closure body unimplemented. The implementation is expected to be provided later in the process by adding bodies to the textual descriptions of the different steps of the story.

Spock (http://code.google.com/p/spock/) is a testing and specification framework for Java and Groovy applications. What makes it stand out from the crowd is its beautiful and highly expressive specification language. As you can see from the following snippet, Spock code tweaks Java syntax quite a bit. It allows you to create several sections describing different aspects of your test, each labeled accordingly, such as `expect:`, `where:`, `when:`, and `then:`.

```
class HelloSpock extends spock.lang.Specification {
    def "can you figure out what I'm up to?"() {
        expect:
        name.size() == size

        where:
        name << ["Kirk", "Spock", "Scotty"]
        size << [4, 5, 6]
    }
}
```

Whereas easyb takes a more traditional approach to defining DSLs in Groovy, Spock relies on compile-time AST Transformations and therefore can stretch the allowed syntax a bit further. While Spock provides syntax that looks different from typical Java or Groovy code, Spock feels comfortable to developers, who are used to unit testing frameworks like JUnit. By leveraging the power of Groovy meta-programming and DSL definition abilities, together with being able to help pure Java shops, both frameworks serve as good examples of typical citizens of the Groovy ecosystem.

9.1.4 Groovy Maven ecosystem

Besides IDE support, build tools also support working with Groovy. Groovy is designed to run alongside Java, so any build tool that works for Java works for Groovy as well. The following listing shows an example Maven POM for compiling Groovy classes.

Listing 9.2 Compiling Groovy with Maven

```
<dependencies>
  <dependency>
      <groupId>org.codehaus.groovy.maven.runtime</groupId>      ⟵   Add dependency
      <artifactId>gmaven-runtime-default</artifactId>                  for compiling
  </dependency>                                                        Groovy artifacts
</dependencies>
<build>
    <plugins>
        <plugin>
            <groupId>org.codehaus.groovy.maven</groupId>      ⟵   Call plug-in's
            <artifactId>gmaven-plugin</artifactId>                  goals in build
            <executions>                                            phase
                <execution>
                    <goals>
                        <goal>generateStubs</goal>
                        <goal>compile</goal>
                        <goal>generateTestStubs</goal>
                        <goal>testCompile</goal>
                    </goals>
                </execution>
            </executions>
        </plugin>
    </plugins>
</build>
```

Groovy is one of the languages you can use to write POM information that Maven supports. If you would prefer to write your POM as source code, as opposed to XML, Groovy supports that approach. A translator tool is also available to translate a given POM into a Groovy derivate by calling `translator pom.xml pom.groovy`.

The following listing shows an example POM written in Groovy.

Listing 9.3 A Maven POM, written in Groovy

```
project {
    modelVersion '4.0.0'
    parent {
        artifactId 'artifact-parent'
        groupId 'group'
        version '1.0.0-SNAPSHOT'
```

```
}
artifactId 'artifact'
version '1.0.0-SNAPSHOT'
name 'name'
url 'http://maven.apache.org'
dependencies {
  dependency { groupId 'junit'; artifactId 'junit';
    version '4.7'; scope 'test' }
  dependency { groupId 'org.hamcrest'; artifactId 'hamcrest-all';
    version '1.1'}
  dependency { groupId 'log4j'; artifactId 'log4j';
    version '1.2.12' }
}
profiles {
    profile {
        id 'development'
        properties {
            'log4j.level' 'DEBUG'
        }
    }
    profile {
        id 'production'
        properties {
            'log4j.level' 'WARN'
        }
    }
}

    properties {
        'log4j.level' 'info'
    }
}
```

Because Groovy is supported in all modern IDEs, writing POMs this way can be even more fun.

Groovy has many interesting applications that can help you support an Agile ALM. Scala/specs2 provide another useful approach that supports BDD.

9.2   BDD with specs2 and Scala

—This section contributed by Radosław Holewa

Scala, which is short for "scalable language," is a statically typed hybrid for object-oriented and functional programming. It runs on the Java platform (JVM) and is interoperable with Java. The Java and Scala languages share the same runtime environment and deployment infrastructure. As a result, you can invoke your existing Java code from inside your Scala methods and also invoke Scala code from Java. Scala, Java, and Groovy can all be used together, so you can choose the language that best fits your particular requirements without leaving the JVM ecosystem.

Scala is popular, and API-breaking changes in new versions are rare. Scala was created at a university, and clarity and richness of features were the goals in mind. Scala is a fully object-oriented language. Every value or variable used in your code is an object. This also holds for Java primitive types, which come with their own Scala wrapper classes. In Scala, functions are first-class citizens. You can create anonymous functions, pass functions as parameters of other functions, and even return functions as method results. But Scala functions are also objects. You can even derive subclasses from function types.

Scala works well in multithreaded environments due to its Actors library, which was inspired by Erlang actors.[3] Hence, multithreading applications written in Scala are often more reliable and scalable than their Java counterparts. For example, using actors prevents data races caused by inconsistent states, because the data is encapsulated within actors and can't be accessed from outside. The only way for actors to cooperate is by sending messages to each other.

Scala is an interesting and important language; it's a generational advance in terms of syntax and programming language approach. Fifty years of programming language design influenced the design of Scala, and the Scala language's origins are a major distinguishing feature as compared to Java. Java has grown over the years to serve as an easy, multipurpose language. Scala, in contrast, represents new ideas that many programmers haven't seen (such as applying functional programming). This can help us all reflect on how we approach BDD and provides new models for abstraction. Scala's core is small but extensible, and its SDK contains many useful libraries that were developed by extending the Scala core, including the Actors and XML libraries. The language's flexibility also helps in creating internal and external DSLs. Scala allows you to develop your own syntax on top of Scala language features, and it also provides combinator passing for processing your own external DSL grammars.

9.2.1   Scala/specs2

specs2 (http://specs2.org) is one of the most popular external Scala libraries. It provides a BDD framework that was created by Eric Torreborre. Specs2 leverages Scala's flexibility and offers many constructions useful in helping to write BDD tests.

Now it's time for some fun. Let's code a Coca-Cola machine example in Scala, using the specs2 framework! (If you're wondering, I don't get any rebates from Coca-Cola for doing this.)

We'll define our specifications within the CocaColaMachineSpec object:

```
import org.specs2.mutable._
object CocaColaMachineSpec extends Specification {
  "coca-cola machine" should {
   "sell one can and return change" in {
   }
   "not sell can because of wrong price and return all money" in {
 }
```

---

[3] For more information on the Erlang programming language and runtime environment, see www.erlang.org.

```
  "not sell can because of missing cans and return all money" in {
    }
  }
}
```

This snippet is written in what specs2 calls *unit specification style*, where the text is interleaved with the specification code. As you can see, we created the specification using almost pure natural language. Thanks to this fact, it's readable not only by developers, but also by other project stakeholders.

The first example could be read as "coca-cola machine should sell one can and return change." This is the specification of the first use case: The Coca-Cola machine will sell the child a can of Coke. This kind of definition obviously helps in understanding what effect the processing should have. It also shows how elegant BDD tests can be.

The body of this example is implemented in the next step. Here is the implementation of the first part of our specification:

```
"coca-cola machine" should {
    def machine = CocaColaMachine.create(5, 2) // some factory

    "sell one can and return change" in {
      val (can, change) = machine.sell(4)
      can must not beEmpty
      change must be_==(2)
    }
}
```

Declaring matchers

There are different ways to declare and use matchers that can look more or less like using the English language. For example, the canonical way of expecting an option to be "not empty" is `can must not beEmpty`.

This can also be written as `can must not be empty` (works with any object that has an `isEmpty` method), but this needs a bit more machinery than creating only a new matcher. Therefore, if you want to create a matcher like this:

`moneyInEur1 must not be matchingMoney(moneyInEur2)`

instead of

`moneyInEur1 must not beMatchingMoney(moneyInEur2)`

you would have to create a new implicit definition:

```
implicit def toMoneyResult(r: MatchResult[Money]) =
  new { def matchingMoney(m: Money) =
  r.apply(beMatchingWith(m)) }
```

Consult the specs user guide (http://code.google.com/p/specs/wiki/UserGuide) for all options.

Let's take a closer look at this example. We invoke the `sell` method on the `machine` object and receive the Coke can and change as a result. Scala/specs2 provides a special internal DSL for writing specifications. As you can see,

- `can must not beEmpty` checks if the machine delivers the can
- `change must be_==(2)` checks if the returned change is 2

Thanks to the internal DSL, the code for final state checking is clear immediately. The whole `CocaColaMachineSpec` object is presented in the following listing.

Listing 9.4   The `CocaColaMachineSpec` object

```
object CocaColaMachineSpec extends Specification {        ❶ Invoke factory
  "coca-cola machine" should {                                method
  def machine = CocaColaMachine.create(5, 2)

  "sell one can and return change" in {          ❷ Invoke sell()
      val (can, change) = machine.sell(4)            method        ❸ Check value of
      can must not beEmpty                                           returned tuple
      change must be_==(2)              Confirm returned
  }                                    ❹ change value
  "not sell can because of wrong price and return all money" in{
      val (can, change) = machine.sell(1)           ◄─❷
      can must beEmpty           ◄──❸
      change must be_==(1)           ◄──❹
  }
  "not sell can because of missing cans and return all money" in{
      val machine = CocaColaMachine.create(0,
      val (can, change) = machine.sell(2)           ◄─❷
      can must beEmpty           ◄──❸
      change must be_==(2)           ◄──❹
  }
  }
}
```

First we use the factory method invocation ❶ to create an instance of the CocaCola-Machine class. For each instance, we invoke the `sell()` method ❷ with the amount of money as the argument, check the first value ❸ of the returned tuple to make sure it isn't empty, and then confirm the value of the returned change ❹.

SPECIFICATION: CLASS OR OBJECT?   A specification can be either a class or an object. Using the class approach, you could execute the class with `scala -cp <...> specs2.run CocaColaSpec`.[4] JUnit can also execute this by appending `WithUnit` to the extended class name: `class CocaColaSpec extends SpecificationWithJUnit`.

---

[4]   The classpath is represented by the `<...>` placeholder.

specs2 is a powerful BDD framework with many useful features. It's also flexible, which means you can easily extend specs2. Let's consider a subset of the previously discussed code snippet:

```
val (can, change) = machine.sell(2)
can must beEmpty
change must be_==(2)
```

You can see what a nice piece of code we've specified using specs2. This code fragment looks friendly and ensures good readability: `can must beEmpty`. The preceding code checks the value against an empty matcher represented by `beEmpty`, which is the special matcher that was created for checking options.

> **MATCHERS**   Matchers as defined in specs and pattern matching are two different things. A specs matcher generally doesn't use pattern matching. You can find more details on general pattern matching with Scala here: www.scala-lang.org/node/120.

Matchers are constructs that simplify the code. Specs offers many predefined matchers out of the box, but you can create a new one, as the following example illustrates. Let's start by creating `Currency` object:

```
object Currency extends Enumeration {
  type CurrencyType = Value
  val EUR, USD, CHF = Value
}
```

This code is an example of an enumeration definition in Scala. It defines an enumeration of currency values: EUR, USD, and CHF. We'll use our currency enumeration as the type of currency value in the `Money` class:

```
class Money(val value: Integer, val currency: Currency.CurrencyType) {
  override def equals(obj: Any) = {
    val money = obj.asInstanceOf[Money]
    value.equals(money.value) && currency.equals(money.currency)
  }

  override def toString = value + " " + currency
}
```

The class overrides two methods. The `equals` method is used by the matcher. The `Money` class contains two overridden methods: `equals()` and `toString()`. The `equals` method will be used to compare `Money` objects that belong to the matcher class. (You could also create the `Money` class as a case class here to avoid `ClassCastException` with `obj.asInstanceOf[Money]`).

Now let's create a new matcher for the `Money` class. There are different ways of creating matchers in specs2, but here is the simplest way:

```
def matchMoney(money: Money): Matcher[Money] = {
  (m: Money) => (m.equals(money),
                 m + " is equal to " + money,
```

```
                 m + " is not equal to " + money)
}
```

The following listing shows how this matcher can be used in a simple specs example.

Listing 9.5   Specs2 in our example

```
object MoneySpec extends Specification {
  "money" should {
    "be not equal" in {                                    Creates instance
      val moneyInEur = new Money(10, Currency.EUR)    ◁──┘ of Money class
      val moneyInChf = new Money(10, Currency.CHF)
      moneyInEur must not matchMoney(moneyInChf)      ◁─┐ Checks if moneyInEur
    }                                                    │ isn't moneyInChf

    "be equal" in {
      val moneyInEur1 = new Money(5, Currency.EUR)
      val moneyInEur2 = new Money(5, Currency.EUR)
      moneyInEur1 must matchMoney(moneyInEur2)
    }
  }

}
```

As you can see, matchers make your code compact by hiding checks inside their implementation and providing intuitive DSL-like constructions that can be reused in specifications.

Another nice and useful feature of specs2 is data tables. Consider a simple test where you want to check whether the sum of two given values was calculated correctly. The simplest way to write such a test is to add two values directly and compare the result with the sum. But what happens if your test is invoked for many different predefined value pairs? This is where the specs2 data table feature enters the game. This example illustrates how to use it:

```
"calculation example" should {
  "add values correctly" in {
    "first value" | "second value" | "sum" |>
        1         !       2        !  3    |
        4         !       5        !  9    | { (value1, value2, sum) =>
          (value1 + value2) must be_==(sum)
      }
    }
  }
```

Here, we define a data table with two rows of data and one row with table column names. The first and second columns contain values that will be added, and the third column contains the sum of the two values. The code (value1 + value2) must be_==(sum) will be invoked for every row in the data table (excluding the column headers row). Obviously, this is a simple and powerful solution for providing a test data set.

Eric Torreborre on the present and future of specification tools

As he reviewed this chapter, Eric Torreborre, the founder of specs/specs2, offered the following comments:

"I built the Forms support in specs2 as an alternative to Fit in the Java world. I wanted to (a) get the specification closer to statically typed code (whereas in Fit the tables can't be type checked); (b) propose more complex forms that can be composed instead of simple tables—this suits better complex domain models; and (c) still allow for simple text to be used with appropriate code inserted to check the literal assertions. There is still a big gap to fill in terms of collaboration with the business analyst (or product owner or whatever role you give her). The big question is, can you let the BA write the specifications and then have the developer instrument them for execution? This point is important, because the person writing the specification ultimately owns it. That's her work, her baby.

But there are fundamental difficulties in putting BDD and acceptance testing tools in the hands of a BA:

- Tools need to live close and evolve with the code. Otherwise it's prone to the same kind of evolution issues that we faced when trying to synchronize UML diagrams with code.
- Specification text needs to be version controlled, which brings in concepts that aren't so easy to understand for the BA (even for developers sometimes).
- Successful specifications need to be constantly refactored like any code. This requires some thinking skills that are close to a developer mindset.

On the other hand, leaving all the BDD artifacts in the hands of the developers is also doomed to fail because it's less easy to use the artifacts as communication and discussion tools.

In conclusion, I think that there is still room for improvement in that space. I can envision tools where the developer would build templates and components for accessing and setting up the business objects, domain, and services, and for checking up on them. Then the BA would use those tools to write up the specification. When those templates or components don't exist, the BA should still be able to create some generic or not executable ones to start off the work."

The last feature I'd like to mention in this context is the support for literate specifications.[5] Suppose you need to handle tests where the test description could also be a part of the code that will be invoked. This way, tests can be described using a natural language. And as another benefit, each change in the description will have an impact on the test execution.

---

[5] For more information about literate specifications, see http://code.google.com/p/specs/wiki/LiterateSpecifications.

9.2.2   *Specs2 forms*

The next example was created using specs2 Forms and creates tables with your custom content in a convenient way.[6]

Listing 9.6   specs2 Forms in action

```
package alm

import org.specs2._
import specification.Forms
import form._

class FormsSpec extends Specification with Forms          ◁─┐ Define class to
{ def is =                                                    use Forms
  "Forms specification".title                                        ^
  details                                                            ^
                                                                    """

### Basic

This is a simple example to show how to mix your
 Scala code and description of your tests.

                                                           """^
                                                           p^     ┌ Create a
"should add two values correctly" !                       ◁─┘    └ simple test
{ 2 + 2 must_== 4 } ^

                                                           p^
                                                           """

### Advanced

An advanced example that shows how to mix calculation
 forms inside of your tests.
                                                           """^
  Form.th("a", "b", "a*b")                  ◁─┐ Invoke form to compute
      .tr(multiply(2, 1, 2))                   multiplications
      .tr(multiply(2, 2, 4))
      .tr(multiply(2, 3, 6))                           ^
                                                       p^
                                                       """

### Failed

This is example of failed test:                        """^
                                                       p^
"**this test should fail**" !          ◁─┐ Define a simple
{ 2 must_== 3 } ^                         test that fails
                                                       p^
                                                       """
because there is a mistake in the code (2 != 3)        """

def details =                              ◁─┐ Define details to be
Form.tr(field("author", "Agile ALM")).        included at top of page
```

```
    tr(field("version", "2.0"))

  def multiply(a: Int, b: Int, result: Int) =
    Row.tr(field(a), field(b), prop(a*b)(result))
}
```
⟵ **Define multiply method
to be used by tests**

With Forms, you can represent domain objects and declare expected values in tables. Forms can be composed of other Forms to accommodate composite information. specs2 allows you to write tests in what specs2 calls *acceptance* style. In a test written according the acceptance style, the implementation is isolated from the specification text and located elsewhere.

When using the acceptance style, a list of "fragments" is concatenated by the special caret character (^). Specification examples are written using the format: `"descrip-tion" ! body`. Other special characters are used by specs2 as well. For instance, surrounding an item with triple double-quotes (`"""`), at its start and its end, allows things written on multiple lines to be treated as continuous strings. Another example are blocks that are separated from each other by introducing "p" as in "paragraph". In the class, these special operations are often aligned on the right to leave the text on the left free from visual markers. For more information on the layout, see http://etorreborre.github.com/specs2/guide/org.specs2.guide.SpecStructure.html#Layout.

Running this example outputs the report that's shown in figure 9.1.

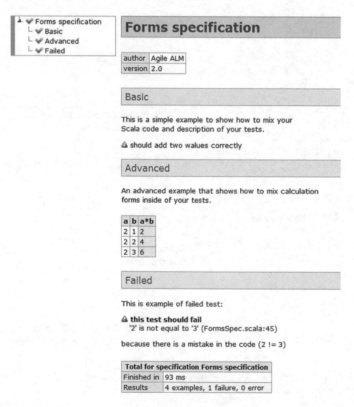

Figure 9.1   A Forms sample,
BDD with Scala

9.2.3 *Scala build ecosystem*

Scala artifacts can be built with Maven. This next listing shows an extract of a Maven POM for processing Scala artifacts.

Listing 9.7 A Maven POM that includes Scala

```
<build>
    <plugins>
        <plugin>
            <groupId>org.scala-tools</groupId>
            <artifactId>maven-scala-plugin</artifactId>
            <executions>
                <execution>
                    <goals>
                        <goal>compile</goal>
                        <goal>testCompile</goal>
                    </goals>
                </execution>
            </executions>
            <configuration>
                <scalaVersion>${scala.version}</scalaVersion>
            </configuration>
        </plugin>
    </plugins>
```

Compile artifacts

Besides Maven, the simple-build-tool (http://code.google.com/p/simple-build-tool), sbt for short, is another powerful option for building your Scala projects. sbt is written in Scala and can be configured and extended by using the Scala language, so you don't need to leave your Scala platform to configure your build scripts. Additionally, sbt supports specs2 as well as advanced dependency management. You can use different dependency declaration types, including Ivy and Maven configuration files. It's also possible to trigger sbt build scripts with Jenkins, using Jenkins' dedicated plug-in (https://wiki.jenkins-ci.org/display/JENKINS/sbt+plugin).

9.3 *Summary*

This final chapter detailed collaborative and barrier-free development and testing. We introduced Groovy and Scala as languages that also run on the Java Virtual Machine. They're part of the polyglot development movement, bridging different languages, technologies, and tools to gain the best benefit for specific project requirements. Both languages, Groovy and Scala, provide features that can bridge the distance between the coding and testing activities.

Roundup

In this book, we discussed what Agile ALM is, and we covered strategies and tools for implementing an Agile ALM. You've seen that ALM evolved from SCM, which in turn evolved from version control. An Agile ALM enriches an ALM with Agile strategies. Concepts are agnostic regarding tools, but I've offered suggestions on how to use and integrate lightweight tools while applying Agile strategies. Concepts, as well as tools, can be aligned with your individual requirements, and the resulting mash-up can form an Agile ALM. I've shown example toolchains along with different aspects of Agile ALM in dedicated chapters in this book.

Consider the following items, which we've discussed in this book:

- Introduce quality gates—milestones in the project where quality requirements must be fulfilled
- Work in isolation and as a team; maintain productive development environments, in order to focus on individual tasks, while also working collaboratively as a team in an efficient way
- Commit early, commit often, to provide your changes to the team and to gain from fast feedback
- Structure work so it's aligned with tasks, to allow humans and tools to link work items to technical artifacts in a traceable way
- Include audits to detect integration issues early and often, and to improve quality
- Follow conventions as a team by aligning your work with standards that were committed to by the team
- Apply barrier-free approaches to avoid silos by integrating tools, project phases, artifact types, activities, and considering polyglot languages and specification by example
- Streamline your work by implementing strategies for building, testing, staging, and configuring artifacts

Also, consider the common questions I pointed to in chapter 1, including:

- How can I improve communication in the team?
- How can I set up a flexible infrastructure to secure the assets of my company?
- What is the state of my software?
- Which changes (requirements, bugs) are implemented in which artifacts?

Step out of your career as a software professional for a moment, and imagine yourself doing something different, perhaps building cars or managing a restaurant. Almost all of these activities involve interacting with a lot of people. These are all universal terms and questions—the ideas in this book can be extended well beyond issues of software development to address corporate challenges and project management.

In this book, we applied these universal principles to the specific instance of software programming. Each instance I picked could be slightly modified for a different managerial environment: For example, "How do I significantly improve the quality of the food I sell at my restaurant?" Obviously, the answers across different fields will differ, but the questions are remarkably similar. Gathering requirements and then testing to ensure that there is acceptable functionality is a good example of aspects that can be applied in many different situations.

In this book, I've developed a set of questions every business owner should be asking, and I've delivered answers for the specific instance of software programming. We've examined many different problem domains, and I've suggested a variety of ways to improve the development process in terms of both productivity and quality. I hope that you have enjoyed the book and will apply these approaches in your Agile ALM.

index

Specicification by Example
How Successful Teams Deliver the Right Software
by Gojko Adzic

  ISBN: 978-1-617290-08-4
  296 pages, $49.99
  June 2011

Camel in Action
by Claus Ibsen and Jonathan Anstey

  ISBN: 978-1-935182-36-8
  552 pages, $49.99
  December 2010

OSGi in Action
Creating Modular Applications in Java

by Richard S. Hall, Karl Pauls,
   Stuart McCulloch, and David Savage

  ISBN: 978-1-933988-91-7
  576 pages, $49.99
  April 2011

Test Driven
Practical TDD and Acceptance TDD
for Java Developers
by Lasse Koskela

  ISBN: 978-1-932394-85-6
  544 pages, $49.99
  October 2007

For ordering information go to www.manning.com

YOU MAY ALSO BE INTERESTED IN

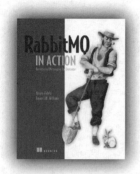

JRabbitMQ in Action
Distributed Messaging for Everyone
by Alvaro Videla and Jason J.W. Williams

    ISBN: 978-1-935182-97-9
    325 pages, $44.99
    October 2011

C# in Depth, Second Edition

by Jon Skeet

    ISBN: 978-1-935182-47-4
    584 pages, $49.99
    November 2010

JUnit in Action, Second Edition

by Petar Tahchiev, Felipe Leme,
   Vincent Massol, and Gary Gregory

    ISBN: 978-1-935182-02-3
    504 pages, $49.99
    July 2010

The Art of Unit Testing
with Examples in .NET
by Roy Osherove

    ISBN: 978-1-933988-27-6
    320 pages, $39.99
    May 2009

For ordering information go to www.manning.com